TEX'

Legal Skills and System

CONSULTANT EDITOR: LORD TEMPLEMAN
EDITORS: JUDITH EVANS LLB, Cert Ed
LINDA PERKS LLB, Cert Ed

OLD BAILEY PRESS

OLD BAILEY PRESS
200 Greyhound Road, London W14 9RY

1st edition 1997

© Old Bailey Press Ltd 1997

Previous editions published under The
HLT Group Ltd.

ISBN 1 85836 226 1

British Library Cataloguing-in-Publication.
A CIP Catalogue record for this book is
available from the British Library.

Acknowledgement
The publishers and author would
like to thank the Incorporated
Council of Law Reporting for
England and Wales for kind
permission to reproduce extracts
from the Weekly Law Reports, and
Butterworths for their kind
permission to reproduce extracts
from the All England Law Reports.

Printed and bound in Great Britain

Contents

Preface

This book seeks to prepare you for the demands of legal study found within the modern undergraduate law courses by combining materials and instruction on legal skills with the substantive knowledge of the operation of our legal system.

Increasingly there has been a wider recognition of the benefits of integrating skills training from the outset of legal studies and as an integral part of it. A significant proportion of legal study now rests on the acquisition of knowledge through the process of personal skills development and this is being reflected in the trend toward student-centred learning techniques both within undergraduate higher education generally, and in the postgraduate legal professional courses. The Legal Practice Course for intending solicitors and the new Bar Vocational Course for intending barristers are both skills based and student centred in terms of teaching and learning methodology.

To reflect this we have taken the opportunity to add skills related material. In addition to the chapters related to the application of skills relevant to the use of legal knowledge in future careers, there are chapters giving advice to assist you with developing successful study and research skills. These include a chapter on how to find the law and chapters that use materials to assist you with learning how to work with case law precedent and statutory provision.

To achieve an increased integration of the skills elements with the substantive legal system aspects, the format of the book has been changed. The chapters providing information on the operation of the legal system are broadly divided into their three main aspects, namely, the sources of law, the jurisdictions and administration of the courts, and the role of the legal personnel. These provide the core information that enable you to understand the way in which our law is made and the way in which it is administered. The skills associated with this are now presented either with the appropriate substantive knowledge legal system text or in the following chapter. Thus, by reading the chapters in conjunction with each other, the reader should more easily gain a fuller understanding of the legal process as a whole.

The editors acknowledge the work of the authors of the chapters in the first edition of the book: D G Cracknell, Peter Handley, Rosemary Higgott, Richard Law, Lynn Leighton-Johnstone, Louise M Miles and Suzanne Woollard. They are experts in the areas to which they have contributed and have a breadth and depth of knowledge and experience which has enabled us to maintain the comprehensive package of materials and exercises contained within this book.

Our editors also thank the editorial staff of Old Bailey Press for their help in the planning and publication of the book.

The developments in this edition represent the law as at 30 April 1997.

Judith Evans and Linda Perks
School of Legal Studies
University of Wolverhampton

1

Introduction to Legal Study

1.1 Introduction

earning a collection of rules. It is equally a
and apply the law. For the most part this is
he separate substantive laws, for example,
so on. The study of the legal principles and
a knowledge of how the various principles of
ds of the subject-matter to which they relate.
ntifying how the law has been applied to the
urts, and the interpretation of the law found
ding of judicial reasoning. A part of this
udy of the operation of the legal system,
dependent upon the source of the law and the
jurisdiction of the court hearing the case. The study of the English legal system is, therefore, an essential foundation for the study of our law. It provides a knowledge of how our law is made and the way in which it is administered. This involves the study of the sources of law, the structure and jurisdictions of the courts, and the role of the legal personnel.

A 'contextual' approach

It is possible to undertake all of the study of the substantive laws and the operation of the legal system from a purely academic basis. This is the traditional approach to learning the law and is a perfectly acceptable activity, but it does not provide certain skills that enhance the understanding of the process of the law. The purpose of this book is to provide a guide to these skills in relation to the study of the English legal system, which is a syllabus that suits this introductory study.

The modern approach to law teaching takes a more critical standpoint. Alongside the study of the various legal principles and the method of their application, there is a consideration of whether that law provides a suitable remedy in today's world, and of whether the machinery for dispute resolution provides an effective system that is suitable for all. The chapters in this book that explain the sources of the law, the structure of the courts, and the role of the legal personnel provide the foundation study necessary to understanding the framework in which the law exists. Consideration is also given to the issues raised by the cumbersome process of litigation and the cost of it. Tribunals and arbitration provide an alternative to hearing matters within the court system, but these are not suitable for dealing with some of the problems of modern life and there is an increasing use of conciliation and mediation. For many the cost of litigation is a very real concern, and so the provision of legal aid must be considered in terms of whether it offers real relief and what the alternatives are for ensuring that all persons have equal access to justice.

The inter-relationship of 'practice' skills

Legal resolution is not always a matter of going to court, and even when it is it involves a great many matters that occur outside of the court. The interpretation and application of the law learnt during the course of academic study is but one part of the work of the practising lawyer. In the past there has been a considerable divide between the academic study of the law and the acquisition of the skills required for professional practice. This is a divide that is rapidly disappearing and the undergraduate law degrees are increasingly incorporating all of the practical skills in preparation for the transition onto the Legal Practice Course (for intending solicitors) and the Bar Vocational Course (for intending barristers). Chapters on mooting, client counselling, and negotiation skills are given in this book as these are the activities that are most usually included as a part of the undergraduate study, either as extra-mural activity or as a part of the assessed work. An exercise on the filling-in of an application to an Industrial Tribunal for a matter involving unfair dismissal is included at the end of the chapter on alternative methods of resolving disputes.

Mooting, which is the holding of a 'mock trial', provides an insight into good practice and a very beneficial understanding of trial procedure and the effect it has on the way in which the law is argued. This serves to improve the way in which you argue the law, and the preparation of the submission tests your ability to research the law from primary sources and your understanding of how to work with precedents and statutory provision. The chapter explaining mooting technique and its complimentary chapter explaining civil and criminal trial procedures are given after the sources of the law and the various courts and tribunals have been identified. To enhance your understanding, visits to the courts to watch the cases is a simple and effective means of discovering how the law is argued and will help to bring your study of the law to life.

The chapters on client counselling and negotiation skills are included after the discussion of the role of the legal profession. The lawyer must be able to communicate effectively with the client to learn all the relevant facts, and be able to explain the law and its implications. It is equally necessary to prevent the parties from getting themselves into entrenched positions and closing their minds to the merits of their opponent's arguments. Negotiation must take place not only between the two opposing sides but also between the lawyer and the client. Clients have to be enabled to see where their own best interests really lie. The foundation knowledge for these skills is acquired during the academic study of the law in relation to ascertaining the material facts underpinning the reasoning for the application of a legal principle. Role-playing interviewing, client counselling and negotiation is beneficial to improving your acquisition of these skills and helps you to improve the way in which you explain the law in the seminar discussions and the assessed work. You should also endeavour to spend some time in an environment that involves legal work. This does not have to be at a firm of solicitors or barristers chambers, it is equally as beneficial to spend some time in a legal department of a commercial or industrial organisation, in the courts administration, or with organisations like the Citizens Advice Bureau.

Study skills

Other skills that are dealt with in this book relate to those that can be termed as 'study skills'. Acquiring an effective study method is essential to the successful study of every part of the study of the law. Advice is given on how to find the law, the most important of all the legal study skills. The method of study at university comprises types of tutor-led study, and a considerable amount of self-driven personal study. For the study of the law much of the personal study time is devoted to reading the cases and the interpretation of the law given in the textbooks and legal reference books. Advice is given on using the tutor contact time to its fullest advantage, and on developing techniques for 'reading' the law and taking concise and relevant notes. Effective time management and the development of accurate search statements aid these tasks. The learning and research skills have to be acquired early on in the study of the law, and if they are not the later study of the law will become increasingly more burdensome.

1.2 The need for law

It is said that we live in a free country, but the freedoms we enjoy are not absolute. There are many limitations placed upon what the individual can do and say. This is an inevitable consequence of living in a society in which what one person does is likely to affect another person to a greater or lesser extent. You may wish to sit on a beach listening to loud music whereas others may wish to enjoy the peace and quiet of the seaside. Clearly some kind of acceptable compromise is needed, but it is unrealistic to expect parties to arrive at individual settlements to deal with each situation when and as it arises. The law provides the necessary rules and balances the various interests of different members of the community. In effect the law determines what the compromises are that we all have to make if we are to live together in a civilised way. Sometimes the law operates by anticipating the sort of conflicts that may arise and providing for their resolution. In other situations what is offered is the machinery for resolving disputes.

Certain activities appear only to affect the participants, and the question then is whether the law should have any application to them. In practice the law often intervenes, perhaps seeking to impose certain standards of behaviour and morality which are deemed necessary for the well-being of society as a whole. For example, consider the law relating to homosexuality or drug-taking. Should private morality be the concern of public law? In reality it is difficult to find an activity which does not have implications, either direct or indirect, for others individually or as members of society. Law offers those perceived as vulnerable protection not only from the actions of others but also from themselves.

Law may be regarded as a set of rules recognised by society as being binding on its members. These rules must:

1. apply to all the members of society;
2. be made by some recognised and accepted authority;
3. be enforced by a court or other body by means of some inescapable sanction if necessary.

If asked, most people would say that they looked for justice and fairness in the law. Obviously this is desirable, but it is not so easy to establish what is just and fair. The rich man might say that it is unfair for the law to impose heavy taxation burdens on him because he works hard for his money. The poor man might reply that the rich man should be taxed at a high rate because he can best afford to make a contribution to the society from which he derives his income. This is an over-simplified example, but the point is that justice and fairness are not objective concepts. Whether we like a particular law or not we are still bound by it, and society is potentially threatened if it can be disregarded with impunity. Even so, a law which is manifestly unfair will fall into disrepute and might in extreme cases cause unrest. The answer must be for there to be proper mechanisms to change the law. The change may be brought about by the law makers responding to various external influences, and in a democracy it should be possible to hand the law-making role to others if those in power at any one time are insufficiently responsive.

There are very few areas of our lives which are not affected by law. Most people are not unduly aware of the law most of the time because it is self-evident that certain forms of conduct are socially unacceptable and so are avoided as a matter of course. Only a very few people are prepared to take the life of another because they realise that to do so is wrong, and the fact that murder is a crime is irrelevant since they would not commit it anyway. The difficulty is that issues are not always so clear-cut, and it is necessary to know the contents of the law on particular matters. There is an assumption that everyone knows what the law is, or, to put it rather differently, ignorance of the law is no defence. Since there are so many laws it is quite unreasonable in practice to expect the ordinary citizen to know about them all. One of the important roles of the lawyer is to advise the layman as to the law in terms that can be easily understood.

If law is to be effective it must be enforced. There must be some forum for the proper debate and resolution of disputes. This forum is provided by the courts which deal with both the civil disputes between one citizen and another and criminal cases involving the citizen and the State.

Just as the contents of the law need to be certain and capable of being known, so the courts need to have known boundaries to their jurisdiction and must follow established and predictable procedures. If law is to have any significance for the ordinary person he or she must have access to the courts; a rule of law which cannot be enforced might as well not exist. It is not reasonable, however, for the layman to know the practices and procedures of the courts, since it is to be hoped that his experiences of them will be limited to rare occasions. Once again, this is an area in which the lawyer can help by offering both advice and guidance as well as actual representation in the courts.

The law regulates the behaviour of individuals and organisations by confining them within a known framework of rules. Operating within this framework means that they can plan and conduct their affairs with confidence and certainty. The obligations imposed upon them and which they can impose upon others are known in advance. Any disregard of such obligations may result in the imposition of a sanction.

Without law society would quickly descend into a state of anarchy and the will of the strong would prevail regardless of the merits of their case. Badly motivated people would not have to be in a majority to bring about this state of affairs. Most of us think that some limitation of our personal freedom is a price worth paying to avoid such a situation and, of course, we obey the law not just because of the fear of sanction or the disapprobation of our peers but because we believe it to be right to do so.

1.3 The distinction between criminal law and civil law

There are a number of different ways of categorising law. It might be done according to source, for example as deriving from the common law or from equity or, perhaps, from statute or from decided cases. The point of reference could be its applicability, for example domestic as opposed to international law. The most useful classification at this stage is according to whether it is civil or criminal.

Criminal and civil laws within our society serve different purposes, and many of the practices and procedures applicable to each are also different.

Criminal law

Criminal law is concerned with the relationship between the State, acting on behalf of us all, and the individual. It concerns itself with conduct which requires regulation and which is disapproved sufficiently to warrant punishment. Breach of the criminal law may take the form of a positive act such as where a person 'dishonestly appropriates property belonging to another with the intention of permanently depriving the other of it' (Theft Act 1968 s1). A crime may take the form of an omission such as failing to submit a tax return when properly required to do so. The disapproval may not be based upon moral considerations but simply upon the fact that disobedience of a duly made law threatens us all to a greater or lesser extent and so must be suppressed.

The sanctions or punishments that may be imposed can take many different forms, ranging from imprisonment for various terms to probation orders or community service orders. These affect the liberty of the individual, and, in addition or as an alternative, a range of fines may also be imposed. The penalty should take account of the particular ends that its imposition seeks to further. These could include, for example, retribution, deterrence, reformation, or the protection of society.

Criminal law has its own terminology. An *accused* person is *prosecuted*. The State will act in the name of the Queen and so the case will be referred to as *R* v *Smith*. 'V' is short for versus, which means 'against', and 'R' is the abbreviation for Regina, which is the Latin word for Queen.

A person is presumed to be innocent, and the prosecution must be able to prove *beyond reasonable doubt* that the accused is guilty in order to secure a conviction. This is quite a high standard of proof, but it must be remembered that the accused's liberty is at stake and so it is appropriate.

The victim of a crime may feel that justice has been done if a criminal is convicted and sentenced, but that is of little consolation if as a result of the crime substantial loss has been suffered. The courts have certain limited powers to order the convicted person to pay compensation, but the basic aim of the criminal law remains to deal with the wrongdoer rather than to help the victim.

Civil law

Civil law is concerned with disputes between individuals or organisations, and the State has no real interest beyond providing the machinery for their resolution. It is in all our interests for legal obligations to be honoured and for compensation to be paid by one who has caused harm in such circumstances as the law recognises as giving rise to a claim. This gives certainty to our lives and helps develop socially responsible attitudes.

The civil law protects many interests. Typically, it deals with alleged breaches of contract or with torts such as negligence, nuisance or defamation; the list of protected interests is very long. There are many different remedies that may be sought, including damages, decrees for specific performance, and injunctions in all their various forms.

In simple terms, damages represent financial compensation for loss sustained, but financial compensation may not be the answer. If, for example, someone is creating a nuisance the person affected does not want money but, rather, wants the nuisance to be stopped. By means of an injunction the court may order the person responsible for the nuisance to cease the activity causing it. If a person fails to honour his contractual obligations there may be circumstances in which damages will not be adequate compensation, in which case the courts might order the party in breach to perform his or her part of the contract.

Civil law is thus concerned with enforcing obligations, resolving disputes and ordering compensation, and not with punishment. The terminology is different from that in criminal cases: the *plaintiff* brings an action against the *defendant*. He sues the defendant. The action will be cited as *Laurel* v *Hardy*, and the 'v' is expressed verbally as 'and'.

As with criminal law, in nearly every case the person who makes an allegation must prove what he alleges, and he must do so on a *balance of probabilities*. This is less demanding than the burden of proof in criminal cases.

The difference between the two branches of the law is underlined by there being separate courts provided to hear criminal and civil cases.

1.4 Origins of the common law

In section 1.3 reference was made to the possibility of classifying law according to whether it derived from the common law or from equity. These two sources of law merit special mention because although the distinction is less important than formerly it does remain significant.

The term 'common law' itself is capable of several meanings:

1. It might mean law that is common to the whole country as opposed to being limited to a particular locality or trade.
2. It might mean law that was developed in the old common law courts.
3. It might mean the rules of law that can be found in decided cases.

However defined, it seems to have its earliest origins in the common customs of the country.

A brief *and simplified* historical review is necessary to explain how equity came into being and developed.

Following the Battle of Hastings in 1066 William, Duke of Normandy, became King William I of England, a position he regarded as his by both legal and moral right. His attitude was proprietorial: the country was a source of revenue and an extension of his power base. If it was to be these things, however, William needed to settle and unify the country by making it secure and stable. His needs were:

1. to secure the loyalty of his barons, themselves rich and powerful men, by giving them an interest in the land, and to bind the indigenous population to the soil;
2. to provide a central administration to give effect to the laws he decreed and to collect revenues;
3. to provide a means of enforcing law and order.

To help fulfil these needs William took an inventory of the country, the Domesday Book, from which he could form a view of the value of his acquisition and the income it should generate.

He introduced a system of land holding which came to be known as the feudal system. He made grants of areas of the country to various of his barons, and in return they paid him in terms of both money and military service. The barons in turn gave sub-tenancies to those below them in the hierarchy and received similar benefits. As the process continued it came to resemble a pyramid with many tenants and sub-tenants, all of whom gave and received money and various services. Except for the very lowest they all had some interest in the continuation of the system, but ultimately all land belonged to the Crown to which it could revert.

The Curia Regis or King's Council, a consultative body made up of the barons as the King's tenants-in-chief, was formed to share some of the burdens of state with the King. Royal Commissioners were sent out to take word of the King's orders to the various parts of the kingdom and to ensure that they were given effect. In time these commissioners assumed a judicial role and became itinerant judges given authority to try cases in the name of the Crown.

These judges played an important part in the development of English law. They found a country which had no one legal system. Each part of the country had its own courts which applied its own local laws and customs. Today such a situation would be regarded as unfair, but in those days poor communications and an immobile population would have made the consequent inequality less of an issue. An individual would accept that the local law was quite simply all that need concern him.

The commissioners, as representatives of the King, would enforce the laws he made, but where appropriate they would adopt the local customs they found. As they moved from one area to another they would take with them the best of the customs and start to apply them over a wider area. When from time to time they returned to the King's Court they would meet and discuss their experiences and exchange views about the cases they had dealt with and the customs they had found and applied. When they went out to the regions again they would apply the best of these rules, and clearly this process started to make the law more 'common'.

The origins of the doctrine of precedent can be found in the practices of these judges. They would consider what had been decided in cases in the past which were similar to the case currently before them. Account would also be taken of what their fellow judges had done elsewhere. It is remarkable that as early as the thirteenth century in the Year Books there was a recognisable form of law reporting developing. These manuscript books recorded the decisions of the courts in important cases, and although they did not provide full reports they would have been of use to contemporary lawyers. The operation of a system of precedent is necessarily dependent upon those implementing it having access to reliable records of what has been previously decided.

1.5 Origins of equity

As early as the thirteenth century defects were perceived in the common law. The precedent system was rigid in application, a price that had to be paid for certainty. Its procedures were also rigid. There was, for example, the writ system with its 'forms of actions'. A writ was needed to start an action; it stated the plaintiff's claim and was issued in the name of the King. It ordered the defendant to do whatever the writ specified. The writs were issued by the clerks in the Chancellor's office and were expensive to obtain, which was in itself enough to deny access to justice to the poor. There was only a remedy if the facts of a claim could fit within an existing writ, and the list of writs was closed: 'no writ, no remedy'. There was no law of contract that would be recognised as such today because there was no writ which covered breach of contract. In other words the law under the Normans quickly became fossilised and did not allow for the natural growth that a developing society required. Consider the following examples:

1. Remedies available were limited: financial compensation has its purposes but it does not meet every need and there was, for example, no injunction.
2. Trusts were not recognised, which meant that there was nothing to prevent those who were in effect trustees from abusing their position.
3. Complicated and technical defences coupled with corruption resulted in long delays.
4. Witnesses who might have been critical in enabling a party to prove his case were not compellable.

The defects in the common law presented a major problem for the would-be litigant who was effectively denied justice. The solution was to by-pass the law! In those early days the King was a far more powerful person than the modern monarc,h and so the custom grew of petitioning the King for a remedy, the King being thought of as the fount of justice. The hope was that by the judicial application of common sense and ordinary fairness the King would give whatever remedy seemed appropriate without being bound by strict legal rules; in other words, that he would deal with the dispute with equity, considering where true justice lay. This obviously paid little regard to precedent and was highly subjective.

By the time of the reign of Henry III (1216–1272), the power to hear petitions was delegated by the King to his Lord Chancellor who was a cleric and who might be expected to dispense justice tempered with mercy. In time it became impossible for the Chancellor to deal with all such matters personally and so a Court of Chancery emerged to dispense equity. At first its rulings, like those of the King and Chancellor before it, were given according to a concept of justice rather than by reference to fixed principles of law. This is what was first looked for when the practice of petitioning the King began, but it did offend against the idea that the law should be certain and uniform in its application. What was needed was a framework of rules allowing for development, within which there was room for the exercise of discretion.

Sir Thomas More (1478–1535) was the first non-clerical Chancellor, and he started to formalise the rules and to adopt a system based upon precedent. As a result a court of equity came into being which, while it applied its own principles, became in time just as rigid and protracted in its procedures as the common law. It did, however, continue to offer solutions to the kind of problems identified earlier.

Thus there were two legal systems in the country offering different procedures and different remedies, which was a recipe for disaster. There was real rivalry between them since then (as now) litigation was a great source of income for the lawyers. A litigant might pursue an action at high cost in terms of both money and time only to find that the remedy he sought was only available in another court, and so the whole action would have to be started afresh.

The conflict could result in absurdity. For example, a defendant who had an award made against him at common law could turn to equity. If persuaded of the justice of the case, equity could issue a common injunction restraining the successful plaintiff from enforcing the award made by the common law court. If the injunction was ignored there was a contempt of court and the plaintiff could be sent to gaol. The common law's response might then be to issue a writ of habeas corpus. Such a state of affairs did not inspire confidence in the law and must have been of far more benefit to the lawyers than the litigants.

The case of *Wood* v *Scarth* (1855) 2 K & J 33 is instructive. It concerned a mistake as to the terms of a contract for the letting of a public house. The plaintiff believed that all he had to pay was an annual rent as set out in a letter of offer which he accepted. The defendant through his agent thought he had made it clear that a premium of £500 was also to be paid. The defendant refused to grant the lease, and so in 1855 the plaintiff sought a decree of specific performance. The court in exercise of its discretion refused to grant the decree having regard to the uncertainty caused by the mistake. Three years later, relying on exactly the same facts, the plaintiff sued again for damages and won. It was held that notwithstanding the mistake the contract must stand, and damages were awarded for the refusal to grant the lease.

1.6 Common law and equity today

The Judicature Acts 1873–1875 fused the common law courts and the equity courts into one High Court. It was the courts that were fused, not common law and equity themselves. In the simplest of terms it meant that both legal systems with their individual characteristics remained in being, with their different remedies being available in the same court. For example, an injunction may be sought in the Queen's Bench Division or the Chancery Division but according to the rules of equity. This is a matter of great convenience to litigants and also saves a waste of court time by avoiding the need to duplicate actions.

The essential difference remains that whereas common law remedies may in appropriate circumstances be demanded as of right, equitable remedies are discretionary. This does not mean that the individual judge has a discretion to grant an equitable remedy depending upon his own caprice but rather that there is a judicial discretion which determines whether or not a remedy will be granted.

The maxims of equity

Equity is still applied in accordance with certain principles which embody concepts of natural justice and which find their expression in a series of maxims. Many of these maxims speak for themselves and have immediate appeal to most people's sense of fairness. The list is quite long and the following are simply offered as examples:

1. 'Equity does not suffer a wrong to be without a remedy.'
   Equity has been prepared to create a new remedy where a common law remedy has seemed deficient.
2. 'He who comes to equity must come with clean hands.'
   This means, for example, that there will be no remedy for someone who has behaved unconscionably, such as a beneficiary who has acquiesced in a breach of trust.
3. 'Delay defeats equity.'
   If a plaintiff has been slow or negligent in pursuing a claim he may be denied the remedy that could have been obtained if it had been sought promptly. The delay might have led the defendant to think the claim was not going to be pursued at all.
4. 'Equity will not assist a volunteer.'
   Although a decree of specific performance may be available to enforce an obligation arising from a contract or a under trust, it will not be awarded to one who has given no consideration for the obligation which is sought to be enforced.
5. 'Equity looks upon that as done which ought to be done.'
   Equity will give effect to people's intentions even though some formality may not

have been met; for example, an agreement to create a formal lease is the equivalent of the lease itself.

The maxims indicate the approach that the courts will adopt when considering whether or not to allow an equitable right or to grant an equitable remedy.

Equitable rights

Perhaps the most important equitable right is that of the beneficiary under a trust.

At common law a person who owns an interest in property is taken to do so absolutely and must dispose of that property absolutely. This means:

1. An owner of property must have the legal right to enjoy the benefit of the property.
2. If it is disposed of by gift, sale or by being devised in a will, conditions – such as, for example, the creation of a life interest – cannot be attached.
3. There cannot be a succession of interests.

This could be a charter for the unscrupulous. If, for example, a person with an infant child left property for the benefit of that child and then died there would be an immediate problem.The child would not be legally capable of holding that property and so somebody else would have to hold it as legal owner on the child's behalf. The common law would only recognise the rights of the legal owner (the trustee), and so the child (the beneficiary) would have no redress if the trustee abused the position of trust and used the property for improper purposes.

Equity recognises the rights of beneficiaries, which dictate that the trustees must hold for the benefit of the beneficiaries. It imposes the necessary duties and obligations on trustees to ensure that this happens.

A trust allows for a succession of interests. For example, a testator can leave property to his wife with the remainder to his children. What he does is to devise his property to trustees to hold it for his wife, remainder to children absolutely; that is, on his death his wife will enjoy the property but cannot alienate it. On her death the trust will end and the property will pass to the children.

Trusts may come into existence without having been expressly established. Constructive trusts are raised by construction of equity to satisfy the demands of justice and good conscience without reference to the presumed intention of the parties.

Another significant equitable right is the right of redemption. A mortgagor has a right to regain his property from the mortgagee before or after the redemption date. Under the common law a mortgage was strictly construed as being a conveyance of land that was subject to a covenant to reconvey to the mortgagor on repayment of the loan and the interest on or before an agreed date. If the date for redemption was passed then the right to redeem the mortgage was lost. This was open to abuse, for example, by mortgagees absenting themselves at the time agreed for redemption so that repayment could not be made. Equity recognises a right to redeem even after the due date for redemption. The maxim 'Equity looks to intention and not to form' applies. It is intended that the property is to provide security for the repayment, and once the repayment is made the property is to be returned notwithstanding that there may have been some failure to comply with the strict letter of the agreement.

Another example of an equitable right is that of lien. By an equitable lien one party acquires a charge on the property of another until a certain claim has been met; for example, an unpaid vendor may have a right to retain goods until payment has been made. At common law the ownership should be with the purchaser.

Equitable remedies

Equitable remedies are appropriate when monetary compensation or damages are inadequate.

Injunctions are orders of the court which restrain a person from acting in a particular way or, sometimes, which compel a particular action. They may be:

1. prohibitory: an order not to perform an act – for example, to stop picketing, not to infringe a patent, not to approach the matrimonial home, not to publish a particular article in a newspaper;
2. mandatory: an order to perform an act – for example, an order that a trespasser should leave land.

Injunctions may take a number of different forms to deal with a range of situations. They are available not only in respect of equitable rights but also for common law rights, for example to prevent a nuisance. Since injunctions are orders of the court, their breach is a contempt of court, the penalty for which can ultimately be imprisonment.

A decree of specific performance is a court order to oblige a person to fulfil some pre-existing obligation into which he or she has entered. Normally damages suffice, but they will not do so where the subject of the contract has some special or rare characteristic which makes it unobtainable from an alternative source. Such decrees will not be granted where their implementation would require an unacceptable level of court supervision. They are suitable if all that is required is a single act, for example signing a conveyance of land.

Rescission may be available. The right to rescind is the right of a party to have a contract set aside and to be restored to his original position. There has to be some inherent defect in the contract which makes it voidable, arising perhaps from a misrepresentation or a mistake. It must be possible for there to be full restitution so that the parties can be restored to the status quo ante. Like all equitable remedies it is discretionary.

Another interesting equitable remedy is that of rectification. At common law, extrinsic parol evidence cannot be introduced to contradict a deed or other written instrument; the court will consider the contract as evidenced by the writing. Equity will allow parol evidence to be introduced if one party argues that the writing does not accurately reflect the actual agreement. Rectification does not vary the contract, only the documents, and it is mainly used to deal with mistakes in the expression of the agreement.

These are only some of the equitable remedies, but they serve to demonstrate the way in which fairness and justice are introduced through the application of equity.

Common law damages

The common law remedy of damages is used in a number of situations. In contract, damages may be ordered to put the injured party in the same financial position that he or she would have been in if the contract had not been broken. In tort, damages attempt to provide financial compensation to put the injured party in the position that he or she would have been in if the tort had not been committed. Although the assessment of damages is difficult the courts normally operate according to known guidelines. There are real problems. It is hard to work out the compensation due to somebody who as the result of another's negligence is confined to a wheelchair. There is no real remedy, but money can provide the means to make life less intolerable. What compensation can there be for the parents of a dead child? So, in many cases, damages are poor compensation but they are the best the law can offer.

1.7 Statute law and case law

Law may be classified according to whether it has its origins in statute or in case law. These will be the subject of detailed examination later. At this stage a brief statement is sufficient.

The classification of the law as statute law and case law is sometimes also referred to as being the distinction between written law and unwritten law. It is a distinction that reflects the difference between the legislative and the judicial functions within our legal system.

Statute

The statute law (also referred to as legislation) is written by Parliament, or by those who derive authority from Parliament. It is found in:

1. the Acts of Parliament (the statutes),
2. statutory instruments,
3. delegated legislation (comprising rules, orders, regulations and by-laws), and
4. by virtue of our membership of the European Union, in the legislation of the Community institutions.

The statute law that you will deal with in the main is that which is found in the

Acts of Parliament. An Act states the law as a series of provisions divided into 'sections' which comprise of rules, principles and tests. These rules are inserted into the pre-existing law as the supreme law and have to be applied by the courts in preference to any common law principles on the same matter.

Parliament is the supreme law-making authority. It is open to Parliament to legislate upon any topic it chooses, and under the constitution there is no provision for legislation properly enacted to be challenged. Sometimes Parliament passes an Act which delegates the making of necessary detailed rules to other bodies such as local authorities. Such delegated legislation may be challenged by the courts on certain specified grounds, for example because the rule made exceeds the power given in the enabling Act itself.

The statute law is not only supreme law but is now, arguably, the *main* source for our law whereas, up to about the middle of the nineteenth century, the common law was undoubtedly the main source for the law. The brief account of the historical development of common law and equity given in sections 1.3 to 1.6 above serves to show the extent to which the judiciary enjoyed dominion over the development of our law for most of our legal history from the eleventh century. At the start of the nineteenth century the statute law still mainly served to guide the development of the common law. At the turn into this century it had become a major source of law transcending common law and equity, and it is really within the last hundred years that it has taken on the full mantle of supremacy that it now has.

The supremacy of the European Union legislation

Although Parliament is our supreme law-making authority, by virtue of our membership of the European Union, sovereignty has been surrendered in respect of specified areas of the law. The primary European Union legislation and much of the secondary legislation is enacted in the UK as Acts of Parliament. The European Court of Justice gives preliminary rulings on questions concerning the applicability of the Community law in any individual case and has consistently held that the Community law takes precedence over the domestic law of any Member State.

Case law

The case law is the term used to describe all decided cases. These are found in the law reports (discussed in Chapter 2, section 2.4, below) and they become *a source of law* by virtue of the role played by our judiciary in the law-making process. The judgments delivered by the judges hearing the cases provide a source of reference for the *judicial reasoning* determining the application of all of our law, irrespective of whether the legal principles involved derive from the common law, equity, or the statute law.

The brief account of the development of common law and equity given in the preceding sections identifies the reasons why the judiciary enjoy a law-making role in relation to those sources of law. The aspect that can be difficult to grasp during the early study of the law is the extent to which their 'law-making' role continues to exist now that the statute law has become the major source of our law. The operation of the doctrine of judicial precedent and the 'rules' for the judicial interpretation of statute have to be studied to gain an appreciation of this role and the following explanation merely provides a summary of the key aspects.

The doctrine of judicial precedent

This is a very important feature of our legal system. The law aspires to certainty so that society can make decisions about what can and cannot legally be done. An essential part of maintaining certainty is consistency of decision-making in the courts and the doctrine of judicial precedent is used to achieve this. Precedent, stated simply, is the practice of re-using past decisions in later similar cases to which they can and should apply. The rule or principle that is applied is found by extracting the ratio decidendi (the reason for the decision) from the judgments. The ratio decidendi will be based upon the facts of the case to which it relates and, within the judgment as a whole, there will be a reasoned explanation of why the rule should apply to those facts. It is this explanation that enables a general principle to be extracted for future use in cases that have a similar basis of factual circumstances. It is not a question of searching for identical facts but of looking for a similarity of fact which is a reasoning process that involves moving from the specific to the more general.

A simple example to help put this reasoning process into some context is the criteria used for the application of the 'invitation to treat' rule in contract law. This rule recognises the need to regard certain activities as being mere pre-contractual negotiations that do not have the status of being contractually binding. The leading case (ie the case cited as the precedent for the rule) is *Pharmaceutical Society of Great Britain* v *Boots Cash Chemists (Southern) Ltd* [1952] 2 QB 795; [1952] 2 All ER 456. It involved the sale of restricted medicines in a pharmacy and it was necessary to establish that the displayed goods did not 'offer themselves for sale' but rather 'invited persons to offer to buy them' so that the pharmacist could refuse to sell them to persons who, by statute law, he was not permitted to sell to. The judicial reasoning for the application of the 'invitation to treat' rule, as it came to be called, relied on the notion that persons have to be able to 'examine' goods before they buy them and it is this that goes forward as the criteria for the application of the rule in future cases. Any form of preliminary consideration about a purchase can fall under the notion of 'examination'; the rule does not merely apply to goods bought in shops, nor to the physical examination of them. Descriptions in advertisements or in catalogues, or representations made in letters, can equally fall under the 'invitation to treat' rule.

Statutory interpretation

Statutory provision is worded so that it may be applied in a general way rather than to sets of precisely defined facts. It is for the judiciary to determine *whether* any part of the statutory provision applies to the facts of a case in hand, and to determine *how* it should be applied. This is carried out in accordance with 'interpretation rules' developed, for the most part, by the judiciary themselves and these provide 'aids' by which the judiciary determine the purpose of the rules and the interpretation of specific words and phrases used in the Acts of Parliament. This means that all statutory provision becomes subject to judicial interpretation and it is necessary to refer to the decided cases to determine how the statute law has been applied.

The key differences between statute law and the common law

The statute law is the means by which change to the law can be initiated quickly, and embodies rules which must be applied in every case. It provides regulation for an activity *in advance of its occurrence* and thereby performs two important functions within a common law system:

1. it is the means by which political, social or economic objectives can be translated into an appropriate legal form for immediate enforcement; and
2. it is the means by which new rules, concepts and tests can be inserted into the legal reasoning process for any pre-existing area of the law as the supreme law.

The common law deals with circumstances *when they arise* and it relies entirely upon a case being brought before the court. The decision given is primarily intended to resolve the dispute that has arisen between the parties and the law is applied in relation to the facts of the case. This limits the ability of the common law to lay down a general legal policy, whereas the statute law can immediately insert new rules and abolish old ones as a matter of general policy without being fettered by the need to consider particular facts. However, the decision in a case does signal to others the way in which the law will treat any matter, and to this extent lays down laws for the future.

The common law does not have the same ability as the statute law to initiate rapid change to the law. It may require several cases before the legal principle is developed in full and it can take some time for a recognisable precedent to emerge. The evolutionary nature of the development of any legal principle in relation to the facts of cases means that the principle of law can be subject to variable development and this substantially reduces the certainty of application of the law and makes it unsuitable for the regulation of many types of activity in modern society.

The application of a precedent found in a previous case is subject to the status of the court that heard the case. Stated broadly, the courts higher in the hierarchy bind those below them, for example, the House of Lords binds the Court of Appeal. This limitation on the ability of the judges to change the law has had important effects on the development of the common law and has been part of the reason for the growth of the statute law.

2

Study Skills

2.1 The learning process

The method of study at university comprises types of tutor-led study, and a considerable amount of self-driven personal study. For the study of the law much of the personal study time is devoted to reading the cases and the interpretation of the law given in the textbooks and legal reference books. Most of the modules or units of study culminate in a form of assessment that: (a) tests the level of understanding you have acquired; and (b) tests your ability to interpret and apply the law.

Each activity is as important as the others in the whole process and they are inter-dependent. The diagram given on page 20 shows the inter-relationship.

18

The lectures have a dual function:

1. they introduce the topic through an identification of the main legal rules and an explanation of their source, scope and purpose; and
2. they identify the ambit of the syllabus, direct your reading and note-taking, and thereby help you to prepare you for the seminars, workshops, and the assessed work.

The seminars and workshops clarify your lectures, reading and note-taking and, through structured discussion or set tasks, they enable a better understanding of the law to be acquired which, in turn, is valuable preparation for the assessed work.

Reading from the literary and the primary sources of information facilitates your understanding of the lectures, and provides the detail of knowledge required for the seminars, workshops and the assessed work.

Your notes serve several purposes. They need to be used for reference in the seminars, for the writing of essays or assignments, and for revision for examinations.

The essays/assignments require you to discuss the law, and in so doing, they help you think about the inter-relationship between legal principles as well as causing you to review and improve your notes.

The examinations test your ability to recall key principles and write about them under time constraint, and the revision for them relies on the notes accumulated during all the aforementioned activities.

The tutor-led study directs your personal study. The course materials and the classes indicate the syllabus and it is important to use this information. It identifies what should be studied, and the depth to which you are required to study it. Researching into information that is beyond the scope of the syllabus may cause you to become confused about the law, and is, in any event, time that is better devoted to acquiring a knowledge of the law that will be discussed in the seminars and that is required for the assessed work.

Contact with a tutor is a valuable part of the learning process. The distance-learning courses generally add tutor contact by holding summer schools, review programmes and revision programmes, and these should be attended whenever possible. Tutor contact for students who are attending at an institution usually takes the form of lectures and seminars and some courses include other forms of study sessions, such as workshops and personal tutorials. Lectures are usually of 50 minutes to one hour duration and seminars are discussion groups comprising of about twelve persons. Workshops vary but usually involve team work for the practical application of the law to typical legal matters.

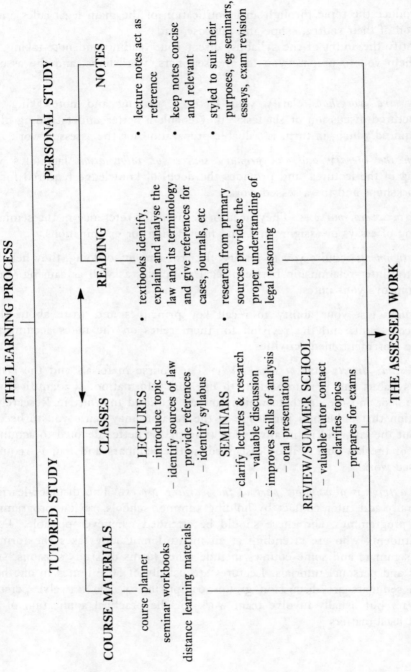

THE LEARNING PROCESS

TUTORED STUDY

PERSONAL STUDY

CLASSES

COURSE MATERIALS
- course planner
- seminar workbooks
- distance learning materials

LECTURES
- introduce topic
- identify sources of law
- provide references
- identify syllabus

SEMINARS
- clarify lectures & research
- valuable discussion
- improves skills of analysis
- oral presentation

REVIEW/SUMMER SCHOOL
- valuable tutor contact
- clarifies topics
- prepares for exams

READING
- textbooks identify, explain and analyse the law and its terminology and give references for cases, journals, etc
- research from primary sources provides the proper understanding of legal reasoning

NOTES
- lecture notes act as reference
- keep notes concise and relevant
- styled to suit their purposes, eg seminars, essays, exam revision

THE ASSESSED WORK

- Unseen/seen examinations test your ability to recall and explain principles under time restraint
- Successful revision relies on good notes made during course
- Written assignments test your understanding of the topic and ability to argue law in a clear and precise way
- Cause you to review and improve your notes

2.2 Gaining the most from the class contact time

As the method of study at university is likely to be different to that which you have previously been used to, learning how to use the class contact time to your advantage is one of the first skills that you have to acquire. Lectures, seminars and other types of classes, such as tutorials and workshops, each serve different purposes within the learning process and demand different forms of preparation and participation. If you learn how to use them properly you will not only understand the law better, but you will also greatly ease the demands that the research into the law places on your limited study time.

The value of lectures

They provide valuable *information* through the identification of:

1. the key principles, leading cases, statutory provision, etc;
2. references for other primary source material, eg supporting or comparative cases;
3. references for secondary source material, eg textbooks that give clear, or interesting, or alternative views, or informative journal articles;
4. a bridged gap between printed textbooks and the present state of knowledge;
5. an introduction to issues that will be discussed further in seminars or dealt with in workshops.

They provide valuable *explanation* of:

1. conceptually difficult rules;
2. the reasoning underpinning judicial dicta;
3. the problems that have arisen with the interpretation of statutory provision;
4. the way that a rule is refined, expanded, or changed in later cases;
5. the differing interpretations that have been given to rules either in the cases or in the textbooks.

To get the most from a lecture

The importance of attending lectures should be obvious but it is important to note that the lectures do not intend to cover the topic in detail and will not provide all of the information that you require to discuss the law in the seminars or to write about it in your assessed work. They introduce the topic and, in as far as time permits, explore central issues.

A common characteristic of a law lecture is that it is a continuous exposition of facts; it can be as densely packed with information as the textbooks it seeks to support. The following advice represents the best way to deal with this quantity of valuable information.

1. Before the lecture, read the topic in the recommended course textbook to

acquaint yourself with legal terminology and gain an overall appreciation of what the subject-matter entails. This will help you to recognise the importance of points raised by the lecturer and enable you to be selective in the points that you take a note of.

2. During the lecture take a minimum amount of notes and concentrate instead on listening to and understanding what is being said. The taking of notes deflects your mind from the overall appreciation of the topic that a lecture gives. Your notes merely need to be an *aide memoir* of the analysis that was given of the cases or the legal rules, and references for cases, statutes, and recommended further reading from textbooks and journals. Their purpose is to assist you when undertaking the detailed research required for the seminars and the assessed work.

3. The taking of lecture notes is a skill that is learnt with practice, and it relies on you developing a 'shorthand' that enables you to get a lot of information down on paper whilst still listening to what is being said. Reduce commonly used words and terms to shortforms, for example, 'the rule in *Rylands* v *Fletcher*' to RVF, 'invitation to treat' to ITT, Unfair Contract Terms Act 1977 to UCTA, and so on. Certain letters could relate to a lot of things so it is best to decide on some format and use them consistently throughout all your notes, for example, use *D* for defendant, *def* for defence, *d* for duty, and *dc* for duty of care – in certain notes you could have all of these on one page!

4. Start your further research as soon as possible whilst the content of the lecture is still fresh in your mind.

The value of seminars

Seminar discussions are an important part of the learning process for several reasons:

1. They enable you to discuss aspects of the topic in a small group with a tutor which is invaluable for helping to sort out in your mind the inter-relationship between the various rules and may also provide you with an interpretation of the law or an analysis of a problem that you may not have thought of yourself.

2. They serve to stimulate your interest and direct your further research into, or revision of, the topic.

3. They require you to present explanations of the law and arguments for its application which is essential training for the type of analysis that you will be expected to give in the written assessed work.

4. They provide an opportunity to clarify any points which you did not fully understand in the lecture or from your reading of the textbook(s) or cases. This, however, is subject to the extent of your misunderstanding and the tutor may suggest other reading that you should undertake, or recommend you to make an appointment for a personal tutorial.

To get the most from the seminars you should:

1. *Prepare* notes to answer the seminar questions or discussion points. Do not rely solely on your lecture notes; these were intended to provide the framework for the seminar preparation, not the answers to the seminar questions. Do the suggested reading and look up as many cases as you can. Most courses expect 40 hours of study per week which includes the class contact time. This usually leaves you 25 hours plus per week to allocate to the advance reading for lectures and preparation for the other classes and assessed work that you have. You should, therefore, have more than enough time to prepare thoroughly for the seminars.

2. *Write a summary* of the key points with a clear reference system to the main material in your file. If you have done thorough research your notes will consist of a number of different papers – see section 2.11 below. Summary sheets enable you to identify relevant judicial dicta from judgments or wording from statutory provision – this level of discussion is much the most beneficial form of seminar debate and should be aspired to.

3. *Always sort out any aspects you do not understand*, either at the seminar or at a mutually convenient time with the tutor afterwards. If you have heard information at the seminar that you have not researched you should follow it up unless the tutor indicates that it is not necessary.

4. *Attend*! You will always benefit from the discussion even if you have not been able to do all the preparation work. In any week that you have unusually limited preparation time do a little bit of research for each discussion point so that you have an overall appreciation of each part of the debate. Ensure that you do finish the required research afterwards. Do not miss selected seminars because you think your own research is sufficient and that the seminar discussion topics will not add much more to understanding. The tutors conduct seminars to suit the topic and experiencing these different styles of discussion is a valuable part of the learning process.

5. *Contribute* to the discussion. Being involved in the debate stimulates your interest and will help you to structure your thoughts on a subject in a way that reading and note-taking cannot. Participation in the debate also enables you to develop the skill of oral presentation of an argument.

2.3 The literary sources of information

The literary sources (also known as the secondary sources) include the textbooks, the legal encyclopaedias, the law dictionaries, and the journals and periodicals. They are books *about* law as distinct from the primary sources which are books *of* law.

The textbooks

The legal textbooks are usually your first point of reference for academic research. They identify the various rules that arise from the statute law and the case law and explain the reasoning underpinning their creation, development, interpretation and application. In choosing which textbooks to read, you should take your direction from those that are recommended for the course that you are taking. The syllabus will relate to the content and type of analysis contained within those recommended books. You will usually be referred to a selection of textbooks, perhaps with one highlighted as being the key recommended book for the course. You are likely to find that a particular book suits you best, but reading generally from all of the titles is advisable because there can be different views and approaches to the interpretation of the law.

Do not confine your reading only to those texts which provide you with material for making notes. A valuable 'overview' of a law is gained by reading several books and journals and then selecting those to make notes from. If you find a book particularly difficult to understand, turn to the shorter works on the subject to gain a feel for the topic, but do not rely on these for all your research. Although they may be easier to understand and helpful in the initial stages of looking up a topic, they do not provide an analysis sufficient for seminar, essay and examination purposes.

Law journals and periodicals

The many law journals provide interesting articles which may give you ideas about a topic that you have not picked up from the textbooks and case reports. Journals such as the *New Law Journal* run articles on all the different laws and are particularly good for the articles discussing new case law or statutes. The usual custom is that laws and legal principles introduced during the duration of the course will not be part of the assessment criteria in an examination, but you should take your guidance on this from your tutor who may indicate that writing about the new law will either be necessary to or advantageous to the final grade. Some journals are specific to a law and contain some highly detailed articles, some of which may delve into the topic in a much more analytical way than you require. Be careful not to allow your reading of such articles to confuse you or to cause you to branch off into lengthy research on an aspect of the law that your course syllabus does not aim to cover.

Journal citations

The journals have their own abbreviated citations and examples are: NLJ for the *New Law Journal*, MLR for the *Modern Law Review*, SJ for the *Solicitors' Journal*, EL Rev for the *European Law Review*.

An example of a reference is: Steiner J. 'From Direct Effects to *Francovich*: Shifting Means of Enforcement of Community Law' (1993) 18 EL Rev 3.

2.4 The primary sources of information: case law

The cases are reported in a variety of series of law reports and the legislation is published in a variety of 'official' and 'unofficial' series of reference works. Finding out what a 'law' is, as stated in its original form, is a matter of referring to the judgments given in the cases and to the statutory provision. In relation to any one task you will have to read several cases and may have to refer to more than one Act of Parliament.

Case reports

The case law is divided into *reported* cases, which are the ones that you will deal with, and the *unreported* cases, which you may use on occasion. The reported cases are found in the law reports. It is neither practical nor necessary to report every case heard and the reporters select those that are important for use as precedents. On occasion an unreported case may turn out to be more important than at first appeared and a copy of the judgment can be ordered from the official shorthand writers. LEXIS, the computerised law information retrieval system (discussed below), carries a large number of unreported cases.

The modern law reports that you will use are:

The Law Reports of the Incorporated Council of Law Reporting
These consist of four series and any series may have more than one volume in any year:

Series	Abbreviation	Cases Reported
Appeal Cases	AC	House of Lords. Privy Council
Chancery Division	Ch	Chancery cases
Queen's Bench Division	QB (or KB)	QBD cases
Family Division	Fam	High Court and Court of Appeal

The Weekly Law Reports (abbreviated as WLR)
These are also published by the Council and aim to provide a comprehensive coverage of all of the important new High Court, Court of Appeal, House of Lords and Privy Council cases. They are useful as a means of keeping up to date with developments in the law. The series is published in weekly parts and as three annual bound volumes. The first volume contains cases which will *not* be included in the Law Reports.

The All England Law Reports (abbreviated as All ER)
These are the most important of the private series of law reports. They are

published by Butterworths in weekly parts and as three annual bound volumes. Their acceptability for citation in court is accorded a considerable status that is barely inferior to that of the *Weekly Law Reports*.

The other modern private law reports

These are published by various bodies and you will come across them in relation to the study of certain laws, for example, the use of the Lloyd's Reports if you study maritime laws, and the Criminal Appeal Reports when you study criminal law.

The reports of the cases heard by the European Court of Justice and the Court of First Instance

These are found in:

1. The *European Court Reports*, the official reports, abbreviated as ECR, and available in all of the languages of the Member States of the Union. An unfortunate effect of this is that there is a delay before the case is reported.
2. The *Common Market Law Reports*, an unofficial series, abbreviated as CMLR which are written in English and published weekly by the European Law Centre.
3. The *Official Journal C Series* (the 'Communications' section) gives the listings of cases to appear before the Court of Justice and a summary of the decisions handed down by the Court, usually before the full report is published in the ECR.

Where the application of the European Union law is by an English court the case will often also be reported in one of the English law reports. This may simply be a report of a case in which European Union law has been applied, or it may be a case where the English court has requested a preliminary ruling from the European Court of Justice under the Article 177 procedure (this is explained in the chapter on the courts).

2.5 Citation of cases

The citations are the reference for the source of information for the law and, apart from being the means by which the law can be found, they indicate the authority of the source that is being used.

Case names in the criminal cases

A criminal prosecution is brought by the Crown and is usually cited as *R* v ... (name of defendant). R is an abbreviation for Rex or Regina (King or Queen) and is said as 'the Crown against ...'; ie the 'R' and the 'v' are not pronounced as initials and 'v' should not be said as versus! On appeal the case may become, eg, *Smith* v *R*. A case shown as *DPP* v .... is being brought by the Director of Public Prosecutions and some cases are brought by the Attorney-General (A-G).

Case names in the civil cases

The name of both parties is given with a 'v' between them, eg, *Smith* v *Jones*, and for civil cases the 'v' is said as 'and' (not as 'against' as in criminal cases). The party named first is the plaintiff (at first instance) or appellant (for appeal cases), and the second party will be the defendant or respondent. Note that the effect of this is that, on appeal, the names of the parties might be reversed depending upon whether it is the plaintiff or defendant who is bringing the appeal, but this name reversal is not a hard and fast rule and sometimes does not occur.

The abbreviation 'Re' is used for some types of cases, notably in relation to trusts and the estates of deceased persons, and indicates 'in the case of', eg *Re Smith*. 'Re' is also used where anonymity for the party is required, such as in cases involving children, and the name of the party is merely indicated as its first letter, eg *Re S*.

In maritime law it is common to refer to the case by the name of the ship, eg *The Julia* rather than *Comptoir d'Achat* v *Luis de Ridder Ltda, The Julia* [1949] AC 293. As those of you who do international trade law, carriage of goods by sea, or maritime law subjects will come to realise, this is very much preferable to remembering the sometimes very long foreign names of the parties to these cases!

R v *Jones, ex parte Smith* is a case that is being brought under the prerogative orders of the Crown, hence the use of 'R', and the ex parte (in part) denotes that Smith is outside the proceedings but made the application for judicial review.

Case law citations for the English law reports

These are a reference to the law report in which the case is reported and use the abbreviation for the law report, its volume number (if required) and the page number.

For example in *Anns* v *Merton London Borough Council* [1978] AC 728; [1977] 2 All ER 492 the AC (Appeal Cases) report does not have a volume and is found by its year, 1978, and at page 728; and the All ER (All England) report is found in volume 2 of the 1977 reports at page 492.

The year is shown either in round ( ) or in square [ ] brackets. Square brackets are used for reports that rely on the year as their reference system, and any volumes published within that year will start as number 1, as in the above example of [1977] 2 All ER which requires you to find the shelf with the 1977 reports and then to select volume 2. Round brackets are used if the reports consecutively number the volumes, eg *Cunningham* v *Munro* (1922) 28 Com Cas 42 is found in volume 28 of Commercial Cases, the year itself is not vital to the reference.

The abbreviations for the law reports are adhered to rigidly and can be checked by referring to the list given in any volume of the *Current Law Yearbook*, and are also given in *Sweet and Maxwell's Guide to Law Reports and Statutes*, and Dane and Thomas' *How to Use a Law Library*.

Where the case is reported in more than one law report there is a hierarchy of citation which is: Law Reports, Weekly Law Reports, All England Law Reports, and then other series, and the citation will also reflect the status of the court, eg *Davis* v *Johnson* [1979] AC 264, [1978] 1 All ER 1132 (HL); [1978] 2 WLR 182, [1978] 1 All ER 841 (CA).

Citation of European Union cases

The case number is the important part of the citation. It gives the list number for the case and the last two numbers of the year in which the application or reference was made. This case number is given first, followed by the name of the case, and the citation for the report comes last, eg 13/61 *Bosch* v *de Geus* [1962] ECR 45.

There are now two courts. Cases listed for the European Court of Justice have the prefix C–, and cases listed for the Court of First Instance have the prefix T–, eg C–150/88 *Parfumerie Fabrik* v *Provide* [1989] ECR 3891; [1991] 1 CMLR 715, and T–51/89 *Tetra Pak Rausing SA* v *EC Commission* [1991] 4 CMLR 334.

Another thing to note is that the number is not necessarily the same year that the judgment was given or that the case was reported. A good example of this is the *Factortame* case which asked for a preliminary ruling in 1989 and is listed as case C–213/89, but the judgment was not handed down until 1990. You will find that cases like these are in sequel so, by 1990, *Factortame* was Case C–213/89 *R* v *Secretary of State, ex parte Factortame (No 3)* [1990] 1 WLR 818.

Finding case law citations and checking for later cases

You should be able to find the citation for most of the cases you use in the case index of the textbooks on the subject. These list the cases in alphabetical name order and if you cannot find it, look for it in reverse name order. The European Union law cases may be listed in chronological date order. The *Current Law Case Citators* list all reported cases in alphabetical order with their citation, plus a reference to a summary of the case in the relevant annual volume of *Current Law*.

2.6 The primary sources of information: legislation

The legislation that you deal with in the main is that found in the Acts of Parliament but you may be referred to other written sources for the law, and in particular to the international Treaties and Conventions. You will come across these in relation to certain substantive law subjects and all of you will be required to study the Treaties that provide the constitution and legal authority for the law of the European Union and its institutions.

Acts of Parliament

These are published by Her Majesty's Stationery Office (HMSO) as individual copies of the statutes as they are passed and are brought together in the annual bound editions of the *Public General Acts and Measures* and in *Statutes in Force*. The Incorporated Council of Law Reporting publishes a series called *Law Reports: Statutes*. The main learning resource is *Halsbury's Statutes of England* which contains an annotated version of all legislation currently in force. *Current Law Statutes Annotated* publishes the Acts in loose-leaf format and provides annotations written by a specialist in the particular area of law that identify the scope and the operation of the provisions.

Statutory instruments

These are bound annually in their own volume called *Statutory Instruments* published by the HMSO and the main alternative source is *Halsbury's Statutory Instruments*.

European Union legislation

This is contained in specific volumes of *Halsbury's Laws* and *Halsbury's Statutes* and, since 1973, in an *Encyclopaedia of European Community Law* which is published in loose-leaf form. The major work is the *Official Journal*. This records all of the legal information for the European Union. The *L Series* contains the record of all of the Community legislation. New legislation is recorded in the *C Series* before it goes into the *L Series*.

2.7 Citation of legislation

Citation of Acts of Parliament

Acts have a long title which include description of the general scope of the Act, and a short title which is used for ease of citation. The same short title will be used in successive Acts, eg a Criminal Justice Act has been passed in 1967, in 1972, in 1982, in 1987, in 1988, in 1991, in 1993, and in 1994. Consequently, it is very important to give the year of the Act! Every Act also has a 'chapter number' which, when used together with the year date, is a precise way of citing the Act, eg 1988 c33 refers only to the Criminal Justice Act 1988.

Regnal years are used for the older Acts, for example, 15 & 16 Geo 5 c20 Law of Property Act 1925 is the 20th statute passed in the parliamentary session which overlapped the 15th and 16th years of the reign of George V. The use of regnal years declined in the post-war years and they were abolished in 1963.

An Act of Parliament is made up of 'sections'; section is abbreviated to 's' and sections is written as 'ss', eg s1, or ss1–4. A section may be divided into subsections, and the subsections may be divided further into paragraphs. For example:

> 37(3) A person shall not be entitled to an allowance ... if
> (a) she is married and either
> (i) she is residing with her husband, or ...

If you wanted to refer to the part of the rule 'she is residing with her husband', you would cite this as s37(3)(a)(i).

Finding statute law citations and checking for later statutes

The *Current Law Statute Citators* offer assistance in identifying what legislation there is in relation to any subject-matter and identify whether an Act has been amended (changed) or repealed (is no longer in force). The Acts are given chronologically by year and chapter number and use the short title.

Citation of European Union legislation

The Treaties, and the international agreements formally amending these, the Conventions, the Rules of Procedure and the UK Acts giving effect to the primary legislation have citations for the *Official Journal L Series* (or for the *C Series* if it is new legislation), and usually also for our reports, for example, *Halsbury's Statutes* (see above).

1. A citation for a Treaty puts the place where the Treaty was signed and the year into the brackets, eg EC Treaty (Rome, 1957; 50 *Statutes* 263) which is a *Halsbury's Statutes of England* reference.
2. For the *Official Journal* the *L series* and the *C Series* are cited as L or C, eg Agreement on the European Economic Area (OJ 1994 L 1/3); Treaty on European Union (Maastricht, 1992; OJ 1992 C 191/1). If a *Halsbury's Statutes* reference is also given it comes after the OJ reference, eg Treaty on European Union (Maastricht, 1992; OJ 1992 C 191/1; 50S *Statutes* 45).
3. A citation of an Act gives the year that the Act was passed after its title and the year of the citation reference even if these are the same, eg Act of Accession (1979) (OJ 1979 L 291/17).

The secondary legislation has three separate forms: the Regulations, the Directives, and the Decisions. Each of these has its own identifying number and the citation gives this, the last two numbers of the year, and the institutional source for the legislation.

1. The Regulations put the year *last*, eg Council Regulation 15/61 (number 15 of 1961); Commission Regulation 99/63 (number 99 of 1963).
2. The Directives and the Decisions put the year *first*, eg Council Directive 64/221 (number 221 of 1964); Council Decision 87/602 (number 602 of 1987).

2.8 The law library

If you have access to a law library you should use it read as many of the sources of information as are relevant to your studies. Students taking their degree by full-time study are expected to spend a lot of time in the library to use the variety of sources of information that it provides. Those of you who are taking the course by part-time or evening study should allocate as much time as is possible to reading the cases in the law reports and some time using the reference books. If you are a distance-learning student you will probably be supplied with extracts from primary source material but do take the opportunity to visit a law library if you can because it will give an appreciation of the true nature of 'manual' research work that the lawyer has to undertake, and of the breadth and variety of legal materials that are available for the identification and the interpretation of the law.

Familiarise yourself with the layout of your library as quickly as possible. Identify where the primary and literary sources are to be found and how they are catalogued. The literary sources will be arranged in a conventional subject-classification. A law library is a reference library rather than a lending library and the reference works, the journals and periodicals, and many of the textbooks will probably be confined to reference sections for use in the library or its reading rooms. Some libraries put the 'set course texts' in a separate short-loan section but you should consider buying a selection of these for your personal use.

All libraries have a catalogue of their collections, either as a card index, or, more usually now, in a computerised form such as the On-Line Public Access Catalogue (OPAC). You will probably also find that you can access this catalogue at terminals located other than in the library itself, for example in your University's student-use computer labs, and it is worth finding out whether your institution has this facility.

The acquisition of effective library research skills is entirely up to you; the use of a law library has to be learnt, it cannot be taught. A comprehensive guide to using a law library is that of *How to Use a Law Library* by Dane and Thomas (1987) 2nd Edition, London: Sweet and Maxwell. Sweet and Maxwell also publish *Where to Look for Your Law, Sweet and Maxwell's Guide to Law Reports and Statutes.*

Most law degrees now include some form of induction programme that gives initial guidance on how to use your university law library, and instruction, often coupled with practical exercises, to introduce you to the use of the primary and the literary sources of the law. These are an invaluable start to your studies; use the opportunity provided by them to the full! Within weeks of the start of the course you will come to discover how useful that guidance has been. The cases are difficult to read, the statutory provision is bewildering, and the textbooks you turn to for help in understanding the primary sources are highly factual and do not represent easy reading. It will take you some time to become familiar with using these sources for the law and you should not expect to be able to use them either easily or quickly in the first few months. They will most likely represent an entirely different sort of research pattern to that which you have previously been used to, and a part of the purpose of the first year studies is to enable you to acquire the skill of reading law.

There is always a large amount and variety of information available on any topic and on occasion you will feel that you have spent hours in the library but 'not got very far'. Do not worry about this because you will have achieved something and it is an invaluable contribution to your future studies; you will have been learning *how* to use the sources for the law. As time goes by, constant practice will be rewarded and you will find that researching the law becomes easier and quicker.

2.9 The computerised information retrieval systems

These include international and national law 'on-line' (telecommunications link-up) databases such as LEXIS, LAWTEL and JUSTIS, the CD-ROM (Compact Disk – Read Only Memory) databases, and materials on the Internet and World-Wide Web.

The advantages of these systems is that they are able to store vast amounts of information and, by comparison to the traditional methods, they provide a thorough and a quicker means of discovering the variety of materials available of any topic. However, using the law is not simply a matter of search and retrieval, it is also a matter of application, and an information retrieval system does not have the capability to handle concepts and make complex value judgments in the same way as the trained lawyer does. The information retrieved has to be treated as no more than an 'information accumulation' exercise and care should be taken not to print off huge amounts of data. The time-consuming research demanded by the traditional sources of information for the law has one advantage; it causes you to be selective in what you read and take notes from. The quick retrieval and print-off facility provided by the computer databases can leave you with what is best described as an excess of information. Use the system in the same way that you would use the traditional reference resources to gain a collection of notes that are relevant and valuable to the study that you are undertaking.

Each system uses its own search methods that work on a variety of input pointers which access the libraries and files or other categories used for the organisation of the data. The type and the use of these input pointers should be carefully studied from the user manual before embarking on the search request and there is a considerable value in attending any 'user sessions' that your institution may offer. There is a substantial difference between using systems such as LEXIS, LAWTEL, and JUSTIS and using the Internet.

Although the systems are interactive and do enable the terms of the search to be amended in response to information received, they are, on the whole, not programmes that are easy to use *effectively* unless a precise search statement has been thought out in advance. If the search parameters are set too wide the exercise becomes useless by virtue of the quantity of loosely related data that is returned. Indeed, the search itself may become unmanageable and excessively time-consuming as the system searches its vast data banks for all information that falls within the parameters of the question. Conversely, it is possible to construct what appears to be a logical and methodical search question and discover that it does not bring back cases that you know exist.

A search request has to be limited to a number of key words so it is sometimes better to break the search problem down into constituent parts and retrieve the information one stage at a time, applying value judgments as to which bits of the information to search on next. Rudimentary guidelines for keeping the search parameters within suitable limits are:

1. *Choose the shortest possible date span*: reducing the search to as little as a two-month period in one year would still bring back huge amounts of data if the search request was for something that occurs frequently in cases.
2. *Find key words that encompass the exact scope of the search required*: eg 'shock at witnessing injury to a child' is a potentially large research request. It can be limited by, for example, by identifying the type of injury (eg head), identifying the cause of the injury (eg swing), more closely defining 'child' (eg infant) and stating who is shocked (eg mother).

AND is used by LEXIS and LAWTEL to produce a search that only looks for data where each component is present. OR can be used to identify the components as an 'either or both' search. Some systems use NOT and JUSTIS uses ! to enable documents that do not contain the word given after NOT to be excluded from the search. The sort of key words that you could use for the start of the search example in 2. above are: mother AND infant AND playground. The parameters could then be modified to restrict the final production of the data to that concerning head injuries/injuries on swings, etc.

LEXIS

This is the largest of the commercial 'on-line' systems. Many educational institutions and most of the larger law firms subscribe to it. Its databanks contain all UK public general Acts and statutory instruments in force, and full text case reports of most cases reported in England and Wales since 1945. It also holds a substantial amount of unreported case decisions, the decisions of the European Court of Justice, and case reports for other common law jurisdictions. There is a considerable amount of American material; it is an American database.

The first level of the search is in the libraries and the second level is in one of the sets of files within that library. Only one file of one library can be searched at a time. To get to the English case law you have to get into the ENGGEN library and then into CASES. The searches are done by typing in key words. The documents can be browsed either as the full text or as KWIC (Key Words in Context) which is a fast means of searching the document to read the key words and the lines of text that immediately surround it. The documents can be printed off either in full or as selected extracts.

LAWTEL

This is an English-based and a considerably smaller data base, containing mainly the UK law, so is considerably cheaper to use and generally sufficient for the type of search problem that an undergraduate student of law would want to make. It is different to LEXIS and JUSTIS in that it works off numbers, and is, thereby, simple to use. A page number is keyed-in to open up the one of the indexes and then other numbers are used to gain access to other parts of the system. Thereafter, the three Subjects Indexes can be used, or the Table of Cases, or the Statute Citator. The main index can always be got back to by keying in 0 until it appears. A feature of the system is the Daily Update which notes legal matters that have arisen in the last 24 hours. Another simple user function is the ability to go backwards and forwards through the pages by keying in 9 (forward) or 8 (back one).

The CD-ROM databases

These are much smaller databases than those described above but searches are done far faster than the 'on-line' systems. They operate from a computer compact disk and examples of them are:

1. There are various CD-ROM databases available that enable identification of texts on subjects, for example: *Bookbank* (books in print); *General Academic Index* (major UK journals on all subjects); *LegalTrac* (US, European and UK law journals); and the *Legal Information Resources*.
2. Other CD-ROMS contain the *Law Reports* and *Hansard* (House of Commons and House of Lords), the full text of major newspapers, such as, *The Times* and the *Sunday Times*, *The Independent* and *The Guardian*, and there information databases such as *Compton's Multimedia Cyclopaedia*.

2.10 The art of reading

The study of the law substantially comprises of a study of the case law. To be more precise, it comprises an examination of the judgments given in the cases to identify the legal reasoning underpinning either the creation or expansion of a common law principle, or the interpretation of the scope and purpose of a statutory provision. The purpose of this examination is the identification of why a principle was applied, and the accumulation of examples of how it has been re-used.

The legal textbooks

These provide you with identification of the cases and statutory provision relating to any topic and with an analysis of the interpretation of the law. They are highly factual and are intended to be used for *reference* rather than for straight reading as such. This is an important part of the art of learning how to 'read' them. You will use them as reference books when you are given fictitious problems to answer, but most courses do not present you with these to start with; they start by laying down the foundations of the law. Thus, the time that you will find the reading difficult is in the early stages of the course when you are trying to find out about a law in general terms. One way of overcoming this is to set yourself tasks to answer, such as the discussion points indicated for a seminar, and use the texts to find the answers to these questions.

The legal textbooks do not teach you the skill of finding the law and knowing how to apply it for yourself. If you intend to qualify for practice this is a skill that you should learn as soon as possible and take every opportunity to perfect during the time of your undergraduate study. You should refer to the actual law reports for as many cases as possible and certainly for all 'leading cases'. In other words, you should not rely solely on the summary and interpretation of cases given in the textbooks and the 'cases and materials' books. Many of the discussions of the cases in the textbooks relate to a particular point dealt with in one of the judgments, whereas the case may have decided a number of different points, and if it was a matter on appeal, may have been heard by as many as five judges. In addition, the textbooks may cite a case in support of a remark without saying that it was given as obiter dictum by the judge (ie was not part of the decision of the case).

'Reading' the statute law

This is an acquired skill, for, as you will discover, an Act of Parliament is most decidedly not a document that can be 'read' as if it were a book. They employ a linguistically difficult and grammatically complex prose and interpretation turns on the precision of the words used. The law is stated as a series of provisions which are separately applicable but which also have an inter-relationship with other provisions. A definition may be set up in one section and interpretation of the individual words and phrases used in it is provided in the following sections. The Acts also provide a variety of interpretation devices like separate interpretation sections, schedules and tables. All of these different parts of the Act have to be referred to so as to build up the picture of what the rule is and how it should be applied. In 'Statutory Reform: the Draftsman and the Judge' (1981) 30 ICLQ 141, Sir William Dale describes the process as being a 'flight from the centre to definition and interpretation clauses'. He called this 'the centrifugence principle'; the centre is the section under consideration and the flight to the other clauses is because they are usually located in very different parts of the Act. He concludes by aptly describing the effect as being: 'an English statute often cannot be read – it must be perambulated'.

Mastering the art of reading and using statutes is, therefore, a major task when you first start to use them. The chapters on judicial interpretation of statute and on working with the sources of law provide an insight into how to interpret the legislative language.

Reading the case law

This is considerably easier than using the statute law but is also an acquired skill. The judgments in the cases provide a lengthy explanation of why certain rules are applicable to the facts of the case and, depending upon the case and the existing law, some cases interpret and develop existing common law principles, some cases are involved in the interpretation of statutory provision, and a few cases create rules to be applied. You read the cases to discover the judicial reasoning for each of these applications. Refer to the chapters on judicial precedent and working with the sources of law to gain an appreciation of how this is done.

The legal terminology

At first you will find the language of the law difficult to understand. You have to master the specialist legal terminology as well as the different styles of language that are used as between the case law judgments and the statute law.

The legal terminology has to be learnt and used. When you come across any term or phrase that you do not understand, you must find out its meaning and take a note of it. Legal terminology often uses words in a different way to the colloquial use of them. Some of it will also use words that you are not familiar with and sometimes the terms are in Latin. The use of the terminology is important to the law because it provides the precise use of words that the interpretation of the law relies on. It also acts as a short form by which sometimes large and conceptually difficult principles of law can be reduced to a key word or short phrase for convenient use.

The textbooks are the best sources for finding the meaning of terminology because, in addition to explaining the term itself, they also identify its use in terms of the case law and the statute law. A judgment may use a recognised term without giving further explanation of it, and the language used in statutes does not provide an immediately understandable interpretation of the terminology. Although the terminology takes some mastering at first, as your studies progress you will find that it is not difficult to use, and will come to appreciate the precision afforded by the established terminology and phrases.

'Skim' reading and an effective search method

Some of the reading you do will not answer the question that you are searching for the answer to. This element of the reading is, of course, not wasted because you are learning about some aspect of the law, but in terms of managing limited time to carry out a specific research task it is vital that you do not spend too much time reading information which is not directly relevant to the task in hand.

The best way to learn to read quickly is to master the art of 'skim' reading which involves trusting your eye to settle on the points that you are looking for. All lawyers rely on this as the means of quickly identifying from the range of legal authority available that which seems to be most relevant to the problem in hand. You must have a clear idea of what it is that you are looking for, especially if you want to 'skim' read the cases. Before starting any research formulate an accurate statement of the search problem and use this to keep your research to precisely what is required, ie:

1. examine the question or the task to identify precisely what has to be researched and decide which aspects should be treated as the focus of the answer, or which ones look more important than others;
2. evaluate the *amount* and the *level* of discussion required for each aspect – the question may indicate this, and your lecture notes should provide clues about the intended scope of the topic;
3. decide upon potential sources of information in relation to both of the above criteria – refer to the suggested reading and case lists given on your seminar sheet, and to textbook, journal and case law references given in the lectures;
4. use the familiarity with the tasks that you have so far gained to 'skim' read at least one of the textbooks to identify cases, statutory provision, references to other reading, and so on;
5. before embarking on the detailed research, critically evaluate the relevance of the material you have found in terms of the decisions made in 1. and 2. above and think about exactly what it is that you will be looking for detail on in each of the sources identified;
6. set aside all materials that are not directly and fully relevant – you may return to them later on to add information to your answer but they should not be used in establishing the core information;
7. decide honestly how much time you have at your disposal and whether you are going to be able to complete the amount of detailed reading that you have set yourself, ie establish an achievable outcome for the completed task – for a seminar, for instance, it might be better to know something about each of the discussion points rather than a lot about two of them;
8. now 'skim' read the final selection of sources of information in accordance with the decisions made in 5. above – you should by now have a sufficient familiarity with the task and the scope of the topic to be able to quickly identify the relevant parts of the judgments, journal articles, or chapters in the reference books;
9. you should now be able to make informed decisions about what you need to take detailed notes on to answer the problem.

With continued practice you will become used to handling quantities of legal data and find that you are able to quickly identify the facts that you require.

2.11 The art of note-taking

Note taking is very much a matter of personal style and the guidance given below is merely intended to assist you in developing a style that suits you. The important thing to bear in mind is the reason why you are taking the notes. Your notes have to serve several purposes. They need to provide quick information retrieval in the seminars, detail for the assessed essays, and be easy to learn when revising for examinations.

The overriding rule is that quality is the key to success not quantity. Large files of notes are not that useful for revision nor for essay-writing, and are too cumbersome to use in the seminars. Maintaining concise and relevant notes is something that you have to consciously think about. More or less every sentence in the leading law textbooks contains an important point and it is easy to fall into the trap of effectively writing out the book again. The same is true of the judgments in the cases. In addition, the method of study involves collecting a variety of notes on any one topic, for example, you may have:

1. lecture notes, seminar notes, and workshop papers;
2. notes taken from two or three textbooks;
3. photocopies of judgments and of Acts of Parliament, plus further hand-written notes on these;
4. photocopies of, or notes taken from, journal articles.

It is necessary to collate the key points from these into simple summary *that uses references to the material in your file*. Examples of the sort of techniques that are useful for these are:

1. *Key words and phrases* that act as a trigger for your memory. Support these with a very brief summary of what it entails and give the references for the source material that cover the points in more detail. Abbreviations and 'mnemonics' are useful but you must use them regularly and consistently or else you may not remember what they mean!
2. *Data ordered under clearly divided headings*. This makes it considerably easier to quickly locate text and is especially useful for quick reference in the seminars as well as for use for revision. Use headings, paragraphs and sub-paragraphs as the way of making points 'stand out' rather than using the coloured pen highlighters – very concise notes simply become a mass of highlights.
3. *Short, simple checklists* are very useful. You can re-use the same data in different ways for use for different purposes, eg a list of the legal rules with the names of the relevant cases given under them, or, conversely, a summary of the cases with brief identification of the principles applied and why they were applied.

4. *Note the source of the information* including page references. This is a good habit to develop. It enables you to return to the source material quickly if something in your notes is unclear. It is also a important resource for compiling a bibliography to attach to assessed work.

Photocopying

Beware of taking too much photocopied material. There are two problems associated with this practice. First, all that you have is a large amount of text that you have still to extract the relevant information from; and second, the exercise in itself has the effect of reassuring you that you 'have the information' when, in fact, it is of not much more use to you than carrying about an unread book.

Although you will intend to read through all your materials, time pressures are likely to work against you. There is no substitute for sitting in the library and making your own usable notes as preparation for your lectures, seminars, assessed coursework and examinations.

2.12 Assessed essays or written assignments

Many law schools now use forms of continuous assessment which frequently includes the submission of an assessed essay or written assignment. The aims of these vary and you must identify why your course is using this as a part of the assessment regime. Some might require a discussion of the sort that would not normally be provided in an examination; others might use the essay as a practice for the examination. This variance of aims and objectives makes it difficult to give advice but certain things are likely to be expected:

1. *Evidence of research*: this relates to the primary sources as well as to the textbooks and it also includes interpretation and analysis extracted from journal articles.
2. *A well structured answer*: the 'identification, analysis, diagnosis and/or conclusion' format suits law answers. (See points 3., 4. and 5. below.) You may have heard this being described as the 'a beginning, a middle and an end' layout but it is a little more than this for law answers.
3. *Identification* involves definitions of, or descriptions of, the legal concepts or rules that are applicable to the question. These do not necessarily have to be given at the start of the essay; they should be given where they are appropriate within the text and can be effective as a 'natural break' in the analysis if used at the start of a paragraph.
4. *Analysis* relates to the use of the authorities for the law. Cite cases, statutes, and other sources of information correctly. Use the discussion of these as the vehicle for the analysis. Do not give long accounts of the facts of cases; it is the legal principle used in them and the reasoning for its use that is important to the

analysis. Selected facts might be used to effect if they establish a similarity to facts given in the problem.

5. *Diagnosis and/or conclusion* depends on the task. All answers benefit from a conclusion that draws together the various lines of argument presented in the answer.

6. *A neat and legible presentation.* Many law schools now expect a word-processed submission, with an attached bibliography. The answer must conform to any word limit that is set. To achieve a proper analysis of the law you should write in prose style. Generally avoid the use of bullet points, numbered lists, tables, charts, and diagrams (other than in appendices), as these prevent you from describing the full scope and purpose of any rule, or their inter-relationship with the other rules stated.

2.13 The types of written examinations

The unseen written examination

This is the traditional method of assessment for law degrees. It provides valuable training for the examinations taken to gain professional qualification either in the law or in other careers. It tests certain abilities of which the two most important ones are the ability to recall information and the ability to apply that information to given problems under time constraint. The papers vary in style, eg a two-part paper requiring answers to be given to questions in each part, or one compulsory question and a free choice for the remainder, or all compulsory questions, or, conversely, an entirely free choice. It is very important to find out what style of paper will be used for each examination you sit. The format of the paper influences the nature of the revision that you should undertake in preparation for it.

The questions fall into two main categories:

1. *The 'fictitious problem' question*: a 'mini case scenario' for which you advise one party. The facts of the problem are often an amalgam of those from decided cases to 'cue' you into the relevant legal principles. The answer to this type of question needs to combine a discussion of the relevant legal principles with a discussion of how that law is likely to be applied to the facts given in the question. Depending on the topic matter, the question may test your knowledge of more than one aspect of the syllabus, eg a combination of the rule in *Rylands* v *Fletcher* and the tort of nuisance.

2. *The 'general discussion' question*: invariably given as a quote from a judgment in a leading case and sometimes followed by words to limit the discussion to certain key aspects. The answer to this type of question is not as specifically directed as the problem-type questions and therefore needs careful planning to ensure that it does remain relevant to the emphasis given in the quote.

The 'seen' examination

The examination paper is issued at a given point before the examination is sat and the level of analysis that you will be expected to give is greater than that expected for unseen examinations. At undergraduate level they are most commonly used where the questions are a series of tasks related to a large fictitious case scenario.

The 'unseen open book' examination

Specified materials can be used in the examination, for example, permission to use *Sweet and Maxwell's Property Statutes*. These do not replace revision for the topic, they merely reflect the fact that the sections of Acts of Parliament cannot be committed to memory. The material is not being provided to help jog your memory or to give you half the answer. It is being provided to test your ability to analyse and apply actual rules and tests and you will not be able to do this if you have not previously learnt how this has been done in the decided cases.

The multiple choice examination

These take the format of setting a question and giving choices of answer that test the precision of knowledge of the candidate. Some lecturers use them as an informal assessment during the course to prepare students for their revision programme. They do not play a major part in the currently used assessment regimes of the UK law schools although they have been used for some time as a part of the assessment of civil litigation, criminal litigation, and evidence in the Bar Finals course.

2.14 Revision for examinations

This is the true test of the extent to which you have kept clear and concise notes throughout the year. The art of examination revision is the identification of what has to be committed to memory.

Some assistance is obtained by looking at past examination papers to identify: the aspects of the syllabus that are commonly questioned; the way in which these are questioned; and the inter-relationship of topic matter, eg how often does 'offer and acceptance' get questioned on its own, and what sort of aspects is it usually combined with?

Check that the format of examination has not been changed for the current year and remember that these are merely clues, they give no certainty of likelihood of question. They do provide a structure around which to plan your revision and are useful titles to plan draft answers in the form of notated plans. These have the advantage of being easy to commit to memory, but you must be ready to adapt them in the examination, or to amalgamate two or more of them, so that what you write relates to the question asked.

Some essential things that aid successful completion of examinations are:

1. *Ensure that you properly recorded the examination date and know where it is to be held*: ie actually know how to get to the building and how long it will take to get there. A surprising number of students get the date wrong or arrive late for examinations because they have got lost, or under-estimated how long it will take to get to the examination building.

2. *Read the instructions for answering the paper given at the top of the paper*. If you do not attempt a compulsory question, or do not choose the right number of questions from the set sections, you will not pass.

3. *Read through all of the questions before starting to answer any*. You should be able to immediately identify those that you like the most but *read through them again* to check that you have not overlooked any part of the question in your relief at recognising a question that you can answer!

4. *Answer the question, the whole question, and nothing but the question*! Marks are allocated to the discussion of the individual parts encompassed within a question and an answer that is off the track, however good it might be, or that misses out certain parts, cannot gain good marks. Quickly jot down the points, cases, statutory sections, etc, that you intend to use and order them into a presentation order – and then keep to this!

5. *Keep the format of examination answer relatively simple*. Lay down definitions at the start of the answer, or at the start of new paragraphs that move over to different principles. Provide a separate discussion of each distinct part of the answer, but also try to maintain a 'thread' of analysis that links related concepts together. Avoid giving lists of cases that do not build up into a full discussion of the principles. Refer to the question and, if it is a fictitious problem type, apply the points to the circumstances of the party you have been asked to advise. It is preferable to give a conclusion that draws together the various lines of argument presented in the answer.

6. *Learn case names, the proper titles of Acts, and the correct spelling of the legal terminology*: if you cannot remember the full name of a case, or an Act, give that which you can remember. The various tricks employed by students to cover up the fact that they do not know case names and titles of Acts do not pass unnoticed by the examiner, eg sentences like, 'in a leading case ...', or 'the main Act relating to this ...', without reference to the name, indicate to the examiner that you do not really know the topic. However, if the discussion given is good, and the lapse of memory relates to supporting information, the omission may be overlooked. Examiners usually deduct marks if legal terminology is mis-spelt; it indicates that the student has not read about the law in the books and cases but has merely relied on what has been heard in lectures.

3

The Court Structure

3.1 Introduction

3.2 Divisions of the courts

3.3 The different courts

3.4 Courts of particular jurisdiction

3.5 Diagrams of the court structure

3.6 Double liability

3.7 Exercises

3.1 Introduction

The present structure of the courts is the result of a long process which began before the rise of the courts of the common law with the customary courts of the shires and hundreds. These courts did not administer a law which was 'common', as our present system of law is, since each shire, each town, each village had its own customary law which was administered by the local courts. The appearance of the 'common law' was the result of a growing interest in justice by the Norman and Plantagenet kings in the twelfth and thirteenth centuries which, since it was administered and produced by the central royal courts (which appeared in the period around 1200 as offshoots of the great council, the Curia Regis, of the Norman kings), was 'common' to the realm and did not undergo regional variations. With the appearance and rapid expansion of royal justice (the common law), local law and the local courts were gradually reduced into insignificance and, eventually, oblivion.

The first courts of common law were the Court of Common Pleas, the Court of King's Bench and the Court of Exchequer, each of which had separate jurisdictions but which, during the course of their history, encroached on each others' specialist jurisdictions. At various times other courts appeared, such as the various courts (largely appellate) which, at different periods, went under the name of the Exchequer Chamber, and courts outside the common law, such as the High Court of Admiralty, the Ecclesiastical Courts and the Conciliar Courts (eg Star Chamber). The most important of the courts outside the common law from the position of the present system was the Court of Chancery (the Lord Chancellor's court), which exercised an extraordinary jurisdiction over the litigants based on principles of conscience and good faith and developed a system of legal principles which both complemented and supplemented the common law – later called 'equity'.

Each of these courts had its own staff and its own complicated procedure, and this could lead to immense problems for litigants, especially as the courts remained largely unreformed from the thirteenth to the nineteenth centuries. Further problems were caused by the Court of Chancery, which could traditionally re-open cases decided at common law and decide them anew on the basis of the rules of equity, which could lead to quite a different result.

Difficulties, delays and abuses finally led to major reform in the nineteenth century, notably the creation of the county courts in 1846 and of the Supreme Court in the Judicature Acts of 1873–75. Further reforms since have resulted in the creation in 1966 of a single Court of Appeal, with two divisions, hearing both civil and criminal appeals (previously the Court of Appeal and the Court of Criminal Appeal), the reorganisation of the divisions of the High Court in 1971, and the abolition of the old criminal courts of assize in the same year, replaced by the Crown Court.

Scotland has a separate system of law and its own courts, and is not part of the English legal system – save that appeals can be made to the House of Lords from the Court of Session in Scotland.

3.2 Divisions of the courts

The two fundamental divisions of the courts are superior and inferior courts, and courts of record and courts not of record.

Superior and inferior courts

Superior courts have unlimited jurisdiction and include the House of Lords, the Privy Council, the Supreme Court and the Crown Court.

Inferior courts have jurisdiction limited either by value or geographically or both (eg county courts, magistrates' courts).

Courts of record and courts not of record

This is a historical division, based upon whether the court kept official records of its proceedings or not, a distinction which no longer applies.

Civil and criminal

English law and procedure are divided into two categories, civil and criminal, and a case must be one or the other. Some courts have jurisdiction over both civil and criminal cases (eg the House of Lords, the Court of Appeal and magistrates' courts).

Courts of common law and equity

Until the Judicature Act of 1873 the common law was administered solely by the courts of common law (see section 2.1 above) and the rules of equity by the Court of Chancery, the two being quite separate – having different procedures, being based on different principles, and offering different remedies. However, ss24–25 of the 1873 Act 'fused' the administration of law and equity. The jurisdiction of both the superior common law courts and the Court of Chancery was transferred to the High Court, and judges are now required to apply both sets of rules, where relevant. Thus the modern Chancery Division of the High Court, though it is assigned some specialist matters once dealt with exclusively by the old Court of Chancery, no longer is the sole administrator of equity. Where the rules of common law and equity are in conflict, those of equity prevail.

3.3 The different courts

The purpose of this section is to give a basic outline of each of the courts in the present court structure.

The European Court of Justice

The EC Treaty gives the European Court of Justice (ECJ) jurisdiction to hear various matters concerning European law, including the power to review the legality of Community legislation (Arts 173–175 of the EC Treaty). However, such actions take place entirely in the ECJ and are of no direct concern to the English courts. Article 177, on the other hand, is of direct interest here since it empowers the ECJ to hear references on questions of European law sent to it by the courts of the various member states, including England: see, for example, *Factortame Ltd v Secretary of State for Transport (No 2)* [1991] 1 All ER 70, *R v Secretary of State for Transport, ex parte Factortame Ltd* [1991] 3 All ER 769 and *Stoke-on-Trent City Council v B & Q plc* [1993] 1 All ER 481; [1993] 2 All ER 297. In the last of these examples the ECJ affirmed, in response to a reference by the House of Lords, that Art 30 of the EC Treaty does not prohibit national legislation (in this case s47 of the Shops Act 1950) prohibiting retailers from opening their premises on Sundays. The reference is not an appeal, and it is inaccurate to describe the ECJ as being situated within the structure of the appellate courts – especially since it may hear references addressed to it from any body exercising a judicial function (not just the House of Lords).

Article 177 gives the ECJ jurisdiction to hear references concerning:

1. interpretation of the Treaty (ie the EC Treaty);
2. interpretation and validity of Acts of the Community institutions (ie Community legislation);
3. interpretation of the statutes of bodies established by the Council.

Any court or tribunal of a member state may make a reference – though if it is a court or tribunal from which there is no 'judicial remedy' (ie no appeal or judicial review), then it must make a reference on a point of European law if it is 'necessary' to reach a decision.

In order to enable the ECJ to provide an interpretation of Community law which will be useful for national judges, it is necessary for the latter to describe the factual and legislative background to the questions which they submit: *Telemarsicabruzzo SpA* v *Circostel* (1993) The Times 10 February. The ECJ so held in refusing to answer questions submitted to it by the Rome District Magistrate's Court for a preliminary ruling pursuant to Art 177.

Where the English court has a discretion whether or not to make a reference, then it must consider the matters set out by Lord Denning MR in *HP Bulmer Ltd* v *J Bollinger SA* [1974] 2 All ER 1226 (CA), reaffirmed by Bingham J in *Customs & Excise Commissioners* v *ApS Samex* [1983] 1 All ER 1042:

1. Only questions of Community law as opposed to domestic law may be referred.
2. An English court will not refer a question unless the answer is 'necessary' to decide the particular case.
3. If 'substantially the same question' has been answered in a previous case by the ECJ, the national court may follow that decision and not refer the matter.
4. If a point is reasonably clear there is no need to refer it.
5. All the other surrounding circumstances must be taken into account (eg the length of time, expense, the importance of not overloading the ECJ, the difficulty and importance of the point and the fact that the ECJ is the most appropriate court to consider European matters).

It may be questioned whether all of these items should legitimately be considered by an English court (eg the workload of the ECJ), given that it is the task of the ECJ to interpret Community law and such matters are better left for it to decide. However, Bingham J in the *ApS Samex* case did stress that it should be remembered that the ECJ is the appropriate court for deciding questions of Community law. When a reference is made the court will stay (ie temporarily suspend) the English proceedings until it receives an answer to the point referred – which it must follow.

To sum up, the court's role is as follows:

1. To quash, at the request of a Community institution, government or individual, any measures adopted by the Commission, Council of Ministers or national governments which are incompatible with the Treaties.
2. To pass judgment, at the request of a national court, on the interpretation or validity of points of Community law. If a legal action produces a disputed point of this kind, a national court can request a preliminary ruling by the European Court. It must do so if there is no higher court of appeal in the Member State concerned.

The court can also be invited to give its opinion – which then becomes binding – on agreements which the Community proposes to undertake with third countries.

The court consists of five judges assisted by eight advocates-general. Usually only seven judges (the minimum number for the full court) will sit to hear a case, assisted by one advocate-general, though four smaller 'chambers' of three judges and one advocate-general also sit. The business of the court is directed by the president of the court, one of the judges elected by his fellows, and each Chamber has its own presiding judge. The judges and advocates-general are appointed from 'amongst persons of indisputable independence who fulfil the conditions required for the holding of the highest judicial office in their respective countries or who are jurists of recognised competence' (Art 167(1) EC Treaty).

Though the advocates-general have the same status as the judges they do not take part in the formal decisions of the ECJ. Their task is to make 'in open court, reasoned submissions on cases brought before the Court of Justice, in order to assist the court ...' (Art 166 EC Treaty). The advocates-general will give an independent opinion on the case which will be considered with great care by the judges, though they do not need to follow it. While the judges tend to be motivated by the needs of Community policy (much more blatantly than an English judge would be by policy considerations), it is the task of the advocates-general to give an impartial view of the case.

Only one judgment (always reserved) is given by the court, which is printed with the submissions of the advocate-general. Most of the representations to the court are in writing, and oral procedure is used merely to expand existing submissions. Where the court requires evidence to be given, this is done at an earlier stage in the preparatory inquiry – though, of course, this is not necessary on an Art 177 reference which is solely on a point of law.

The Court of First Instance

A Court of First Instance was established in 1988 under the Single European Act. It has jurisdiction in actions relating to, inter alia, the enforcement of the rules on competition and disputes between the Community institutions and their staff. Since 1993 the court has dealt with cases brought by individuals or companies against the Community. Appeals against its decisions may be brought before the ECJ only on points of law.

The European Court of Human Rights

The ECJ (and its Court of First Instance) at Luxembourg should not be confused with the European Court of Human Rights (ECHR) at Strasbourg. The European Convention for the Protection of Human Rights and Fundamental Freedoms was brought into being by the Council of Europe (to be distinguished from the European Community), and any alleged infringement of the Convention may be referred ultimately to the ECHR. For example, it was the ECHR which decided (by five votes to four) that corporal punishment (slippering) inflicted on a boy in a United Kingdom private boarding school did not constitute degrading punishment under the Convention as it had not reached the required minimum threshold of severity: see *Costello-Roberts* v *United Kingdom* (1993) The Times 26 March.

Litigants have to exhaust legal processes in their own country before resorting to the court at Strasbourg. Decisions of the ECHR are binding on UK governments in international law but have no binding force on UK judges unless and until the Convention is incorporated into UK law by Act of Parliament.

The House of Lords

Originally Parliament was a court which exercised certain judicial functions, but by Tudor times this jurisdiction came to be exercised exclusively by the House of Lords. Until the Appellate Jurisdiction Act 1876 – which created Lords of Appeal in Ordinary, appointed from eminent judges and lawyers, to hear appeals – any peer could hear appeals and vote on the decision, and often the only lawyer present was the Lord Chancellor. One result of this was that House of Lords decisions before 1876 carried very little legal authority, except in cases where the judges were invited to advise the House of the law.

Appeals are heard by at least three, and usually five, judges who must be drawn from the Lords of Appeal in Ordinary, the Lord Chancellor and any other peer who has held 'high judicial office', which is defined by the 1876 Act. In practice only the Lords of Appeal ('law lords') normally sit, although some Lord Chancellors do so. There are 12 Lords of Appeal in Ordinary and they are usually appointed from Lord Justices of Appeal, although there are usually two who were Scottish judges because the House of Lords is also the final appeal court for Scotland.

Appeals are heard generally in a committee room and their lordships do not wear robes. Strictly the lords do not give 'judgments' but instead give 'opinions' stating the reasons for their vote whether to allow or dismiss the appeal. If the House is equally divided the appeal is dismissed, and while normally this situation does not arise because an uneven number sits, it can occur – such as when a law lord dies before giving judgment and the House is otherwise equally divided: see *Kennedy* v *Spratt* [1972] AC 83 (Lord Upjohn died).

The House of Lords has very little original jurisdiction. The trial of one of its members 'by his peers' was abolished in 1948, and impeachment (prosecution of political offenders) is obsolete. The only remaining matters of original jurisdiction are breaches of privilege and disputed claims to peerages.

The jurisdiction of the House is almost entirely appellate, hearing appeals from (mainly):

1. the Court of Appeal (with the leave of either the Court of Appeal or the Appeals Committee of the Lords);

2. the High Court ('leap frog' procedure, with leave of the House of Lords, on a point of law of general public importance);
3. a Divisional Court of the Queen's Bench Division in a criminal cause or matter, with the leave of that court or the House;
4. the Inner House of the Court of Session (Scotland);
5. the Court of Appeal (Northern Ireland);

The general criminal appellate jurisdiction of the House was only created in 1907 by the Court of Criminal Appeal Act.

Note that the House of Lords is not part of the Supreme Court, even though it is the highest appellate court. This is due to the fact that when the Supreme Court was formed it was intended to abolish the Lords. This was only reversed by the 1876 Act.

One important factor in favour of the current system is that whereas the Court of Appeal is bound by its own previous decisions the House is not. The reluctance of the House to do this unless it can be shown that it is necessary is discussed in detail in Chapter 4 and there are very few examples. In *Murphy* v *Brentwood District Council* [1990] 2 All ER 908 the House of Lords (which included, it should be noted, Lord Mackay of Clashfern LC) overruled its previous decision in *Anns* v *Merton London Borough* [1977] 2 All ER 492. As to the need for a final court to review these decisions, Lord Diplock (see *Davis* v *Johnson* [1979] AC 264 at p326) stated:

> 'In an appellate court of last resort a balance must be struck between the need on the one side for the legal certainty resulting from the binding effect of previous decisions and on the other side the avoidance of undue restriction on the proper development of the law. In the case of an intermediate appellate court, however, the second desideratum can be taken care of by appeal to a superior appellate court if reasonable means of access to it are available ...'

However, it is not impossible that the House of Lords could be abolished and the Court of Appeal reconstituted so that, in certain cases, its own previous decisions could be reviewed. Difficulties arise, however, with the growing size of the Court of Appeal and the huge volume of work with which it must deal – with possibly a consequent lack of time to consider matters to the same extent as the House of Lords.

The Court of Appeal

This is the highest of the three courts which constitute the Supreme Court of England and Wales, the others being the High Court and the Crown Court. The Lord Chancellor is president of the Supreme Court.

The Court of Appeal is composed of (1) ex officio judges who are the Lord Chancellor, the Lord Chief Justice (the president of the Criminal Division), the Master of the Rolls (the president of the Civil Division), the president of the Family

Division, Lords of Appeal in Ordinary and former Lord Chancellors, and the Vice-Chancellor, and (2) the Lords Justices of Appeal (as at 1 February 1997 there are 35 Lords Justices of Appeal in post). In practice only the Master of the Rolls and the Lord Chief Justice of the ex officio judges sit in the Civil and Criminal Divisions respectively. High Court judges may also sit with Lords Justices, and frequently do so in the Criminal Division. The normal number is three, but when a difficult and important point of law is in issue the court may consist of five. Interlocutory appeals may now be heard by a single judge sitting in chambers (in private). Further, appeals from county courts are now usually heard by two judges, though three should sit if a difficult point arises. The administrative work of the divisions is supervised by two registrars.

Section 8(1) and (2) of the Courts and Legal Services Act 1990 provide that in any case where the Court of Appeal has power to order a new trial on the ground that damages awarded by a jury are excessive or inadequate, rules of court may provide for the Court of Appeal to have power, in place of ordering a new trial, to substitute for the sum awarded by the jury such sum as appears to the court to be proper. Accordingly, and pursuant to RSC O.59, r11(4), in *Rantzen* v *Mirror Group Newspapers* (1993) The Times 6 April the Court of Appeal reduced a jury's award of libel damages from £250,000 to £110,000.

Since the Criminal Appeal Act 1966 the Court of Appeal has consisted of two divisions. The Civil Division has the jurisdiction exercised by the old Court of Appeal which is exclusively civil (see eg *Re O* [1991] 1 All ER 330) and almost entirely appellate. Appeal is by rehearing, but normally the only evidence given is the written transcript of evidence given at the trial.

The Criminal Division replaces the old Court of Criminal Appeal which was set up in 1907. Its jurisdiction is exclusively criminal and appellate, hearing appeals from the Crown Court and considering points of law referred by the Attorney-General when the Crown Court trial ends in an acquittal.

The Court of Appeal is a creature of statute and its powers are those conferred by the relevant Acts of Parliament: see *R* v *McIlkenny* [1992] 2 All ER 417 and *R* v *Blandford Magistrates' Court, ex parte Pamment* [1991] 1 All ER 218.

The High Court

This was created in 1873 as a part of the Supreme Court of Judicature and, following a reorganisation in 1970, it now has three administrative divisions:

1. the Chancery Division;
2. the Queen's Bench Division;
3. the Family Division.

There were originally five divisions which reflected the old courts that had been abolished, but these were almost immediately reorganised in 1880 into the three divisions that we had until 1970, namely, the Chancery Division, the Queen's Bench

Division, and the Probate, Divorce and Admiralty Division. The Administration of Justice Act 1970 disbanded the Probate, Divorce and Admiralty Division and created the Family Division which kept the divorce work and all other matters relating to matrimonial disputes and children, including the jurisdiction over wards of court formerly dealt with by the Chancery Division. The admiralty work was transferred to the Queen's Bench Division, and contentious probate work to the Chancery Division.

High Court judges are called puisne (pronounced 'puny') judges from the law French for 'junior' or 'inferior'. The volume of litigation has steadily increased and there are now 96 High Court judges in post, most of whom sit in the Queen's Bench Division. Before the Courts Act 1971 the High Court sat solely in the Law Courts in the Strand, although High Court judges also tried civil cases on Assize. That Act abolished the assizes and instead provided that the High Court could sit at other locations. In practice these are the first tier Crown Courts (see below, *The Crown Court*) but it can and does sit elsewhere when necessary.

The High Court has both civil and criminal jurisdiction, original and appellate. Procedure in the High Court and the Court of Appeal is governed by the Rules of the Supreme Court (conveniently to be found in *Supreme Court Practice*: the 'White Book'). Although all three divisions have equal competence, in practice they have separate jurisdiction laid down partly by the rules and partly by statutory provisions. There are no financial or geographical limitations to the High Court jurisdiction (except that its jurisdiction is confined to England and Wales, as Scotland and Northern Ireland have their own laws and legal systems).

The Queen's Bench Division

The president of this division is the Lord Chief Justice. It has the largest number of puisne judges and the widest jurisdiction of the three divisions. Its original civil jurisdiction includes tort and most contract actions; it also deals with commercial and admiralty actions. It has a lesser civil appellate jurisdiction, its divisional court hearing appeals by way of case stated from magistrates' courts (except in matrimonial matters) and from the Crown Court. It also hears appeals from district judges. More important is its criminal appellate function, as most of the appeals by case stated from magistrates' courts and the Crown Court are in criminal matters. The division exercises the supervisory jurisdiction of the old Court of King's Bench by means of the prerogative orders granted by the divisional court.

Judges of this division also spend part of their time trying serious criminal matters in first tier Crown Courts and hearing Queen's Bench Division actions in the same locations.

There are two specialist courts of the Queen's Bench Division with specialist judges assigned to them: the Commercial Court and the Admiralty Court. These two 'courts' have procedures which differ from those in general operation in the division; they deal more efficiently with the specialist nature of the subject matter. There are also courts in certain cities that hear commercial cases. These are presided over by a circuit judge and, to avoid confusion with the Commercial Court, they are known as the mercantile courts.

The Chancery Division

The president of this division is the Lord Chancellor, who in practice never sits, so the effective head is the Vice-Chancellor, who is now also an ex-officio judge of the Court of Appeal. Most chancery actions are heard in London, but chancery actions are also tried at certain centres in the north of England by the Vice-Chancellor of the County Palatinate of Lancaster (who is officially a circuit judge) and in other major centres (eg Birmingham). This division tries most matters concerned with land and is given jurisdiction over contentious probate, bankruptcy, revenue matters, trusts, company matters and winding up, and patent and trade mark actions (which are heard in the Patents Court).

The Chancery Division divisional court has appellate jurisdiction in relation to bankruptcy appeals from the county courts and land registration. Income tax appeals from the Special Commissioners of Inland Revenue are heard by a single judge.

The Family Division

The head of this division is the president of the Family Division. Its jurisdiction includes all defended matrimonial causes, declarations of legitimacy and of validity of a marriage, proceedings for a decree of presumption of death, wardship, adoption, guardianship and certain matrimonial property matters. It deals with all proceedings under the Child Support Act 1991. The divisional court of the division hears appeals from magistrates' courts and county courts in adoption, guardianship proceedings and appeals by way of case stated in matrimonial proceedings in magistrates' courts.

The Crown Court

History

Before 1972 the courts where trials on indictment took place were the 61 Assize Courts and the 173 Quarter Sessions together with the Central Criminal Court, commonly known as 'the Old Bailey', and the Crown Courts of Liverpool and Manchester. Both Assizes and Quarter Sessions had a local jurisdiction, so that in general they could only try crimes committed within their locality, and also the methods of court administration varied from area to area.

The Assize system was founded by Henry II in the twelfth century. The most serious offences were tried at Assize by a judge sitting not by virtue of his normal office but under royal commissions of oyer and terminer and gaol delivery, and included at each Assize two or more High Court judges who tried the most serious cases and also heard civil cases. The Assizes were grouped into circuits, and the judges and the Assize court staff moved round this circuit on a fixed timetable. This caused a great deal of inconvenience and inefficiency.

Less serious offences were tried on indictment by the Quarter Sessions. These were held at least four times a year and were composed of the justices of the peace for the locality presided over by a legally qualified chairman. Many of the towns had a borough Quarter Session presided over by a recorder, a qualified lawyer, who sat alone.

The present structure

The Courts Act 1971 abolished Assizes (both criminal and civil sides) and Quarter Sessions. All serious crime is tried on indictment in the Crown Court (which is a single court sitting in many locations composed of many judges). Civil work is now separate (see above, *The High Court*) but in practice civil cases are heard by High Court judges sitting as part of the High Court in one of the centres designated by the Lord Chancellor as a first-tier Crown Court.

There are four types of judge in the Crown Court:

1. High Court judges;
2. circuit judges;
3. recorders;
4. assistant recorders/deputy circuit judges.

The High Court judges are usually those attached to the Queen's Bench Division. Circuit judges are full-time judges who sit in both the Crown Court and county courts, and recorders are part-time judges appointed for a limited period. When the Crown Court is hearing an appeal from a magistrates' court, lay justices of the peace sit with a single circuit judge. Deputy circuit judges and assistant recorders are ad hoc appointments for a very short period, though used to a great extent. Assistant recorders are persons who have a ten-year Crown Court or county court qualification within s71 of the Courts and Legal Services Act 1990.

The Crown Court has exclusive jurisdiction over all criminal trials on indictment for offences wherever committed. Procedure is governed by Crown Court Rules, which are delegated legislation made by the Crown Court Rule Committee under s84 of the Supreme Court Act 1981. The Crown Court is part of the Supreme Court and is a superior court of record, but it is under the supervisory jurisdiction of the High Court as expressed by the issue of prerogative orders, and a circuit judge is not a High Court judge.

As a concession to the City of London the Central Criminal Court retained certain privileges after 1971. All very serious crimes committed in London are tried there, the Lord Mayor and Aldermen of the City are still entitled to sit as judges (although they do not sit in practice), and the judges wear the same court robes as High Court judges and are addressed as 'My Lord' (other circuit judges being addressed as 'Your Honour'). The two senior judges are still called the Recorder and the Common Serjeant and are appointed in consultation with the City.

England and Wales are divided into six administrative regions called circuits, with at least two presiding judges. Crown Court cases are allocated according to the composition of the court: that is, High Court judge, circuit judge or recorder, or a court comprising justices of the peace. Allocation is made by the Lord Chief Justice with the concurrence of the Lord Chancellor (s75 of the Supreme Court Act 1981) and comprehensive distribution was made (under the Courts Act 1971) by *Practice Note* [1971] 3 All ER 829. *Practice Note* [1993] 1 All ER 41 contains directions with regard to the place of trial for cases of serious and complex fraud transferred to the Crown Court under the Criminal Justice Act 1987.

County courts

Although there were county courts in earlier times, the present-day county courts were established by statute in 1846 and are now governed by the County Courts Act 1984 which consolidated earlier legislation. They were introduced to provide local courts for the adjudication of relatively minor civil matters and have become an important part of the court structure because they offer a comprehensive, speedy and relatively cheap procedure.

Procedure is governed by the County Court Rules (made pursuant to the 1984 Act) and may be found in *County Court Practice*, known as the 'Green' Book. County courts also have the power to issue their own local practice directions provided that these are not inconsistent with statute or with the statutory rules of court.

County court jurisdiction is limited by financial and geographical criteria but their jurisdiction has been enlarged steadily over the years and broadly covers actions arising in contract, tort, probate, property, bankruptcy, insolvency, and family law matters. Significant changes were introduced by the Courts and Legal Services Act 1990 and Statutory Instrument 1991 No 724. Section 3 of the 1990 Act gives the county courts virtually the same powers as the High Court so that they can now deal with most civil litigation, but there are rules governing the differentiation between matters that are to be heard by the county court and those that are to be heard by the High Court. In exercise of the power conferred on him by s1 of the 1990 Act, the Lord Chancellor made the High Court and County Courts Jurisdiction Order 1991. This reflects proposals made in the *Report of the Review Body on Civil Justice* (Cm 394, 1988).

The *general* provision for the allocation of business between the county court and the High Court is:

1. actions for which the value is £25,000 or less must be tried in a county court;
2. actions for which the value is £50,000 or more must be tried in the High Court;
3. cases in which the value of the action is between £25,000 and £50,000 can be tried in either the county court or the High Court;
4. under the County Courts Act 1984, a county court has jurisdiction 'whatever the amount involved in the proceedings and whatever the value of any fund or asset connected with the proceedings' for: contract and tort (s15), recovery of land (s21), and the Inheritance (Provisions for Family and Dependants) Act 1975 (s25);

5. proceedings in which county courts have jurisdiction and which include a claim for damages in respect of personal injuries must be commenced in a county court, unless the value of the action is £50,000 or more, but a case involving a fatal accident will be tried in the High Court;
6. a county court has jurisdiction under certain provisions of, inter alia, the Law of Property Act 1925 and the Land Charges Act 1972 where, generally, the value of the land does not exceed £30,000;
7. a county court has jurisdiction under certain provisions relating to local land charges and rent charges where the sum concerned or amount claimed does not exceed £5,000;
8. county courts do not normally have jurisdiction to try cases involving defamation, professional negligence, allegations of fraud or undue influence, malicious prosecution or false imprisonment, claims against the police;
9. a county court does not have jurisdiction to hear any application for judicial review (s1(10) of CLSA 1990), nor power to grant the prerogative remedies of mandamus, cetiorari, and prohibition, and cannot grant Anton Piller orders, nor, generally, Mareva injunctions (*Practice Direction, ex parte Mareva Injunctions and Anton Piller Orders* (1994)).

The purpose of this allocation of the business is to enable the High Court and its judges to try the more important cases. A plaintiff who has a cause of action for more than the county court limit may abandon the excess so as to give the county court jurisdiction. It is not lawful for a plaintiff to divide a cause of action for the purpose of bringing two or more actions in one or more of the county courts. An action commenced in a county court may be transferred to the High Court under s42 of the County Courts Act 1984 if the court considers that it ought to transfer the case and the High Court considers that it ought to try the case. Proceedings commenced in the High Court can be transferred to a county court under s40 of the 1984 Act. The High Court can do this on its own motion or on that of one of the parties. Where the High Court is satisfied that any proceeding brought before it is required by any enactment to be in a county court, it must order the transfer of the proceedings to a county court. When considering whether to exercise their powers of transfer, the High Court and the county courts must have regard to the following criteria:

1. the financial substance of the action, including the value of any counterclaim;
2. the importance of the action and, in particular, whether it raises issues relevant to third parties or points of general public interest;
3. the complexity of the facts, legal issues, remedies or procedures invovled;
4. whether transfer is likely to result in a more speedy trial of the action, though no transfer can be made on this ground alone.

Section 4(8), (9) of the Courts and Legal Services Act 1990 allows the court to penalise a party bringing an action in the High Court which it considers should have been commenced in a county court. The normal penalty is a reduction in costs which may be by as much as 25 per cent, but there is also power to strike the proceeding out. A general policy of the courts is not to strike out a proceeding because of some mistake in procedure on the part of the plaintiff or his advisors. In *Restick* v *Crickmore* [1994] 2 All ER 112, Stuart-Smith LJ stressed that proceedings wrongly begun in the High Court should not be struck out unless the court is satisfied that the person bringing the proceedings knew, or ought to have known, of the requirement to bring the case in a county court.

The division of the business between the High Court and the county courts seems to be rather complex but, in the interests of a better provision for civil litigation, it intends to promote the commencement of most civil actions in a county court. A question that remains is the extent to which the county courts can continue to take on the ever-increasing load of work without a significant improvement in their resources to meet it. At present there are about 280 courts in England and Wales and they are grouped for administrative purposes into the same circuits as the Crown Courts. They are served by circuit judges and district judges and each court has at least one specifically assigned circuit judge. The district judges are appointed by the Lord Chancellor from persons who hold a seven-year general qualification within s71 of the Courts and Legal Services Act 1990. The district judge can try cases where the amount involved is £5,000 or less (see also 'small claims procedure' below) and also deals with procedural matters. Where there is concurrent jurisdiction, to achieve maximum flexibility the business is listed before either the circuit judge or the district judge according to availability, but where a case appears to contain issues of particular importance or complexity it will usually be reserved for a circuit judge: *Practice Direction* [1991] 3 All ER 722. Appeal from the district judge is to the circuit judge, and from there to the Court of Appeal. Leave is required to appeal to the Court of Appeal in many cases, for example, in contract or tort where the amount involved is below £5,000, and in equity and probate matters below £15,000: County Courts Appeals Order 1991.

The designated divorce county courts

Some of the county courts are designated divorce county courts which deal with undefended divorces and related matters, and this jurisdiction is not geographically limited. Section 9 of the Courts and Legal Services Act 1990 empowers the Lord Chancellor, with the concurrence of the President of the Family Division, to allocate family proceedings which are within the jurisdiction of county courts. Section 11 enables him, in relation to the proceedings specified in s11(2), by order to provide that there shall be no restriction on the persons who exercise rights of audience, or rights to conduct litigation, in relation to proceedings specified by the order.

The Patents County Court

This was established by the Lord Chancellor under powers conferred on him by s287 of the Copyright, Designs and Patents Act 1988. It is intended as an alternative to the High Court to resolve disputes relatively quickly and inexpensively and patent agents have a right of audience. The Court now sits in the Central London Civil Trial Centre in the West End of London Patents, which opened in June 1994. Cases lasting more than a day, which would otherwise be tried in London's 12 county courts, are also heard there and two of the courts are set aside for business disputes, using a simplified procedure giving the judge greater control over the management of the proceedings.

The small claims procedure

This is a form of arbitration for money claims that are valued at £3,000 or less. It is a default action which means that the plaint note gives the defendant notice that judgment in default may be entered if s/he does not either pay the claim (plus costs) or file a defence or counterclaim within 14 days. If no defence or counterclaim has been filed the claim is assessed by the district judge. If a defence is filed the claim is automatically referred to arbitration by the district judge. This uses an informal procedure and the strict rules of evidence do not apply. The arbitrator may adopt any method of procedure which s/he considers to be convenient and to afford a fair and equal opportunity to each party to present their case. The hearing is usually in chambers (private) and the decision of the district judge can be set aside only if there is an error of law or a misconduct in the proceedings.

The Lay Representatives (Rights of Audience) Order 1992, made under s11 of the Courts and Legal Services Act 1990, gives lay representatives rights of audience, but they cannot be heard if the person represented does not attend the hearing. The removal of the complex rules of evidence and procedure are intended to encourage the litigant to bring the matter in person and the use of legal representatives is discouraged. This is supported by the costs rules: solicitors' charges on an arbitration are not allowed except for the cost of commencing proceedings and of enforcing the district judge's award; and costs occasioned by the unreasonable conduct of the other party. For this reason legal aid is not available.

An application can be made to rescind the reference to arbitration in order for legal representation to be obtained and the costs of the proceedings recovered. The district judge has a discretion to rescind the reference on one or more of the following grounds:

1. a difficult question of law or exceptionally complex issue of fact is involved;
2. there is a fraud charge in question;
3. the parties agree to rescinding the reference;

4. it would otherwise be unreasonable to proceed to arbitration having regard to the subject-matter of the claim, the circumstances of the parties, or the interests of other persons likely to be affected by the award.

The district judge may rescind the reference on his/her own motion but, if a party requests it, a hearing takes place at which the district judge reviews his/her decision. If the reference is rescinded the district judge refers the matter to a full trial in open court. In *Pepper* v *Healey* [1982] RTR 411 (CA) a reference was rescinded in a road accident case because the defendant would be represented at the insurer's expense. However, it is clear from the cases heard during the 1990s that there must be substantial reason for the reference to be rescinded. In *Afzal and Others* v *Ford Motor Company* [1994] 4 All ER 720 the Court of Appeal allowed an appeal by Ford against a district judge who had rescinded the reference in respect of claims by employees for damages for personal injuries on the basis of grounds 1. and 4. above. In respect of point 4. the employees, who were represented by their trade union, had argued that the denial of the right to recover the costs of representation would deter the trade unions from assisting their members in the future. In *Joyce* v *Liverpool City Council* [1995] 3 All ER 110 the action against the defendant for damages and an order for specific performance in relation to the authority's statutory housing repair obligations was heard in ordinary county court proceedings. The plaintiff succeeded but was awarded only fixed costs on the ground that the action should have been heard in arbitration under the small claims jurisdiction. The Court of Appeal dismissed the plaintiff's appeal against the costs order on the grounds that the district judge had the power to award remedies of specific performance and/or injunction in housing disputes heard under the small claims procedure and therefore reference to arbitration was appropriate. The order for costs reflected that position.

These two cases indicate the general policy to promote reference to arbitration under the small claims procedure and of the estimated 500,000 claims made each year, only about one-tenth of them lead to a full hearing. The small claims procedure has been extensively used for resolving consumer disputes involving faulty goods and is well suited to this because the legal points and the facts involved are not too difficult for the litigants to argue for themselves. It is now used for a variety of matters and it is expected that the use of the procedure will increase considerably, partly because of the cost of legal representation, but also because of the increased financial limit. The Courts and Legal Services Act 1990 raised the financial limit from £500 to £1,000 and, following the recommendation of the interim report of the Woolf Committee on Civil Justice in 1995, the Lord Chancellor acted to raise the small claims limit to the present £3,000 (effective as from 8 January 1996).

Magistrates' courts

Magistrates' courts are composed of justices of the peace or, in the big cities, a stipendiary (professional salaried) magistrate. A stipendiary magistrate must have a seven-year general qualification within s71 of the Courts and Legal Services Act 1990. For trying an information summarily there must be at least two and not more than seven justices of the peace (in practice there are usually three) or one stipendiary. A lay justice may hear committal proceedings for cases which are going for trial at the Crown Court on his own.

Magistrates' courts have a very wide and varied jurisdiction, only part of it being criminal, but their jurisdiction is limited geographically and is confined to minor matters.

The criminal jurisdiction has two aspects, trial and committal proceedings. Certain offences can only be tried summarily (ie in a magistrates' court), and certain other offences may be tried either on indictment or summarily. Where a case is to be tried on indictment in the Crown Court then the other aspect of the jurisdiction arises. Before a case can be tried at the Crown Court it must have been sent there by a magistrates' court by means of committal proceedings. However, where a person is charged with certain offences involving children, sexual offences and offences involving violence or cruelty, in certain circumstances, and before the magistrates' court has begun to enquire into the case as examining justices, the Director of Public Prosecutions may by notice have the proceedings transferred to the Crown Court: s53 of the Criminal Justice Act 1991 as amended. By virtue of *Practice Note* [1992] 3 All ER 922, the transfer is to be made to a Crown Court centre equipped with live television link facilities.

Magistrates also issue summonses and warrants, which start the whole criminal process, and grant bail.

There are special magistrates' courts, known as youth courts, which deal with people under the age of 17 who commit offences. A youth court is composed of at least three lay justices from a special panel, at least one of whom must be a woman. The youth court must not sit in any place where an adult court has been sitting within the last hour and, unlike those of adult courts, the proceedings are not in public.

The magistrates' courts also have a very varied civil jurisdiction. Probably the most important is over family proceedings (in family proceedings courts), under which the court can grant maintenance and custody and make a non-cohabitation order, but complex cases under the Children Act 1989 should be transferred to the nearest county court: *Essex County Council* v *L* (1992) The Times 18 December. Magistrates' courts can also deal with adoption proceedings, and are responsible for the recovery of a large number of debts such as outstanding council tax payments, gas, electricity and water charges, income tax and National Insurance contributions. They also grant and revoke several kinds of licences, especially licences to sell alcohol. Appeals on family matters go to the divisional court of the Family Division.

Magistrates can award compensation (maximum £5,000 for any one offence) for personal injury, loss or damage.

Coroners' courts

The coroner was originally the King's official responsible for ensuring that the King got the revenue due to him, including treasure trove and possible fines arising from unexplained deaths.

The coroner's jurisdiction is now statutory. He must have a five-year general qualification within the meaning of the Courts and Legal Services Act 1990 or be a legally qualified medical practitioner of at least five years' standing. His main jurisdiction is inquests into the deaths of persons who appear to have died violent or unnatural deaths, or sudden deaths of which the causes are unknown, or when the deaths occurred in prison. He also has jurisdiction over treasure trove.

The purpose of an inquest is to establish the cause of death of the deceased. The coroner is not concerned with any question of civil or criminal liability for the death. The coroner may summon a jury of between seven and eleven members to hold an inquest, and he must do so in certain circumstances (eg where a death occurred in prison or in police custody: see s8(2) of the Coroners Act 1988). The procedure is inquisitorial, which means that the coroner conducts the proceedings and questions the witnesses. Formerly, if the jury returned a verdict of murder, manslaughter or infanticide the coroner could commit the person named for trial. This power was abolished by s56(1) Criminal Law Act 1977. Whenever a person has been charged with a crime, the practice is to adjourn the inquest until after the trial. There is no appeal, but the coroner's court is subject to control by the High Court by means of prerogative orders.

Judicial Committee of the Privy Council

The Privy Council is the last remnant of the great council of the monarch (the Curia Regis). The Curia Regis was the source of most modern governmental and administrative institutions (eg Parliament, the courts, the revenue) which gradually separated from it and became established in their own right. However, the Privy Council retains a small judicial jurisdiction which is exercised, on behalf of the monarch, by the Judicial Committee (usually staffed by the Law Lords). This jurisdiction consists of:

1. Hearing appeals from outside the United Kingdom. The Privy Council hears appeals from the Channel Islands, the Isle of Man, British colonies and protectorates, and the highest courts in those Commonwealth countries which have not abolished the right to appeal to the Privy Council.
2. Admiralty jurisdiction. This is now limited only to appeals from the Admiralty court when sitting as a prize court (ie a court which determines issues concerning the ownership of ships and cargo captured by enemy warships).
3. Appeals from ecclesiastical courts.
4. Appeals from medical tribunals.

The Judicial Committee may also advise on matters of law relating to the Commonwealth and colonies. Membership includes all persons who have held high judicial office in the Commonwealth, but in practice the court is generally composed of Law Lords, the usual number being five. When the Privy Council sits to hear ecclesiastical appeals, one archbishop (or the Bishop of London) and four other bishops sit as assessors, to advise. Only one majority opinion is given by the committee, though dissenting opinions are recorded. The committee does not give judgment, but simply advises the sovereign who implements the recommedation by convention by Order in Council. The committee may also be required by the sovereign to advise on particular legal matters.

3.4 Courts of particular jurisdiction

The Court of Protection

An office of the Supreme Court, this court protects and manages the property and affairs of persons who, by reason of mental disorder, are incapable of dealing with them without assistance. The Lord Chancellor nominates one or more judges of the Supreme Court for the purpose, and he appoints the Master of the Court of Protection. In practice the court is administered by the master and his staff and is not a court in the normal sense, although the judge has the same powers as are vested in the High Court in respect of securing the attendance of witnesses and the production of documents. Its jurisdiction is confined to dealing with the property of mental patients.

Restrictive Practices Court

The Director-General of Fair Trading may refer agreements to this court, which must then decide whether or not any restrictions or information provisions are contrary to the public interest. On a positive declaration, the restrictions or information provisions in question are void.

A superior court of record, the Restrictive Practices Court consists of three puisne judges of the High Court, one judge of the Court of Session and one judge of the Supreme Court of Northern Ireland, together with not more than ten appointed members who are qualified by virtue of their knowledge of or experience in industry, commerce or public affairs. In England and Wales, appeal lies to the Court of Appeal.

Courts martial

These exercise jurisdiction over members of the armed forces under the Army and Air Force Acts 1955 and the Naval Discipline Act 1957. Murder, manslaughter, treason and rape committed within the United Kingdom must be tried in the ordinary criminal courts. For other offences the military and civilian courts have a concurrent jurisdiction, but a person tried in one cannot be subsequently tried by the other.

The trial procedure is very similar to that in the civilian courts. There is a preliminary enquiry and the accused is sent for trial at the court martial on a charge sheet (similar to an indictment). The trial is before three or five officers assisted by a judge advocate who is a lawyer. Proceedings are in open court, and counsel and solicitors have a right of audience. Normally the prosecution is conducted by an officer from the service legal department, and the accused is defended by an officer, but in serious cases a civilian lawyer is paid by the service to defend the case. There is no jury; the judge advocate sums up and advises on the law, and the other members of the court arrive at a majority decision. If the accused is found guilty the findings must be confirmed by a superior officer who can remit the decision to the court for further consideration or even refuse to confirm it.

Appeal is to the Courts Martial Appeal Court, the judges of which are the ex officio and ordinary judges of the Court of Appeal, nominated High Court, Scottish and Northern Irish judges and 'other persons ... of legal experience' if the Lord Chancellor decides to appoint them.

With leave, there is a further appeal to the House of Lords, but leave is not granted unless the appeal court certifies that a point of law of general public importance is involved and it appears to the appeal court or the House that the point is one which the House ought to consider.

The ecclesiastical courts

The powers of ecclesiastical courts were seriously curtailed in the sixteenth century during the Reformation and have been further reduced by statute. In each diocese there is a consistory court with a judge called a chancellor, who has a seven-year general qualification within s71 of the Courts and Legal Services Act 1990 and is appointed by the bishop. Its jurisdiction is mainly concerned with investigating allegations against the clergy and with the granting of faculties. For example, in *Re St Bartholomew's, Aldbrough* [1990] 3 All ER 440 the York Consistory Court granted a faculty, ie gave permission, for the sale of a fourteenth-century helmet in order to relieve the church's finances. Appeal lies to the Court of Arches in the province of Canterbury and to the Chancery Court of York in the Province of York, and further appeal is to the Privy Council. Jurisdiction over bishops and archbishops is exercised by Commissions of Convocation. The courts may be controlled by the prerogative orders.

Section 3.5 (following) gives a complete overview of the court structure in diagrammatic form.

3.5 Diagrams of the court structure

The civil courts

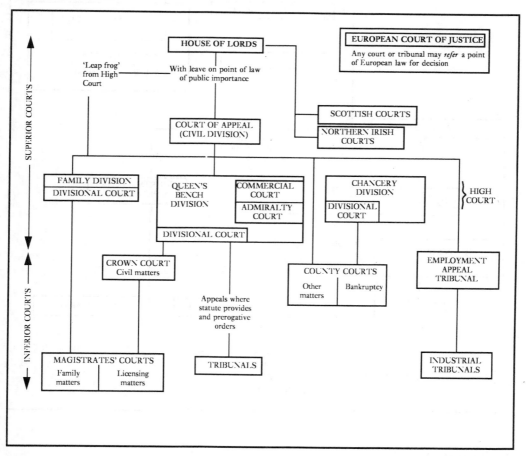

The criminal courts

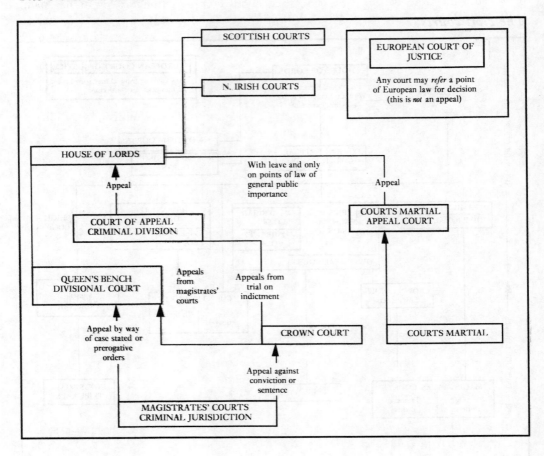

3.6 Double liability

From the analysis of the court structure it can be seen that the division is between civil and criminal matters. However, while it is good to isolate the structures and procedures, in real life it may often happen that one event in an individual's life may incur visits to courts within both structures. A scenario involving the two structures is known as double liability. An example of this would be where, say, a vehicle driven dangerously by yourself runs into another vehicle causing damage to it and injury to the other driver.

Here the outcome, subject to questions of insurance, is that the police may well be interested in bringing a prosecution against yourself for dangerous driving. A prosecution will be followed through the magistrates' court. However, while your victim may well be happy to think that justice has been done, and you have been punished, he or she will also be concerned about compensation for his or her pain, suffering, injury and loss. In order to do this it will be necessary for him or her to bring an action in the county court, or the High Court if the amount claimed is over £50,000.

If you were a lawyer acting for a client in the situation given you would have to advise on both the civil and criminal implications of the case. Remember that s11 of the Civil Evidence Act 1968 would allow, in the above scenario, the successful prosecution to be pleaded in the civil case, thus saving time in establishing liability.

3.7 Exercises

1. What types of action would be heard in the following courts?

   a) Chancery Division of the High Court;
   b) Family Division of the High Court;
   c) county court;
   d) Queen's Bench Division;
   e) magistrates' court;
   f) Court of Appeal;
   g) House of Lords;

2. Where would the following matters be heard?

   a) a claim for damages for £50,000 in a non-personal injury case;
   b) an appeal on a point of law from the decision of a county court;
   c) a claim concerning matrimonial property;
   d) committal proceedings;
   e) a claim that the Secretary of State for Education has exceeded his powers;
   f) an undefended divorce;
   g) a criminal trial before a judge and jury;
   h) an appeal from an overseas country which recognises our jurisdiction.

3. Which of the following statements is correct?

   a) A breach of contract should be brought in the Crown Court.
   b) A criminal prosecution must be brought in the High Court.
   c) It is always possible to appeal to the House of Lords.
   d) A claim for damages for breach of contract should be brought in the county or the High Court.

4

The Doctrine of Judicial Precedent

4.1 Stare decisis and res judicata

4.2 Ratio decidendi

4.3 Ascertaining the ratio decidendi

4.4 Judicial precedent within the court hierarchy

4.5 Persuasive precedents

4.6 Advantages and disadvantages of the doctrine of binding precedent

4.1 Stare decisis and res judicata

Binding judicial precedent involves case law and the fundamental element of stare decisis, which means following the decisions of previous cases. Accordingly, a judge will decide a case in the same way that another judge has decided a previous similar case; that is, like cases should be treated alike.

Where judicial precedent is binding, a judge will have an obligation to follow a previous case, whether or not he or she approves of the decision. On some occasions, however, judicial precedent may be not binding but persuasive, and a judge will not then be under the same obligation. Persuasive precedent is discussed further in section 4.5 below.

Binding judicial precedent means *consistency* in decisions and provides *certainty* for the future. This ensures a solid basis for legal advice and enables people to organise their lives and arrange their business affairs on sound legal footings. Two other important points should be borne in mind: first, a case itself can be termed a 'precedent' which may be relied on subsequently, and secondly, there is no legislation either to guide or to specify as to how judicial precedent should be applied. Accordingly, understanding the application and effect of judicial precedent provides both a challenging and a fascinating task for any student embarking upon a study of the law.

As has been said above, a consideration of the doctrine of binding judicial precedent involves the application of the principle of stare decisis. A distinction should initially be drawn between stare decisis and the doctrine of res judicata which means that the court's order is binding on the *parties* and they cannot reopen the issue unless an appeal is possible. In criminal law, however, even when the right of appeal has been exhausted, there is an exception to res judicata where there has been a miscarriage of justice. In contrast, the doctrine of stare decisis means that a decision has an effect in the future, *on everyone else and especially on the courts*, and not only on the specific parties to the original case.

Accordingly, in civil cases there will be judgment for the plaintiff or defendant, eg judgment for £5,000. This decision *binds the parties* – res judicata – but does not, in itself, bind others in the future.

To illustrate the distinction between stare decisis and the doctrine of res judicata further, consideration may be given to:

Re Waring, Westminster Bank Ltd *v* Awdry *[1942] Ch 426*

The Court of Appeal decided that income tax had to be deducted from an annuity which had been left to a Mr Howard by Mr Waring. Another annuity had been left to a Mrs Louie Burton-Butler, but she was not a party to the appeal. The House of Lords refused leave to appeal. Later, in the case of *Berkeley* v *Berkeley* [1946] AC 555, the House of Lords overruled the *Awdry* case. Subsequently, in *Re Waring, Westminster Bank Ltd* v *Burton-Butler* [1948] Ch 221, it was held that, in respect of Mr Howard, the *Awdry* case was res judicata (binding on those parties) despite the fact that the latter case had been overruled by *Berkeley* v *Berkeley*. However, with regard to the annuity left to Mrs Burton-Butler, on the basis of stare decisis the *Berkeley* case was the leading authority. Mrs Burton-Butler had not been a party to the *Awdry* case, and therefore the doctrine of res judicata was not appropriate.

By virtue of stare decisis, therefore, a decision will have a subsequent effect on others and, in particular on the courts. The following question may now be asked about a decision: what *is* the core element which is so influential? The answer is: the rule or principle of law which is the basis of the decision, and such a principle of law is called the ratio decidendi (pronounced rayshio desseedendye). Judges decide cases on the basis of principles of law contained in earlier decisions, and therein lies the foundation of the doctrine of binding judicial precedent.

Generally, therefore, the *judgment* in a case binds the parties, but such a judgment does not, in itself, bind others in the future. It is the *ratio decidendi* which provides the binding element to be followed by others, particularly by the courts.

4.2 Ratio decidendi

The reasons for judges' decisions provide principles of law which are the rationes decidendi (the plural of ratio decidendi), broadly described as principles of law which are applied to resolve the legal issues arising from the material facts and are also the reasons for the decisions. Put in another way, they are the principles of law which are the bases of or reasons for the decision. To encapsulate this, the ratio decidendi is the reason for the decision and it is this fundamental element which *may* be binding in later cases.

There are many definitions of the ratio decidendi. Professor Michael Zander, in *The Law-Making Process*, defines it at 249 as 'a proposition of law which decides the case, in the light or in the context of the material facts'. It can be seen that the material facts of the case have to be ascertained, but of great importance is the reference to a proposition (or principle) of law which decides the case and therefore, by inference, is the reason for the decision. Professor Zander also states at 248: 'The ratio ... of a case is its central core of meaning, its sharpest cutting edge.' This is indicative of the importance of the ratio decidendi.

In Cross and Harris, *Precedent in English Law* (4th edition), at 72, there is the following description:

> 'The *ratio decidendi* of a case is any rule of law expressly or impliedly treated by the judge as a necessary step in reaching his conclusion, having regard to the line of reasoning adopted by him, or a necessary part of his direction to the jury.'

This is perhaps a wider description, bearing in mind the words 'expressly or impliedly'. Nevertheless, there is reference to 'any rule of law' which is a 'necessary step' in the decision or a 'necessary part' of the judge's direction to the jury. Cross and Harris also refer to Professor Neil MacCormick's 'Why Cases have *Rationes* and What These Are' (in Goldstein (ed), *Precedent in Law*, at 179), in which he points out that instead of a 'rule of law' there should be reference to a 'ruling on a point of law'. To support this point of view, where the interpretation of a statutory rule *is not in question* (no ruling or decision having to be given), then although the rule may well be an essential part of a judge's reason, it will not be a ratio decidendi, whereas *if the meaning of the rule is disputed* then the judge's ruling as to its meaning will be ratio decidendi if that ruling is part of the basis of the decision. Nevertheless, generally, it could be said that the ratio decidendi is any rule of law regarded by the judge as a very necessary element in the decision itself or in the direction to the jury. By way of further reference, Cross and Harris (op cit) state at 63:

> 'According to Dr Goodhart the *ratio decidendi* of a case is determined by ascertaining the facts treated as material by the judge. It is the principle to be derived from the judge's decision on the basis of those facts. Any court bound by the case must come to a similar conclusion unless there is a further fact in the case before it which it is prepared to treat as material, or unless some fact treated as material in the previous case is absent.'

A decision is therefore made on the material facts, and the principle of law derives from that decision. In effect, the ratio decidendi is the principle of law *necessary* for the decision on those material facts.

In addition to the many definitions of ratio decidendi there are various descriptions or methods to assist in determining it, and for a detailed examination of this area the student is referred again to Cross and Harris (above). It is submitted that once the material facts have been clarified, together with the legal issue arising from them, the principle of law used by the judge to resolve that issue and to reach his decision will be the ratio decidendi – the reason for the decision.

Once the concept of the ratio decidendi has been grasped, a distinction has to be drawn between a ratio and an obiter dictum, the plural of the latter being obiter dicta. An obiter dictum is a statement or principle of law which is not a necessary part of nor the reason for the judge's decision. There are various types of obiter dictum; for instance, a judge may hypothesise in the sense that he states the principle of law which would have been applicable had the material facts been different. As such a principle of law would not relate to the actual material facts of the case, then clearly it could not be the reason for the decision. In these circumstances the principle of law would be an obiter dictum – something said 'by the way' and therefore not binding. Other examples of obiter dicta will be considered later. Basically, although an obiter dictum is not binding it will have a persuasive influence.

The astute reader will have noted that the final part of the first paragraph under the heading 'Ratio decidendi' refers to the reason for the decision (the ratio decidendi) being the fundamental element which *may* be binding in later cases. This alludes to the very important point that a ratio decidendi is *capable* of being binding, and whether or not it *is* binding will be determined by the court hierarchy. This involves the position of courts in relation to each other, and generally higher courts bind lower courts. A comparison is made between the position of the court which made the original decision (including the ratio decidendi) and that of the court which is now being called upon to decide a particular case. Will the latter court be bound by the original decision, bearing in mind that higher courts bind lower courts?

Thus the operation of the doctrine of binding precedent is dependent upon the court hierarchy, which is one of the most important factors in its development. (The court hierarchy is dealt with fully at pp195–204.) Where there *is* a binding precedent then it must be followed by a court even though it may cause injustice.

4.3 Ascertaining the ratio decidendi

A judge may have stated a principle of law in wide or narrow terms – will the ratio decidendi be the words as stated by the judge? The traditional view has been 'yes'. The modern approach, however, is that the ratio in the *original* case is ascertained by a court in a *later* case. This means, in effect, that the court in the later case considers the earlier case and endeavours to clarify the ratio decidendi, and the later judge is able to restrict or enlarge the scope of the ratio. To explain this further, the facts of two cases will not be identical; therefore if the judge decides that the ratio does not apply to the *current* facts he restricts the ratio, whereas if he applies the ratio to these current different facts he is thereby enlarging it. A ratio will also be restricted or enlarged depending upon whether the material facts are few or many. For instance, A, B, C, D, E and F are facts in a case, and if the judge considers that A, B and C are the *material* facts then this will result in a wide ratio. If, however, A, B, C, D, E and F are *all* material facts, then the ratio will be narrowed considerably. By way of example, let us consider the following:

A drunken person who drives a blue car negligently, thereby injuring someone, will be liable for compensation for personal injury. If only some of these facts are material, then the ratio is widened – a person who drives a car negligently, thereby injuring someone, will be liable for compensation for personal injury. The ratio decidendi has been widened to cover persons who need not necessarily be drunk and who drive cars, no matter what colour the cars are.

The case of *Rylands* v *Fletcher* (1868) LR 3 HL 330 is a good example of this:

1. A reservoir was built on the defendant's land.
2. It was negligently built by a contractor.
3. There was an escape of water and the plaintiff's mine was flooded.

The defendant was held liable, but item 2 above was considered to be immaterial. The result was a wide ratio, ie strict liability (liability without fault) for the escape of water. The defendant was liable despite the fact that it was his contractor who had been negligent.

In *Donoghue* v *Stevenson* [1932] AC 562 the plaintiff drank some of the contents of an opaque bottle containing ginger beer and the decomposed remains of a snail. The beer was manufactured by the defendant, and the plaintiff was harmed. In essence, these were the material facts and the House of Lords did not, inter alia, consider it material that there was no contract between the plaintiff and defendant. There was, therefore, a wider ratio, and furthermore it was clearly not intended to relate only to snails in bottles of ginger beer. This can be seen from the rule laid down by Lord Atkin:

> '[A] manufacturer of products, which he sells in such a form as to show that he intends them to reach the ultimate consumer in the form in which they left him with no reasonable possibility of intermediate examination, and with the knowledge that the absence of reasonable care in the preparation or putting up of the products will result in an injury to the consumer's life or property, owes a duty to the consumer to take that reasonable care.'

Although words which are not the basis for a decision must be obiter, it is important to note that there may be two or more reasons for a decision, and they will be rationes decidendi and not obiter dicta. In the case of *Ashton* v *Turner* [1980] 3 All ER 870 the plaintiff was in a car driven by the defendant while they were making their getaway from the scene of a burglary. The plaintiff was injured by the known drunken driver's negligent driving and claimed compensation. Ewbank J found against the plaintiff on the following grounds:

1. Ex turpi causa non oritur actio (no action may be brought on an illegal/immoral cause).
2. Volenti non fit injuria (there is no injury to one who consents).
3. Contributory negligence.

When there is an appeal in the Court of Appeal or House of Lords, the judges may come to the same decision – ie judgment for one particular party – *but* their reasons may differ. The ratio decidendi will be what was agreed by the majority, and if there is no majority for any one reason then the case will be a very weak precedent. Does this mean that a subsequent court will have to decide which of the alternative reasons it considers to be a ratio? The case of *Bell* v *Lever Bros Ltd* [1932] AC 161 is a good illustration of the difficulties. In this case there was a three-to-two majority decision in the House of Lords, although the majority of three did not decide on the same ratio. The decision has continued to cause problems, leaving lower courts to pursue one of two different interpretations.

As noted above, a case may have two or more rationes decidendi. In *Jacobs* v *London County Council* [1950] AC 361 the House of Lords accepted that two reasons given by the House itself for its decision in *Fairman* v *Perpetual Investment Building Society* [1923] AC 74 were binding.

A rare difficulty which may arise is where two judges express a view of the law which differs from the view of two further judges, and a fifth judge wishes to decide the appeal in the same way as the first two judges but for the reasoning of the latter two judges. This was the situation in *Central Asbestos Co Ltd* v *Dodd* [1973] AC 51. Subsequently, in *Harper* v *National Coal Board* [1974] QB 614, the Court of Appeal held that because there was no clear ratio in the *Central Asbestos* case, the court would return to the law which had been decided in earlier cases.

4.4 Judicial precedent within the court hierarchy

The binding of judges by precedents developed over several centuries. During the eighteenth century precedents would be followed unless they were absurd or unjust, and in the nineteenth and twentieth centuries the development continued; precedents became binding even if they were 'unreasonable and inconvenient'. Improved law reporting was a beneficial factor in this development, and the reorganisation of the courts into a sound, hierarchical structure during the late nineteenth century was also of considerable importance.

Reversing, overruling and distinguishing

Reversing
When a case is taken on appeal and a higher court overturns the decision, it thereby *reverses* the decision.

Overruling
When a *principle of law* laid down by a lower court is overturned by a higher court in a *later different case*, it is *overruled*. In English courts there is *retrospective* overruling, and the earlier principle of law is deemed never to have existed. This earlier principle of law is not applied either in the case currently being dealt with (the instant case) or in later cases. It is argued that this causes injustice as the parties

in the instant case relied on the law as it stood, only now to be told that it never has been the law.

In other countries, in particular the United States, there is *prospective* overruling. By this practice, the earlier case containing the principle of law is overruled. However, this overruled case *is* applied in the instant case but not in future cases. Put another way, *prospective* overruling means that the decision to overrule (resulting in the overruled case) applies in the future but not to the present, ie the instant, case.

Distinguishing

A case may be *distinguished* on the facts or the point of law involved. Accordingly, an otherwise binding decision is thereby avoided.

Court of Justice of the European Communities (The European Court of Justice)

With regard to matters of Community law, decisions of the European Court of Justice bind English courts, including the House of Lords. Although it will generally follow its own previous decisions, the European Court of Justice is not bound to do so.

House of Lords

In *London Tramways* v *London County Council* [1898] AC 375 the House of Lords ruled that it was bound by its own decisions. Cases of individual hardship, and also erroneous judgments, would have to be accepted because, first, certainty was of overriding importance, and, secondly, it was in the public interest for there to be an end to litigation.

Despite criticism, the House of Lords continued to be bound by its own decisions until July 1966 when Lord Gardiner, the then Lord Chancellor, read *Practice Statement* [1966] 1 WLR 1234 (Judicial Precedent) on behalf of the Law Lords. In this they recognised the 'indispensable foundation' of the use of precedent, as certainty assisted individuals in conducting their affairs, and precedent provided 'a basis for orderly development of legal rules'. Nevertheless, their Lordships recognised 'that too rigid adherence to precedent may lead to injustice in a particular case and also unduly restrict the proper development of the law'. Former decisions would be treated as normally binding, but the House of Lords would 'depart from a decision when it appears right to do so'. Their Lordships would be mindful of disturbing retrospectively the basis of contracts, property settlements and fiscal arrangements, and they would bear in mind the need for certainty in the criminal law.

The *Practice Statement* was not intended to affect the use of precedent other than in the House of Lords. Departing from their previous decisions would not be a frequent occurrence. It might happen where conditions which had influenced an earlier decision no longer prevailed and the law ought to be different. The House of Lords could also adapt English law to meet changing conditions. Furthermore, greater attention could be paid to judicial decisions in the superior courts of the Commonwealth where decisions were not rigidly binding.

When it is relevant in an appeal to the House of Lords, a party must make it very clear that their Lordships are to be asked to depart from an earlier decision. The *Practice Statement* was considered to be an event of notable consequence, but the freedom to depart from previous decisions has been used very sparingly, especially where cases have related to the construction of statutes and documents. A case which highlighted reticence in this area was *Jones* v *Secretary of State for Social Services* [1972] AC 944, which involved the interpretation of a statutory provision regarding injury benefit in the light of the prior decision of the House of Lords in *Re Dowling* [1967] 1 AC 725. There were seven Law Lords sitting in this case; four of them considered *Dowling* to be wrong, but only three of those four were prepared to use the *Practice Statement*. The remaining three Law Lords thought *Dowling* was correct, but reflected upon what they would have thought if *Dowling* was wrong – they indicated that they would *not* have departed from the decision. It appeared that the fact that a decision was wrong was not enough to justify use of the *Practice Statement*. It would seem, therefore, that there has to be a practical side to its use, and issues of only academic interest will not be entertained.

The power to depart from a previous decision was first exercised in *Conway* v *Rimmer* [1968] AC 910, where the case of *Duncan* v *Cammell Laird & Co* [1942] AC 624 was unanimously overruled. In that case, a minister's affidavit had been sufficient for the Crown to claim privilege not to disclose documents in civil litigation. In *Conway* v *Rimmer* it was held that an affidavit would no longer be final. Prejudice to the State would be balanced against injustice to the individual.

In certain cases between 1966 and 1975, Lord Reid outlined criteria in respect of use of the *Practice Statement*. These were:

1. The right to depart should be used sparingly.
2. If the legitimate expectations of people would be upset, then there should be no overruling. This encompassed people who had, for example, entered into contracts or organised their affairs on the basis of a specific decision.
3. As regards the construction of statutes or documents, any appropriate decision should only be overruled in rare and exceptional circumstances.
4. If it would be difficult for the Lords to foresee the consequences of departing from a decision, then it should not be overruled. Similarly, if a change should be part of a comprehensive reform of the law, then legislation would be more appropriate.
5. Just because a decision was wrongly decided was not enough to overrule it. The reasoning behind this was certainty. There must be other arguments to justify overruling a decision.

6. A decision *should* be overruled if it had caused great uncertainty in practice, in other words if advisers were unable to indicate what the law would be in the courts.
7. A decision *should* be overruled where it was out of step with social conditions or public policy.

In the period 1966–1980 there were 29 cases when the House of Lords considered overruling one of its own precedents, but only eight were successful. It should be noted, however, that in a large number of cases it seems that the House of Lords has preferred to distinguish previous decisions as opposed to overruling them. It appears that the *Practice Statement* has thus had an important indirect influence.

There are some other interesting cases: *Robert Addie & Sons (Collieries) Ltd* v *Dumbreck* [1929] AC 358 involved a trespassing child, but there would only be liability where the occupier acted intentionally or recklessly. In *British Railways Board* v *Herrington* [1972] AC 877 the House of Lords overruled, or at least modified, the *Addie* case. Conditions had changed, and the House of Lords said that there was a test of 'common humanity' – had the occupier done everything that a humane person would have done to protect the safety of the trespasser?

The case of *Re United Railways of Havana and Regla Warehouses Ltd* [1961] AC 1001 decided that damages in a civil case could only be in sterling. However, in *Miliangos* v *George Frank (Textiles) Ltd* [1976] AC 443 the House of Lords overruled *Havana Railways* and held that damages could be in the currency of any foreign country specified in the contract.

Vestey v *Commissioners of Inland Revenue* [1979] 3 All ER 976 was an income tax case involving the interpretation of a statute. The House of Lords overruled its decision in *Congreve* v *Commissioners of Inland Revenue* [1948] 1 All ER 948 which had stood for thirty years. It will be recalled that the criteria in respect of the use of the *Practice Statement* said that a decision relating to the construction of a statute should only be overruled in rare and exceptional circumstances. How was this criterion reconciled with the *Vestey* case? The House of Lords considered that the *Congreve* case would produce 'startling and unacceptable consequences' in circumstances which had not been foreseen when the case was decided. Accordingly, the decision seemed to involve a broad issue of justice or public policy.

An interesting situation developed through the decision in *Anderton* v *Ryan* [1985] AC 560. This case involved the Criminal Attempts Act 1981. The appellant thought that some goods had been stolen, but there was no evidence that this was so. The appellant was held not guilty of attempting dishonestly to handle stolen property. However, *R* v *Shivpuri* [1986] 2 All ER 334 overruled *Anderton* v *Ryan* within a year. This case also involved the Criminal Attempts Act. The appellant thought that he was carrying drugs, but in fact he was carrying a harmless substance. He was held to be guilty of attempting to commit a drug offence. Despite the need for certainty in criminal law, Lord Bridge of Harwich said: 'If a serious error embodied in a decision of this House has distorted the law the sooner it is corrected the better.'

In *Anns* v *Merton London Borough Council* [1978] AC 728 the House of Lords held that a local authority had a duty to take reasonable care to ensure that the foundations of a building complied with building regulations. There was criticism of the decision because the loss was pure economic loss, in other words the cost of putting right the defect as opposed to physical loss (meaning damage to persons or property). The latter would involve straightforward tortious claims. However, in *Murphy* v *Brentwood District Council* [1990] 2 All ER 908 the House of Lords was invited to reconsider *Anns*. The House took into account the reluctance of English judges to provide a remedy in tort for pure economic loss, compared with occasions when there was physical loss. *Anns* was unanimously overruled. Accordingly, where there was a defect but it was discovered before there was any harm, then the loss was pure economic loss and a consumer's remedy lay in contract and *not in* tort.

The Court of Appeal (Civil Division)

The Court of Appeal is bound by the decisions of the House of Lords, and it in turn binds the High Court and county courts. As to whether the court is bound by its own decisions, consideration must be given to some important cases.

In *Young* v *Bristol Aeroplane Co Ltd* [1944] KB 718 it was decided that the Court of Appeal was bound by its own decisions subject to three exceptions:

1. Where there are previous conflicting decisions, the Court of Appeal decides which decision to follow and rejects the other; for example, in *Tiverton Estates Ltd* v *Wearwell Ltd* [1975] Ch 146 the Court of Appeal avoided following its recent decision in the controversial case of *Law* v *Jones* [1974] Ch 112 because it was inconsistent with earlier decisions of the court.
2. Where a Court of Appeal decision cannot stand with a later decision of the House of Lords.
3. The court does not need to follow a Court of Appeal decision that was given per incuriam, that is through lack of care. This would involve the court being in ignorance of, or failing to consider, a relevant statutory provision or a binding precedent of the House of Lords or Court of Appeal. Such cases will be rare, and per incuriam does not mean, inter alia, that counsel did not argue to his or her best ability.

In *Dixon* v *British Broadcasting Corporation* [1979] QB 546 a decision regarding the construction of a statutory provision was considered per incuriam because other relevant provisions which helped to clarify the words in question had not been brought to the attention of the court.

Since the *Bristol Aeroplane* case a fourth exception has emerged: the Court of Appeal is not bound to follow an interlocutory order (an order which leaves something further to be done, as opposed to a final order) made by two judges in the Court of Appeal. The authority for this is *Boys* v *Chaplin* [1968] 2 QB 1, although this area of law is unsettled in the light of subsequent obiter in *Langley* v *North West Water Authority* [1991] 3 All ER 610.

It can be argued that there is a fifth exception: that the Court of Appeal should be free to depart from a previous decision of its own which is inconsistent with Community law.

Sixthly, and finally, consideration should be given to the case of *Doughty* v *Turner Manufacturing Co Ltd* [1964] 1 QB 518. In this case the Court of Appeal applied the Privy Council decision in *Overseas Tankship (UK) Ltd* v *Morts Dock Engineering Co Ltd* [1961] AC 388 (*The Wagon Mound No 1*) in preference to its own decision in *Re Polemis* [1921] 3 KB 560. In *Worcester Works Finance Ltd* v *Cooden Engineering Co Ltd* [1972] 1 QB 210 the Court of Appeal again preferred a Privy Council decision to its own previous conflicting decisions. Lord Denning MR said (at 217):

> 'Although decisions of the Privy Council are not binding on this Court, nevertheless when the Privy Council disapproves of a previous decision of this Court or casts doubt on it, we are at liberty to depart from the previous decision.'

It is arguable that this statement was part of Lord Denning's campaign against the Court of Appeal being bound by its own previous decisions. (Consideration has to be given as to whether this statement is still authoritative in view of the decision in *Davis* v *Johnson* (see below).)

Lord Denning's campaign

With regard to the *Practice Statement* not being intended to affect the use of precedent anywhere other than in the House of Lords, it appears that Lord Denning took this to mean that the House of Lords was only considering precedent in the Lords and not its use elsewhere. He based his campaign on the *Practice Statement*, and there was a twofold attack:

1. Lord Denning maintained that the Court of Appeal was no longer bound by the decisions of the House of Lords.

    He voiced his dissent in *Conway* v *Rimmer* [1967] 2 All ER 1260 – he did not agree that the Court of Appeal was still bound by *Duncan* v *Cammell Laird & Co Ltd* [1942] AC 624 and said: 'This is the very case in which to throw off the fetters.' The House of Lords did overrule *Duncan* v *Cammell Laird* but expressly stated that the Court of Appeal had been bound by that case.

    In *Broome* v *Cassell & Co Ltd* [1971] 2 QB 354 the Court of Appeal (led by Lord Denning) refused to follow the House of Lords' decision in *Rookes* v *Barnard* [1964] AC 1129, maintaining that the House of Lords had acted per incuriam by ignoring two of its own previous decisions, namely *Hulton* v *Jones* in 1910 and *Ley* v *Hamilton* in 1935. On appeal to the House of Lords, the Court of Appeal was severely rebuked by Lord Hailsham. He said ([1972] AC 1027 at 1054):

'... it is not open to the Court of Appeal to give gratuitous advice to judges of first instance to ignore decisions of the House of Lords in this way ... The fact is, and I hope it will never be necessary to say so again, that in the hierarchical system of courts which exists in this country, it is necessary for each lower tier, including the Court of Appeal, to accept loyally the decisions of the higher tiers.'

In *Schorsch Meier GmbH* v *Hennin* [1975] QB 416 the Court of Appeal did not follow the decision of the House of Lords in *Havana Railways* and held that damages for breach of contract could be awarded in a foreign currency which was the currency of the contract. The basis for Lord Denning's view was cessante ratione cessat ipsa lex – when the reason for the rule goes, the rule lapses. This case did not go on appeal to the House of Lords. The issue arose again, however, in *Miliangos* v *George Frank (Textiles) Ltd* [1976] AC 443, and the trial judge followed *Havana Railways*. The Court of Appeal said that it was bound by its own decision in *Schorsch Meier*. The House of Lords *did* overrule *Havana Railways* but said that the Court of Appeal had been wrong in what it had done. Lord Cross (at 495–6) said:

'In the *Schorsch Meier* case [1975] QB 416, 425, Lord Denning MR, with the concurrence of Foster J, took it on himself to say that the decision in the *Havana* case that our courts cannot give judgment for payment of a sum of foreign currency – though right in 1961 – ought not to be followed in 1974 because the "reasons for the rule have now ceased to exist". I agree with my noble and learned friend, Lord Wilberforce, that the Master of the Rolls was not entitled to take such a course. It is not for any inferior court – be it a county court or a division of the Court of Appeal presided over by Lord Denning – to review decisions of this House. Such a review can only be undertaken by this House itself under the declaration of 1966.'

In his subsequent book *The Discipline of Law* Lord Denning indicated that if in the *Schorsch Meier* case the Court of Appeal had held itself bound by the *Havana Railways* case, the plaintiff in *Miliangos* v *George Frank (Textiles) Ltd* would automatically have taken judgment in sterling also, and the House of Lords would not have had the opportunity of overruling *Havana Railways*.

'The law would still have been that an English court could only give judgment in sterling. That would have been a disaster for our trade with countries overseas.'

Finally, the Court of Appeal may distinguish a decision of the House of Lords on the facts or the law, but this should not be done just to avoid a decision which the Court of Appeal considers to be wrong or troublesome.

2. Lord Denning maintained that the Court of Appeal should not be bound by its own decisions.

In *Gallie* v *Lee* [1969] 2 Ch 17 he said (at 37):

'I do not think we are bound by prior decisions of our own, or at any rate, not absolutely bound. We are not fettered as it was once thought. It was a self-imposed limitation: and we who imposed it can also remove it. The House of Lords have done it. So why should not we do likewise?'

The remaining two judges disagreed with him.

In *Davis* v *Johnson* [1979] AC 264 there was an application under the Domestic Violence and Matrimonial Proceedings Act 1976 for an injunction to restrain the respondent from using violence and to order him to vacate the council flat where the appellant and respondent had been cohabiting as man and wife. Two previous decisions of the Court of Appeal, namely *B* v *B* [1978] Fam 26 and *Cantliff* v *Jenkins* [1978] QB 47, decided that a person who had a proprietary interest in property could not be excluded by an injunction granted under the 1976 Act. The Court of Appeal granted an injunction and did not follow *B* v *B* and *Cantliff* v *Jenkins*, which it said were wrong.

Lord Denning made various points. He maintained that the House of Lords might not have another opportunity to correct an error which otherwise would be continued. He pointed out that it was 60 years before the erroneous decision in *Carlisle and Cumberland Banking Co* v *Bragg* [1911] 1 KB 489 was overruled by the decision of the House of Lords in *Gallie* v *Lee*. A party might be outside the legal aid limits, and not be able to afford to take the case to the House of Lords, especially bearing in mind the risk of failure. And what of cases which were settled before they reached the House of Lords? An insurance company or large employer might obtain a decision of the Court of Appeal in its favour and then settle the case, thereby avoiding any further appeal. Such a body would also have a legal precedent in its favour. In this way an erroneous decision on a point of law could be perpetuated forever.

Since time elapsed before a case was resolved by the House of Lords, Lord Denning asked where that left the lower courts – they had either to apply the erroneous decision of the Court of Appeal, or adjourn fresh cases, or await the decision of the House of Lords. There was a delay in justice and often a denial of justice because of the lapse of time before an error was corrected.

Lord Denning maintained that the Court of Appeal should apply guidelines which were similar to those adopted in 1966 by the House of Lords. When the Court of Appeal considered that a previous decision was wrong, it should be at liberty to depart from it if it thought it right to do so. Normally it would adhere to a decision, but in exceptional cases it would be at liberty to depart from it.

Alternatively, Lord Denning considered that the exceptions in *Young* v *Bristol Aeroplane Co Ltd* should be extended. In support of this contention, Lord Denning referred to new exceptions *since* the *Bristol Aeroplane* case, including, inter alia, the Court of Appeal being able to depart from its own previous decision in a criminal matter. He also referred to the principle cessante ratione cessat ipsa lex which he had used in the *Schorsch Meier* case (see 1. above). Although this had been criticised in *Miliangos* v *George Frank (Textiles) Ltd*, Lord Denning considered that if that step had not been introduced then the House of Lords would not have had an opportunity to reform the law.

Although, on appeal, *B* v *B* and *Cantliff* v *Jenkins* were overruled, nevertheless the House of Lords rejected what the Court of Appeal said about stare decisis. The House of Lords made it clear that the Court of Appeal should abide by its own previous decisions, subject to the exceptions in the *Bristol Aeroplane* case. Lord Diplock said (at 328):

> 'In my opinion this House should take this occasion to re-affirm expressly, unequivocally and unanimously that the rule laid down in the *Bristol Aeroplane* case as to stare decisis is still binding on the Court of Appeal.'

Lord Denning has described this as a 'crushing rebuff'.

Accordingly, the Court of Appeal is bound by decisions of the House of Lords, and furthermore it is bound by its own decisions, subject to the exceptions in the *Bristol Aeroplane* case and, arguably, other exceptions referred to above.

The Court of Appeal (Criminal Division)

Inferior courts, including the divisional court of the Queen's Bench Division, are bound by the decisions of the Criminal Division of the Court of Appeal. The Criminal Division regards itself as bound by decisions of the Civil Division of the Court of Appeal, subject to the exceptions in *Young* v *Bristol Aeroplane Co Ltd.*

With regard to its own previous decisions, however, precedent is not applied so rigidly because a person's liberty may be at stake. The principle emanated from the former Court of Criminal Appeal. Lord Goddard CJ stated the rule in *R* v *Taylor* [1950] 2 KB 368:

> 'This court, however, has to deal with questions involving the liberty of the subject, and if it finds, on reconsideration, that, in the opinion of a full court assembled for that purpose, the law has been either misapplied or misunderstood in a decision which it has previously given, and that, on the strength of that decision, an accused person has been sentenced and imprisoned, it is the bounden duty of the court to reconsider the earlier decision with a view to seeing whether that person had been properly convicted. The exceptions which apply in civil cases ought not to be the only ones applied in such a case as the present.'

The Criminal Division of the Court of Appeal adopted the rule in *R* v *Gould* [1968] 2 QB 65.

Divisional courts

They are bound by the House of Lords and the Court of Appeal in civil and criminal cases. They are usually bound by their own previous decisions, subject to the exceptions in the *Bristol Aeroplane* case.

The High Court of Justice (Queen's Bench, Family and Chancery Divisions)

A High Court judge is bound by the decisions of the House of Lords and the Court of Appeal and by the divisional court of his or her particular division (probably also by the divisional court of another division). The decisions of a High Court judge are binding on county courts but are persuasive in respect of other High Court judges.

The Crown Court

This Court is bound by decisions of the House of Lords, the Court of Appeal and the divisional court of the Queen's Bench Division. There is no obligation on a Crown Court judge to follow other Crown Court judges. However, it should be noted that inconsistent Crown Court decisions produce uncertainty and should be resolved as soon as possible by an appellate court.

Consider that for well over two centuries it was accepted at common law that a husband could not be guilty of raping his wife because on marriage she was deemed to have given him an irrevocable consent to sexual intercourse – the marital exemption rule. This was an extra-judicial statement (ie not made in court) of Sir Matthew Hale, contained in his *History of the Pleas of the Crown*. However:

1. In *R v R (rape: marital exemption)* [1991] 1 All ER 747 Owen J reluctantly accepted that consent was implied but denied that it was irrevocable.
2. In *R v C (rape: marital exemption)* [1991] 1 All ER 755 Simon Brown J went further, and Hale's proposition was rejected entirely.
3. In *R v J (rape: marital exemption)* [1991] 1 All ER 759 Rougier J did not follow *R v C (rape: marital exemption)* and doubted *R v R (rape: marital exemption)*.

When *R v R (rape: marital exemption)* was appealed, the House of Lords held that the marital exemption rule no longer existed as it was an anachronistic and offensive common law fiction which did not reflect the status of wives in contemporary society.

County courts and magistrates' courts

Their decisions are not binding and are not usually reported in the law reports.

The Judicial Committee of the Privy Council

These decisions, although not binding, are very persuasive. Reference may be made to the Court of Appeal case of *Doughty* v *Turner Manufacturing*, where the Privy Council decision in *Wagon Mound No 1* was preferred to the Court of Appeal's own decision in *Re Polemis* (see above, page 76).

4.5 Persuasive precedents

Persuasive precedents are those which are *not* binding but are influential, or persuasive, and may be applied by a court. They comprise the following:

1. Decisions of English courts which are lower in the court hierarchy.
2. Privy Council decisions.
3. Decisions of Scottish, Irish and Commonwealth courts (particularly in Australia, Canada and New Zealand) and also decisions of courts in the USA. In *Murphy* v *Brentwood District Council* [1990] 2 All ER 908 the House of Lords preferred an Australian case, *Sutherland Shire Council* v *Heyman* (1985) 60 ALR 1, to its own decision in *Anns* v *Merton London Borough Council* (see above, p198).
4. Obiter dicta which can be characterised as follows:

   a) Expressions of opinion or a statement of law based upon facts which were not found to exist, or, if they did exist, were not material. This area covers the hypothetical situation sometimes raised by a judge. In *Central London Property Trust Ltd* v *High Trees House Ltd* [1947] KB 30 the equitable doctrine of promissory estoppel was obiter as it concerned facts which were not found to exist in the case. In *Rondel* v *Worsley* [1969] 1 AC 91 the House of Lords held that a barrister was not liable in tort for negligently presenting a case in court and also in respect of preliminary work connected with the case (eg drafting pleadings). It was also stated, obiter, by four Law Lords that a solicitor acting as an advocate was entitled to the same immunity.

   b) Expressions of opinion on a point specifically argued before the court. Such expressions carry greater weight.

   c) A statement of law based upon facts, *but* which does not form the basis of the decision. An example here would be a principle of law in support of a dissenting judgment. Also, it should be noted that in *Hedley Byrne & Co Ltd* v *Heller & Partners Ltd* [1964] AC 465 there was a proposition of law that the maker of a statement owed a duty of care to persons when there was a special relationship between the parties. This, however, was strictly obiter, as in this case there was an effective disclaimer of responsibility. The proposition of law was not therefore essential to the decision.

   d) A principle of law which is too wide for a decision. This would result in part ratio and part obiter. The wider principle is obiter, but that part of the principle of law appertaining to the actual facts of the case is ratio decidendi. In *Hillyer* v *St Bartholomew's Hospital* [1909] 2 KB 820 the Court of Appeal specified a broad principle, namely that because the hospital was not able to control the way in which a doctor performed his work, the hospital was not vicariously liable for the negligence of any doctor. This case concerned liability for a consultant surgeon's negligence, and therefore the broad principle was wider than was necessary for the decision. In the subsequent case of *Cassidy* v *Ministry of Health* [1951] 2 KB 343, the Court of Appeal limited the principle to liability for consulting surgeons.

House of Lords dicta are the most persuasive

In *Saif Ali* v *Sydney Mitchell and Co* [1980] AC 198 there were obiter dicta to the effect that a solicitor, when acting as an advocate, should have the same immunity as a barrister. This was, in effect, accepted as being the law, thereby confirming the persuasiveness of the dicta. Again, in *Saif Ali* certain other dicta were followed and became ratio decidendi. These dicta had emanated from *Rondel* v *Worsley* (above) and related to a barrister's lack of immunity when dealing with matters which were *not* connected with cases in court together with the accompanying preliminary work.

Weight of persuasive precedents

Factors
1. Position of the court – the higher the court, the greater the weight. In *Hedley Byrne* v *Heller* (above) the principle of law relating to negligent misstatement and a special relationship being necessary for a duty of care was strictly obiter. It should be noted, however, that the dicta were in the reserved opinions of five Law Lords. In effect, the dicta were ratio and have been followed in other cases.
2. Prestige of the judge. In *Donoghue* v *Stevenson* (see above, p193) Lord Atkin's neighbour principle was obiter, but it has been adopted in subsequent cases.
3. The date of a case may be used as the basis for an argument in one of two ways:

   a) an old case has stood the test of time, but is it out of touch?
   b) a new case is up to date, but has stood for an insufficient length of time.

4. Was judgment reserved? Where there has been reflection and consideration of authorities, then the judgment will carry more weight. The House of Lords always reserves judgment, although initially the decision itself may be given without the reasons.
5. Was there a dissenting opinion? If there was, then the weight of a persuasive precedent will be reduced.
6. Was the case contested or the point in question argued? If not, then the case has not been subjected to close scrutiny.

Other persuasive authorities

Roman law and legal writings in textbooks and periodicals are persuasive in the absence of any specific authority from statute or decided cases.

4.6 Advantages and disadvantages of the doctrine of binding precedent

Advantages

Certainty

Bearing in mind the court hierarchy, where there is a binding precedent then a previous case must be followed in a subsequent similar case. This gives greater certainty, and people can organise their affairs with confidence. A judge also has a guide by virtue of precedent and is therefore less likely to make a mistake. Binding precedent also helps to ensure the impartiality of a judge.

Precision

This can be achieved through the volume of precedent cases. Furthermore, there is a wealth of experience which is contained in actual cases, as opposed to legal theory. A Continental code will not provide the amount of detail found in precedent cases.

Flexibility

a) Overruling and distinguishing.
b) The principles of law should be stepping-stones – there should *not* be a mechanical exercise.
c) There are opportunities for development of the law – the courts can adapt principles to new circumstances.

Disadvantages

Despite certainty

Although binding precedent gives greater certainty, there *are* too many cases and the result may be confusion. Furthermore, it is argued that where there is certainty then there is rigidity.

Despite precision

The volume of precedent cases may provide precision in respect of ascertaining a principle of law, but nevertheless there are both bulk and complexity by virtue of approximately 350,000 decided cases. It may, therefore, be an easy error to overlook a precedent.

Despite flexibility

Overruling and distinguishing are the pillars of flexibility. However, there is reticence as regards overruling, as is evidenced by the relatively few occasions when the House of Lords has exercised the *Practice Statement* to depart from one of its previous decisions. In addition, retrospective overruling may result in injustice. The problem with distinguishing a precedent is that the distinction may be somewhat strained. *Walker and Walker's The English Legal System* illustrates this point by referring to two cases, *England* v *Cowley* (1873) LR 8 Exch 126 and *Oakley* v *Lyster* [1931] 1 KB 148, both concerned with the tort of conversion. Walker and Walker state at 143:

> 'In *England* v *Cowley* the defendant refused to allow the plaintiff to remove goods from his, the defendant's, premises. This was held not to be conversion since there was no absolute denial of title. This case was distinguished by the Court of Appeal in *Oakley* v *Lyster* in which the defendant refused to allow the plaintiff to remove material from his, the defendant's, land and, in addition, asserted his own title to the material. This was held to be an act of conversion, the assertion of title apparently making the denial of title absolute.'

Generally, there is a centralised system in England with a relatively small number of courts. Precedent is therefore perhaps easier to utilise than in other countries; for example, in the United States of America there are millions of cases decided in federal and state courts – stare decisis is accordingly modified. With codified Continental law, no decision is absolutely binding.

5

Legislation

5.1 Introduction

A dictionary definition of legislation is 'the enacting [making] of laws'. As we saw in Chapter 4, rules of law have also emanated from cases, thereby providing the solid foundation for binding judicial precedent. The shaping and development of case law is a continuing, although perhaps protracted, process. Accordingly, where the House of Lords exercises its freedom, granted by the *Practice Statement* (see Chapter 4, section 4.4), to overrule one of its own precedents, a considerable amount of time and legal argument will have been expended before the case ever reaches those exalted heights. Bearing such a process in mind, it is therefore not surprising that legislation is arguably the main source of legal rules in present times.

There are, in turn, various sources of legislation. These include bills arising from manifesto commitments, government departments and Royal Commissions and also from bodies such as the Law Reform Committee and the Criminal Law Revision Committee which advise on civil and criminal law reform respectively, and, of great importance, the Law Commission.

Furthermore, with regard to legislation, there is a general background which must be borne in mind: the growth of society, ie, the community as a whole. Where there is an increase in population together with urban development and extensive industrialisation, there are inevitably social, economic and human problems. All of this leads, in turn, to the government having to consider the welfare state, education, public health, housing, transport and the economy. Legislation has played a very important part in such areas, and legal rules have been created by a vast number of statutes.

Basically, there are three types of legislation. They are as follows:

1. Acts of Parliament (statutes);
2. delegated legislation;
3. European Community legislation.

5.2 Acts of Parliament

Parliament is sovereign, or supreme. This means that it is not subject to legal limits and thereby has the power to create, alter and repeal English law (if you use the initial letters CAR then you have a simple example of a mnemonic – a memory aid).

It is generally the *legislature* which brings about appropriate changes in the law; the *courts* will only have an opportunity to *change* it in cases which specifically come before them and are thereby restricted. There has to be litigation for the proper development of case law, and even where there is such litigation a distinction has to be made between a ratio decidendi and an obiter dictum to ascertain the true reason for a decision. A clear statute, however, can clarify unsettled areas of law relatively quickly; indeed, Parliament is able to make any law it wishes as it does not have the courts' constraints.

Importantly, Parliament is able to overrule by statute. Legislation may therefore step in where precedent has resulted in an unjust decision.

Acts of Parliament

These originate from many sources, including:

1. *Political party manifestos*, ie legislation which is passed to implement a party's election manifesto. Such legislation involves party political commitments (eg the privatisation of industry).
2. *Incidents occurring during a political party's period of office* from which pressure to legislate may arise. In 1984 there was the miners' strike, involving violence. Political pressure resulted in public order legislation in 1986 whereby the police received greater powers to control demonstrations.
3. *Pressure groups*: such groups may be representative of specific *sections of the community*, eg the Law Society. Or a group may have a specific *area of interest*; for example:

    a) the Legal Action Group is concerned with the operation of the legal system, especially in the area of welfare law, and Shelter specialises in housing conditions. This latter group helped to exert pressure which resulted in the Housing (Homeless Persons) Act 1977 whereby local authorities had a duty to house the homeless unless they were intentionally homeless; and

b) Another example is the case of *R* v *Secretary of State for the Environment, ex parte Greenpeace (No 2)* [1994] 4 All ER 329 in which leave was granted to the pressure group to seek judicial review on behalf of people living near Sellafield power station following a decision to allow nuclear tests on the site.

4. Sometimes pressure may originate not from a group but because of a *specific person*. By way of example, Mary Whitehouse was in many ways responsible for the Protection of Children Act 1978. She wrote letters to newspapers urging people to crush child pornography, she lobbied Members of Parliament, spoke herself and found a Member to sponsor a Private Member's Bill.

5. *Civil service departments* will press for legislation which will assist them to achieve their aims. In this context, note especially the Lord Chancellor's Department and the Home Office. Both the Lord Chancellor and the Home Secretary are responsible for the law generally, and also for its administration, although the division of responsibility is not without complexity. The Lord Chancellor is responsible for civil law and civil procedure, civil and criminal legal aid, administration of the courts and the appointment of judges and magistrates, while the Home Secretary is responsible for criminal law and criminal procedure, for security of the realm, the protection of human rights, immigration control, prisons, the police and magistrates' courts. Basically, there is too great a volume of work for both ministers' departments.

6. *Tragedies and disasters* can initiate inquiries such as the one which took place as a result of the tragedy at Hillsborough Stadium. Pressure may also arise from public concern stemming from incidents such as that which occurred in Hungerford, when the issue which arose was whether there should be a tightening of the gun laws. The later tragic deaths of sixteen children and their teacher at Dunblane Primary School in 1996, and the 'copy-cat' events at the Wolverhampton Primary School, increased this pressure to a sufficient extent for consideration of the reform of the law to be considered again. Pressure for reform was initiated by the people of Dunblane in an action group called The Snowdrop Appeal, and Lord Cullen was appointed by the Scottish Secretary of State, Mr Michael Forsyth, to conduct an inquiry into the law. This lasted five weeks and resulted in a 174-page report that included recommendations relating to the amendment of the statutory provision on firearms that represents some of the toughest gun control law in the world. There was considerable opposition to some of the recommendations that were raised by groups such as the British Shooting Sports Council, the gun manufacturers, and the gun dealers. There was concern that reform enacted too hastily as a reaction to the exceptionally tragic nature of the Dunblane disaster would introduce law that was neither necessary nor practicable. Society's concern, however, was apparent and voiced by the Members of Parliament representing their constituents as well as in several other ways. The Dunblane disaster also serves as an illustration of the fact that the pressure for reform arising out of events such as these involves several issues that

run deeper than the 'surface' issues. Dunblane, for example, triggered a call for the improved regulation of school security and for the keeping of 'paedophile registers'. Both of these issues were considered in the Cullen Report. Other calls for new law included compulsory checking of criminal records of people to be appointed either as employees or volunteers in work that will bring them into contact with children, and some discussions extended this requirement to 'all susceptible groups within the community', for example, the elderly.

In November 1993 there was a terrible coach crash in Kent. Dr Susan Brooks, who was treating survivors, said that she had no doubt that many lives would have been saved and injuries prevented by seatbelts. In addition, ministers were urged to bring in immediate legislation to ban buses and coaches from the fast lanes of motorways and to bring forward plans to reduce their speeds from 70 mph to 65mph. The Royal Automobile Club (RAC) said that it would welcome a hasty introduction of the measures. Reference may also be made to the tragic minibus crash which killed 11 children and their teacher who were returning from a schools' prom concert. It is argued that the rules governing the safe use of minibuses are anomalous, drawing an arbitrary distinction between vehicles driven for hire or reward and those driven by voluntary groups. In effect, there should be a review of outdated regulations which are still applicable to a growing area of the transport market.

7. *Private Members' Bills.* Most bills are introduced by government ministers. However, time is reserved for Private Members' Bills to be introduced into Parliament by an individual Member of Parliament as opposed to a minister. The time available is very limited, and there is a difficult procedure to overcome. Examples of major legislative changes achieved through this source include:

a) the Abortion Act 1967, sponsored by David (now Sir David) Steel MP, through which the abortion laws were liberalised;

b) the Public Bodies (Admission to Meetings) Act 1960, sponsored by Margaret (now Lady) Thatcher MP; and

c) the Indecent Displays (Control) Act 1981, sponsored by Timothy Sainsbury MP.

Since that period there have been few major statutes introduced by way of Private Members' Bills.

The Wild Mammals (Protection) Bill was put forward by the Labour MP Kevin McNamara, but, despite cross-party support, it was defeated in the Commons by 12 votes on 14 February 1992. The main provision was to ban the use of dogs in hunting wild animals, and this encompassed fox hunting. Angela Rumbold, who was the Home Office Minister, said that the government had reservations about the effect of the bill upon farmers. It would be difficult to control agricultural pests effectively, and the proposal to issue licences would mean a large workload and huge costs. She said:

'Normal agricultural practice would be severely disrupted. The need for a farmer to protect his crops or livestock from pests is crucial and something this bill doesn't quite recognise.'

Labour's Home Affairs spokesman was Robin Corbett, who said that hunting with hounds was

'organised ritual destruction of wildlife carried out in fancy dress and amid great ceremony by those who pretend they have care for wildlife and their habitat. It degrades and disgraces the name of legitimate sport.'

In February 1993 the Labour MP Mark Fisher's 'right to know' bill was given an unopposed second reading in the Commons. He maintained that the bill emphasised in law the following principle:

'Free access to information should be a basic, fundamental right in a democracy. Britain is still one of the most secretive societies in the western world and one of the very few democracies not to have some form of freedom of information legislation.'

A minister, William Waldegrave, indicated that more needed to be done to increase the flow of information to the public but that Mr Fisher's bill was not the way for this to be done. Accordingly, although there was strong and widespread support for the bill, without government backing there was little hope of it reaching the statute book.

In April of the same year Tory MPs talked out a bill which had been proposed by Labour's Clive Soley to force newspapers to correct mistakes. It was reported that this would have imposed peacetime controls on newspapers for the first time for 300 years. Editors, journalists and publishers fiercely opposed the bill and maintained that it would hamper investigative reporting.

5.3 The process of legislation

While a statute is progressing through its Parliamentary stages it is known as a bill. Prior to a bill there may well have been a Green and/or a White Paper.

In *The Labour Government 1964–70* (1971) Harold Wilson wrote at 380:

'A White Paper is essentially a statement of government policy in such terms that withdrawal or major amendment, following consultation or public debate, tends to be regarded as a humiliating withdrawal. A Green Paper represents the best that the government can propose on the given issue, but, remaining uncommitted, it is able without loss of face to leave its final decision open until it has been able to consider the public reaction to it.'

Basically, a Green Paper sets out proposals for discussion and a White Paper is a statement of policy which the government proposes to implement by legislation.

With regard to bills themselves, there are public bills, where the subsequent Acts will affect the general public, and private ones, where the subsequent Acts may, for example, benefit nationalised industries, universities or local authorities and possibly, albeit rarely, individuals. A distinction must, however, be drawn between private bills and Private Members' Bills; the latter are introduced by private Members of Parliament – those who are not ministers. Time is reserved for the introduction of such bills but is very limited. In view of the various procedural hazards, to achieve important legislative changes by Private Members' legislation is no mean feat. Major successes have included the Abortion Act 1967, the Sexual Offences Act 1967 and the Divorce Reform Act 1969.

As a bill passes through Parliament, prior to becoming law, there is an opportunity for debate, and it may be criticised and amended. Approval has to be given by both Houses of Parliament, and when a bill receives the Royal Assent it becomes an Act of Parliament.

Most statutes are introduced by the government, and the bills are drafted by parliamentary counsel to the Treasury. Legal language is used because the object of legislation is generally to use precise words covering each and every conceivable situation. However, despite the precise drafting of bills and the scrutiny carried out in parliamentary stages, the problem is that occasionally statutes can be unintelligible, even to lawyers. The conventions of legislative drafting are discussed below and the rules for statutory interpretation are discussed in the next chapter.

5.4 The commencement of an Act of Parliament

An Act consists of sections, subsections and paragraphs. A 'commencement section' may specify a date on which it comes into force. There may, however, be an 'appointed day section' – this will authorise the implementation of an Act by way of Statutory Instrument. In addition, different parts of an Act may come into effect on different dates. In the absence of either of the above sections, an Act will come into force on the day on which it receives the Royal Assent, and it is deemed to have been in force for the whole of that day.

As Parliament is sovereign (supreme) an Act of Parliament can abrogate (cancel, do away with) a previous statute or case, ie abrogate any rule of law. Usually a rule of law is abolished by Parliament *in respect of the future* and therefore previous transactions (based on the old rule) would not be affected. There is a presumption against there being a retroactive statute.

Sometimes a statute will be given *retrospective* effect, but the statute itself must make this very clear; an example is the War Damage Act 1965, which was passed to overrule the House of Lords' decision in *Burmah Oil Co Ltd* v *Lord Advocate* (see the discussion of this in Chapter 6, section 6.7). The possibility of retrospective legislation will only occur occasionally. This area should not be confused with the retrospective effect of an English court overruling a previous *case*. Such a retrospective effect is the norm and not the exception, and it should be noted that judges do *not* have any similar power as regards a *statute*.

5.5 Codifying and consolidating legislation

Consolidating statutes

The existing law contained in several different statutes is consolidated into one statute (a consolidating statute) and, basically, this is done *without* changing the law. Examples are:

1. the County Courts Act 1984;
2. the Companies Act 1985;
3. the Insolvency Act 1986.

In certain circumstances there are procedures which allow corrections and minor improvements and also amendments. Generally, where there is a consolidating bill full debate will not be necessary, and therefore its passage through Parliament will be more rapid than that of other bills.

Codifying statutes

Such a statute embraces both previous statutes and common law principles from previous cases; in other words, it codifies both statute law and case law. Examples are:

1. the Partnership Act 1890;
2. the Sale of Goods Act 1893;
3. the Theft Act 1968.

With a codifying statute the law should be easier to apply, although codificiation of the law is a complicated process. It is, in fact, one of the objectives of the Law Commission, although there have been disappointments in respect of its achievements (see section 5.8 below).

Codification is similar to consolidation in the context of simplifying and clarifying existing law. In essence, however, codification and consolidation differ because, with regard to a particular area of law, codification will replace existing legislation *and case law* with one statute. If necessary, the law may be altered.

France has a code of law drafted on the basis of broad principles, and Germany has a far more detailed code. English law is not contained in a code, although there have been the notable examples of codifying statutes stated above. In addition, the Theft Act 1968 endeavoured to codify the law relating to theft.

In 1966 Mr Justice Scarman (as he then was) said that judicial *precedent* was development of the law by lawyers. Codification, however, was a true law making process. It involved study, research, consultation and planning. On the other hand, in 1967 Professor H R Hahlo indicated that it would be time-consuming to prepare a code. The legal profession would have to learn different techniques, and there would be increased uncertainty that would have to be clarified by the courts. In 1968, Professor Aubrey Diamond specified arguments for codification: first, it makes the law accessible to both lawyers and the public; secondly, it facilitates law reform as the content of the law can be improved by a code and subsequently further improved by revision of the code.

Section 3(1) of the Law Commissions Act is very pertinent here – note the words 'in particular the codification of such law'. Accordingly, codification was an objective of the Law Commission. However, codification of the law of contract was abandoned, as was that of the law of landlord and tenant. But codification of the general principles of criminal liability did result in a draft Criminal Code Bill in 1985. Overall, though, codification by the Law Commission has not been a great success.

5.6 Delegated legislation

Apart from Acts of Parliament there is a vast amount of delegated legislation (comprising rules, orders, regulations and by-laws) which is passed under the auspices of statutes. Parliament authorises law (ie delegated legislation) to be made by some person or other body. These include:

1. ministers of the Crown who make regulations by way of Statutory Instrument;
2. the Privy Council – this involves Orders in Council, but in practice an Order in Council is made by the government and sanctioned by the Privy Council;
3. local authorities, which make by-laws;
4. public corporations (eg British Rail), which also make by-laws;
5. the Supreme Court Rule Committee, which makes rules of court governing procedure under powers conferred by the Supreme Court Act 1981. There are rule committees in respect of other courts.

There are clear *advantages* resulting from delegated legislative powers having been conferred by Parliament. First, local, specialist knowledge may be used. Secondly, Parliament's time is saved, as clearly the Members cannot discuss everything in detail. Thirdly, Parliament does not have to concern itself with technical details. Finally, rules can be changed quickly, which is particularly useful when an emergency presents itself. There are arguably *disadvantages*, and these include the delegated powers being set out in such wide terms that a body may have powers which almost equal those of Parliament itself. Furthermore, whereas an Order in Council is generally made by the government and just sanctioned by the Privy Council, in effect wide powers are conferred upon government departments. Walker & Walker's *The English Legal System* provides an excellent example by referring to s2(2) of the European Communities Act 1972:

> 'Subject to Schedule 2 to this Act, at any time after its passing Her Majesty may by Order in Council, and any designated Minister or department may by regulations, make provision – (a) for the purpose of implementing any community obligation of the United Kingdom, or enabling any such obligation to be implemented, or of enabling any rights enjoyed or to be enjoyed by the United Kingdom under or by virtue of the Treaties to be

exercised; or (b) for the purpose of dealing with matters arising out of or related to any such obligation or rights or the coming into force, or the operation from time to time, of subsection (1) above;
and in the exercise of any statutory power or duty, including any power to give directions or to legislate by means of orders, rules, regulations or other subordinate instrument, the person entrusted with the power or duty may have regard to the objects of the Communities and to any such obligation or rights as aforesaid.'

There has been wide criticism of the above provision because the legislative power conferred is so extensive that only Parliament should properly exercise this power directly. Schedule 2 does, however, limit the powers in various ways.

Control of delegated legislation

It must be emphasised that the courts are able to question the validity of delegated legislation by the doctrine of *ultra vires*, which means 'beyond the power' – an act which is in excess of authorised powers is invalid. For example, the Supreme Court Rule Committee is limited to making rules of procedure. If the Committee made a rule which was basically a rule of law and not a rule of practice, then it would be ineffective, and in an appropriate action it would be declared ultra vires by a court. Furthermore, if a minister acted beyond his or her powers, a court *could*, for example, declare void any regulation which the minister had no power to make. In *Chester* v *Bateson* [1920] 1 KB 829 DC, regulation 2A(2) of the Defence of the Realm Regulations 1914 was held to be ultra vires the Defence of the Realm Consolidation Act 1914.

Accordingly, delegated legislation will only be valid if it is *intra vires*, that is, within the legislative powers authorised by Parliament.

5.7 European Union legislation

European Community law is concerned, inter alia, with agriculture, coal, steel and the free movement of labour. Accordingly, a great deal of English law (eg tort, contract, criminal and family law) is not affected by United Kingdom membership of the European Community.

There is *primary legislation* comprising three main treaties:

1. the Treaty of Paris (1951) which established the European Coal and Steel Community (ECSC Treaty);
2. the Treaty of Rome (1957) which established the European Economic Community (EEC (now EC) Treaty);
3. the second Treaty of Rome (1957) which established the European Atomic Energy Community (Euratom Treaty).

There is also *secondary legislation* which includes regulations, decisions, directives, recommendations and opinions.

Section 2(1) of the European Communities Act 1972 should be noted. The effect of this provision is that present and future Community law which is *directly applicable* will be incorporated into English law without any further enactment being necessary. The question then arises as to what Community law is directly applicable? Generally, the position is as follows:

1. Provisions of the treaties referred to above are directly applicable.
2. Regulations are directly applicable.
3. Decisions may be directly applicable.
4. Directives are usually not directly applicable.
5. Recommendations and opinions are not directly applicable.

Control

Neither national courts nor the European Court of Justice can review the validity of *primary* legislation. However, secondary European Community legislation equates to domestic delegated legislation and may be judicially controlled. This means that national courts and the European Court of Justice may challenge the validity of secondary Community legislation. Article 173(1) of the EC Treaty sets out the grounds for challenge; these include lack of competence, infringement of an essential procedural requirement and the misuse of powers, all of which equate to various aspects of the doctrine of ultra vires.

Human rights

The European Convention on Human Rights is not part of English law but does have a very considerable influence. *Malone* v *United Kingdom (Application 869/79)* (1984) concerned art 8 of the European Convention on Human Rights, and it was decided that telephone 'tapping' was in violation of that Article. The eventual outcome to this case was the passing of the Interception of Communications Act 1985.

With regard to human rights, a question for consideration is whether the United Kingdom should have a *Bill of Rights*. In February 1987 the House of Commons voted on Sir Edward Gardner's Private Member's Bill to incorporate the European Convention on Human Rights into the law of the United Kingdom. This appeared to be the way to adopt a Bill of Rights. There was considerable support for the bill, but the votes fell six short of the number required.

Should a Bill of Rights be available as a remedy in the United Kingdom courts instead of just in Strasbourg where the European Commission of Human Rights and the European Court of Human Rights are based? The purposes of such a remedy in the United Kingdom courts would be not only to reduce cost and time but also, in effect and more importantly, to give a citizen the ability to pursue an action to court and *require* a response from the State.

The government has to explain itself. A citizen may attract public and political support to such an extent that, even if a case is lost, the government may change its mind. Where there is no Bill of Rights then a citizen will be limited in respect of pursuing his or her grievance against injustice. He or she will be left to write letters to the press, complain to his or her Member of Parliament, encourage public campaigns and pursue any rights in the existing law.

5.8 Legislation and law reform agencies

Standing committees

In 1934 the Lord Chancellor set up the Law Revision Committee. It was revived in 1952 by Viscount Simonds as the Law Reform Committee, and the Lord Chancellor makes references to it for advice on the reform of civil law matters. The Law Reform Committee has been responsible for important legislation, eg the Occupiers' Liability Act 1957, the Misrepresentation Act 1967 and the Civil Evidence Act 1968.

In 1959 the Home Secretary set up the Criminal Law Revision Committee, to which he could refer matters of criminal law for examination. The Theft Act 1968 was one resulting statute.

Both these standing committees meet only periodically, and they are composed of part-time volunteers – judges, academics, barristers and solicitors. They do not, however, have any initiative of their own.

Ad hoc committees

Ad hoc committees are established with clear terms of reference within which they have to act. Such a committee will come to an end when a report has been submitted.

An example from 1974 involved safety legislation. At that time there was public concern because of the Aberfan disaster, with both group pressure (from the TUC) and civil service pressure to update legislation. Barbara Castle, the then Minister of Labour, appointed Lord Robens, a highly respected person with National Coal Board experience, to lead an investigating committee – the Robens Committee. Its recommendations were accepted by the TUC, CBI and main political parties.

An ad hoc investigation may involve not a committee led by an expert but a group of non-experts who are given a *Royal Commission* to investigate a problem. Financial and human resources will be provided, and a number of civil servants will work for the commission. Royal Commissions are impartial and non-political, and their membership consists of a wide cross-section of people whose interests and views are balanced. A commission's recommendations are considered by a minister, and if he or she is satisfied, then proposals can be placed before Parliament. Sometimes the balance of a commission will result in a report which reflects compromise; this, in turn, could mean a lack of political support and failure to implement recommendations. A Royal Commission can be a time-consuming exercise, during which public interest may diminish and the government may even change.

Examples of Royal Commissions and their reports are:

1969	Report of the Royal Commission on Assizes and Quarter Sessions	Beeching Commission
1978	Report of the Royal Commission on Civil Liability and Compensation	Pearson Commission
1979	Report of the Royal Commission on Legal Services	Benson Commission
1980	Report of the Royal Commission on Criminal Procedure	Philips Commission

The Law Commission

Consideration has to be given to the necessity for a full-time law reform body. The courts themselves cannot be the prime centres of law reform, and the legislative process itself may have more than enough to contend with. This, in turn, may prevent time-consuming research into possible areas for reform of the law. So does the justification for a full-time law reform body stem not only from the problems experienced by our courts and the judges (including judicial precedent) but also from the problems of a legislative process lacking time for in-depth studies leading to proposals for law reform? In addition, is there liaison between the courts and the legislature?

The notion of a 'permanent body' in respect of a review of the law was referred to in 1921 by a highly respected American judge, Benjamin Cardozo. He felt that the courts and legislature worked 'in separation and aloofness'. In the 1930s a New York Law Revision Commission was set up. About 30 years later the cause was taken up in England by Gerald Gardiner QC, who subsequently became Lord Gardiner. In 1964 Lord Gardiner became Lord Chancellor in Harold Wilson's government – on condition that a Law Commission was implemented.

In 1965 there was a White Paper, *Proposals for English and Scottish Law Commissions*, which referred, inter alia, to the fact that English law contained 3,000 Acts of Parliament, many volumes of delegated legislation and over 300,000 reported cases, and that, furthermore, it was difficult to ascertain the law, and even then at times it might be obsolete or unjust. It also stated:

'English law should be capable of being recast in a form which is accessible, intelligible and in accordance with modern needs ...'

Reference was made to a Royal Commission, or to the setting up from time to time of independent committees with a view 'to examine and make recommendations on particular subjects'. The Law Reform Committee and the Criminal Law Revision

Committee, and their tasks of reviewing areas of law referred to them from time to time, were mentioned. There had been important changes in the law because of recommendations by these committees, but this work had been piecemeal – fragmented and not comprehensive.

In effect the proposal was that there should be one body with the task of achieving comprehensive reform. This body should have an appropriate professional staff. A Law Commission was proposed for England and Wales consisting of five lawyers (the Commissioners) plus a legal staff. English law was to be kept under review and programmes submitted for the examination of areas of law, the purpose being reform.

The Lord Chancellor would consult appropriate ministers, and if a programme was approved by him it would be laid before Parliament. Detailed proposals for reform would be prepared by the Commissioners or an appropriate body. They would be published and, if they were accepted by the government, legislation would be introduced. The Commissioners would have the duty of pressing forward the task of consolidation and statute law revision, and distinguished lawyers would be appointed to the Commission.

The Law Commissions Bill which resulted from the 1965 White Paper received the Royal Assent during that same year (1965). The result of the Law Commissions Act 1965 was both an English and a Scottish Law Commission.

The Law Commissions Act 1965
Section 3 of the Act sets out the duties and functions of the Law Commissions. Under s3(1) there is a duty to keep the law under review, the objective being

> 'its systematic development and reform, including in particular the codification of such law, the elimination of anomalies, the repeal of obsolete and unnecessary enactments, the reduction of the number of separate enactments and generally the simplification and modernisation of the law ...'.

To achieve this purpose the Law Commissions have to carry out the following functions:

1. consider law reform proposals which are submitted;
2. prepare and submit to a minister, from time to time, programmes relating to the examination of areas of law, with a view to reform;
3. undertake the examination of specific areas of law and make reform proposals which could include draft bills;
4. prepare programmes of consolidation and statute law revision;
5. provide advice and information to government departments, together with proposals for reform;
6. acquire information about the legal systems of other countries which might be beneficial.

As proposed in the White Paper, prepared programmes of reform which have been approved by the relevant minister, and proposals arising therefrom, are laid before Parliament by that minister. Accordingly, the Commission advises both government and Parliament, thus covering both the planning of law reform and the formulation of detailed proposals.

The first chairman of the English Law Commission was the then Mr Justice Scarman, who stated in 1968:

> 'The theory that underlies the Act is that law reform should be the province of the legislature; that the legislature requires specialist advice in the planning and formulation of law reform; and that this advice should be provided by a body independent of the executive and of Parliament ...'

It should be noted that the Law Commission has statutory existence and cannot be terminated by a minister; Parliament would have to intervene.

The first programme of work, in 1965, included codification of the law of contract, the law of landlord and tenant, and family law. In the same year there were proposals involving consolidation and statute law revision, ie the repeal of obsolete or unnecessary statutory provisions.

Procedures

A detailed working paper is prepared with recommendations. Following discussion by the Commission there is distribution to the judiciary, lawyers, the national press, lay organisations and government departments.

Consideration is given to the comments received and a draft report is prepared. The report and a draft bill will subsequently be presented to the Lord Chancellor.

Problems

In 1979 Lord Scarman (as he had become) indicated that there were several problems. For example, it was too time-consuming for the Law Commission to deal with requests for advice and assistance from official agencies. Moreover, as far as a programme was concerned, the Lord Chancellor was able to exercise a veto but could not specify what the Commission should put into its programme.

Lord Scarman showed that the government was largely determining what the Commission undertook (eg references in respect of draft EEC Conventions), and questioned if this was law reform. He considered that company law, labour law, and constitutional and administrative law were being 'kept firmly away from the Commission', and said that, except for divorce reform, the Commission had 'been steered away from socially or politically controversial questions'. Successes had been achieved in family law, criminal law, consumer protection and the statute law revision programme.

It is, however, sometimes questioned whether lawyers are the most suitably qualified people to make recommendations in, for instance, the sphere of matrimonial and family law reform. Furthermore, recommendations for reform in the law of conveyancing have not been forthcoming, but in his article 'Commission's sterling effort' (*The Times* 26 June 1990), Brian Davenport QC said:

'... perhaps the years of dedicated work in this field have proved only that "there is no cure for this disease" or, as some might add, "at least while reforms are left in the hands of conveyancers".'

He also said:

'Perhaps the most valuable contribution the commission has made is not in law reform but in giving birth to the idea, revolutionary in its simplicity and outrageous in its naivety, that before proposing a change it is right to ask those affected what they want.'

By way of comparison, the Australian Law Reform Commission had dealt with various interesting issues including complaints against the police, drugs and driving, human tissue transplants, and defamation. Further, a great proportion of the Australian Commission's reports had been implemented, either wholly or in part, or given active consideration.

To return to the United Kingdom, by 1980 various issues, including, inter alia, civil and criminal procedure, had not been dealt with by the Commission but had been left to government departments. In 1984, however, the Commission proved to be an initiating force by organising a seminar on civil procedure, and subsequently the Lord Chancellor's department set up the Civil Justice Review. This involved studies by management consultants under the general supervision of an independent advisory committee and encompassed personal injuries, small claims, commercial cases, debt enforcement and general issues relating to civil litigation. Attention was directed to jurisdiction, procedure and court administration.

Following the complaint by the Law Commission that millions of pounds of taxpayers' money was being wasted because law reform proposals were being left to gather dust, a City law firm held a seminar in April 1993. It was considered that the failure to implement law reform or to give it high priority was unecessary. Derek Wheatley QC, the organiser of the seminar, said:

'The remedy is to instigate a shortened procedure for uncontroversial law reform. An all-party committee could monitor law reform measures with power to call for explanations and further consultation by the Law Commissioners where necessary.
Once past the committee, the measure would go straight to a third reading as a formality, and then become law. The committee could refer a measure for Parliamentary debate on the rare occasion when agreement could not be reached.'

The Law Commission continues to be very active. In April 1993 a consultation paper, 'Mentally Incapacitated Adults and Decision-Making', was published proposing laws to help doctors who are faced with difficult ethical decisions.

An area of law where there had been considerable criticism involved businesses which had sold their leases but nevertheless could subsequently be sued by landlords for rent. The Law Commission made recommendations for reform in 1988, but its proposals were only adopted in 1993. The Lord Chancellor, Lord Mackay of Clashfern, announced at the end of March that the law would be reformed. Although there was no indication as to when the legislation would come into effect, the reform will mean that, as regards new leases, business tenants will be liable while they are the tenants. They will be asked to guarantee the obligations of a person to whom they pass on the lease, if these are reasonable. However, the liability of tenants will cease after their buyers have sold on the lease to someone else.

Judicial review has become of increasing importance; it endeavours to ensure that central and local government and public bodies exercise their powers in a way which is lawful, rational and fair. The number of judicial review cases has considerably increased. The Law Commission published a consultation paper, *Administrative Law: Judicial Review and Statutory Appeals*, raising central issues for discussion.

In November 1993 the Law Commission said that the laws against personal violence were a disgrace and should be replaced by new legal definitions in simple language, to increase conviction and prevent costly miscarriages of justice. The Commission recommended three new offences: intentionally causing serious injury, recklessly causing serious injury and intentionally or recklessly causing injury. The Chairman, Mr Justice Brooke, said that the 1861 Offences against the Person Act used antiquated and obscure language and caused constant argument and confusion.

It was questioned whether the Law Commission would, in effect, put an end to judicial law making, but it appeared that this was not so – the common law was of value, slowly developing the law. Lord Reid associated 'orderly growth' with the common law, while legislation was more of an 'instant solution'.

Nevertheless, although the main justification for the existence of the Law Commission is that government departments and the legislature lack time to formulate proposals for law reform, the shortcomings of the court system are also a major factor.

6

Judicial Interpretation of Statutes

6.1 Introduction

In studying the subject of statutory interpretation, students must endeavour to understand the various difficulties which sometimes arise in cases and the ways in which judges may resolve them. It should then be borne in mind that a common failing of many students is not to apply their knowledge in answering either 'problem-based' or 'essay-type' questions. The sensible student should not only familiarise him or herself with the wide range of rules, intrinsic (internal) aids, extrinsic (external) aids and presumptions, but also apply this knowledge logically and use cases in support of his or her reasoning. Many students merely provide information (in itself often incomplete) without any attempt to answer the question. In other words, the actual question is discarded, and the examiner is presented with as much information about statutory interpretation as the writer can muster. This is not the way to achieve good marks. Students should bear these points in mind when studying the rules and aids to statutory interpretation.

Statutes, of course, may be in existence for a substantial period of time, and accordingly, for obvious beneficial reasons, they should be understood. However, *Smith & Bailey's The Modern English Legal System* (2nd Edition 1991) says at 315:

> 'The user tends to be the public official charged with the duty of implementation, the lawyer or the non-legal professional adviser, and statutes tend to be drafted accordingly: by experts for experts.'

6.2 Drafting conventions

The courts fulfil an important function in dealing with legislation because although an Act of Parliament states what the law *is*, the courts have to decide what the words *mean*, and this involves the study of the perhaps perplexing and yet intriguing area of statutory interpretation. By interpreting a statute the courts are, of course, carrying out their obligation to apply a statute, and it is important to bear in mind that the validity of any statute cannot be challenged in court. The authority for this latter statement is *British Railways Board* v *Pickin* [1974] AC 765 which involved the challenging of the validity of a private Act of Parliament (the British Railways Act 1968). It was held that the validity of the statute could not be challenged, and the claim was struck out as being frivolous, vexatious and an abuse of the process of the court.

In *R* v *Royle* [1971] 3 All ER 1359, s16 of the Theft Act 1968 was described by Edmund Davies LJ (as he then was) as having 'created a judicial nightmare'. Furthermore, in *Central Asbestos Co Ltd* v *Dodd* [1973] AC 518, Lord Reid said that the Limitation Act 1963 had 'a strong claim to the distinction of being the worst drafted Act on the statute book'.

Interestingly, on 4 January 1993 *The Times* reported that Martin Cutts, a co-founder of the Plain English Campaign and a director of Words at Work (based in Whaley Bridge, Derbyshire), had rewritten an Act of Parliament, the Timeshare Act 1992. In 1987 the government lawyer who prepared legislation challenged Mr Cutts to rewrite an Act of Parliament if he thought that the lawyer's laws were unclear. Mr Cutts chose the Timeshare Act because it was 'recent, brief, gives new rights to thousands of people and is already spoken of as a model for EC-wide legislation'. By way of illustration, s5(4) of the original Act reads:

> 'The offeree's giving, within the time allowed under this section, notice of cancellation of the agreement to the offeror at a time when the agreement has been entered into shall have the effect of cancelling the agreement.'

This was rewritten as follows:

> 'An agreement is cancelled if the customer gives the seller notice of cancellation within the time this section allows.'

Both versions of the Act were printed in a discussion paper, *Unspeakable Acts*, and Mr Cutts proposed to ask judges, lawyers and timeshare customers if they understood his version.

After completing their studies in respect of statutory interpretation, students should consider whether the use of plain English would not only be beneficial to the reader but also assist in reducing legal disputes.

Although statutes only consist of words, unfortunately it is not always clear as to what the words mean. This may be because of a poorly drafted statute (see 11.2 above), or there may even be printing errors. Various factors have been identified by F A R Bennion in *Statute Law* (3rd edition 1990). Briefly these are:

1. *Ellipsis.* A draftsman may regard certain words as necessarily implied, and so he omits them from the statute. This may not be realised by others.
2. *Broad terms.* Where such terms are used it is left for others to decide what situations would be covered. Smith and Bailey, op cit state at 316: 'Most words can be said to have a core of certain meaning surrounded by a penumbra of uncertainty.' Consider the word 'vehicle', which obviously covers motor cars. Does it, however, cover an invalid carriage? Further, would 'a mechanically-propelled vehicle' include a car with no engine or a car with parts missing?
3. *Politic (deliberate) uncertainty.* Here ambiguous words are deliberately used, inter alia, to minimise the risk of a legal challenge.
4. *Unforeseeable developments.* A statute may not cover every conceivable situation which may arise.
5. *Inadequate wording.* Ambiguity may arise because of a drafting error giving alternative meanings that were not intended by the draftsman or the legislature.

In addition a provision may be too narrow or too wide for the object of the legislation. It may be that there is a conflict within the statute or, indeed, a conflict between different statutes.

It can be seen, therefore, that various problems may arise, but the courts nevertheless have to decide what the words in a statute mean. It is often maintained by judges that a court's objective is to ascertain the *intention* of Parliament from the words which are specifically used. This immediately causes difficulty – for example, some Members of Parliament may have opposed the original bill, while others may have voted for it not through enthusiasm but more out of party loyalty. Accordingly, it would seem to be impracticable to try to ascertain the intention of *all* MPs. Should a judge speculate as to Parliament's intention, or should he or she just seek the true meaning of the wording of the statute, as indicated by Lord Reid in *Black-Clawson International Ltd* v *Papierwerke Waldhof-Aschaffenburg Aktiengesellschaft* [1975] AC 591? He said at 613:

> 'We often say that we are looking for the intention of Parliament, but that is not quite accurate. We are seeking the meaning of the words which Parliament used. We are seeking not what Parliament meant but the true meaning of what they said.'

On the other hand, the 'intention of Parliament' can involve the statute's intended objective with appropriate interpretations to support such an objective. It is argued that this approach equates to the intentions of the supporters of the bill.

In studying the rules and aids to interpretation, consideration should be given to whether the courts will *always* ascertain the intention of Parliament. Furthermore, with regard to the rules used by judges, it should be noted that they are not regulated and have been developed by the judges themselves. Accordingly, it would perhaps be more accurate to say that the rules equate to general approaches.

6.3 The literal rule

Words must be given their literal, ordinary or plain (LOP is the mnemonic here) meaning. The literal rule is inapplicable if there is ambiguity, in other words if the words are capable of more than one meaning.

In *R v Judge of the City of London Court* [1892] 1 QB 273 at 290 Lord Esher stated:

> 'If the words of an Act are clear, you must follow them, even though they lead to a manifest absurdity. The Court has nothing to do with the question whether the Legislature has committed an absurdity.'

So if the words are quite clear they must be applied, even though this leads to absurdity or hardship.

In the past the courts took a strict view of words and would not countenance the statutory language being altered where the words did not specifically cover the facts of a case. In *R v Ann Harris* (1836) 7 C & P 446 the accused was indicted under the statute 9 Geo IV c31, s12, for wounding a female by biting off the end of her nose. The first part of the section spoke of shooting at and drawing a trigger upon a person, and attempting to discharge loaded arms at a person, and then proceeded to say, 'or shall unlawfully and maliciously stab, cut, or wound any person'. Patteson J informed the jury of what was then a recent case, *R v Stevens*, where the prisoner had been indicted under the same section for biting off the joint of a policeman's finger. It had been determined that biting off the joint of a finger did not come within the words 'stabbing, cutting, or wounding' on the basis that it was evidently the legislature's intention that the wounding should be inflicted with some instrument, and not by the hands or teeth. Therefore biting off the end of a person's nose was not within the section, and Patteson J told the jury that they must acquit the prisoner 'who, however, would not escape punishment if she was guilty, as she would be indicted for an aggravated assault'. Justice, it seems, would prevail at the end of the day.

Cases

R v Maginnis [1987] AC 303 involved interpretation of the Misuse of Drugs Act 1971, which states in s5(3):

> '... it is an offence for a person to have a controlled drug in his possession, whether lawfully or not, with intent to supply it to another ...'

The defendant said that a package of cannabis resin found in his car had been left there by his friend for later collection. He was convicted and appealed on the basis that to return the drug to its owner would not equate to an intention to supply it to another. The Court of Appeal allowed the appeal. The case was taken to the House of Lords, where the defendant was held to be guilty of the offence. There was an 'intent to supply it to another' if the intention was to return the controlled drug to the other person and for that other person's purposes. Their Lordships endeavoured to apply the ordinary meaning of the word 'supply'. Lord Goff of Chieveley dissented – he referred to the *Shorter Oxford English Dictionary* and maintained that 'supply' was not appropriate where A handed goods back to B which B had previously left with A. Lord Goff considered that it was for Parliament to expand the definition of supply. Does a shoe repairer supply his customers with their shoes?

In *Unwin* v *Hanson* [1891] 2 QB 115 a borough surveyor was sued because he had cut off the tops of the plaintiff's trees, whereas the Highways Act 1835 referred to 'prune and lop'. In the context of forestry terms, 'prune' involved surplus branches being removed so that growth was improved and 'lop' involved branches being cut from the side of a tree. In effect, the defendant had cut off the *tops* of trees when he did not have authority to do so. The principle illustrated by this case is that when a technical word is being interpreted, its literal ordinary meaning will be technical.

Inland Revenue Commissioners v *Hinchy* [1960] AC 748 concerned s25(3) of the Income Tax Act 1952, which provided that if a person delivered an incorrect tax return there should be a forfeiture of '... treble the tax which he ought to be charged under this Act'. The House of Lords held that the literal meaning was treble the whole amount of tax payable by him for the year, but was the *intention* of Parliament for the penalty to be treble the *unpaid* tax? Following the decision in *Hinchy* the law was changed by the Finance Act 1960.

The case of *Fisher* v *Bell* [1961] 1 QB 394 concerned s1(1)(a) of the Restriction of Offensive Weapons Act 1959:

> '1(1) Any person who manufactures, sells or hires or offers for sale or hire, or lends or gives to any other person –
> (a) any knife which has a blade which opens automatically by hand pressure applied to a button, spring or other device in or attached to the handle of the knife, sometimes known as a "flick knife" ... shall be guilty of an offence ...'

The defendant had placed a flick knife in his shop window and was charged with offering it for sale contrary to s1(1) of the above statute. The defendant was found not guilty because in the light of the general law of contract there was no offer for sale, just an invitation to treat. This was another example of the application of the literal rule, but what had been the *intention* of the legislature? The Restriction of Offensive Weapons Act 1961 reversed the actual decision in the case.

In *Magor and St Mellons Rural District Council* v *Newport Corporation* [1950] 2 All ER 1226, Newport Corporation had expanded its boundaries by taking in large parts of two neighbouring rural districts. The Local Government Act 1933 provided for reasonable compensation to be paid. A minister, however, made an order amalgamating the two rural district councils into one. Newport Corporation used this to argue that the new council could claim no compensation at all. The corporation said that the statute provided for compensation only to a surviving council, whereas here the two old councils no longer existed and the claim was therefore invalid.

The trial judge and the Court of Appeal agreed with the corporation. Lord Denning dissented. He considered that the intention of Parliament was obvious, and said:

'We sit here to find out the intention of Parliament and of Ministers and carry it out, and we do this better by filling in the gaps and making sense of the enactment than by opening it up to destructive analysis.'

The trial judge and the Court of Appeal were upheld by the House of Lords. Referring to 'filling in the gaps', Viscount Simonds said:

'It appears to me to be a naked usurpation of the legislative function under the thin disguise of interpretation ...'

He further indicated that where there was a gap the remedy lay in an amending Act. The literal rule was strictly applied.

Lord Denning's involvement concerned the court being faced with a factual situation for which statute had not provided – a casus omissus. The argument against this was that a casus omissus attributes to Parliament an intention which Parliament never had and amounts to a legislative act by the judiciary. Lord Denning's view was not upheld.

Interestingly, in a report, *The Interpretation of Statutes*, in 1969, the Law Commission stated:

'To place undue emphasis on the literal meaning of the words of a provision is to assume an unattainable perfection in draftsmanship; it presupposes that the draftsman can always choose words to describe the situations intended to be covered by the provision which will leave no room for a difference of opinion as to their meaning. Such an approach ignores the limitations of language, which is not infrequently demonstrated even at the level of the House of Lords when Law Lords differ as to the so-called "plain meaning" of words.'

Furthermore, in *The Law-Making Process* Michael Zander states at 107:

'The literal approach is based on a narrow concentration on the actual words used, to the exclusion of the surrounding circumstances that might explain what the words were actually intended to mean.'

Accordingly, on the one hand the literal rule has encouraged precision in drafting, and any change in statutory language could be seen as non-elected judges usurping the legislative function of Parliament. On the other hand, a literal meaning could be emphasised to an extreme without considering the meaning of statutory words in a wider context. In *Bourne (Inspector of Taxes)* v *Norwich Crematorium Ltd*

[1967] 2 All ER 576 the question arose whether a crematorium was an 'industrial building or structure' within s271(1)(c) of the Income Tax Act 1952, which states:

'(1) Subject to the provisions of this section ... "industrial building or structure" means a building or structure in use ... (c) for the purposes of a trade which consists in the manufacture of goods or materials or the subjection of goods or materials to any process ...'

The crematorium was managed by a company that would be entitled to a tax allowance if the crematorium was such an 'industrial building or structure'. The court had to resolve whether cremating humans was 'the subjection of goods or materials to any process'. Stamp J rejected the contention that cremation was a process within the definition of 'industrial building or structure'. He said at 578:

'I protest against subjecting the English language, and more particularly a simple English phrase, to this kind of process of philology and semasiology. English words derive colour from those which surround them. Sentences are not mere collections of words to be taken out of the sentence, defined separately by reference to the dictionary or decided cases, and then put back again into the sentence with the meaning which you have assigned to them as separate words, so as to give the sentence or phrase a meaning which as a sentence or phrase it cannot bear without distortion of the English language.'

Students are, of course, advised to clarify the meaning of 'philology and semasiology' as part and parcel of improving their knowledge and understanding of the English language! As a final observation on this case, consideration may be given as to whether it is not justifiable and worthy of *more* credence to argue that the phrase 'goods or materials' does encompass a dead body and, furthermore, that cremation is a process.

As to whether the outcome of a case will always reflect the intention of the parties, consideration may be given to the judicial decisions in, first, *Re Rowland* [1963] 1 Ch 1 and, secondly, *In the Estate of Bravda (deceased)* [1968] 2 All ER 217. In *Re Rowland* there were difficulties over interpreting a will rather than a statute, but nevertheless the case is an interesting one to study when contemplating a literal, as opposed to a liberal, approach to interpretation. A doctor made a will leaving his property to his wife, but if she died 'preceding or coinciding' with his own death then his estate was to go to his brother and nephew. The doctor's wife made a similar will, but if her husband died 'preceding or coinciding' with her own death then her estate was to go to her niece. Both wills were on printed will forms. In July 1958 they were passengers on a small ship in the South Pacific. The ship apparently sank suddenly, and there were no survivors. The issue arose whether the doctor's net estate belonged to his wife's estate or did it pass to his brother and nephew? Section 184 of the Law of Property Act 1925 had to be borne in mind:

'In all cases where ... two or more persons have died in circumstances rendering it uncertain which of them survived the other ... such deaths shall ... for all purposes affecting the title to property, be presumed to have occurred in order of seniority, and accordingly the younger shall be deemed to have survived the elder.'

In this particular case the wife was younger than her husband. If the wife's death did not coincide with her husband's death then s184 would take effect. It was held at first instance that the husband's estate passed to his wife's estate and, in turn, to the wife's niece. The doctor's brother and nephew appealed and had to show that the deaths did 'coincide'. What did the word 'coincide' mean? Lord Justice Russell gave the leading judgment for the majority. He said at 15–16:

> 'I see no room, therefore, for "coinciding", in its normal and natural meaning, to involve some broad conception of overlapping or of occurring within a particular period. In my judgment the normal and natural meaning of "coinciding with" in relation to deaths occurring is the same as "simultaneous" ...'

He further said, at 17:

> 'Counsel for the appellants could not suggest, in the case of either spouse, whether the correct inference was death by drowning, trapped in the ship, or death by drowning, sucked down by the sinking ship after going overboard, or death by shark or similar fish, or by thirst, or by drowning after swimming about or floating for a greater or less period with or without a lifebelt. This makes it plain that there is no evidence at all that the deaths were coincident in point of time (in the natural sense of simultaneous) in the mind of the ordinary man.'

His judgment was that there was not sufficient evidence that the wife's death either preceded or coincided with that of her husband and, because of the statutory assumption of her survival by s184, her neice was entitled to the estate and the appeal failed. Lord Justice Harman agreed, but Lord Denning MR dissented and said at 11:

> 'I decline, therefore, to ask myself: What do the words mean to a grammarian? I prefer to ask: What did Dr Rowland and his wife mean by the word "coincide" in their wills? When they came to make their wills it is not difficult to piece together the thoughts that ran through their minds: the doctor might well say: "We are going off for three years to these far-off places and in case anything happens to either of us we ought to make our wills. If I die before you, I would like everything to go to you: but if you die before me, I should like it to go to my brother and his boy." She might reply: "Yes, but what if we both die together. After all, one of those little ships might run on the rocks or something and we might both be drowned: or we might both be killed in an aeroplane crash." "To meet that," he would say, "I will put in that if your death coincides with mine, it is to go to my brother and his boy just the same." He would use the words "coinciding with," not in the narrow meaning of "simultaneous," but in the wider meaning of which they are equally capable, especially in this context, as denoting death on the same occasion by the same cause. It would not cross Dr Rowland's mind that anyone would think of such niceties as Mr Knox [counsel for the wife's personal representatives] has presented to us. I decline to introduce such fine points into the construction of this will. I would hold that Dr Rowland, when he made his will, intended by these words "coinciding with" to cover their dying together, in just such a calamity as in fact happened: and that we should give his words the meaning which he plainly intended they should bear.'

Could the inherent problem in this case have been avoided by the draftsman of the printed wills using more appropriate wording? In *The Law-Making Process* Michael Zander says at 106:

'There can be no doubt that the draftsman in the *Rowland* case used the word "coinciding" inappropriately. Had he thought more carefully about the problem he might have used a phrase such as "if we die in or as the result of the same accident" or, better still, he might have said, "if my wife does not survive me by thirty days".

In the second case, *In the Estate of Bravda (deceased)*, a testator made a will which was signed by two independent witnesses. The main beneficiaries were the testator's two daughters, who also signed the will 'to make it stronger'. By s15 of the Wills Act 1837 a beneficiary could not take a gift under a will if he or she had signed the will as an attesting witness. To attest means to witness any act or event, for example the signing of a will by a testator.

Could s15 be construed so that a benefit to an attesting witness would not be destroyed if without that witness there were not less than two other witnesses to whom no benefit was given? It was considered that the words of the section were too plain and that, when a beneficiary was an attesting witness, s15 deprived the beneficiary of his benefit and defeated the testator's intention. Obviously the outcome of the case was contrary to the intention of the testator, but Parliament had made it clear that when a testator intended to benefit a person who signed the will as a witness, the testator's intention should be defeated. Following this decision, the defect in the law was quickly corrected.

Varying judicial approaches may be seen in *Kammins Ballrooms Co Ltd v Zenith Investments (Torquay) Ltd* [1971] AC 850 where consideration was given to the interpretation of s29(3) of the Landlord and Tenant Act 1954. In essence, this was that no application for the grant of a new tenancy should be entertained unless it was made not less than two nor more than four months after the tenant requested a new tenancy. The House of Lords held that the court *did* have power to consider an application which was made less than two months after the request of the tenant. Viscount Dilhorne dissented and said (at 869):

'The appellants' contention here is that the words "no application ... shall be entertained" must be interpreted as meaning that an application shall in certain circumstances be entertained notwithstanding that it is made too early or too late. That seems to me to involve implying something wholly inconsistent with the words expressly used. True it is that English is a flexible language but that does not mean that one can disregard the natural and ordinary meaning of the words used unless it is apparent that some other meaning was intended.'

Lord Diplock, however, moved away from a rigid literal interpretation. He said (at 880):

'Upon the literal approach, semantics and the rules of syntax alone could never justify the conclusion that the words "No application ... shall be entertained unless" meant that some applications should be entertained notwithstanding that neither of the conditions which follow the word "unless" was fulfilled ... It can be justified only upon the assumption that the draftsman of the Act omitted to state in any words he used in the subsection an exception to the absolute prohibition to which Parliament must have intended it to be subject.'

A conclusion that an exception was intended by Parliament, and what that exception was, can only be reached by using the purposive approach.'

Accordingly, in view of the cases referred to above, it has to be concluded that there is diversity of judicial approach over the literal rule. Furthermore, it must be borne in mind that, as previously indicated, the literal rule is inapplicable if there is ambiguity. Likewise, the rule provides no panacea where the courts have to resolve a conundrum such as that in the case of the *Commissioners of Customs and Excise* v *Savoy Hotel* [1966] 2 All ER 299. The question arose whether a hotel guest who ordered orange juice and received the juice of an orange, unsweetened, and freshly pressed for his benefit, was provided with chargeable goods within Group 35(a) of Schedule 1 to the Purchase Tax Act 1963, as being within the description 'Manufactured beverages, including fruit juices' in that group. While it is somewhat doubtful that it was uppermost in the minds of hotel guests as to whether portions of delivered orange juice were 'chargeable goods' for the purposes of the statute, it was an issue which the commissioners wished to be determined. It was held by Sachs J that such a prepared and served portion of orange juice was not a manufactured beverage, and the description 'including fruit juices' was to be construed in the context of the words which preceded it, and on this basis the orange juice was not chargeable goods.

6.4 The golden rule

The golden rule means that as far as possible words should be interpreted by their ordinary and grammatical meaning unless there is a manifestly absurd result. Parke B in *Becke* v *Smith* (1836) 2 M & W said (at 195):

'It is a very useful rule in the construction of a statute to adhere to the ordinary meaning of the words used, and to the grammatical construction, unless that is at variance with the intention of the legislature to be collected from the statute itself, or leads to any manifest absurdity or repugnance, in which case the language may be varied or modified so as to avoid such inconvenience, but no further.'

That Parke B became Lord Wensleydale assists the consideration of the following statement. In *Grey* v *Pearson* (1857) 6 HL Cas 61, Lord Wensleydale said at 106:

'I have been long and deeply impressed with the wisdom of the rule, now, I believe, universally adopted, at least in the Courts of Law in Westminster Hall, that in construing wills and indeed statutes, and all written instruments, the grammatical and ordinary sense of the words is to be adhered to, unless that would lead to some absurdity, or some repugnance or inconsistency with the rest of the instrument, in which case the grammatical and ordinary sense of the words may be modified, so as to avoid that absurdity and inconsistency, but no farther.'

Lord Blackburn seemed actually to attribute the golden rule to Lord Wensleydale by virtue of what he himself said in *River Wear Commissioners* v *Adamson* (1877) 2 App Cas 743, at 764–5:

'... I believe that it is not disputed that what Lord Wensleydale used to call the golden rule is right, viz, that we are to take the whole statute together, and construe it all together, giving the words their ordinary signification, unless when so applied they produce an inconsistency, or an absurdity or inconvenience so great as to convince the Court that the intention could not have been to use them in their ordinary signification, and to justify the Court in putting on them some other signification, which, though less proper, is one which the Court thinks the words will bear.'

Narrow and broad applications

Where ambiguity provides alternative meanings there is a narrow application of the golden rule. Arguably, this is a commonsense approach.

Where there is one possible interpretation, the literal rule should be applied even although there may be an absurd result *unless*, because the result would be so undesirable, the court is persuaded to adopt the broader application of the golden rule.

Narrow application

If there are ambiguous words an interpretation should be adopted which produces the least absurd result. It is the narrow application which is mainly used. Section 57 of the Offences against the Person Act 1861 provides that 'whosoever, being married, shall marry any other person during the life of the former husband or wife' shall be guilty of bigamy. 'Marry' could mean 'contracts a valid marriage' or 'goes through a ceremony of marriage'. The former meaning would have produced an absurd result in R v Allen (1872) LR 1 CCR 367, and therefore the latter meaning was applied.

In *Adler* v *George* [1964] 1 All ER 628, under the Official Secrets Act 1920 it was an offence to obstruct HM forces 'in the vicinity of' a prohibited place. The defendants had actually obstructed the forces *in* a prohibited place, but nevertheless they were guilty of the offence. Despite the seemingly plausible defence, common sense surely prevailed. Lord Parker CJ said at 629:

'For my part I am quite satisfied that this is a case where no violence is done to the language by reading the words "in the vicinity of" as meaning "in or in the vicinity of". Here is a section in an Act of Parliament designed to prevent interference with, amongst others, members of Her Majesty's forces who are engaged on guard, sentry, patrol or other similar duty in relation to a prohibited place such as this station. It would be extraordinary, and I venture to think that it would be absurd, if an indictable offence was thereby created when the obstruction took place outside the precincts of the station, albeit in the vicinity, and no offence at all was created if the obstruction occurred on the station itself.'

Broad application

This occurs where the statute has only one literal meaning, but the court rejects that meaning in favour of a more rational construction. In these circumstances, the golden rule is used in *preference* to the literal rule. There are not many cases where this broad approach has been applied. It should be noted that there is an involvement of public policy to discourage objectionable interpretations.

In *Re Sigsworth* [1935] Ch 89, by virtue of the Administration of Estates Act 1925 the residuary estate of someone who had died intestate was to be divided among the 'issue'. Mrs Sigsworth died intestate leaving one son, but he had murdered her. It was held that he could not inherit. In effect, the golden rule was applied *in preference* to the literal rule, bearing in mind that the only possible *literal* interpretation of 'issue' must include a son.

In *Federal Steam Navigation Co Ltd* v *Department of Trade and Industry* [1974] 2 All ER 97, s1 of the Oil in Navigable Waters Act 1955, as amended by the Oil in Navigable Waters Act 1963, read in part:

> '(1) If any oil to which this section applies is discharged from a British ship registered in the United Kingdom into a part of the sea which, in relation to that ship, is a prohibited sea area ... the owner or master of the ship shall, subject to the provisions of this Act, be guilty of an offence under this section.'

The owners *and* the master of a British ship, the *Huntingdon*, were each charged with an offence against s1(1). It was argued that, since the Act provided that the 'owner *or* master' should be guilty of an offence, both could not be found guilty. The appellants *were* found guilty, and the convictions were upheld by the Court of Appeal. There was a further appeal to the House of Lords, but this was dismissed by a majority of three-to-two (Lord Reid and Lord Morris of Borth-y-Gest dissenting) as the word 'or' in s1(1) was used conjunctively and not in an alternative and exclusionary sense. Therefore, the owners and the master could each be convicted of an offence.

Lord Wilberforce said at 110:

> 'It seems clear enough that where the law says that something is to happen to 'A or B', if what is intended is an exclusionary alternative (ie one, but not the other), the law must state either some qualification by which the affected person may be determined, or must name a third person by whom the choice may be made. The Act does neither of these expressly; so on any view some addition to the statutory words is required.'

He further said, at 111:

> 'To substitute "and" for "or" is a strong and exceptional interference with a legislative text, and in a penal statute one must be even more convinced of its necessity. It is surgery rather than therapeutics.'

6.5 The mischief rule

This rule is otherwise known as the rule in *Heydon's* case (1584) 3 Co Rep 7a. Four aspects are considered:

1. the common law prior to the Act;
2. the mischief in respect of which the law was inadequate;

3. Parliament's remedy;
4. the true reason for the remedy.

The aim is to ascertain Parliament's intention from what it has said, *not* from what it meant to say or would have said in certain circumstances.

In *Maidstone Borough Council* v *Mortimer* [1980] 3 All ER 552 the respondent cut down an oak tree, but, unknown to him, this particular tree was the subject of a Tree Preservation Order made by the local council under s60(1) of the Town and Country Planning Act 1971. He was prosecuted, but the magistrates dismissed the case on the basis that knowledge of the order was an essential part of the offence. The council appealed, and the divisional court held that the offence was committed whether or not there was knowledge of the Tree Preservation Order. The Act was trying to prevent the mischief of cutting down protected trees without the local authority's consent.

The case of *Kruhlak* v *Kruhlak* [1958] 2 QB 32 concerned s3 of the Bastardy Laws Amendment Act 1872:

'Any single woman who may be ... delivered of a bastard child ... may ... make application ... for a summons to be served on the man alleged by her to be the father of the child.'

On 2 December 1953 the appellant gave birth to a girl, and it was alleged that the respondent was the father. Later that same day a decree nisi was made absolute in favour of the appellant's former husband, and on 19 December 1953 the appellant and respondent married. In March 1957 the appellant obtained a separation order on the ground of the respondent's persistent cruelty. In April 1957 the appellant issued a complaint under s3. The issue was whether the appellant could be said to be a single woman within the meaning of the statute despite the fact that she was married to the respondent by whom she had previously had an illegitimate child. The case involved certain legal intricacies but, basically, it was held that a married woman with no husband to support her could be regarded as a single woman for the purposes of the statute.

Devlin J (as he then was) said at 37:

'The artificiality of the construction which the courts have given to the expression "single woman" is brought into high relief when a wife asserts against her own husband that she is a single woman. Nevertheless, once the point is reached when the fact of singleness is determined by looking at the actual state to which the woman has been reduced and not at her status in the eyes of the law, it seems to me that a woman whose husband has deserted her or cast her off can say to him, with as much force as she can say it to anyone else, that he reduced her to living as a single woman.'

Pearson J said at 40:

'It is clear from the many cases decided under the Bastardy Laws Amendment Act, 1872, that the expression "single woman" cannot be interpreted literally but has an extended meaning including some married women. In my view, the principle to be deduced from the previously decided cases is simply that a married woman who is for the time being effectively separated from her husband may be regarded as a single woman for the purposes of the Act of 1872, and the material time is the time of the application. Here we have a married woman who was living apart from her husband under a separation order. There could be no more effective separation than that.'

The mischief aimed at being remedied was the possibility of a wife having an illegitimate child with no means of support.

Under s12 of the Licensing Act 1872 a person found drunk in charge of a 'carriage' on the highway could be arrested without a warrant. In *Corkery* v *Carpenter* [1951] 1 KB 102 a man was arrested for being drunk in charge of a bicycle on the highway. Under the literal rule it was arguable that a bicycle was not a carriage. The mischief, however, which the Act was trying to prevent was drunken people being in charge of some form of transport on the highway. It was held by the divisional court that a bicycle was a carriage under the Licensing Act 1872.

The case of *Royal College of Nursing of the United Kingdom* v *DHSS* [1981] AC 800 involved the Abortion Act 1967. No criminal offence is committed 'when a pregnancy is terminated by a registered medical practitioner'. In 1972 surgical abortions were replaced by medically induced abortions, and these had not been in Parliament's contemplation when the Act was passed. At the first stage, doctors inserted a catheter into the womb. The second stage was carried out by *nurses* under a doctor's instructions, with the doctor absent but on call. Was the pregnancy terminated 'by a registered medical practitioner'? At first instance the decision was yes. The Court of Appeal unanimously reversed this decision. The House of Lords, by a three-to-two majority, held that the procedure was lawful. Interestingly, as regards the judges in all three courts, five considered the procedure to be unlawful and four considered it lawful. The House of Lords said that the 1967 Act was to be construed in the light of the intention to amend and clarify the unsatisfactory state of the law, and also in the light of the policy of the Act, which was to broaden the grounds for abortion and to ensure that they were carried out with proper skill in hygienic conditions, involving the entrusting of tasks to nurses under the instructions of the doctor in charge.

Under the Local Government (Miscellaneous Provisions) Act 1982 it is an offence knowingly to use premises as a sex encounter establishment without a licence from the local authority. In defining such an establishment the statute referred to performances, services, and entertainments 'which are not unlawful'. The appellant in *McMonagle* v *Westminster City Council* [1990] 1 All ER 993 raised a somewhat interesting defence, namely, that at his premises the activities *were* unlawful and therefore following a strict statutory interpretation he did not need a licence. The conviction was upheld. A literal interpretation would have produced an absurd result. The mischief to be dealt with related to uncontrolled sex establishments, and, in furtherance of this, the words 'which are not unlawful' had to be ignored. As a result of the mischief rule the words were mere surplusage.

In conclusion it is arguable that the mischief rule improves upon the previous two rules because it looks at the purpose of a statute and not just at the words themselves. Once the purpose of a statute is clear – in other words, the mischief intended to be remedied has been ascertained, the words are interpreted to give best effect to that purpose and thereby correct the mischief. To assist in ascertaining the mischief a judge may consider intrinsic and extrinsic sources or aids (see below, pp247–48).

6.6 Other approaches

Consideration may be given to a unified approach originating from Sir Rupert Cross:

1. A judge must give effect to the grammatical and ordinary or technical meaning of words in the general context of the statute.
2. If the result would be contrary to the purpose of the statute, the judge may apply the words in any secondary meaning which they would be capable of bearing.
3. A judge may read in words which he feels are necessarily implied by the words already in the statute.

There is also the possibility that, to prevent a statutory provision from being, for example, unintelligible, absurd, unworkable or totally irreconcilable with the rest of the statute, a judge has a limited power to add to or alter words.

Noscitur a sociis

This maxim means that the interpretation of a word can be ascertained from its context. In *Bourne* v *Norwich Crematorium Ltd* (see below p234) Stamp J said that words 'derive colour from those which surround them'. By way of example, the words 'floors, steps, stairs, passages and gangways' may be found in s28(1) of the Factories Act 1961, but in *Pengelley* v *Bell Punch Co Ltd* [1964] 1 WLR 1055 the word 'floors' was held not to apply where the floor was used for storage as opposed to passage.

Expressio unius est exclusio alterius

The meaning of this maxim is that 'the mention of one thing is the exclusion of another'. Accordingly, when a person or thing is particularly mentioned, then, by implication, this will exclude other persons or things which have not been specified. The Statute of Frauds 1677 referred to a contract for the sale of 'goods, wares and merchandise'. In *Tempest* v *Kilner* (1846) 3 CB 249 stocks and shares were not 'goods, wares and merchandise'. They were excluded by implication because they received no express mention.

Eiusdem generis rule

This rule of language means 'of the same kind': where particular words are followed by general words, then the general words must have a similar meaning to the particular words. The Betting Act 1853 prohibited the keeping of a 'house, office, room or other place' for the purpose of betting. *Powell* v *Kempton Park Racecourse Co* [1899] AC 143 concerned Tattersall's Ring, which was an uncovered enclosure. Did this outdoor place fall within the words 'other place'? It was held not to do so because the specific words created a genus of indoor places, and 'other place' had to be interpreted eiusdem generis.

In *DPP* v *Jordan* [1977] AC 699 the appellant was charged with possessing obscene films, books and magazines for publication for gain, contrary to the Obscene Publications Act 1959. Section 4(1) of this says that there should be no conviction if it is proved that publication of an obscene article

> 'is justified as being for the public good on the ground that it is in the interests of science, literature, art or learning, or of other objects of general concern'.

The appellant raised the defence of public good and sought to present expert evidence that the obscene articles were of psychotherapeutic value for sexual deviants. The House of Lords held that such evidence had been rightly excluded at the trial. Specific aspects of scientific, literary or artistic merit were not put forward. The House of Lords considered that the obscene articles did not fall within the general words which had to be construed within the same sphere as 'science, literature, art or learning'.

The Interpretation Act 1978

This Act provides definitions of words and phrases which are often found in statutes; it stipulates that the masculine gender will include the feminine gender, singular words will include the plural, and the plural shall include the singular. It should, however, be noted that the definitions in this Act are presumptive – the presumption is that they apply in the absence of any indication to the contrary. They will therefore be superseded by a contrary intention, whether express or implied, in the Act which is being interpreted.

6.7 Presumptions

Osborn's Concise Law Dictionary (7th edition 1983) states that a presumption is

> 'a conclusion or inference as to the truth of some fact in question drawn from other facts proved or admitted to be true'.

In statutory interpretation there are various presumptions which are applied by the courts. For such a presumption to be rebutted (this means disproved by evidence to the contrary) Parliament's words in the statute must be expressed in clear terms.

Presumption against alteration of the law

Unless the words of the statute clearly specify that the common law is changed, the words must be interpreted so that the law is *not* altered. The presumption is that Parliament did *not* intend to alter the common law. In *Leach* v *R* [1912] AC 305 consideration was given to s4(1) of the Criminal Evidence Act 1898. At common law a wife could not be compelled to give evidence against her husband. Section 4(1) provides:

'The wife or husband of a person charged with an offence under any enactment mentioned in the schedule to this Act may be called as a witness either for the prosecution or defence and without the consent of the person charged.'

The House of Lords held that s4(1) only made the wife a competent witness for the prosecution in the scheduled cases – she could not be compelled to be a witness. Lord Atkinson said at 311:

'The principle that a wife is not to be compelled to give evidence against her husband is deep seated in the common law of this country, and I think if it is to be overturned it must be overturned by a clear, definite, and positive enactment, not by an ambiguous one such as the section relied upon in this case.'

Presumption against liability without fault

The legislature does create offences of strict or absolute liability, but a statute's intention must be clear and unambiguous. The leading case is *Sweet* v *Parsley* [1970] AC 132 in which Lord Reid said (at 148):

'Our first duty is to consider the words of the Act; if they show a clear intention to create an absolute offence, that is an end of the matter. But such cases are very rare. Sometimes the words of the section which creates a particular offence make it clear that mens rea is required in one form or another. Such cases are quite frequent. But in a very large number of cases there is no clear indication either way. In such cases there has for centuries been a presumption that Parliament did not intend to make criminals of persons who were in no way blameworthy in what they did. That means that, whenever a section is silent as to mens rea, there is a presumption that, in order to give effect to the will of Parliament, we must read in words appropriate to require mens rea.'

Presumption against ousting the courts' jurisdiction

A contract to oust the jurisdiction of the courts cannot be entered into. If Parliament wishes to remove an individual's right to take action in the courts, then this must be made very clear and with no ambiguity.

Presumption that a statute does not bind the Crown

This applies unless the statute clearly says otherwise *or* there is a necessary implication. Statutes where the Crown is expressly bound include the Occupiers' Liability Acts of 1957 and 1984 and the Limitation Act 1980.

Presumption against retrospective effect

There is a presumption against the retrospective operation of statutes. If Parliament does wish to pass retrospective legislation then, again, clear words must be used.

In 1942 British forces destroyed the Burmah Oil Company's oil installations in Burma to prevent the installations from being captured by the Japanese. The company sued the Crown for compensation. In *Burmah Oil Co Ltd* v *Lord Advocate* [1965] AC 75 the House of Lords held that compensation should be paid, but the War Damage Act 1965 was passed specifically to remove the right to compensation from the Crown.

Presumption against depriving a person of a vested right

A statute will not be construed so as to deprive a person of a right which was vested in him or her prior to the statute coming into force.

If there is an infringement of his or her right to the use and enjoyment of a person's own land then there may be an action in nuisance or trespass. If an act was carried out with statutory authorisation, but that act was a nuisance, then removal of the plaintiff's right of action would specifically have to be made clear by the statute.

6.8 Intrinsic aids

These aids are found within a printed copy of a statute. Certain elements, however, are not actually part of the Act itself. Accordingly, those parts which have not been specifically incorporated into the text of the enactment are not strictly aids to interpretation. They may, however, assist in cases of ambiguity.

Short title

It is part of the statute, but it is descriptive and is not a great deal of use as regards interpretation.

Long title

This is part of the statute and begins with the words 'An Act'. It is a useful guide to the objectives or general effect of the statute. It is, however, not so helpful with regard to specific provisions, and it cannot prevail over such a provision in the main body of the Act. In *Royal College of Nursing of the United Kingdom* v *DHSS* (see above, p241), four out of five Law Lords referred to the long title of the Abortion Act 1967.

Preamble

This is part of the statute but is not often found in modern ones. A preamble sets out the background and purpose of the Act, but it is only used as a guide.

Punctuation

Old statutes were not punctuated, but there is punctuation in modern ones. In *Hanlon* v *The Law Society* [1981] AC 124 the House of Lords held that punctuation could and should be considered by judges when interpreting statutes.

Headings

Basically they are not part of the enactment, but they may be an aid in cases of ambiguity or uncertainty.

Marginal notes

They are not part of the Act and are inserted for reference purposes. Although they may be looked at in cases of ambiguity, they do not have any great influence.

Schedules

They are situated at the end of an Act, and they are part of the enactment if a section of the Act specifically incorporates them. They ease complexity in the main body of an Act as well as assisting in any uncertainty. Schedules comprise, inter alia, minor amendments, forms, illustrations and repealed enactments.

Examples

They are part of the Act and may illustrate the use of terminology and how the statute operates.

Interpretation sections

A statute will generally have a section which defines or provides a guide to the interpretation of words and phrases used in the Act. This is, in effect, an intrinsic or internal aid (see above) but is worthy of separate mention. It should be noted, however, that it is the *context* of a word which primarily determines its interpretation, as opposed to an interpretation section. Furthermore, where there is inconsistency it is the main body of the Act which will prevail. Examples of interpretation sections are s14 of the Unfair Contract Terms Act 1977 and s61 of the Sale of Goods Act 1979.

6.9 Extrinsic aids

The strict practice had been that as judges should not examine the political history of a statute, they would not look at *Hansard,* or reports of commissions and official committees, or international conventions. This practice has been relaxed in recent years, especially with a view to discovering the mischief which an Act was intended to remedy. Accordingly, judges have looked at reports of the Law Commission, of the Law Reform Committee and of royal commissions.

Hansard (reports of Parliamentary debates)

The position until recently was that *Hansard* strictly speaking should not be considered with regard to domestic legislation. In *Davis* v *Johnson* [1979] AC 264 Lord Denning looked at the reports. The House of Lords did not agree with what he had done; Lord Scarman considered such material to be an unreliable guide, and also counsel were not permitted to refer to *Hansard*. (This Parliamentary rule was, in fact, abolished in 1980.) Lord Denning subsequently pursued the matter, and, although direct reference was not allowed, he maintained that there could be indirect reference; that is, where *Hansard* was quoted in a textbook or speech then a judge could look at the textbook or speech.

The modern position in respect of *Hansard* now has to be considered in the light of *Pepper* v *Hart* [1993] 1 All ER 42. The House of Lords held that the courts could refer to the reports of debates or proceedings in Parliament as an aid to construing legislation which was ambiguous or obscure, or the literal meaning of which led to absurdity. Such a reference, however, should only be permitted if it disclosed the mischief aimed at, in, or the legislative intention lying behind, the ambiguous or obscure words. For further study there is a reference by Victor Tunkel in the *Law Society's Gazette* 12 May 1993 at 17–19.

Travaux préparatoires (preparatory works leading to legislation)

In *Fothergill* v *Monarch Airlines Ltd* [1981] AC 251 Lord Denning considered that travaux préparatoires could be used as an aid to the construction of an international convention. The House of Lords agreed with Lord Denning that, as regards *international conventions only*, travaux préparatoires could be looked at *in a general way*. In respect of domestic legislation, travaux préparatoires could be looked at *only to ascertain the mischief* which was intended to be remedied in the statute.

Dictionaries

These are relevant as regards the ordinary meanings of words, that is, where they have no special legal meanings. In *Re Rippon (Highfield) Housing Confirmation Order 1938* [1939] 2 KB 838 the *Oxford English Dictionary* definition of 'park' was accepted. However, in *Mills* v *Cooper* [1967] 2 QB 459 the *Shorter Oxford English Dictionary* definition of 'gipsy' was rejected. The problem is that the dictionary meaning may not be the one intended by Parliament.

Judicial precedents

An inferior court is bound to adopt a superior court's interpretation of an Act's specific words if the inferior court is dealing with those same words in the same Act.

Other statutes

Where words are ambiguous, there can be assistance from consideration of words in other statutes *as long as* the statute is in pari materia (in an analogous case). In *R v Wheatley* [1979] 1 All ER 954 there was the question whether fire-dampened sodium chlorate mixed with sugar was an 'explosive' substance within the meaning of s4 of the Explosive Substances Act 1883. This Act was intended to amend the Explosives Act 1875, and the Acts were in pari materia. Accordingly, what was an explosive substance within s4 of the 1883 Act was to be determined by applying the definition of 'explosive' in s3 of the 1875 Act.

6.10 Development prospects

Criticism may be levelled at the rules of statutory interpretation. The literal approach lays great importance upon the specific words themselves at the expense of their context which may clarify the meaning. By virtue of such an approach, a judge applies the law as stated by Parliament and does not involve himself in any legislative function. Parliament is sovereign, and Parliament's will should be made clear in a statute, but where there is a failure to do so the remedy lies with the legislature. It is not the role of a judge to correct a statute. This is all very well, but, *prior* to the remedy being effected, the literal interpretation of a statutory provision may not, in fact, give the best result. Michael Zander (op cit) also considers that the literal approach is 'defeatist and lazy'. He further says, at 108:

> 'The judge gives up the attempt to understand the document at the first attempt. Instead of struggling to discover what it means, he simply adopts the most straightforward interpretation of the words in question – without regard to whether this interpretation makes sense in the particular context. It is not that the literal approach necessarily gives the wrong result but rather that the result is purely accidental. It is the intellectual equivalent of deciding the case by tossing a coin. The literal *interpretation* in a particular case may in fact be the best and wisest of the various alternatives, but the literal *approach* is always wrong because it amounts to an abdication of responsibility by the judge. Instead of decisions being based on reason and principle, the literalist bases his decision on one meaning arbitrarily preferred.'

The golden rule has also been the subject of criticism. A court has the problem of deciding when there is *such* an absurdity that the literal meaning must be discarded so that the court arrives at another solution. The lack of criteria for deciding *when* there is such an absurdity does not encourage objectivity among the courts themselves. Different judges will reach different conclusions.

As regards the mischief rule, the courts have experienced difficulties in where they may look to ascertain why a statute has been passed. Consideration may be given here to the extent that judges are able to use the intrinsic and extrinsic aids referred to above.

Generally, it should be borne in mind that there is no compulsion to use the literal, golden or mischief rules nor, indeed, is there any order of priority when they *are* used. Furthermore, this means that one court may apply one rule and another court a different rule. Compare, for example, the decisions of the Court of Appeal and the House of Lords in *Royal College of Nursing of the United Kingdom* v *DHSS* (see above, p241). It should also be noted that a court may not, in fact, specify the rule which it is applying.

In 1969 the English and Scottish Law Commissioners published a report, *The Interpretation of Statutes*, which maintained that the literal rule placed too much emphasis on the narrow meaning of words without taking into account their context. Furthermore, the golden rule did not provide a way to test the existence of absurdity, inconsistency or inconvenience. The Law Commissions preferred the mischief rule to either the literal or the golden rule, but considered that it needed to be adapted to modern conditions. Quite apart from this, the Law Commissions recommended, inter alia, that there should be an explanatory statement drafted by a bill's promoters. Although such a statement would not be binding upon the courts, nevertheless it would assist them to clarify in what context the words should be read when the bill had become law.

The Law Commissions' proposals have not been pursued. With regard to the explanatory statement in particular, it appears that first there was concern as to the amount of Parliamentary time which would be required to consider such a document, and, secondly, it was queried whether an explanation of the explanatory statement itself would be necessary.

Lord Scarman did endeavour to bring about legislation to implement the Law Commissions' proposals, but in the face of opposition from various quarters, including judges, he did not succeed. Lord Denning also made attempts to improve interpretative skills. He maintained that the aim of statutory interpretation was to seek the intention of Parliament, and that the words in a statute were just the starting point, not the finishing point. In Europe, statutory interpretation involves a *purposive* approach, in other words, to apply the *spirit* as opposed to the *letter* of the law, and Lord Denning considered that, instead of a literal approach, a purposive approach should be adopted in English courts. In *Nothman* v *London Borough of Barnet* (1978) 1 All ER 1243, he said at 1246:

'The literal method is now completely out-of-date. It has been replaced by the approach which Lord Diplock described as the "purposive" approach. He said so in *Kammins Ballrooms Co Ltd* v *Zenith Investments (Torquay) Ltd* ... In all cases now in the interpretation of statutes we adopt such a construction as will "promote the general legislative purpose underlying the provision". It is no longer necessary for the judges to wring their hands and say: "There is nothing we can do about it." Whenever the strict interpretation of a statute gives rise to an absurd and unjust situation, the judges can and should use their good sense to remedy it – by reading words in, if necessary – so as to do what Parliament would have done had they had the situation in mind.'

This view was criticised in the House of Lords. However, that having been said, when English courts interpret European Community legislation they pursue a purposive approach, and perhaps this will subsequently extend to the interpretation of English statutes. The effect of the decision in *Shah* v *Barnet LBC* [1983] 1 All ER 226 restricts the judges to adopting the purposive approach only when a clear statement of the purpose of the legislation is expressed in the Act of Parliament itself, though this statement may also be found in extrinsic material to which they may legitimately refer for guidance. It will be interesting to see whether the decision in *Pepper* v *Hart* [1993] 1 All ER 42 (see section 6.9 supra) will have an effect now that reference may be made to *Hansard* to discover the legislative intention lying behind ambiguous or obscure words.

6.11 Interpretation of European Union legislation

In England great care is taken in drafting legislation. Community legislation, however, is expressed in terms of broad principle, and the courts provide the detail by giving effect to the general legislative purpose. The literal rule has little significance. Continental judges go further than the mischief rule and adopt a purposive approach, their aim being to apply the spirit of the law.

It would appear that English judges should use the same approach when interpreting Community legislation. In *HP Bulmer Ltd* v *J Bollinger SA* [1974] Ch 401, Lord Denning MR, in referring to the EC Treaty, said at 425:

'What then are the principles of interpretation to be applied? Beyond doubt the English courts must follow the same principles as the European Court. Otherwise there would be differences between the countries of the nine. That would never do. All the courts of all nine countries should interpret the Treaty in the same way. They should all apply the same principles. It is enjoined on the English courts by section 3 of the European Community Act 1972 ...

What a task is thus set before us! The Treaty is quite unlike any of the enactments to which we have become accustomed. The draftsmen of our statutes have striven to express themselves with the utmost exactness. They have tried to foresee all possible circumstances that may arise and to provide for them. They have sacrificed style and simplicity. They have foregone brevity. They have become long and involved. In consequence, the judges have followed suit. They interpret a statute as applying only to the circumstances covered by the very words. They give them a literal interpretation. If the words of the statute do not cover a new situation – which was not foreseen – the judges hold that they have no power to fill the gap. To do so would be a "naked usurpation of the legislative function": see *Magor and St Mellons Rural District Council* v *Newport Corporation* [1952] AC 189, 191. The gap must remain open until Parliament finds time to fill it.

How different is this Treaty! It lays down general principles. It expresses its aims and purposes. All in sentences of moderate length and commendable style. But it lacks precision. It uses words and phrases without defining what they mean. An English lawyer would look for an interpretation clause, but he would look in vain. There is none. All the way through the Treaty there are gaps and lacunae. These have to be filled in by the judges, or by Regulations or directives. It is the European way.'

With regard to Community secondary legislation, Lord Denning said at 425–6:

'Likewise the Regulations and directives. They are enacted by the Council sitting in Brussels for everyone to obey. They are quite unlike our statutory instruments. They have to give the reasons on which they are based: article 190. So they start off with pages of preambles, "whereas" and "whereas" and "whereas". These show the purpose and intent of the Regulations and directives. Then follow the provisions which are to be obeyed. Here again words and phrases are used without defining their import ... In case of difficulty, recourse is had to the preambles. These are useful to show the purpose and intent behind it all. But much is left to the judges. The enactments give only an outline plan. The details are to be filled in by the judges.

Seeing these differences, what are the English courts to do when they are faced with a problem of interpretation? They must follow the European pattern. No longer must they examine the words in meticulous detail. No longer must they argue about the precise grammatical sense. They must look to the purpose or intent ... They must divine the spirit of the Treaty and gain inspiration from it. If they find a gap, they must fill it as best they can. They must do what the framers of the instrument would have done if they had thought about it. So we must do the same.'

Finally, when interpreting Community legislation, an English judge must abide by the decisions and opinions of the European Court of Justice. In this context, s3(1) and (2) specifically provide as follows:

'(1) For the purposes of all legal proceedings any question as to the meaning or effect of any of the Treaties, or as to the validity, meaning or effect of any Community instrument, shall be treated as a question of law (and, if not referred to the European Court, be for determination as such in accordance with the principles laid down by and any relevant decision of the European Court).

(2) Judicial notice shall be taken of the Treaties, of the Official Journal of the Communities and of any decision of, or expression of opinion by, the European Court on any such question as aforesaid; and the Official Journal shall be admissible as evidence of any instrument or other act thereby communicated of any of the Communities or of any Community institution.'

7

Working with Precedent

7.1 Introduction

The discussion of the doctrine of judicial precedent given in Chapter 4 identifies what 'stare decisis' (standing by past decisions) means and the key aspects associated with defining ratio decidendi (the reason for the decision). This information acts as the basis for understanding how judicial precedent operates, but a further examination is required to acquire an understanding of how these two concepts inter-relate when faced with the problem of deciding *why* two cases are sufficiently similar that the rule of law applied in the earlier case should also be applied in the later case.

The material contained in this chapter aims to provide practical examples of how to use the cases to 'find' the law contained within the judgments and how to apply that law to other sets of facts. These examples are given in relation to the theoretical basis on which they rest to indicate the way in which the English legal reasoning process works in practice.

There are a number of variable factors taken into consideration by the judges in their determination of why any rule of law should be applied to any given fact or combination of facts. Of these the three main aspects underlying the legal reasoning process are:

1. the concept of the sufficiency of similarity of material facts; and
2. the 'fact to law' reasoning process; and
3. the interpretation of the intended scope of the rule.

Although each of these is separated for discussion below, it is an artificial division because all three aspects are inter-dependent and co-exist within the legal reasoning process. The ratio decidendi of any case rests on their existence and contains evidence of consideration of each, although this may have to be extracted rather than found as a clear statement of intention to incorporate them.

7.2 The three main aspects of the legal reasoning process

1. *The concept of the sufficiency of similarity of material facts*

Individuals undertake their activities in a wide and varied way and no case involves precisely the same facts as another case. Whilst the English law recognises the uniqueness of the facts of each case, it cannot rely on creating entirely 'fact specific' rules. If the law were to do this there would be no certainty of application of any rule unless it happened to be that the present case had the same combination of facts as the earlier case. In addition, the substantive law would have to be made up of innumerable rules, most of which would lie dormant because the unique combination of facts they relate to might never arise again. What the English legal reasoning process actually relies on is finding a *sufficient similarity* between the facts of the cases. The clues as to a sufficient similarity are found by interpreting *why* the judge decided that any particular fact, or combination of facts, was relevant to the *reason to apply* the legal rule. It is these facts that are *material* to the case because they are the facts that determined the application of the rule.

An example of sufficiently similar material facts can be found by looking at how the case of *Grant* v *Australian Knitting Mills* [1936] AC 85 (Privy Council) fell to be determined under the principle laid down in *Donoghue* v *Stevenson* [1932] AC 562.

The material facts of *Donoghue* are that a friend of the appellant purchased for her a bottle of ginger beer manufactured by the respondents and contained in a dark opaque bottle sealed with a metal cap, and that the appellant suffered shock and gastro-enteritis by the effects of a half-decomposed snail that was not detected until the greater part of the ginger beer had been consumed.

The material facts of *Grant* are that an undetectable excess of sulphites in undergarments that should have been washed out in the manufacturing process caused Mr Grant severe dermatitis.

For the purposes of this discussion of sufficiently similar material facts the part of Lord Atkin's judgment in *Donoghue* v *Stevenson* that we shall examine is:

'... a manufacturer of products, which he sells in such a form as to show that he intends them to reach the ultimate consumer in the form in which they left him with no reasonable possibility of intermediate examination, and with the knowledge that the absence of reasonable care in the putting up of the products will result in any injury to the consumer's life or property, owes a duty to the consumer to take that reasonable care.'

(*Note*: this rule is referred back to later and for simplicity of reference is referred to as 'extract 1'.)

The wording used to lay down this rule does not restrict the application of it to half-decomposed snails found in opaque ginger beer bottles. Neither does it confine the liability to the causing the sort of nausea and shock claimed by Mrs Donoghue. The language used is general enough to allow for a very much wider interpretation of the sort of *sufficiently similar* facts that may fall under the scope of the rule. For example,

The bottle of ginger beer becomes '*a product*'.

The nausea and shock becomes '*an injury to the consumer's life or property*'.

The half-decomposed snail is not directly referred to and thereby becomes an undefined thing that is responsible for causing the injury and which cannot be detected on reasonable examination.

The opaque nature of the bottle and its sealed metal cap are material to the ratio decidendi because they are the key reasons why 'there is no reasonable possibility of intermediate examination' of the contents of the bottle. They are, therefore, the facts of the case that establish the manufacturer's liability because they dictate why the manufacturer has a duty to take reasonable care. In this context the duty to take reasonable care, and the knowledge that there is no reasonable possibility of intermediate examination, combine to give the manufacturer a *legal duty* to take that care.

The fact that the rule refers to the manufacturer of products and the ultimate consumer, keeps the scope of this statement within the realms of defective consumer products. In this context it is a logical step to apply the rule to the facts found in *Grant* v *Australian Knitting Mills*. Although these are wholly different facts to those in *Donoghue*, they are sufficiently similar in context in that:

a. the undergarments left the manufacturer in the form in which they were intended to reach the ultimate consumer; and
b. the defect could not be detected by reasonable intermediate examination; and
c. there is an injury to the consumer; and
d. the defect is attributable to the lack of care of the manufacturer.

2. The 'fact to law' reasoning process

In the four-point list given immediately above, points a. to c. relate to the sufficiently similar *facts*: they are the facts of *Grant* that are contextually the same as the facts of *Donoghue*. Point d. relates to the *legal reasoning* that is attached to facts such as these under the *Donoghue* principle. In every case there will be questions of fact to answer and questions of law to answer. In *Donoghue* v *Stevenson* there was an important issue in terms of the legal debate that arose from the fact that Mrs Donoghue had no contractual relationship with either the retailer or the manufacturer: the bottle of ginger beer was purchased for her by her friend. The rule of privity of contract prevents a claim by a person who is not a party to the contract. In 1932, to establish a case for negligence, Mrs Donoghue had to avoid the application of this rule (as per the operation of precedent) by proving that the manufacturer had breached a duty of care owed to her.

The essence of the question before the court was whether the rule of privity of contract should apply in these circumstances, or whether the existing cases were capable of establishing a remedy direct against the manufacturer.

The question of law was whether there was a duty of law governing the manufacturer. The question of fact was whether, on the facts of this case, the manufacturer had broken that duty. Lord Atkin expressed this as:

> 'The question is whether the manufacturer of an article of drink sold by him to a distributor, in circumstances which prevent the distributor or the ultimate purchaser or consumer from discovering by inspection any defect, is under any legal duty to the ultimate purchaser or consumer to take reasonable care that the article is free from defect likely to cause injury to health.'

In the discussion in 1. above, the opaque nature of the bottle and its sealed metal cap were identified as being key determinants in the establishing of the legal duty to take care. This can now been seen as being a part of the fact to law reasoning process inherent in legal reasoning. The question that Lord Atkin addresses is asking about the sort of circumstances that will put the manufacturer in a direct relationship, founded on a duty to take care, with the ultimate consumer. The answer to that question is found in the wording used in 'extract 1' above, namely, that the manufacturer *'owes a duty to the consumer to take that reasonable care'* where there is *'no reasonable possibility of intermediate examination'*, provided that there is *'knowledge'* that *'injury'* will result.

In terms of a statement of the law, this is commonly stated as being:

1. a duty of care owed to the plaintiff by the defendant; and
2. a breach of *that* duty; and
3. an injury or damage resulting from *that* breach.

3. *The interpretation of the intended scope of the rule*

The statement of the law given immediately above is applicable to any combination of facts. It is not confined to manufactured products containing hidden defects. *Grant v Australian Knitting Mills* can thereby be seen as falling within the original use of the legal principle in *Donoghue*, but the extrapolated legal principle does not, in itself, dictate that this must always be the case.

Therefore, the notion that the case law proceeds from case to case on the basis of simply finding a similarity in the material facts and applying a fact to law reasoning is obviously not the whole story of how legal reasoning operates. Another essential ingredient is the way in which the scope of the legal rule has to be found. In respect of the *Donoghue* case the answer to this lies in the use of what has come to be called the 'neighbour test' which is a part of the reasoning used by Lord Atkin in his judgment.

'The rule that you are to love your neighbour becomes in law, you must not injure your neighbour; and the lawyer's question, "Who is my neighbour?" receives a restricted reply. You must take reasonable care to avoid acts or omissions which you can reasonably foresee would be likely to injure your neighbour. Who then in law is my neighbour? The answer seems to be – persons who are so closely and directly affected by my act that I ought reasonably to have them in contemplation as being so affected when I am directing my mind to the acts or omissions which are called in question ...'

This test defines the scope of the duty of care owed and it has the effect of widening the ambit of application of the *Donoghue* ratio beyond that which we have so far examined by reference to 'extract 1' above. It is the interpretation of the 'neighbour test' that enables the expansion of the rule into the considerably wider applications that it took, eg liability for negligent misstatement and other acts or omissions causing economic loss, liability in nervous shock, liability for professional negligence, and so on.

The 'neighbour test', when taken on its own, provides a different interpretation of the possible scope of application of the duty of care principle. It does not confine the use of the principle to the manufacturer of products and a purchaser or ultimate consumer, and it provides a test that can be used for a much wider class of actions (a much wider variety of fact situations) than hidden defects in manufactured products. This is because the wording provides for a determination of the facts by the use of a wholly objective test.

- It does not specify who the class of injured persons are: they are simply '... *persons* who are so closely and directly affected ...'.
- It does not limit the liability to any type of activity: they are any '... *acts* or *omissions* which are called in question ...'.

For these reasons the 'neighbour test' is different to the rule stated in 'extract 1' above which does specifically relate to the manufacturer and to the ultimate consumer and is a liability in relation to the 'putting up of the products'.

The question needs to be asked as to whether the 'neighbour test' should be used to broaden the scope of the 'extract 1' rule in this way. An important characteristic of any rule is that its scope must be co-extensive with its purpose, or, in other words, it must be formulated in such a way that it is applied only to those circumstances that it is right to apply it to. The rule that is created should be:

(1) specific enough to limit the type of actions that may fall within the ambit of the principle; and

(2) general enough to apply to the wide variety of circumstances that may arise in the cases which *ought* to fall under the principle.

The facts that the judge treats as material have a direct bearing on how wide or how narrow the ratio is and examples of this can be found in the explanation of ratio decidendi given in Chapter 4, section 4.3, above. In the example of the drunken driver the colour of the car is not treated as material for the obvious reason that the rule would be so limited as to be useless if its application were restricted to blue cars. Conversely, the opaque nature of the bottle in *Donoghue* is material to the ratio decidendi because it is one of the reasons why 'there is no reasonable possibility of intermediate examination' of the contents of the bottle. If the rule is too narrow cases that ought to fall under it will be excluded, and if it is too wide those that ought not to fall under it will do. Either situation usually results in difficult consequences for the future development of the law.

There is a preamble to the 'neighbour test' that is contained within the same paragraph and which recognises the potential wideness of creating a duty relationship between the parties:

> 'At present I content myself with pointing out that in English law there must be, and is, some general concept of relations giving rise to a duty of care ... But acts or omissions which any moral code would censure cannot in a practical world be treated so as to give a right to every person injured by them to demand relief. In this way rules of law arise which limit the range of complainants and the extent of their injury. The rule that you are to love your neighbour ... [etc, see above]
> ... There will no doubt arise cases where it will be difficult to determine whether the contemplated relationship is so close that the duty arises.'

These are indications of a need to limit the application of the duty of care principle but they do not, in themselves, provide a limitation on its application. They do not indicate what types of facts might, or might not, fall within the scope of the duty. The element that specifically relates to a *legal* duty, as opposed to notions of a moral duty, is found in the 'neighbour test' itself, ie:

- 'The rule that you are to love your neighbour *becomes in law*, you must not injure your neighbour', and
- 'Who then *in law* is my neighbour? The answer seems to be – ...'.

Accordingly, the test assumes the status of a test in law and has been used as such. In addition, Lord Atkin's judgment contains sufficient indication that application of the 'extract 1' rule is not intended to be limited to manufacturers, ultimate consumers, and hidden defects in products. Although the various illustrative examples that he gives are of other products, and are used to establish the likelihood of there being an injured party who is not the actual purchaser, his reasoning of the applicability of the previous case law cited in support of the negligence claim indicates a willingness to expand the class of actions if the essential elements of the liability are present.

The wideness of the rule that arises out of the highly general and objective wording of the 'neighbour test' has caused problems. Various cases have attempted to define the scope of its application, of which the 'Anns test' is one (*Anns* v *Merton London Borough* [1978] AC 728). This was applied for several years. It shifted the emphasis from using Atkin's proximity test if there were good policy reasons to do so, to a mere foreseeability of harm test unless there were policy reasons not to do so. There were problems with this approach and it was eventually overruled in *Murphy* v *Brentwood District Council* [1990] 2 All ER 908.

NB Atkin's test is not for the mere foreseeability of a harm per se; it is a test of harm which the defendant, as a 'reasonable man', could anticipate as being likely to injure the plaintiff(s) in the way that it has. A re-statement of this principle in the context of economic loss arising out of negligent statements, is given in *Caparo Industries plc* v *Dickman and Others* [1990] 1 All ER 568 and has done much to resolve the problems in this area of the law.

7.3 Interpreting the ratio

The discussion of ratio decidendi given in Chapter 4 identifies some of the difficulties in defining what is meant by the ratio of a case and this lack of definition makes the early study of the cases a difficult task. The things that can be stated with certainty about ratio decidendi are:

1. it is the ratio alone that is binding on future courts (within the hierarchy of the courts) and no matter how difficult it is to find that ratio, it has to found and applied to any later case which is not reasonably distinguishable;
2. only pronouncements of law can be ratio;
3. only those reasons (or reason) which are necessary to reach the decision in the particular case can be ratio.

The ratio is, in other words, the reasoning for why the case was decided as it was, and if this reasoning could not be applied to the facts of the case treated as material by the judge, the case would have to have been decided otherwise.

The following extracts taken from the judgement delivered by Lord Goddard in *Pharmaceutical Society of Great Britain* v *Boots Cash Chemists (Southern) Ltd* [1952] 2 QB 795 provide an example of how to interpret the way in which his reasoning is applied to the facts of the case.

The material facts included the following. The defendant chemists shop had been changed into a 'self-service' store which contained a 'chemist's department' that was under the control of a registered pharmacist who was responsible for the sale of the drugs and proprietary medicines listed in Part I of the Poisons List compiled under s17(1) of the Pharmacy and Poisons Act 1933. The goods displayed in the shop had their price clearly marked on them. The buyer took the selected goods to the cashier who stated the total price for them and received the money, but the pharmacist supervised that part of every transaction involving the sale of a drug which took place at the cash desk and was authorised to prevent any customer from removing any drug from the premises.

The question for the opinion of the court was whether particular sales that had taken place were 'effected by, or under the supervision of, a registered pharmacist' in accordance with the provisions of s18(1)(a)(iii) of the Pharmacy and Poisons Act

1933. *The question for the law to determine was* when the point of sale was effected. In the words of Lord Goddard (at p800):

> 'The question which I have to decide is whether the sale is completed before or after the intending purchaser has passed the scrutiny of the pharmacist and paid his money, or, to put it another way, whether the offer which initiates the negotiations is an offer by the shopkeeper or an offer by the buyer.'

The following extract is found at the end of Lord Goddard's judgment at pp802–3. Note the way in which key facts of the case are used to establish the reason why the rule is applied.

> '... the mere fact that a customer picks up a bottle of medicine from the shelves in this case does not amount to an acceptance of an offer to sell. It is an offer by the customer to buy and there is no sale effected until the buyer's offer to buy is accepted by the acceptance of the price. The offer, the acceptance of the price, and therefore the sale, take place under the supervision of the pharmacist. That is sufficient to satisfy the requirements of the section, for by using the words "the sale is effected by, or under the supervision of, a registered pharmacist" the Act envisages that the sale may be effected by someone not a pharmacist. I think too that the sale is effected under his supervision if he is in a position to say "You must not have that: that contains poison" so that in any case, even if I were wrong in the view that I have taken on the question as to when the sale was completed, and it was completed when the customer took the article from the shelf, it would still be effected under the supervision of the pharmacist within the meaning of section 18.'

TASK A

The following questions should be answered by reference only to the information given above and you may use your own words, or those of Lord Goddard, or a combination of your own words and those of Lord Goddard.

1. The question for the law to determine was when the point of sale was effected. State in one sentence what the legal answer to this question is.
2. Under s18(1)(a)(iii) of the Pharmacy and Poisons Act 1933 the sale has to be 'effected by, or under the supervision of, a registered pharmacist'. Explain why Lord Goddard's decision accords with the precise wording used in this phrase.
3. Refer to the description of the facts given above under the heading '*The material facts included the following*' and identify whether any of these facts have not yet been addressed by the extracts from the judgment of Lord Goddard given above.

The legal principle that is found in the *Boots Cash Chemists* case is known as the 'invitation to treat' rule and when you undertake your study of the contract law you will find an alternative principle that is known as 'the offer to the world at large rule' which was laid down before the *Boots Cash Chemists* case in *Carlill* v *Carbolic Smoke Ball Co* [1893] 1 QB 256. This case concerned an advertisement placed in various newspapers in which the defendants claimed that their Carbolic Smoke Ball had been used by many thousands of people and that in no ascertained case had any user contracted influenza. It was stated that a £100 reward would be paid to anyone who used the smoke ball properly and who still contracted influenza or any one of the other many illnesses that were also listed. The defendants also stated that they had deposited £1,000 with a well-known bank 'showing our sincerity in the matter'. Mrs Carlill purchased a smoke ball, used it in accordance with the instructions, and caught influenza. It was the view of the court that in so doing she had fully completed all that was required of her in respect of the instructions on how to accept the offer stated in the advert. The defendants promise that £1,000 had been deposited in the bank was also treated as being an indication of intention to form a contract. Accordingly, the defendants argument that the advert was not an offer but a mere 'advertising puff' and that it did not show any intention to enter into a contract was unsuccessful.

In *Boots Cash Chemists* the plaintiffs cited *Carlill* as a part of their argument for proposing that the self-service system of trading *inherently invites the customer to purchase* so that the taking of an article by a customer is an acceptance of the offer. The key fact that was relied on for this argument was that the price was fully displayed on the articles which were offered for sale.

This provides two other facts that have not yet been addressed in the extracts selected from Lord Goddard's judgment, namely, it was a self-service store and the goods had their price marked on them. If it was 1952 and you were reading the judgment of Lord Goddard in the first report printed of it, these are two facts that you might think were very important. Speculate, for instance, on the approach that you would take if you had before you set of facts that were the same in all respects to that of the *Boots Cash Chemists* case except that the goods selected by your client (the customer) did *not* have the price marked on them. Alternatively, the shop in your new set of facts might not be a 'self-service store' as such but the goods selected by your client and taken into the shopkeeper may have been laid out on a table in front of the shop. In addition, it may or may not be the case that these goods indicated the price that had to be paid for them.

TASK B

Forming an initial view on the minimum of information about cases is a valuable skill to acquire because it allows you to target your attentions onto cases that look as if they may be relevant rather than in wasting valuable time reading cases in detail that turn out to be inapplicable. Using only the information that is presented above for the cases of *Boots Cash Chemists* and *Carlill*, form an initial view on whether the following set of facts would fall under the invitation to treat rule or the offer to the world at large rule. (*Note*: attempt not to let any other knowledge intrude upon the reasoning that you use.)

X, the owner of an antique shop, placed an advert in the local newspaper which was headed 'Midsummer Madness! One day sale of genuine antiques at unrepeatable prices.' One of the articles was described as 'An original 1940's Swiss Army knife –

£15.' Z took time off from work to be at the shop as it opened that day. The Swiss Army knife was displayed in an open-backed cabinet and he picked up the knife and took it to X together with £15 in cash. X refused to sell him the knife saying that the price was printed wrongly in the paper and the knife was actually £150.

Now consider whether your initial view of the applicable rule would differ if X had refused to sell the knife because Z was only 15 years of age.

These sort of variations on the facts give examples of need to determine the *sufficiently similar material* facts that enable you to identify whether any a new set of facts is likely to fall under the invitation to treat rule or the offer to the world at large rule. The antique shop is not a self-service store in the sense that the Boots Cash Chemists store was, and the indication from the facts is that the price was not written on the knife. The question is whether either of these facts changes the applicability of the invitation to treat rule. On reading the judgment of Lord Goddard you would find the following reasoning (at page 801–2):

> 'I think that it is a well established principle that the mere exposure of goods for sale by a shopkeeper indicates to the public that he is willing to treat but does not amount to an offer to sell. I do not think that I ought to hold that that principle is completely reversed merely because there is a self-service scheme, such as this, in operation. In my opinion it comes to no more than that the customer is informed that he may himself pick up an article and bring it to the shopkeeper with a view to buying it, and if, but only if, the shopkeeper then expresses his willingness to sell, the contract for sale is completed. In fact, the offer is an offer to buy, and there is no offer to sell; the customer brings the goods to the shopkeeper to see whether he will sell or not.'

And in relation to the specific fact of the presence of the pharmacist he says:

> 'The very fact that the supervising pharmacist is at the place where the money has to be paid is an indication to the purchaser that the shopkeeper may not be willing to complete a contract with anybody who may bring the goods to him.'

An examination of the inter-relationship of fact and law contained within the first of these quotes reveals the generality of the rule that has been laid down. The first part of it is related to establishing that the exposure of goods for sale by a shopkeeper is a mere invitation to treat. There is no offer to sell; the customer offers to buy. This statement of the law is not confined to being applicable to self-service systems, nor to the sale of 'poisons' under the supervision of the pharmacist. Note the sentence structure and the wording of the text. The concept of invitation is introduced as being 'a well established principle' before reference is made to the self-service system. The self-service system is a fact that does not alter the principle, ie the principle should not be '... completely reversed merely because there is a self-service scheme ...'. This is supported later in the judgment. For example, at the start of the third paragraph on p802, he says:

> '... the transaction is in no way different from the normal transaction in a shop in which there is no self-service scheme.'

A part of the submission made by the plaintiff relied on the contention that the self-service scheme was an innovation that represented a new system of trading which was a variant of an automatic sale. The defendants challenged this by using a variety of examples of trading that involved the customer inspecting goods without help from a sales assistant and then either replacing them or taking them to be purchased. Lord Goddard referred to some of these in his judgment and in particular to the example of browsing through books before deciding to purchase them. Illustrations such as these can provide useful information about the legal reasoning which can be of importance in establishing whether the precedent established in the case ought to be applied to the facts of some future case.

A part of the legal debate involved the issue of when property in the goods passed, and whether goods that offered themselves for sale had the dual effect of preventing the customer from putting them back, and entitled the shopkeeper to insist that they must be bought. Two policy issues are involved in this: the purpose of the contract law as regulation consistent with commercial practice, and the consideration of the affect of a decision such as this on the future development of the law.

Lord Goddard dealt with this by saying (at p802):

'Ordinary principles of common sense and of commerce must be applied in this matter, and to hold that in the case of self-service shops the exposure of an article is an offer to sell, and that a person can accept the offer by picking up the article, would be contrary to those principles and might entail serious results.'

He then went on to give reasoning for why the property should not pass when the article is picked up and as part of this said:

'... I am quite satisfied it would be wrong to say that the shopkeeper is making an offer to sell every article in the shop to any person who might come in and that that person can insist on buying any article ...'

TASK B revisited:

It can now be deduced that the sample facts given in Task B above would be treated as falling under the invitation to treat rule. The effect of the reasoning given to support the rule is that it marginalises the offer to the world rule to being applicable only to exceptional cases that contain an offer which waives the need to communicate acceptance in the way that the advert in *Carlill* v *Carbolic Smoke Ball* did. This is supported by later cases that expand the use of the invitation to treat rule and, in relation to the Task B facts, two that are relevant are:

1. a flick knife displayed in a shop window (for which a shop cabinet would be sufficiently similar): *Fisher* v *Bell* [1961] 1 QB 394;
2. classified advertisements: *Partridge* v *Crittenden* [1968] 2 All ER 421.

Fisher v *Bell and Partridge* v *Crittenden – examples of the breadth of application of the invitation to treat rule*

Both these cases are unusual in that they involved criminal prosecutions. The application of the invitation to treat rule in these cases reflected the importance that the rule had assumed within the contract law. To hold that the defendants in these cases had 'offered to sell' would have been incompatible with the reasoning used in the contract law cases to establish that the same circumstances of sale would be an invitation to treat. In both cases it was decided that it was more important to preserve the use of the invitation to treat rule and to leave Parliament to change the wording used in the statutory sections that gave rise to the problem.

In the case of *Fisher* v *Bell* [1961] 1 QB 394 the rule was applied in relation to statutory provision under the Restriction of Offensive Weapons Act 1959. The defendant had displayed a 'flick knife' in his shop window and was charged with a criminal offence under s1(1)(a) of the Act. The wording in the first part of the section referred to 'sells ... or offers for sale' and the defendant successfully argued that the invitation to treat rule should be applied; in other words, that he had not offered the knife for sale by displaying it in the window. The section had to be amended by the Restriction of Offensive Weapons Act 1961.

The case of *Partridge* v *Crittenden* [1968] 1 WLR 1204; [1968] 2 All ER 421 is similar but involved a prosecution under the Protection of Birds Act 1934, which also used the words 'offer for sale', in relation to an advertisement that stated 'bramblefinch cocks, ditto hens 25s each'. Following this case Parliament passed the Trades Descriptions Act 1968 which effectively legislated that in all instances of this sort the activity is to be treated as offers for sale. This does not affect the application of the invitation to treat rule in respect of those cases in contract to which it should apply.

Other applications of the 'invitation to treat' rule

The 'invitation to treat' rule found in Lord Goddard's judgment has sufficient generality to be applied to the variety of circumstances that arise to be determined under the contract law and it has come to be a major principle in determining the formation of a legally binding contract.

There are a number of cases involving correspondence that provide a good illustration of how the courts have applied the rule to the particular facts of the cases of which the following are selected to provide this illustration.

In *Clifton* v *Palumbo* [1944] 2 All ER 497 the use of the words 'I am prepared to offer you ...' was not an offer having regard to the other uncertainties still unresolved in the negotiations.

By comparison, in *Bigg* v *Boyd Gibbins Ltd* [1971] 1 WLR 913 the words 'For a quick sale I would accept ...' was an offer as all other arrangements were complete.

In *Gibson* v *Manchester City Council* [1978] 2 All ER 583 a confusion of correspondence between Gibson and the council for the sale of a house contained technical counter-offers on the price as well as an agreement to pay the full price. The debate turned on whether a letter from the council that used the words '... may be prepared to sell to you at ... if you return the application form ...' was an invitation to treat. The Court of Appeal took the view that this was an offer on the grounds that the use of 'may be' instead of 'are' was irrelevant having regard to the later conduct of the council and reasonable assumptions of the buyer. The House of Lords did not agree and held that the Council had merely made an invitation to treat evidenced by the vague words and the invitation to apply to buy the house.

7.4 Selecting the right rule

It should by now be clear that the application of the English law is not simply a process of selecting ready made legal concepts and tests and applying them to the problem in hand. Reference to the previous case law is merely the means by which the lawyer can determine what the possible legal resolution *might* be. There are so many variable considerations that may be taken into account by a judge that it is impossible to say with certainty what the outcome of a case will be. Where the real skill of the lawyer lies is in putting together a collection of cases that give a high probability of bringing about the desired resolution. However, where the parties have gone into court voluntarily to argue out their case, it has to be assumed that each believes that there is a good chance that the law will be construed in their favour. This is an interesting notion because it means that at the outset of the case the opposing sides must each have viewed the risk of losing as being a risk worth taking and the quantification of that risk lay in the evaluation of the scope for interpretation provided by the cases to be used in support of their submission.

If this is looked at the other way round, what it reveals is that the case law always leaves a sufficient ambiguity to give scope for further interpretation of how the law should be applied. The practising lawyer relies on this ambiguity and scope for further interpretation to formulate a good argument in favour of the client, but when you are a student new to the study of the law, the ambiguity and the subtlety of re-interpretation that occurs in the cases is a most confusing thing. The development of the various tests applied in the nervous shock cases provides an example of how the law creates a number of different rules within an area of the law to meet the variety of circumstances that arise to be determined. The judgments delivered in the Court of Appeal in *McLoughlin* v *O'Brian* [1981] QB 599; [1981] 1 All ER 809 also provide an example of judges reaching the same decision but for different reasons (see Task 3 below).

Gaining an appreciation of the topic

The first thing to note is that we are now no longer looking at how to find the law contained within one judgment but are moving over to dealing with several judgments that contain different interpretations of how the law is to be applied. You would not start such a task by reading the cases first! An appreciation of the ambit of the topic would have been gained from the reading of the textbooks and from the lectures.

The main purpose of reading the textbooks is to gain:

1. an identification of the legal principles involved in the topic;
2. a familiarity with the legal terminology specific to that topic;
3. a list of the leading cases together with some appreciation of what each decides.

A familiarity with the terminology applicable to the topic is essential before detailed examination of the case law can be undertaken. The terminology is a form of legal shorthand: it conveys a conceptual meaning in a precise way. You must become as familiar with its use as the lawyers are that use it as most of the reasoning given in a judgment assumes such knowledge.

The knowledge of which rules you should be working with is vital if any case that you read contains other rules or aspects of law. It is the only means by which you will be able to decide which parts of the judgments you should be reading and analysing.

Reading a case in a law report is obviously made much easier if you already have some idea of what it is about from reading the explanation given of it in your textbook. Equally as important though is the priority list for the cases that you can derive from the emphasis that is given to them in the textbook.

Determining how far into the chapter you should read in any week might already be indicated for you in your course/module guidebook or on the seminar sheets that you are given. Do remember to refer to any guidelines of this nature that you have been given as they are of invaluable benefit to structuring your studies to what is required.

Your reading is likely to provide you with a lot of information on each of the concepts involved in the topic. The notes that you will find most useful when reading the cases in the law reports are those that are in the nature of checklists that:

1. briefly define the interpretation(s) of each case given in the textbook(s) you have read; and
2. identify the relationship between the cases, eg the rule is first formulated in case A in the Court of Appeal; is next used in case B in the House of Lords and note any refinements made to the rule; is distinguished from in case C, and so on.

Notes like this help you to make value judgments about what you should read and in what order. For example, from the information given in 2. above it would seem that Case B would be the best one to read first, followed by a quick reference to case A, then a reading of Case C. If you come across something in a judgment that you do not fully understand, the brief notes made as per 1. above may help you to sort this out quickly so that you can carry on with the minimum of delay.

Organise your notes into a format relevant to the topic. Notes on nervous shock should:

1. clearly identify the gradual development of this law;
2. isolate those tests specific to nervous shock;
3. indicate further future trends.

TASK 1

Make brief notes from the following passage that:

1. identify the main terminology and tests; and
2. pinpoint the key stages in the development of this law.

> An action in nervous shock is unusual in that the plaintiff need not have been directly injured by the defendant's actions. The plaintiff's shock can arise as a result of witnessing injury to someone who is sufficiently proximate to him or her. Thus, the plaintiff is claiming that he or she is also owed a duty of care by the defendant on the grounds that the defendant ought to have reasonably foreseen that such shock would be caused as a probable or natural result of the defendant's negligent act or omission.
>
> The early cases in nervous shock relied on establishing the plaintiff's immediate proximity to the ambit of the act, and his or her reasonable fear of bodily injury to him or herself or to others. The standard of susceptibility was that which the reasonably strong-nerved person situated in the position of the plaintiff would experience. The question was always whether the extent of the defendant's duty of care brought the plaintiff within its ambit. Thus, it was a debate about neither causation nor remoteness of damage but instead about whether the plaintiff belonged to that class of persons to whom the defendant owed a duty of care. In other words, it was a debate about the special relationship between the plaintiff and the defendant and was therefore in the nature of a policy decision.
>
> Later cases retained all of these tests but included in the criteria a wider definition of the shock that could be sustained. The transition from 'the impact theory' to 'the shock theory' was swift, and the emergence of the proximity-in-time-and-space test can be viewed as a natural development from this. After the duty principle had been extended thus far, it was only a short step to move over into the aftermath principle and its resultant extension of the class of persons to whom a duty will be owed.

Identifying the inter-relationships between the cases and their tests

The following passages are taken from the judgment of Lord Wilberforce given in *McLoughlin* v *O'Brian* [1982] 2 All ER 298 (House of Lords). They provide a summary of the legal position and the leading cases decided prior to 1982 and an indication of the facts involved in the *McLoughlin* case.

> 'The critical question to be decided is whether a person in the position of the appellant, ie one who was not present at the scene of grievous injuries to her family but who comes on those injuries at an interval of time and space, can recover damages for nervous shock. ...
>
> Although in the only case which has reached this House (*Hay (or Bourhill)* v *Young* [1942]) ... a claim for damages in respect of "nervous shock" was rejected on its facts, the

House gave clear recognition to the legitimacy, in principle, of claims of that character. As the result of that and other cases, assuming that they are accepted as correct, the following position has been reached:

1. While damages cannot, at common law, be awarded for grief and sorrow, a claim for damages for "nervous shock" caused by negligence can be made without the necessity of showing direct impact or fear of immediate personal injuries for oneself ...
2. A plaintiff may recover damages for "nervous shock" brought on by injury caused not to him or herself but to a near relative, or by the fear of such injury. So far (subject to 5 below), the cases do not extend beyond the spouse or children of the plaintiff (*Hambrook* v *Stokes Bros* [1925] ... *Boardman* v *Sanderson* [1964] ... *Hinz* v *Berry* [1970]) ... including foster children (where liability was assumed), and see *King* v *Phillips* [1953] ...
3. Subject to the next paragraph, there is no English case in which a plaintiff has been able to recover nervous shock damages where the injury to the near relative occurred out of sight and earshot of the plaintiff. In *Hambrook* v *Stokes Bros* an express distinction was made between shock caused by what the mother saw with her own eyes and what she might have been told by bystanders, liability being excluded in the latter case.
4. An exception from, or I would prefer to call it an extension of, the latter case has been made where the plaintiff does not see or hear the incident but comes on its immediate aftermath. In *Boardman* v *Sanderson* the father was within earshot of the accident to his child and likely to come on the scene; he did so and suffered damage from what he then saw. In *Marshall* v *Lionel Enterprises* (1971) ... the wife came immediately on the badly injured body of her husband. And in *Benson* v *Lee* [1972] VR 879 a situation existed with some similarity to the present case. The mother was in her home 100 yards away, and, on communication by a third party, ran out to the scene of the accident and there suffered shock. Your Lordships have to decide whether or not to validate these extensions.
5. A remedy on account of nervous shock has been given to a man who came on a serious accident involving people immediately thereafter and acted as a rescuer of those involved (*Chadwick* v *British Transport Commission* [1967] ... "Shock" was caused neither by fear for himself nor by fear or horror on account of a near relative. The principle of "rescuer" cases was not challenged by the respondents and ought, in my opinion, to be accepted. But we have to consider whether, and how far, it can be applied to such cases as the present.

Throughout these developments, as can be seen, the courts have proceeded in the traditional manner of the common law from case to case, on a basis of logical necessity. If a mother, with or without accompanying children, could recover on account of fear for herself, how can she be denied recovery on account of fear for her accompanying children? If a father could recover had he seen his child run over by a backing car, how can he be denied recovery if he is in the immediate vicinity and runs to the child's assistance? If a wife and mother could recover if she had witnessed a serious accident to her husband and children, does she fail because she was a short distance away and immediately rushes to the scene? (cf *Benson* v *Lee*). I think that, unless the law is to draw an arbitrary line at the point of direct sight and sound, these arguments require acceptance of the extension mentioned above under principle 4 in the interests of justice.

If one continues to follow the process of logical progression, it is hard to see why the present plaintiff also should not succeed. She was not present at the accident, but she came very soon after on its aftermath. If, from a distance of some 100 yards (cf *Benson* v

Lee), she had found her family by the roadside, she would have come within principle 4 above. Can it make any difference that she comes on them in an ambulance, or, as here, in a nearby hospital, when, as the evidence shows, they were in the same condition, covered with oil and mud, and distraught with pain? If Mr Chadwick can recover when, acting in accordance with normal and irresistible human instinct, and indeed moral compulsion, he goes to the scene of an accident, may not a mother recover if, acting under the same motives, she goes to where her family can be found? ...'

TASK 2

1. Extract from the above all of the facts of the case of *McLoughlin* v *O'Brian* that are referred to by Lord Wilberforce.
2. Identify his reasoning for arguing that Mrs McLoughlin does fall within the class of persons to whom the duty was owed.
3. Make a list of all of the other cases cited and note any indication of the facts of those cases that is given. *Note*: leave a large margin at one side to use for the answers to the next question.
4. Add the *McLoughlin* case to the end of your list and in the margin that you have left by the cases write in whichever of the following statements you think relate best to the cases (*Note*: some cases may have more than one relevant statement):

   - immediate proximity to the act
   - proximity in time and space
   - interval in time and space
   - the unaided senses rule
   - direct impact or fear of immediate personal injuries for oneself
   - fear of injury to a spouse or child of the plaintiff
   - out of sight and earshot
   - out of sight but within earshot
   - in the immediate vicinity
   - immediate aftermath
   - the rescuer principle

Policy considerations

A matter of particular concern in the development of the liability for nervous shock has been the question of where the boundary should be drawn for fixing the defendants' liability for acts of negligence. The reasoning that is used to establish liability for negligence has been discussed in section 7.2 above. The duty of care exists in relation to acts or omissions that the defendant 'can reasonably foresee would be likely to injure' the plaintiff. In addition, the plaintiff has to be someone who is '... so closely and directly affected by [the defendant's] act that [the defendant] ought reasonably to have them in contemplation as being so affected ...'.

Nervous shock cases are unusual in that the plaintiff is not normally the person who was directly injured by the defendant's act but is instead a person who was shocked by the injuries that the defendant caused to another person. The debate therefore becomes a rather complex one about the reasonable foreseeability that the defendant should have of causing shock to the plaintiff when carrying out the act or omission which harms the directly affected victim.

Some further passages taken from the judgement of Lord Wilberforce in *McLoughlin* v *O'Brian* (above) serve to show the difficulties that arise.

On the point of *foreseeability of harm* to Mrs McLoughlin, the following passages indicate the view that was taken at first instance and by the Court of Appeal:

'Boreham J gave judgment for the respondents holding ... that the respondents owed no duty of care to the appellant because the possibility of her suffering injury by nervous shock, in the circumstances, was not reasonably foreseeable.'

'On appeal by the appellant, the judgment of Boreham J was upheld, but not on the same ground ...'

'Stephenson LJ took the view that the possibility of injury to the appellant by nervous shock was reasonably foreseeable and that the respondents owed the appellant a duty of care. However, he held that considerations of policy prevented the appellant from recovering ...'

'Griffiths LJ held that injury by nervous shock to the appellant was "readily foreseeable" but that the respondents owed no duty of care to the appellant. The duty was limited to those on the road nearby.'

'Cumming-Bruce LJ agreed with both judgments.'

On the point of *the duty of care owed*, the following passages indicate the view that was taken by Stephenson and Griffiths LJJ:

'Stephenson LJ considered that the defendants owed a duty of care to the plaintiff, but that for reasons of policy the law should stop short of giving her damages: it should limit relief to those on or near the highway at or near the time of the accident caused by the defendants' negligence ...'

'Griffiths LJ took the view that, although the injury to the plaintiff was foreseeable, there was no duty of care. The duty of care of drivers of motor vehicles was, according to decided cases, limited to persons and owners of property on the road or near to it who might be directly affected. The line should be drawn at this point. It was not even in the interest of those suffering from shock as a class to extend the scope of the defendants' liability: to do so would quite likely delay their recovery by immersing them in the anxiety of litigation.'

Lord Wilberforce's view is indicated by these words:

'... in my opinion the boundaries of a man's responsibility for acts of negligence have to be fixed as a matter of policy ... looking with hindsight at an event which has occurred, is a formula adopted by English law ... for limiting the persons to whom duty may be owed
...
... the statement that there is a "duty of care" (owed to a person or a class) denotes a

conclusion into the forming of which considerations of policy have entered. That foreseeability does not of itself, and automatically, lead to a duty of care is, I think, clear.'

TASK 3

1. By reference to the reasoning that is given in the above passages, identify the extent to which the criteria for determining the foreseeability of harm is distinct from the criteria for determining that the duty of care is owed.
2. Make a brief note that identifies the essence of the differences in reasoning employed by Stephenson and Griffiths LLJ.

Note: the judgments given in the Court of Appeal provide an example of judges coming to the same decision but for different reasons – an example of the ambiguities and scope for judicial interpretation referred to in the opening paragraphs of this section.

Lord Wilberforce deals with the policy considerations involved in the *McLoughlin* case by discussing them under four heads as follows:

'We must then consider the policy arguments ... damages must be confined to those within sight and sound of an event caused by negligence or, at least, to those in close, or very close, proximity to such a situation.

The policy arguments against a wider extension can be stated under four heads. First, it may be said that such extension may lead to a proliferation of claims ... Second, it may be claimed that an extension of liability would be unfair to defendants as imposing damages out of proportion to the negligent conduct complained of ... Third, to extend most direct and plain cases would greatly increase evidentiary liability beyond the difficulties and tend to lengthen litigation. Fourth, it may be said (and the Court of Appeal agreed with this) that an extension of the scope of liability ought only to be made by the legislature.

Fraudulent claims can be contained by the courts, which, also, can cope with evidentiary difficulties. The scarcity of cases which have occurred in the past, and the modest sums recovered, give some indication that fears of a flood of litigation may be exaggerated: experience in other fields suggests that such fears usually are. If some increase does occur, that may only reveal the existence of a genuine social need ...

... because "shock" in its nature is capable of affecting so wide a range of people, (there is) a real need for the law to place some limitation on the extent of admissible claims. It is necessary to consider three elements inherent in any claim: the class of persons whose claims should be recognised; the proximity of such persons to the accident; and the means by which the shock is caused.

As regards the class of persons, the possible range is between the closest of family ties, of parent and child, or husband and wife, and the ordinary bystander. Existing law recognises the claims of the first; it denies that of the second, either on the basis that such persons must be assumed to be possessed of fortitude sufficient to enable them to endure the calamities of modern life or that defendants cannot be expected to compensate the world at large. In my opinion, these positions are justifiable, and since the present case falls within the first class it is strictly unnecessary to say more. I think, however, that it should follow that other cases involving less close relationships must be very carefully scrutinised. I cannot say that they should never be admitted. The closer the tie (not merely in relationship, but in care) the greater the claim for consideration. The claim, in any case, has to be judged in the light of the other factors, such as proximity to the scene in time and place, and the nature of the accident.

As regards proximity to the accident, it is obvious that this must be close in both time and space. It is after all, the fact and consequence of the defendant's negligence that must be proved to have caused the "nervous shock". Experience has shown that to insist on direct and immediate sight or hearing would be impractical and unjust and that under what may be called the "aftermath" doctrine, one who, from close proximity comes very soon on the scene, should not be excluded. In my opinion, the result in *Benson* v *Lee* [1972] VR 879 was correct and indeed inescapable. It was based, soundly, on "direct perception of some of the events which go to make up the accident as an entire event, and this includes ... the immediate aftermath".

Finally, and by way of reinforcement of "aftermath" cases, I would accept, by analogy with "rescue" situations, that a person of whom it could be said that one could expect nothing else than that he or she would come immediately to the scene (normally a parent or a spouse) could be regarded as being within the scope of foresight and duty. Where there is not immediate presence, account must be taken of the possibility of alterations in the circumstances, for which the defendant should not be responsible. Subject only to these qualifications, I think that a strict test of proximity by sight or hearing should be applied by the courts.

Lastly, as regards communication, there is no case in which the law has compensation for shock brought about by communication by a third party ... the shock must come through sight or hearing of the event or of its immediate aftermath. Whether some equivalent of sight or hearing, eg through simultaneous television, would suffice may have to be considered.

My Lords, I believe that these indications ... to be applied with common sense to individual situations in their entirety, represent either the existing law, or the existing law with only such circumstantial extension as the common law process may legitimately make. They do not introduce a new principle ... I find on this appeal that the appellant's case falls within the boundaries of the law so drawn. I would allow her appeal.'

TASK 4

1. What are, the three elements inherent in any claim that the law needs to consider?
2. Why does Mrs McLoughlin fall within the class of persons that the law is willing to recognise?
3. Why is Mrs McLoughlin sufficiently proximate to the accident?
4. Identify the reasons why Lord Wilberforce agrees with the decision in *Benson* v *Lee*.

Using extracts from the judgments as vehicles for analysis

Reading the judgments in the law reports gives you a detailed analysis of why the principles were formulated and applied as they were. You have to incorporate this information in your written analysis of the law. The following examples are taken from the House of Lords judgements in *Bourhill (or Hay)* v *Young* [1943] AC 92; [1942] 2 All ER 396. Prior to 1943 the courts were reluctant to allow claims in shock, fearing a 'flood' of fraudulent claims, but this gradually gave way to the qualified application of the neighbour principle to this type of harm. *Bourhill* laid down a test, based on the 'unaided senses' rule, as to who may fall within the class of persons to whom a duty is owed which became the foundation for the legal reasoning used in the later cases.

The key facts of the case are:

1. The plaintiff saw neither the defendant nor the collision in which he was killed, but she did hear the crash and later saw blood on the road.
2. The plaintiff admitted that she was not in fear of bodily danger to herself or to others; she claimed instead that her peculiar susceptibility to shock at the time of the act (she was eight months pregnant) brought her within the ambit of care owed by the defendant.

The House of Lords unanimously dismissed her appeal. The following is an example of the points that may be extracted from the judgments and of the quotes that could be selected to illustrate the reasoning.

1. The plaintiff must be in reasonable fear of bodily danger either for herself or for others. In this case the plaintiff was not 'closely and directly affected by the act' either geographically or out of reasonable fear for others – she was therefore outside of the ambit of proximity.

   'The duty is not to the world at large. It must be tested by asking ... was a duty owed to [the appellant]. If [the appellant was not] in such a position that direct physical injury could reasonably be anticipated to them or their relations or friends ... no duty (will) be owed' (per Porter LJ).

   '[The appellant was] not within his line of vision ... did not see the accident and ... [was not] in reasonable fear of immediate bodily injury to herself. She was not so placed that there was any reasonable likelihood of her being affected by the deceased's careless driving' (per Macmillan LJ).

   'If [the appellant] has a cause of action, it is because of a wrong to herself. She cannot build on a wrong to someone else' (per Wright LJ).

2. The plaintiff, as a 'person of normal nervous strength', must reasonably have suffered the shock that has been sustained in these circumstances – in other words, the reasonable man test establishes the standard of care owed by defendant.

   '... whether there is a duty owing to members of the public who come within the ambit of the act, must generally depend on a normal standard of susceptibility' (per Wright LJ).

   'It is not every emotional disturbance or every shock which should have been foreseen. ... [the user of a highway] even though careless is entitled to assume that the ordinary frequenter of the streets has sufficient fortitude to endure such incidents as may from time to time be expected to occur in them, including the noise of a collision and the sight of injury to others, and is not to be considered negligent towards one who does not possess the customary phlegm ...' (per Porter LJ).

3. The nervous shock sustained must be a medically recognised psychiatric illness or disorder. Mere sensations of fear, mental distress or grief that would ordinarily be experienced by the reasonably strong-nerved person situated in the position of the plaintiff are not actionable. Lord Wright illustrated this in his judgment by phrasing his definition of liability in terms of it being determined by 'the standard of the normal person':

'The question of liability must generally depend on a normal standard of susceptibility... a reasonably normal condition, if medical evidence is capable of defining it, would be the standard.'

4. For the plaintiff to establish that her peculiar susceptibility to shock falls within the defendant's ambit of care, this extraordinary risk must:

a) either be known to the defendant; or
b) be one which he could reasonably be taken to have foreseen.

'It is ... a question of what the hypothetical reasonable man, viewing the position, I suppose ex post facto, would say it was proper to foresee. What danger of particular infirmity that would include must depend on all the circumstances; but generally ... a reasonably normal (medical) condition ... would be the standard. The test of the plaintiff's extraordinary susceptibility, if unknown to the defendant, would in effect make the defendant an insurer' (per Wright LJ).

TASK 5

Devise your own version of notes like these for *McLoughlin* v *O'Brian* using the notes made for the Tasks given above and the various extracts from the judgment of Lord Wilberforce. Also look up the case in the law report to choose quotes from the other judgments, or from parts of Lord Wilberforce's judgment that are not reproduced in this chapter.

7.5 Final considerations of the doctrine of stare decisis

Stare decisis is generally defined as 'standing by past decisions', but stare decisis is actually an abbreviation of 'stare rationibus decidendi' which reflects the fact that what actually occurs is an agreement with the judicial legal reasoning used in the previous case. In terms of a discussion of how to work with precedent, this is the more accurate description of what 'standing by past decisions' really means.

In the discussion of how to work with judgments that is given in this chapter, the emphasis has been on 'finding' the ratio decidendi. The nature of the problem of learning the law causes this to be the primary consideration but the law in practice has to also give equal weight to the importance of preserving the integrity of the doctrine of stare decisis. Clues as to this are found in all of the judgments and are therefore present in those that have been dealt with in this chapter. For example, look again at the final paragraph of Lord Wilberforce's judgment in *McLoughlin* v *O'Brian* and note that he says:

> '... I believe that these indications ... represent either the existing law, or the existing law with only such circumstantial extension as the common law process may legitimately make. They do not introduce a new principle ... I find on this appeal that the appellant's case falls within the boundaries of the law so drawn.'

Also note the words of Lord Goddard in *Pharmaceutical Society of Great Britain* v *Boots Cash Chemists (Southern) Ltd* when he says:

> 'I think that it is a *well established principle* that the mere exposure of goods for sale by a shopkeeper indicates to the public that he is willing to treat but does not amount to an offer to sell. *I do not think that I ought to hold that that principle is completely reversed* merely because there is a self-service scheme, such as this, in operation.' (*Note*: italics are added for emphasis.)

Their concern for establishing that, in their opinion, their reasoning is consistent with that used in earlier cases arises out of the long-standing view that it is the role of judges to declare the existing law rather than to create new law. Consistently re-applying legal principles gives the law its strength because it maintains certainty, predictability and fairness (this is explained in more detail in Chapter 4). The notion of stare decisis is inextricably intertwined with the ratio decidendi and is found in the following conventions:

1. a primary consideration of the judiciary is to maintain certainty and consistency of application of the law by reapplying the well-established principles of law to new combinations of facts that arise in the cases brought before the courts;
2. a departure from the application of a previous legal principle can only arise if the earlier case and the previous case can be distinguished on their facts, either because there is some further fact in the case that the court is prepared to treat as material, or because some fact treated as material in the earlier case is absent in the present case.

All of this relates to the discussion given in the opening paragraphs of section 7.4 above. When lawyers argue a case in court they do not ask the judge to formulate some new principle on behalf of their client. As was described in those paragraphs, the skill of the lawyer lies in selecting reasoning from the decided cases that supports a *particular interpretation* of the law. Keep this in mind when you read Chapters 10 and 11 to learn about trial procedure and mooting technique, and participate in a moot if you have the opportunity to do so as it is by far the best way of learning how to acquire this skill of moving from the knowledge provided in the cases to the answer that you desire to achieve.

8

Working with Statutory Provision

8.1 The language of the statute law

English legislative drafting relies on recognised conventions that date back to the late nineteenth century. The conventions relating to matters of form and the rules for the interpretation of statute are discussed separately in Chapters 5 and 6. This Chapter looks at the nature of the legislative language used and the extent to which it reduces ambiguity of meaning of words.

The linguistic and grammatical style

The style of language used in Acts of Parliament reflects the purpose of our statute law. Our Acts do not intend to provide all of the law on any one aspect. The provisions are inserted into the law either as a supplement to, or as a replacement of, the existing common law. They are presented as a series of definitions, rules, and tests and are written in a language that intends to convey the rules in a precise, unambiguous and clear way. The following example taken from ss1 to 3 of the Summer Time Act 1972 (1972, c6) shows the nature of the language used.

Advance of time during period of summer time.

1. – (1) Subject to section 2 below, the time for general purposes in Great Britain shall, during the period of summer time, be one hour in advance of Greenwich mean time.

(2) Subject to section 2 below, the period of summer time for the purposes of this Act is the period beginning at two o'clock, Greenwich mean time, in the morning of the day after the third Saturday in March or, if that day is Easter Day, the day after the second Saturday in March, and ending at two o'clock, Greenwich mean time, in the morning of the day after the fourth Saturday in October.

Extension of period, and double summer time.

2. – (1) In relation to any year Her Majesty may by Order in Council direct –

(a) that the period of summer time for the purposes of this Act shall be such period as may be specified in the Order instead of the period specified in section 1 above;

(b) that the time for general purposes in Great Britain shall, during any part of the period of summer time, be two hours instead of one hour in advance of Greenwich mean time.

(2) ...

[*Note*: subsections (2) and (3) deal with how the Order is made, varied or revoked]

Interpretation of references.

3. – (1) Subject to subsection (2) below, wherever any reference to a point of time occurs in any enactment, Order in Council, order, regulation, rule, byelaw, deed, notice, or other document whatsoever, the time referred to shall, during the period of summer time, be taken to be the time as fixed for general purposes by or under this Act.

(2) Nothing in this Act shall affect the use of Greenwich mean time for purposes of astronomy, meteorology, or navigation, or affect the construction of any document mentioning or referring to a point of time in connection with any of these purposes.

The wording is in the flat prose style typical of Acts of Parliament. This was laid down in the nineteenth century and there is a tendency toward a rigid adherence to it. Francis Bennion, a parliamentary draftsman, whose nine targets of legislative drafting are identified in Chapter 6 describes it as being the 'acceptable' language of the statute law. The somewhat complicated syntax takes a bit of getting used to but it is used for a purpose. Note how in s1(2), above, the period of summer time is given in its entirety within one sentence, including the problem of the difference for

Easter Day. It is a precise statement of when summer time starts and when it finishes. This makes the sentence appear long and cumbersome and is not the way that it would be written in an 'everyday' text. An explanation given in a textbook, for example, might choose to state the Easter Day element of the rule separately because it comes into play only as an exception in some years. At first sight it might seem that greater clarity could be achieved by doing this. In terms of the *application* of the law, however, it is an *integral part* of the rule relating to the start of the period of summer time. To provide a comprehensive statement of that part of the rule, the standard application and the exception have to be given together. A person who is trying to establish when summer time starts is immediately alerted to the fact that there is this exception.

'Subject to ...'

A linguistic convention that is used throughout the statute law is the phrase 'subject to ...'. This enables rules to be identified separately whilst also indicating any inter-relationship that they might have with other rules. (*Note*: unless otherwise stated the sections referred to below are those of the Summer Time Act 1972 given above.)

- *Subject to other parts of the same section*, eg s3(1) states that it is 'Subject to subsection (2) below ...'

  The subsections within a section divide the rule up into its component parts. Section 3(1) applies the provisions of the Act to all forms of other enactments and documents, except those that are stated in subs(2). In s1, the rule is given in two parts: (1) the statement as to the one hour advancement, and (2) the statement for the period of summer time. The rule contained in subs(2), therefore, relates to a *one hour* advancement in time. The second form of time advancement – double summer time – is not dealt with within s1 but in s2.

- *Subject to other parts of the same Act*. Both subsections of s1 start with the words 'Subject to section 2 below, ...'. This means that their application is affected by the 'double summer time' rule that is stated there and the two sections need to be read in conjunction. Each provision must have one clear and certain meaning and the *division into sections is used as the means of dividing up the rules into their separate applications*. The provision for double summer time is dealt with separately because it requires an Order in Council, whereas the one hour advancement provided for in s1 is applied by virtue of the Act. Therefore, to clarify the separate operation of the double summer time rule its component parts are dealt with separately to the component parts of the one hour advancement rule.

  The inter-relationship may not just be with another section. Some sections may start with the words 'Subject to the provisions of this Act ...'. Section 1(2) of the Unfair Contract Terms Act 1977 (1977, c50) provides a different illustration. It states:

'This Part of the Act is subject to Part III; and in relation to contracts, the operation of sections 2 to 4 and 7 is subject to the exceptions made by Schedule 1.'

8.2 Devices used to aid the interpretation of the language used

The rules laid down by ss1 and 2 of the Summer Time Act 1972 are simple enough to be stated in a precise way and no further definition of the phrase 'summer time' is required. Acts that have to deal with more complex concepts and rules do rely on a variety of different ways of providing interpretation advice for the words and phrases used. These seek to reduce the ambiguities that arise as an inescapable outcome of the imprecision of the written word.

As has been identified in section 8.1, one of the features of the language is its flexibility, but this also means that it is not a precise tool with which to convey the precise meaning intended by any statutory provision. Specific interpretation of the language used in the sections is usually found in separate interpretation sections, and in devices such as tables or schedules attached to the back of the Act. However, general indication as to the interpretation of the provisions is given throughout the Act. Indeed, one can take the view that the whole Act is in itself an 'interpretation device' by virtue of the fact that it states the law without application to particular facts. The rules take full form and meaning when they are applied to the facts of cases by courts that use the statements given in the Act to interpret how the provisions should do this.

There is such a variety of examples of how the legislative language, grammatical structure, and section structure can be used to aid interpretation that it is impossible to show them in a book such as this. It would require the reproduction of large extracts from many different Acts. A browse through any of the statutes textbooks that are available for the substantive laws will reveal the density of prose and the variety of layouts for the sections that Acts employ. When you start to use the statute law in your studies you will discover that Acts cannot be read as such; they have to be used in relation to sets of facts that require legal resolution. The entire language of the statute is directed at fulfilling this aim. The examples given in the following sections are, therefore, but a small sample of the way in which the legislative language is used to lessen ambiguity.

8.3 Subsections and paragraphs

Draftsmen have a wholly different task to that which a judge has. Judges decide how the law should be applied to the facts of a case and they can use the facts as the vehicle for the explanation of how and why the law is applied. Acts of Parliament are written in isolation from the circumstances to which their rules will eventually be applied. They are a general statement as to the law on any given matter. This generality conflicts with need to provide precise instruction as to purpose, scope and intended application of the law. The draftsmen attempt to overcome this by writing long provisions that use subsections to divide the rule into its related component parts and paragraphs within those subsections to give clarification to the elements contained within the subsection. The inevitable result of this is that the provision has to be interpreted, it cannot simply be read. A part of s1 of the Unsolicited Goods and Services Act 1971 (1971, c30) is given to illustrate this:

> '1. Rights of recipient of unsolicited goods.
> (1) In the circumstances specified in the following subsection, a person who ... receives unsolicited goods, may as between himself and the sender, use, deal with or dispose of them as if they were an unconditional gift to him, and any right of the sender to the goods shall be extinguished.
> (2) The circumstances referred to in the preceding subsection are that the goods were sent to the recipient with a view to his acquiring them, that the recipient has no reasonable cause to believe that they were sent with a view to their being acquired for the purposes of a trade or business and has neither agreed to acquire nor agreed to return them, and either –
> (a) that during the period of six months beginning with the day on which the recipient received the goods the sender did not take possession of them and the recipient did not unreasonably refuse to permit the sender to do so; or
> (b) that not less than thirty days before the expiration of the period aforesaid the recipient gave notice to the sender in accordance with the following subsection, and that during the period of thirty days beginning with the day on which the notice was given the sender did not take possession of the goods and the recipient did not unreasonably refuse to permit the sender to do so.
> (3) ...'

This provision is not easy to read, though it is simpler than some! It has to be remembered that it would be read in connection with its application to some set of facts and these would serve to help with unravelling the structure of the rule. For example, the facts may relate to trade or business goods, and the wording in subs(2) would catch the eye, ie 'sent with a view to their being acquired for the purposes of a trade or business'.

It then becomes clear, despite the initially confusing structure of the sentence, that it is necessary to establish that the recipient had 'no reasonable cause to believe' that they were such goods. The same process would repeat itself with other parts of the section, such as the six month and the thirty day rules.

Other parts of the rule have to be extracted without immediate help from the facts. For instance, it is necessary to notice that subs(2)(b) lays down a requirement to give notice to the sender, and (a) and (b) both require that the recipient did not 'unreasonably refuse to permit' the sender to repossess the goods. The circumstances of the dispute would have to be checked to see whether they relate to these factors.

8.4 Sections that use long sentences with dependent clauses

Most sections use subsections and paragraphs to present the parts of the rule, but in some instances the nature of the subject-matter may not lend itself to this and the rule is instead given as densely packed text. The key features of these sections are their long sentences and a grammatical construction that employs dependent clauses. These sort of sections are usually not that easy to use and time has to be spent breaking the rule up into its constituent parts. Holland and Webb in *Learning Legal Rules* at p149 give as an example of this the especially cumbersome statement as to the entitlement to invalidity allowance for a person in receipt of an invalidity pension given in s16(1) of the Social Security Act 1975. This is a particularly good example of a section presented entirely as prose, that relies on a difficult grammatical construction and which refers in part to other provisions. Its scope and purpose are not immediately ascertainable. It reads:

'If a person is more than 5 years below pensionable age on the qualifying date in any period of interruption of employment then, subject to the following provisions of this section, in respect of every day of that period in respect of which he is entitled to an invalidity pension, he shall also be entitled to an invalidity allowance at the appropriate weekly rate specified in relation thereto in Schedule 4, Part I, paragraph 3; and "the qualifying date" means the first day in that period (whether before the coming into force of this section or later) which is a day of incapacity for work or such earlier day as may be prescribed.'

The only way to handle a rule like this is to separate the various parts of the text by reference to factual questions.

1. who it applies to? – a 'person more than 5 years below pensionable age';
2. when it applies? – 'on the qualifying date in any period of interruption of employment';
3. how is that defined? – 'the first day in that period' that is the 'day of incapacity for work' or is 'such earlier day as may be prescribed';
4. what limitations there may be? – it operates irrespective of whether this 'qualifying date' falls before s16 was brought into force;
5. for what length of time it applies? – 'in respect of every day of that period' for which the person would be 'entitled to an invalidity pension';
6. what the person is entitled to? – 'shall also be entitled to an invalidity allowance at the appropriate weekly rate specified in relation thereto in Schedule 4, Part I, paragraph 3'.

So, it is really a straightforward rule – the most difficult part comes when you try to work out the weekly rate as per Schedule 4, Part I, paragraph 3. It is the way that it is presented that makes it seem so complicated. Although the wording of 'in respect of every day of that period in respect of which ...' is an accepted and precise form of joining the two elements together, in this sentence structure it is initially confusing. One also wonders whether the words 'subject to the following provisions of this section' are entirely necessary since it is obvious that that is what it is subject to.

Phrases like 'specified in relation thereto' are also somewhat archaic – what it actually means to say is 'given in' Schedule 4, etc. The continuing use of these sort of phrases is connected to the notion of the 'acceptable' language of the statute law identified by Bennion (supra), and there is a slow acceptance of any attempts to modernise it. Bennion himself was criticised by the House of Commons for using the more modern phrase of 'tried his best' instead of the conventionally used phrase 'used his best endeavours'. The theory is that the Act should have applicability without the need for its interpretation by the judiciary which is an unfortuantely simplistic view that ignores the law making abilities of our judiciary. Section 16(1) of the Social Security Act 1975 is an example of an over-concern to insert precision and comprehensibility into a provision.

8.5 Sections that allow for judicial discretion

In contrast to s16(1) above, the Unfair Contract Terms Act 1977 provides an example of wording that allows for considerable judicial interpretation of the application of the rule. The 'reasonableness test' set up in s11(1) states:

> 'In relation to a contract term, the requirement of reasonableness ... is that the term shall have been a fair and reasonable one to be included having regard to the circumstances which were, or ought reasonably to have been, known to or in the contemplation of the parties when the contract was made.'

Subsection (2) provides that in the determination of this:

> '... regard shall be had in particular to the matters specified in Schedule 2 to this Act; but this subsection does not prevent the court or arbitrator from holding, in accordance with any rule of law, that a term which purports to exclude or restrict any relevant liability is not a term of the contract.'

Subsection (4) gives further assistance as to application by indicating the sort of circumstances that should be considered where the clause seeks to restrict liability to a specified sum of money.

Schedule 2 is entitled: 'GUIDELINES' FOR APPLICATION OF REASONABLENESS TEST and starts with the phrase: 'The matters to which regard is to be had in particular ...'. The entire application of the s11 reasonableness test is, therefore, very much at the discretion of the court to determine.

8.6 Identifying which parts of the Act the interpretation of the words relates to

The meaning of words or phrases might be explained in a subsection and this interpretation is usually intended to relate only to words and phrases contained elsewhere within that section. The wording will make it clear which parts of the section it does relate to.

It might be the whole section, eg

> (3) In this section –
> 'competent authority' means ...
> 'enactment' means ...

or it might relate to specific words used in this subsection and another subsection, eg

> (6) In subsection (3) above and this subsection –
> (a) 'credit broker' means ...
> (b) 'credit brokerage' means ...

or it might give the meaning of a term found in the preceding subsection and be dealt with in this way so as to reduce the amount and complexity of explanation given there, eg

> (3) In section 14(2) above 'corresponding hire-purchase agreement' means ...

or the section might re-use a term used in another section and so the 'interpretation' subsection will refer to its previous definition, eg s15(3) of the Sale of Goods Act 1979 (1979, c54) re-uses a definition given in s14(6):

> (3) In subsection (2)(c) above 'unmerchantable' is to be construed in accordance with section 14(6) above.

The meanings of words or phrases might be given in separate interpretation sections and these are found as two main types.

1. *The section that lists several words/phrases and their intended meanings*, eg s14 of the Unfair Contract Terms Act 1977 gives the meanings of most of the key words and phrases used in Part I of the Act. An example of part of it shows the style of language and presentation used:

> '14. In this Part of this Act –
> 'business' includes a profession and ... [*etc*];
> 'goods' has the same meaning as in the Sale of Goods Act 1893;
> 'negligence' has the meaning given by section 1(1);
> 'notice' includes an announcement, ...'

Note the different types of assistance given. The terms 'goods' and 'negligence' are defined by reference to the meaning given to them in other sources, and 'business' and 'notice' are defined by listing the activities that they *include*.

This indicates that the list is not definitive and can be compared with another example that you will come across in your study of torts, namely, s11 of the Animals Act 1971 (1971, c22), which describes itself as a 'General interpretation' section. The generic titles given for animals in the Act (eg 'livestock' and 'poultry') are defined by giving long lists of the related animals that fall under these titles and the word that is used at the start of these lists is *'means'*, ie it does not say 'includes' in the way that 'business' and 'notice' do in the example above. Thus, 'livestock' *means* cattle, horses, asses, etc and does not include an animal that is not listed there. The definitive effect of lists like these can be reduced by more general words added at the end. For example the list for livestock could (but does not) give at the end the words 'and other animals' which would enable other non-specified animals to be included, provided that they were of a similar kind to those listed.

There are various types of this 'specific words followed by general words' style of description given in the statute law and they tend to become subject to lengthy interpretation.

2. *The section that deals with the meaning of an important concept*, eg the phrase 'dealing as a consumer' used in Part I of the Unfair Contract Terms Act 1977 is not included in the s14 list but is explained separately in s12 and is in three subsections, and subs(1) has two further paragraphs. Accordingly, it could not be dealt with appropriately in the s14 'list' style.

These 'concept' interpretation sections always tend to be lengthy and some are quite complicated. An example of this is found in the s29 explanation of the 'Meaning of trade disputes' of the Trade Union and Labour Relations Act 1974 (1974, c52).

Another example that you could look up is s15 of the Supply of Goods (Implied Terms) Act 1973 (1973, c13) which uses a mixture of the two types of sections, ie lists and explanation of key phrases. You will deal with this Act when you study the sale of goods law.

Some Acts use section 1 as a definition section, for example, s1 of the Torts (Interference with Goods) Act 1977 (1977, c32) defines what is meant by 'wrongful interference with goods' by listing the types of actions that fall under it, rather by actually providing a definition of it, whilst s2 abolishes one of the old forms of action. Section 1 of the Unfair Contract Terms Act 1977 gives the scope of Part I of the Act and starts with a definition of what negligence means for the purposes of the Act, which may seem rather suprising for an Act that by name appears to be about contract, but, as one quickly discovers, 'negligence' and 'reasonableness' are central to the provisions of the Act.

8.7 Identification of how the rules are to be applied

All Acts contain references throughout the provisions that identify the application of the rules or parts of them. This may be that they do apply or that do not apply, for example, an instruction that losses and liabilites stated in (1) do not apply to (2). The application of the provisions of other enactments to the Act are usually stated in separate sections. Most Acts do not provide all of the law on any one subject and there can be a relationship to rules found in Acts relating to other parts of the same broad subject matter, or, to Acts regulating completely different subject matter. In both instances the rule and legislative language is being re-used to provide a consistency of application throughout the statute law. There will also be statements, if relevant, of the application of this Act to other enactments. For an example of this see s3 of the Summer Time Act 1972 given above. Although the sections are not printed above, the Summer Time Act 1972 repeals various other enactments (s6) and applies to Northern Ireland (s4), and, subject to stated exceptions, to the Channel Islands and the Isle of Man (s5).

The use of the word 'shall' is important; it is an instruction to apply something. It is used throughout the statute law and in a variety of contexts. One example of its use is that given in s1(1) of the Equal Pay Act 1970 (1970, c41) which states:

> 'If the terms of a contract under which a woman is employed at an establishment in Great Britain do not include (directly or by reference to a collective agreement or otherwise) an equality clause they shall be deemed to include one.'

Other examples of the form of phrase in which it is used are: '... shall be taken into account ...' meaning that it must be; '... that term shall be of no effect ...' meaning that it will not have effect; 'All floors, steps, stairs, passages and gangways shall be of sound construction ...' meaning that they must be; and so and so forth.

8.8 The conditions of doubt

It can be seen from the preceding section that statute law can present the judiciary with some difficulties in determining the true scope and intention of the legislators. The need for so many aids to interpret statutes begs the question 'could legislation be better drafted, and if so, how?'. This section explores further the factors that give rise to the ambiguities inherent in written rules by reference to the fact that no written codes of law can be 'perfect' becuase the conditions under which they are written do not afford a perfect medium; these are 'the conditions of doubt'.

The essence of the problem, stated very simply, is that written rules should regulate conduct 'unambiguously and in advance'. The examples given in Chapter 6 illustrate that this is not always achieved. Indeed the aids for statutory interpretation exist because:

1. The written word is an imperfect medium; words can be ambiguous and/or may not easily convey all the subtleties of criteria that ought to be embodied within a rule.
2. The rule maker cannot anticipate all the contingencies that may arise to be determined under the rule.

One argument is that statutory interpretation is the best means of overcoming the difficulties of legislative drafting because the alternative remedy – improving the way in which they are drafted – is difficult to achieve. This argument is based on the debate over whether 'statutes are drafted by experts for experts', a question raised in Chapter 6 and there illustrated by reference to the factors identified by Bennion.

Those factors are directly related to the ones given in 1. and 2. above. If it is accepted that statute law cannot always achieve all of the objectives that it should (due to both verbal imperfections and the impossibility of foreseeing to what contingencies the rule will be applied in the future), then it follows that the best remedy is to draft those statutes using language that an 'expert' judiciary can interpret fairly and appropriately in the future. Therefore aids to statutory interpretation that interpret individual words or phrases as a whole, find the purpose of the rule, and mitigate any harshness or injustice that may arise, are an effective method of eliminating the faults in statutes.

The counter-argument to this is that statute law is supreme and will continue to operate for a long time into the future, so it ought to be drafted in such a way that it requires the minimum of interpretative aids. An analysis of the viability of this contention requires a definition of the technically perfect rule and a statement of criteria for legislative drafting.

Definition of a rule, for the purposes of law

'A rule is a general prescription guiding conduct or action.' The elements contained within this definition are as follows:

1. It is prescriptive, in other words, it is not a mere factual description of behaviour. It embodies notions of what ought or ought not, may or may not, can or cannot be permitted in relation to the behaviour described. This requires complex interpretation.
2. It is general; in other words, it does not govern a unique event. It should be applicable to a variety of different types of behaviour performed in various circumstances. It therefore generalises and simplifies.
3. It guides behaviour by promoting or preventing specific conduct, eg some rules prohibit, some confer powers, some specify conditions to be satisfied.

In the search for the 'perfect' rule a model of such a rule is needed.

The 'technically perfect' rule

The 'technically perfect' rule should contain:

1. a single clear and acceptable aim, and
2. a scope that is confined to the purpose of the rule,

and should be drafted to be:

1. so clearly and precisely expressed that it is certain to achieve its purpose without undesirable side-effects, with
2. no room for doubt about its application in any possible case, and
3. no loopholes for those who might wish to escape its effects.

To achieve this model the 'perfect' rule maker would need to know:

1. all the possible combinations and permutations of circumstances that might fall within the scope of the rule;
2. the details of the situation that he or she is trying to influence;
3. the likely effects the rule(s) will have on the situation; and
4. the way in which the situation is likely to develop so that the rule can continue to influence behaviour.

Obviously legislators cannot always know all of these things, and H L A Hart in *The Concept of Law* describes this as being the 'handicap of the human rule maker'. Greatly simplified, his identification of these handicaps can be summarised as:

1. relative ignorance of fact: the rule maker cannot anticipate all the possible combinations of circumstances to which the rules might be applicable; and
2. relative indeterminacy of aim: the rule maker cannot anticipate all the contingencies that might arise to be determined.

In conclusion, the statement of criteria for a 'perfectly' drafted set of rules is that they:

1. identify the mischief(s) requiring regulation;
2. define the 'scope' of the rule (the fact-situations it governs);
3. state the intention or purpose of the rule; and
4. influence certain kinds of behaviour in a particular way.

The wording and the layout are important because they must clarify:

1. the problem that the rule maker intends to solve;
2. the division of those problems into their categories of regulation;
3. how any one rule is to be interpreted in the light of any other rule(s);
4. the criteria for determining what conduct is or is not acceptable under any rule(s).

Finally, the overriding criterion that the Act as a whole must recognise is that its rules are to be interpreted by persons other than those who wrote them. Therefore, the 'perfect' Act should leave no doubt in the mind of the interpreter as to the true extent of the intended scope and purpose of the rules, and should include clear indications of the following factors:

1. circumstances that ought not to be determined under the rule;

2. the leeway that may be exercised to mitigate an unduly harsh or unjust result caused by the literal application of the provisions of the Act.

8.9 Some of the drafting techniques used in the Unfair Contract Terms Act 1977

Despite its title, this Act applies to the purported exclusion of tortious as well as contractual liability. Furthermore, its effect is not restricted to terms expressly inserted into bilateral agreements; implied terms and the unilateral exclusion of liability by means of a notice are also provided for. The Act therefore has a considerable complexity of purpose, which in part contains concepts difficult to reduce to precise rules. In particular, those rules which involve the tortious obligation to exercise reasonable care or skill required careful drafting.

To overcome this, the Act does not describe exclusions that could be determined as either fair or unfair, but instead includes the following provisions:

1. The 'reasonableness' test (s11) for use with certain sections: a clause must be a

   'fair and reasonable one to be included having regard to the circumstances which were, or ought reasonably to have been, known to or in the contemplation of the parties when the contract was made'.

2. Guidelines for the application of the reasonableness test (Schedule 2) to some of those sections: eg the relative strength of the bargaining position of the parties; inducements given to agree to the term; ability to contract elsewhere, etc.

The intended application of both the s11 test and the Schedule 2 guidelines is clearly indicated, but the wording used for some aspects gives an overall presumption that the test for reasonableness and the guidelines for that test are relevant, at the discretion of the court, to other provisions within the Act. For example, the Schedule 2 guidelines state that they are the matters to be considered 'in particular' for the purposes of named sections. This is a clear indication that they are not 'exclusive' to those sections.

Section 11(2) refers the determination of the provisions contained within ss6 and 7 to the guidelines given in Schedule 2 but, by its wording, leaves the determination of these guidelines to the discretion of the court:

'Regard shall be had in particular to the matters specified in Schedule 2 of this Act; but this subsection does not prevent the court or arbitrator from holding, in accordance with any rule of law, that a term which purports to exclude or restrict any relevant liability is not a term of the contract.'

Two examples of how the courts have been able to use the reasonableness test and Schedule 2 guidelines are to be found in the following cases:

In *Levison* v *Patent Steam Carpet Cleaning Co Ltd* [1978] QB 69; [1977] 3 All ER 498, the defendants, who were specialist carpet cleaners, had lost a valuable Chinese carpet belonging to the plaintiff and relied on a clause which the plaintiff had not read limiting their liability to £40. It was held that the plaintiff had reasonably relied on the defendant's skill and expertise; the plaintiff could not easily contract elsewhere for such specialist cleaning as this, and the clause was not negotiated nor one which the plaintiff would reasonably suppose was operating in a contract of this nature. Denning LJ united the themes of the Act when he said:

> 'If a party uses his superior power to impose an exemption ... on the weaker party, he will not be allowed to rely on it if he has himself been guilty of a breach going to the root of the contract.'

In *Woodman* v *Photo Trade Processing Ltd* [1981] (unreported) a film, being the only pictures of a wedding, was lost by the defendants, who relied on the usual trade clause limiting liability to replacement of a film only. The defendants' argument that the plaintiff benefited from the clause because it enabled them to run a cheap mass-production technique failed. On a construction of s11 and Schedule 2, the clause was unreasonable because:

1. The entire industry used this clause, so the plaintiff had no real alternative but to entrust his film to a firm using the clause
2. The plaintiff had chosen the defendants in reliance on their known skill and expertise.

Where the provisions are not intended to be subject to an 'open' interpretation, the Act employs a more rigid structure for the provisions and definitions. For example, s12 gives the criteria for determining whether a person 'deals as a consumer'. The Act is intended to relate only to business liability, with an application to private consumers only in so far as the clause is connected to a 'business party', so the classification of those persons who 'deal as a consumer' is important if the Act is to be properly interpreted. Section 12 achieves this by breaking down the subject matter as follows:

1. The provision is in three clear sub-sections.
2. Sub-section (1) divides again into three parts to identify clearly what 'dealing as a consumer' entails by specifying who the 'consumer' can be, who the 'other party' must be, and what 'type of contract' it must be, as follows:

   a) He neither makes the contract in the course of a business nor holds himself out as doing so.
   b) The other party makes the contract in the courts of a business; and
   c) '... for sale of goods or hire purchase ... the goods ... are of a type ordinarily supplied for private use or consumption.'

Section 12 is intended to be a precise rule and indicates in its style of drafting that it is not open to a subsequent interpretation which would allow classes of person not identified to be included.

The layout of the Act is another indication of how the legislators intended the provisions to be interpreted and applied. The subject matter is divided into three parts, and within those parts there are sections identifying:

1. the scope of that part;
2. the interpretation of terminology used;
3. clarification of the effect of these rules on other legislation.

Two schedules give further guidelines:

1. Schedule 1 gives detail on the scope of ss2–4.
2. Schedule 2 gives the guidelines for the application of the s11 reasonableness test.

Within each part, the subject matter is further divided into categories of regulation under separate sections; for example s2 regulates negligence liability, s3 regulates liability in contract and s6 regulates sale and hire purchase.

The identification of the effect of a rule on other statutory provisions is given where it relates. For example, the s11 'reasonableness test' expressly includes s3 of the Misrepresentation Act 1967. The use of s11, with its guidelines for application in Schedule 2, is a technique that is especially suitable for the already discretionary nature of the existing common law. Other areas of the law require similar discretionary interpretation. For example, the provisions of the road traffic legislation prohibit vehicles from travelling through a red stop light at a traffic light. The proper construction of the statutory provisions is that no vehicle is permitted, under any circumstances, to contravene this red stop light. There is no express exemption or exclusion for, say, a fire brigade engine answering an emergency call, nor is any discretionary interpretation of this rule afforded by any other part of this or any other statute law.

The problem is that of drafting provisions that exclude persons and activities such as the emergency services on duty, but which will not bring unwanted categories of exemption into the new rule. A possible solution is to use a technique similar to the s11 reasonableness test supported by guidelines like those in Schedule 2.

TASK

Without reference to the actual provisions contained within the Road Traffic Acts, draft three types of statutory rule: first, one which would automatically prohibit the contravention of the red stop light in all cases except those identified as exempt, and secondly, the reverse of this, a rule that indicates only when a contravention of the red stop light will be unlawful. To do this:

1. Identify as many examples as you can of when 'a vehicle' might contravene a red stop light.
2. Categorise these examples into those that might be appropriate for exclusion or exemption from the rule, and those that ought not to be included.
3. Consider what words you would use to define separate classes of person or behaviour falling within the categories you identified in item 2.

Critically examine the two rules you have written to identify all the harsh or undesirable outcomes that may arise from their interpretation.

Now consider how the s11 and Schedule 2 techniques of the Unfair Contract Terms Act 1977 could be adopted to ensure that the courts use an application of the rules and exemptions which reflect the discretionary criteria required for cases involving contravention of the red stop light. Then, thirdly, draft a section for a Road Traffic Act and a schedule of guidelines for its application.

8.10 Writing rules unambiguously and in advance

The task contained in section 8.9 above is directly concerned with the problem of writing a rule with a scope that is wide enough to meet the purpose of the rule, but not so wide that it covers circumstances not intended to fall within the rule.

However, as was noted in section 8.8 above, another facet of a good rule is that it should regulate conduct 'unambiguously and in advance'. This means that the scope and purpose of the rule need to be definite rather than indefinite. The rules for games are good examples of definite rules. The conduct that is to be guided is easily identifiable, and the various circumstances that may arise are usually predictable.

TASK 1

Draw up a set of rules for a simple game that you already know, eg Noughts and Crosses or a Patience card game. Use these rules to the letter to play the game and note any ambiguities that arise in interpreting how each rule is to be applied. Consider how the rule(s) could be better drafted to eliminate these ambiguities.

Of course not all human conduct is so easy to predict, which makes the task of writing suitable laws 'in advance' of the event a much more complex task. Indeed, not all games are so easy to regulate unambiguously and in advance; the games of chess and golf, for instance, have lengthy and complex rules which can become matters of debate and discretionary application. So when legislation is being drafted, it is not simply a case of predicting all the types of conduct and legislating for these. The rule maker has to limit the scope and purpose of the rule(s) by carefully chosen words that will serve to stop the rule being used for any conduct which it is not intended to regulate. Herein lies the real art of written law making; the words chosen can produce very different provisions, remedies and sanctions.

TASK 2

Consider the following two sets of rules regulating the use of a private car park. In each set the rule maker intends to regulate the use of the car park in a specific way, and this purpose would have to be identified and used as the benchmark for any future interpretation of the application of that rule.

Set 1

'This is a private car park and may only be used by persons holding permits. Parked vehicles which do not display valid parking permits may be wheel-clamped. The removal of a wheel-clamp requires a written application to the site manager's office and the payment of a £30 penalty. Unauthorised vehicles left for longer than 48 hours will be removed from the car park and if left unclaimed for a period of seven days thereafter will be disposed of at the discretion of the site-manager.'

Set 2

'This car park may only be used by persons holding valid parking permits. All vehicles must be parked in the designated parking bays and are left at their owners' risk.

Warning: wheel-clamping is used in this car park. The removal of a wheel-clamp is subject to the payment of a £30 penalty.'

Identify the purpose or purposes of each set of rules. Consider how each set of rules can be interpreted so as to apply to the following incident:

X parks his car, which does display a valid parking permit, on the pavement, so that it obstructs the pedestrian access to the building. The site manager wheel-clamps the vehicle. X refuses to pay the £30 penalty.

Identify other problems that might arise in the use of the car park which are not covered by a literal interpretation of either rule. Write a new rule or set of rules that would regulate 'unambiguously and in advance' all the types of usage of the car park that you have identified.

8.11 Dealing with complex rules – an example

Many legal rules are very complicated, involving exceptions, qualifications, provisos and so on. At a first reading the rule may leave a doubt about the relationship between its various parts. In order to understand it we have to break it down into its constituent parts – we examine its 'structure'.

Presented with s20(1) of the Powers of Criminal Courts Act 1973, for instance, we are aware of a number of negatives. The structure of the rule obscures an immediate understanding of what the rule covers. Section 20(1) reads:

'No court shall pass a sentence of imprisonment on a person of or over twenty-one years of age on whom such sentence has not previously been passed by a court in any part of the United Kingdom unless the court is of the opinion that no other method of dealing with him is appropriate ...'

An aid to understanding such a rule is to present it in a schematic form. We can rewrite s20(1) in such a way:

No court shall pass a
sentence of imprisonment
on a person ...

> ... of or over twenty-one years of age on
> whom such a sentence has not previously
> been passed by a court of the United
> Kingdom ...

> > ... unless the court is of the opinion
> > that no other method of dealing with
> > him is appropriate

This separates the conditions under which the provision operates; it makes a form of simple checklist, and as such it provides some help with the tasks of:

1. identifying the purpose of the rule; and
2. checking whether the rule applies to the problem in hand.

However, it is of limited assistance in determining whether you are actually applying the rule correctly to the problem. In other words, it is still a complex structure.

The rule can be broken down further into a simple set of instructions for solving the problem by employing the algorithm. An algorithm is a diagrammatic presentation of a rule (or rules) in the form of a structured series of questions with answers providing instructions for the total, or partial, resolution of the problem (partial resolution is when more questions need to be answered).

Section 20(1) in algorithmic form is:

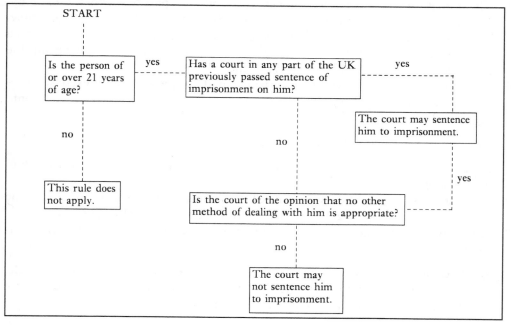

This is a sequence of questions to which the answer is either 'yes' or 'no', each answer automatically taking the reader to the next question relevant to his or her case. At any point in the sequence the reader may find that the rule does not apply, or that he or she has reached a conclusion for his or her case. Indeed, if the algorithm has been constructed properly it should not be possible to proceed any further than that conclusion. Therefore, he or she does not need to read the whole rule but only those parts which apply to his or her case. The other parts of the rule, which might be a source of confusion to him or her, are eliminated from his or her sequence of answers. There are no choices: the algorithm eliminates these. The sequence proceeds on a 'yes-no' basis – only one option can apply to the case.

In summary, the basic rules for algorithm construction are as follows:

1. To each question there can only be one 'yes' and one 'no'. Each answer takes the reader automatically to the next relevant question. Only one question can follow after each answer – in other words, there is no choice as to the next question.
2. Therefore there can only be one question following each answer.
3. When an answer leads to a conclusion (an outcome), that part of the algorithm is complete. No more questions need or can be asked.

The advantages of the algorithm are:

1. It presents rules in a visibly more comprehensible form than conventional prose.
2. Its clarity can help the reader to establish quickly whether the provisions of the rule applies to his or her case.
3. The structure eliminates the problem of, and the possible errors caused by, having to understand the whole provision when only a part of it is applicable. The construction of an algorithm is an intellectual discipline – anyone who presents a rule in this way must first be in a position to understand the interrelationship of the different parts of the rule.
4. It is adaptable. It is possible to move from simple to more difficult exercises.
5. It is very useful for organising large quantities of data or other material into manageable form.

The disadvantages of the algorithm are:

1. It can only be used for a well-defined problem because it is a precise set of instructions.
2. It is therefore a simplified statement of the requisites of the law involved – the reader would have to obtain the detail by reading the textbooks, cases etc.
3. It merely arranges the parts of the rule into a schematic form and therefore has the following drawbacks:

    a) It cannot resolve all doubts that may arise as to the interpretation of a rule; doubts about the interpretation of words, or as to the rule's policy, are entirely omitted from the question/answer sequence.

b) It cannot provide a complete answer to any problem. Any one rule is likely to be just a part of a set of rules that need to be applied to the problem. The algorithm isolates one section and constructs a simple set of questions to work through that rule alone. In application to the problem, it would have to be used with regard to a much wider range of provisions that also apply to the problem.

c) It can become cumbersome, either when applied to lengthy rules or when the interpreter is seeking to provide a comprehensive statement of a rule. With the latter he or she would have to account for the wider range of provisions that might also affect the solution to the problem. These would have to be referred to either in the text or in some other way.

d) It can take a long time to construct.

e) Its utility diminishes as one becomes familiar with the particular rule.

8.12 Dealing with complex rules – theory into practice

The following sections are from the Animals Act 1971 and are the statutory provisions for the killing or injuring of dogs that have worried, or are about to worry, livestock. They illustrate a typical method of referring the reader from one section to another within the Act to piece together the liability or rights given by the statute. In this example the main provision is found in s9; s9(2)(b) refers to s5(4), which in turn refers to s3 of the Act.

First, read the three extracts from the statutory provision to familiarise yourself with its content and to identify the extent to which the regulation is clear upon first reading.

'9. Killing of or injury to dogs worrying livestock.

(1) In any civil proceedings against a person (in this section referred to as the defendant) for killing or causing injury to a dog it shall be a defence to prove –

(a) that the defendant acted for the protection of any livestock and was a person entitled to act for the protection of that livestock; and

(b) that within forty-eight hours of the killing or injury notice thereof was given by the defendant to the officer in charge of a police station.

(2) For the purposes of this section a person is entitled to act for the protection of any livestock if, and only if –

(a) the livestock or the land on which it is belongs to him or to any person under whose express authority he is acting; and

(b) the circumstances are not such that liability for killing or causing injury to the livestock would be excluded by section 5(4) of this Act.

(3) Subject to subsection (4) of this section, a person killing or causing injury to a dog shall be deemed for the purposes of this section to act for the protection of any livestock if, and only if, either –

(a) the dog is worrying or is about to worry the livestock and there are no other reasonable means of ending or preventing the worrying; or

(b) the dog has been worrying livestock, has not left the vicinity and is not under the control of any person and there are no practicable means of ascertaining to whom it belongs.

(4) For the purposes of this section the condition stated in either of the paragraphs of the preceding subsection shall be deemed to have been satisfied if the defendant believed that it was satisfied and had reasonable ground for that belief.

(5) For the purposes of this section –

(a) an animal belongs to any person if he owns it or has it in his possession; and

(b) land belongs to any person if he is the occupier thereof.

5. Exceptions from liability under sections 2 to 4.
...

(4) A person is not liable under section 3 of this Act if the livestock was killed or injured on land on to which it had strayed and either the dog belonged to the occupier or its presence on the land was authorised by the occupier.

3. Liability for injury done by dogs to livestock.

Where a dog causes damage by killing or injuring livestock, any person who is a keeper of the dog is liable for the damage except as otherwise provided by this Act.'

To make the rule clearer, break down s9 (incorporating s5(4) and s3) into its constituent parts in the same way as shown above (p258–259) for s20(1) Powers of the Criminal Courts Act 1973 (*Note*: you may need more than the three constituent parts shown for that example). Prepare this breakdown of material for the construction of an algorithm by reducing each constituent part to a checklist of information. Now construct an algorithm suitable for the general purpose use of the provisions and check whether it works by applying to it the problem given below.

Farmer Giles grazes his sheep on land which he rents from Farmer Smart. It is adjacent to a camp site which is also owned and run by Smart. The Careless family are staying at this camp site and they keep their Alsatian dog, Rover, tied up outside the tent. The dog slips its leash on two occasions, and on one of these has to be chased from among Giles's sheep by the shepherd, George. Rover then escapes for a third time and again starts to chase Giles's sheep. George attempts to catch Rover, but the dog growls and snarls at him so ferociously that he gives up the attempt. Smart hears the commotion and comes to George's assistance, bringing a rifle which he shoots into the air to scare Rover away. However, Rover instead becomes uncontrollable and chases the badly frightened sheep, whereupon Smart aims the rifle directly at the dog and shoots it dead.

9

Alternative Methods of Resolving Disputes

9.1 Introduction

9.2 Tribunals

9.3 Arbitration

9.4 Conciliation and mediation

9.5 Exercise

9.1 Introduction

There are many alternatives to pursuing a matter through the court system in order to bring a dispute to a resolution. One such way is for the parties to settle the matter between themselves, without recourse to a third party. In many cases, however, this is not possible, and so other methods of dispute resolution may be used. Examples include mediation or conciliation in family disputes, taking matters before tribunals or referring disputes to an arbitrator. Other forms include the involvement of the Advisory Conciliation and Arbitration Service (ACAS) in industrial disputes, the work of the Equal Opportunities Commission and the Commission for Racial Equality, the work of ombudsmen in banking and insurance disputes, the referral of commercial disputes to arbitration and the work of trade associations in consumer disputes, eg the Association of British Travel Agents (ABTA).

These alternative methods of dispute resolution are regarded by many as the way forward in the future, especially as the costs of litigation continue to rise and the time taken to bring a matter to trial also continues to increase.

9.2 Tribunals

The word 'tribunal' is defined by the *Oxford English Dictionary* as a 'judgment seat ... a court of justice; a judicial assembly'. It is thus possible, if confusing, for an ordinary court of law to be referred to as a tribunal. The word now tends to be used in a different context from the normal court system to mean a panel to resolve disputes between, for example, a citizen and an officer of a government agency, or between individuals in an area of law in which the government has legislated the conduct of their relations. These tribunals may be conveniently called 'administrative tribunals'.

Tribunals exist alongside the courts in the English legal system for a number of reasons: first, in order to resolve disputes between private citizens and a central government department, eg in social security benefit claims; secondly, in order to deal with disputes requiring the application of special knowledge or expertise, eg the assessment of compensation following a compulsory purchase order; thirdly, in order to deal with disputes which are considered unsuitable for hearing by the courts, eg the fixing of a 'fair rent' for the benefit of a tenant; fourthly, sometimes to deal with disputes between two private citizens, eg matters between employer and employee.

Tribunals ease the congestion in the ordinary courts of law by dealing with the kinds of dispute which would otherwise have to be taken to court. Although their workload far exceeds that of the courts, tribunals provide a more speedy and efficient way of dealing with such cases.

Tribunals are of statutory origin, and the appointment of the members of a tribunal usually falls to the minister of the central government department responsible for the service to which the tribunal's jurisdiction relates.

Usually there are no appeals from tribunals on questions of fact. Appeals on points of law may go to the High Court under s13 of the Tribunals and Inquiries Act 1971. Applications for judicial review may go to the Queen's Bench divisional court.

Tribunals are generally governed by the Tribunals and Inquiries Act 1992 and by the basic characteristics of openness, fairness and impartiality. By virtue of the Franks Report of 1957 tribunals have proliferated, and it is generally thought not only that their expertise and expedited process make them invaluable to the already overburdened courts but also that they perform a useful function in themselves. Unfortunately legal aid is not often available in tribunals, but there is more opportunity for representation of a party by a non-lawyer, and many individuals have the benefit of advice and assistance from, for example, trade unions.

Domestic tribunals

These have been set up by private or professional bodies in order to resolve disputes between their own members, or to exercise a disciplinary role over them. The jurisdiction of such non-statutory tribunals is derived from contract; in other words, employees submit to the jurisdiction of a particular tribunal by agreeing to be bound by a contractual clause to that effect. There is no appeal as such from domestic tribunals to a court, although the High Court exercises a supervisory jurisdiction and may intervene to uphold the principles of natural justice.

Some domestic tribunals exist on a statutory basis, eg the Solicitors' Disciplinary Tribunal established by the Solicitors Act 1974, and so there are rights of appeal to the courts.

Inquiries

When matters of great public significance arise, Parliament will resolve to establish a tribunal of inquiry to investigate the matter. The Secretary of State may then set up a tribunal which will have powers to call witnesses, order discovery of documents and require evidence to be given on oath.

Composition of tribunals

Every tribunal varies in terms of composition, but generally speaking tribunals have a chairman and a number of wingmen.

The role of the chairman is to ensure that proceedings are conducted with fairness to all parties, and to find a balance between formality and informality. Clearly, a tribunal does not operate with the same formalities as a courtroom (for example, the rules of evidence are relaxed in most cases), but some formality must be observed in order to provide a suitable forum for the consideration of the issue in hand. The chairman will ensure that the parties understand the issues involved, especially when they are not otherwise represented. He will also ensure that each party has an adequate opportunity to present its case and that both are given a fair hearing (ie that the rules of natural justice are observed).

The wingmen who sit as part of a tribunal are usually people with special skills or expertise in the subject matter which comes before the tribunal. For example, in the Industrial Tribunal the wingmen will be, inter alia, employers' representatives, employees' representatives and people with a background in industry or trade unions.

Similarities between courts and tribunals

In brief, these are as follows:

1. Both courts and tribunals are usually established by statute.
2. Both interpret laws made by or under statute in addition to having their own case law.
3. Both are chaired by people appointed by the Lord Chancellor.

Differences between courts and tribunals

These are set out below:

1. The tribunal bench has a wider range of skills than a court-room bench.
2. The decision makers in a tribunal are lawyers, laymen or a combination of both. Generally speaking, in a court room, the decision maker is professionally qualified, with the exception of the magistrates' court where lay people sit on the bench.
3. The decision makers in tribunals have special skills and expertise in relation to the issue under consideration; this may not be so in a court.

4. Tribunals are said to be cheaper, speedier (meeting by appointment) and more efficient to utilise than the courts. However, some tribunals may be as expensive as a court (eg the Lands Tribunal).
5. Civil courts tend to charge court fees, whereas most tribunals do not.
6. Civil courts generally operate the rule that the loser pays the winner's costs. In tribunals, this rule does not operate.
7. Tribunals are far more informal than courts; for example, barristers representing clients will not wear wigs and gowns as they would in a court room. There is a clear attempt to make people feel at ease in a tribunal, although the presence of legal representatives and a legally qualified chairman may hinder this.
8. There are more restricted rights of appeal from tribunals. In some cases appeals must go to the minister concerned, eg appeals from tribunals under the National Health Service. In other cases they will go to a special commissioner, eg appeals from the Social Security Appeals Tribunals.
9. The work load of tribunals far exceeds that of the courts. The Royal Commission on Legal Services concluded that in 1978 the number of cases heard by tribunals was six times the number of civil cases heard by the High Court and county courts (Cmnd 7648, 1979, para 15.1 and Tables 2.1 and 2.2).
10. Generally tribunals tend to deal with smaller cases than the courts. Some, however, do deal with substantial amounts of money (eg the Industrial Tribunal).
11. The functions of a tribunal are regarded by some as administrative rather than judicial.

Problems with the tribunal system

1. Although legal representation is permitted in most tribunals, it is not permitted in a small number.
2. Except for tribunals such as the Lands Tribunal and the Common Commissioners, legal aid is not available to the parties, although green form advice and assistance may be available.
3. Some tribunals decide disputes between a minister and a citizen, even though the same minister appointed the members of the tribunal. Therefore it is difficult to create the appearance of impartiality.
4. Usually, written reasons for a tribunal decision are available, but there are a few tribunals where this is not so. Lack of written reasons may make it difficult for a party to appeal against a decision.
5. In some cases there is no right of appeal from a tribunal, although the right to judicial review remains unaffected.

The Council on Tribunals

The Council consists of 16 part-time members, including the Chairman of the Council. It was set up by the Tribunals and Inquiries Act 1958 and now operates under the Tribunals and Inquiries Act 1992. The members of the Council include senior lawyers, legal and non-legal academics, magistrates, accountants, representatives of trades unions and civil servants. The role of the Council is to advise on the procedural rules relating to tribunals, and on the procedural rules made by the Lord Chancellor in connection with statutory inquiries. The Council also takes an interest in many features of tribunals, for example, delays, the training of tribunal members and the role of clerks. The Council is required to make an Annual Report to the Lord Chancellor and the Lord Advocate, which usually deals with any matters that have arisen and are a cause for concern, as well as the main consultations and business covered in the preceding year.

The Industrial Tribunal

The Industrial Tribunal (IT) was first established by the Industrial Training Act 1964, and since then its jurisdiction has been extended considerably to include complaints for unfair dismissal, equal pay, unlawful sex or race discrimination, maternity pay, unlawful deduction of wages and so on. No jurisdiction lies in relation to common law claims arising out of breaches of contract of employment, nor over tortious claims following accidents at work.

The IT sits at over 50 centres and is administered by 16 regional offices under the control of the Central Office of Industrial Tribunals. Each individual IT has a legally qualified chairman who sits with two other members representing the interests of employers and employees. The chairman must have a seven-year qualification under s71 of the Courts and Legal Services Act 1990. Lay members are selected from panels appointed by the Secretary of State for Employment. An applicant to the IT may be represented by a solicitor, barrister, trade union representative or any person whom he or she desires as a representative. Awards of costs will not be made unless the person has acted frivolously or vexatiously. Appeals from the tribunal lie either to the Employment Appeal Tribunal or to the Queen's Bench Division.

The Employment Appeal Tribunal

The Employment Appeal Tribunal (EAT) was established by the Employment Protection Act 1975. At that time the trades unions did not like the label 'court', as they were reacting against the ill-fated National Industrial Relations Court (NIRC), and therefore it was decided that the new court was to be known as a 'tribunal'. Despite its name, the EAT is a superior court of record; in other words, permanent records of proceedings are kept. The EAT has power to punish for contempt of court and is not subject to the supervisory jurisdiction of the Queen's Bench Division of the High Court.

The personnel of the EAT are High Court and Court of Appeal judges (nominated by the Lord Chancellor) who sit with two or four lay wingmen. These are employers' or employees' representatives who have special expertise, and there are no independent lay members. The judge will act as chairman. The decision of the EAT is by a majority, and the lay members can outvote the judge even on points of law.

The workload of the EAT is mostly comprised of appeals from the Industrial Tribunal, eg on matters of redundancy, unfair dismissal or equal pay. It has a very limited original jurisdiction, for example in cases where compensation is being sought by a person who has been unreasonably excluded or expelled from membership of a trade union.

Decisions of the EAT are final on any question of fact. On questions of law, appeals will go to the Court of Appeal, with leave. Further appeals go to the House of Lords, with leave.

The procedure adopted in the EAT is largely quick, cheap and informal. There is no rigid adherence to the strict rules of evidence. The EAT can order witnesses to attend, and also order the discovery of documents. The usual rule for costs in civil proceedings (loser pays winner's costs) does not operate, and each party usually bears his or her own costs. The EAT will order a person's costs to be paid by his or her opponent when, for example, it deems that proceedings have been vexatious or unwarranted.

Social Security Tribunals

These tribunals were established to determine questions arising from the administration of benefits available under the social security legislation. Examples of these benefits include unemployment benefit, invalidity benefit, widows' benefit, income support etc. Various tribunal jurisdictions have been amalgamated, and the tribunals have now been integrated within the court system. Appeals against the decisions of adjudication officers lie to the Social Security Appeal Tribunal, which cosists of a chairman and two other members. Appeals from the Social Security Appeals Tribunal lie to the Social Security Commissioners, from whom there is a right of appeal on a point of law to the Court of Appeal, with the leave of either the Court of Appeal or the Commissioner.

In the Social Security Appeals Tribunal the applicant is usually appealing against the decision of an adjudication officer who is an employee of the Department of Social Security. The officer may have decided that the applicant is not entitled to unemployment benefit, and the applicant is informed with the adjudication officer's decision that there is a right of appeal. This is conducted by the independent tribunal, usually composed of three persons, of whom the chairman has a five-year general qualification within s71 of the Courts and Legal Services Act 1990.

Although the location and general appearance of the tribunal may make it seem as if it is an offshoot of the civil service department from which the appeal is being made, it is stressed to the appellant that the tribunal is, in fact, totally independent. Appeals from the decisions of immigration officers would be in the same category of a tribunal which deals with matters where the individual is challenging the decision of the state.

The Lands Tribunal

The Lands Tribunal was formed in 1949 to determine disputes concerning the assessment of compensation following the compulsory acquisition of land. It consists of a president, someone who has held a judicial office or a barrister of at least seven years' standing, together with a number of members who are barristers or solicitors of seven years' standing and a number of persons who have experience in land valuation (eg qualified surveyors). The jurisdiction of the tribunal can be exercised by any one or more of its members as selected by the president. The permanent offices of the tribunal are in London, although it may sit in the provinces.

The tribunal also has jurisdiction to determine disputes as to the valuation of land for taxation, and it hears appeals from local valuation courts. It deals with disputed assessments of land and building values for rating purposes, hears appeals from leasehold validation tribunals and has a discretionary power to vary, modify or discharge restrictive covenants under s84 of the Law of Property Act 1925. Appeals lie to the Court of Appeal by way of case stated.

9.3 Arbitration

Arbitration is the referral of a dispute to a third party for determination and is one of the oldest forms of settling disputes in the English legal system. Since medieval times courts have recognised agreements which seek to resolve disputes in this way. Nowadays they continue to recognise agreements of this nature, and the present law in relation to arbitration is contained in the Arbitration Act 1950 (as amended).

Generally speaking, arbitration is a popular alternative to a court action. This is due to a variety of reasons, such as the fact that proceedings are held in private and are of an informal nature. The arbitrators and assessors are people with expert skills and special knowledge of the industry or trade concerned. In addition, the cost of arbitration will generally be less than the cost of a court case, although this is not necessarily true in the case of large commercial disputes. The jurisdiction of arbitrators usually arises out of contracts, but some statutes provide for disputes to be referred to arbitration. Arbitration is used widely in shipping, commerce and the building and engineering professions.

The parties may nominate any person to act as arbitrator, and it is not uncommon to request a member of the Bar to act in this way. Judges of the Commercial Court may act as sole arbitrators if the criteria set out in s4 of the Administration of Justice Act 1970 are satisfied. The Arbitration Act 1950 by s10 gives the High Court various powers to appoint arbitrators in default of appointment by the parties. The governing statute must be decided according to the ordinary rules of English law (unless otherwise provided). The contract provides how the arbitrator is to be appointed, and a common provision is that if the parties cannot agree on an arbitrator then some body or person such as the president of the Law Society shall appoint an arbitrator. In building disputes the person nominated to appoint the arbitrator, in the event of there being no agreement between the parties, is often the President of the Royal Institute of British Architects. As to the filling of vacancies for arbitrators, perhaps by the High Court, see s10 of the Arbitration Act 1950 as amended by s101 of the Courts and Legal Services Act 1990. For arbitration by an official referee, see now s11 of the Arbitration Act 1950 as substituted by s99 of the Courts and Legal Services Act 1990.

In order for a dispute to be referred to arbitration, there must be an agreement to this effect, which may be expressly set out in the original contract between the parties, or reached once the dispute has arisen and proceedings become likely. In both cases, clearly the parties have agreed to waive their right to go to court.

Even if a contractual clause exists it is still open to the parties to go to court if they agree to waive the arbitration clause. However, if one party goes to court without an agreement to waive the arbitration clause then the other party can apply to the court for the proceedings to be stayed (s4(1) Arbitration Act 1950). This right will be lost if the party who wishes to insist on arbitration takes any step in the action (eg files a defence). Any provision in a contract which purports to oust the jurisdiction of the courts is void, but it is usual for a contract (or sometimes a lease) to provide that a dispute be referred first to arbitration. If one party commences court proceedings without arbitration the other may, if he has taken no step in those proceedings, apply to the court to stay the proceedings until after arbitration, and this order is usually granted. On the other hand, if all parties agree, the High Court may exercise the arbitrator's powers: see s43A of the Supreme Court Act 1981 as inserted by s100 of the Courts and Legal Services Act 1990.

Where a contract containing an arbitration clause provides for some preliminary step (eg reference to a panel of experts for settlement) before there is an arbitration, the fact that the preliminary step has not been taken does not prevent the court from ordering a stay under s1 of the Arbitration Act 1975 of any action brought by a party to the contract: *Channel Tunnel Group Ltd* v *Balfour Beatty Construction Ltd* [1992] 2 All ER 609.

The procedure in relation to arbitration is governed by the Arbitration Acts 1950 and 1979. Issues arising are dealt with according to the ordinary rules of English law, and the usual judicial procedures will apply, including the rules of evidence, although these may be disposed of by agreement. The arbitrator has the power to question witnesses, and to order discovery of documents, pleadings and so on. An arbitrator may not, however, dismiss a case for want of prosecution (*Bremer* v *South India Shipping Corp* [1981] AC 909).

The decision of the arbitrator is known as an award, and this deals with all of the issues on which the reference is made. The award may contain provision for the payment of money, costs, or an order for specific performance (except for a contract relating to land). The award may, with leave of the High Court, be enforced in the same way as a judgment or order of the High Court.

The Arbitration Act 1979 s1(2) provides for an appeal to a judge of the Commercial Court within 21 days on any question of law arising out of an award made where all the parties agree, or the court gives leave. In addition, there is an appeal from the High Court to the Court of Appeal in certain circumstances, but only with leave of the High Court and if the High Court certifies that there is a question of law of general public importance at issue or a question which for some other special reason should be considered by the Court of Appeal (Arbitration Act 1979 s1(7)).

What are the advantages of arbitration?

The following, inter alia, are advantages of using arbitration:

1. It is said that arbitration is less expensive than going to court even though the arbitrator must be paid a fee. In practice, of course, cost is related to the time spent on the matter by legal advisers, participants and so on, so it may be that arbitration is cheaper due to a reduction in the total time required for the hearing of the case compared with court proceedings. It may also be cheaper due to lack of court fees and the avoidance of solicitors' and barristers' fees.
2. The proceedings are held in private and are less formal and complicated than court proceedings.
3. The arbitration will take place at a fixed time and place, and therefore waiting times (which can be considerable if a case is in the court list) will be kept to a minimum.
4. The arbitrator is able to use his or her personal knowledge and experience in dealing with proceedings. He or she will already be familiar with the practice of a particular profession, its trade customs, technical terms and so on, and this will speed up the proceedings. By contrast, a judge may not be familiar with these.
5. The decision of the arbitrator is usually given immediately, whereas the judgment of a court may be reserved.

Disadvantages of arbitration

1. Parties may be forced to go to arbitration against their wishes, if they are bound by an arbitration clause.
2. It may be that having a professional to decide the dispute (eg a judge) is more desirable, especially in cases where there is a great body of evidence or where evidence is disputed.
3. Legal aid is not available to any party for arbitration proceedings. This is a great problem, especially for parties who would otherwise be eligible for civil legal aid.
4. Questions of law or appeals against arbitration awards can only be settled by an

appeal to a court. The court will not look into questions of fact as these are deemed to have been decided by the arbitrator. If the proceedings had been held in court initially, then the court would already be in possession of these facts and could make a decision accordingly.

5. Arbitration may not be cheaper than litigation (see above).

Arbitration: county court small claims

A form of arbitration for small claims is operated in the county court, with district judges acting as arbitrators. Claims up to the value of £3,000 are automatically referred to arbitration, instead of going to a full county court trial. In cases where the value exceeds £3,000 the district judge may order the case to go to arbitration if the parties agree.

Where a case is referred to arbitration the district judge has a discretion to rescind the reference if he is satisfied that:

1. A difficult question of law or a question of fact of exceptional complexity is involved; or
2. A charge of fraud is in issue; or
3. The parties have agreed that the dispute should be tried in court; or
4. It would be unreasonable for the matter to proceed to arbitration having regard to its subject matter, the circumstances of the parties or of any other person likely to be affected by the award.

Legal aid is not available for small claims, and the usual rule that costs follow the event does not operate. A party may, however, be ordered to pay for some items such as the summons fee or witnesses' expenses. As stated above, most arbitrations are conducted by a district judge, although he may refer the matter to a circuit judge or outside arbitrator, on the application of the parties.

The small claims proceedings are informal, and the usual rules of evidence are relaxed. If a party wishes to be represented by a solicitor or a barrister he or she must pay for this luxury, and most applicants represent themselves before the district judge.

9.4 Conciliation and mediation

The Conciliation Act 1896 gave power to the Board of Trade to inquire into the causes of any dispute and to take 'such steps as seem expedient'. Conciliation as a method of settling disputes is not new and centres on providing a forum for discussion and procedural guidance in bringing the parties together. It does not involve suggesting solutions that are then considered by the parties. Mediation is a more active and searching process than conciliation, and the mediator will be actively involved in discussions and in suggesting possible solutions to the problems raised.

In cases of divorce in which children's arrangements are in dispute a variety of conciliation schemes operate. These aim to avoid unnecessary bitterness between the divorcing couple, and to save both the parties and the court unnecessary time and expense. The schemes vary in the way that they operate, but they all have a common aim in that they seek to reduce acrimony and to finalise the arrangements in relation to the future of the children concerned.

The practice and procedure in relation to this matter are set out in *Practice Direction* [1992] 1 WLR 147 which states, inter alia, that the district judge may order conciliation at any time when considering arrangements for children under s41 of the Matrimonial Causes Act 1973, or where an application is made for an order for residence or contact under s8 of the Children Act 1989.

The scheme operating at the Principal Registry is that a conciliation appointment will be fixed before a district judge whenever a contested application for a residence or contact order is made. On the day of the appointment both parties attend before the court with their legal advisers. Sometimes the children will attend as well. The district judge and a court welfare officer will hear details of the nature of the dispute. If the parties cannot reach an agreement straight away they will retire to a private room to discuss matters further. If no subsequent agreement is reached the district judge will make directions and will order a welfare officer's report.

Mediation at work: a case study

The Birmingham Family Mediation Centre is a small organisation aiming to help families at the time of family breakdown. It deals with both married couples who are seeking divorces and unmarried couples wishing to separate. The service is an independent charity funded almost entirely by local government – a fragile existence for the workers at the centre, with the constant threat of closure if local government funding should be withdrawn.

The centre is staffed by a full-time co-ordinator and a part-time administrative assistant, together with several part-time mediators from varied backgrounds but with a good deal of mediation experience. Clients are referred by many different agents, such as solicitors, the local social services department, Relate, the Citizens' Advice Bureau, a local children's psychiatric unit, and, of course, by friends and relatives who have themselves been clients of the centre.

Clients may attend the centre for mediation sessions alone or with their partners, and they are invited to bring their children along if they wish to. Clients attending the first session alone are encouraged to bring their partners along to subsequent sessions. Each session lasts approximately one hour and, on average, couples attend the centre for three sessions in all.

Each couple works with an individual mediator whose aim is to enable them to discuss their difficulties openly. The best interests of the children are of paramount importance. Other matters such as maintenance and property are only discussed in the context of the welfare of the children. In approximately 15 per cent of cases at the Birmingham Centre, couples are reconciled after attending the sessions. In the other cases, once agreement has been reached, the centre writes to the solicitor concerned setting out the fine details of the arrangements decided upon. The solicitor will then in turn advise the court of this.

Clients who can afford to pay for mediation are invited to make a contribution of about £10 per session to cover the costs of the service. The costs of those who cannot afford to pay are covered by the Green Form Scheme or by a Legal Aid Certificate.

The centre is run by a management committee which consists of, inter alia, four solicitors, a barrister, a psychologist, an accountant, a Methodist minister, a representative of Families Need Fathers, a magistrate and a social worker. It is chaired by a Circuit judge. The committee meets every three months to take any necessary decisions in relation to the running of the centre.

The work done by the centre is, to some extent, duplicated by the probation service in the local magistrates' court. In divorce cases where there are problems with the children's arrangements, the district judge will refer the matter to probation officers who will then mediate the problem. If no satisfactory arrangements are reached, then a welfare report must be obtained. The in-court mediation service differs from the work done by the centre in that couples are required by the court to attend mediation together, rather than as individuals. In addition, the court probation officers are prohibited from discussing matters other than children.

The Advisory and Conciliation Service (ACAS)

ACAS is a government service which assists in cases of industrial dispute. Until 1974 this role was carried out by the Commission for Industrial Relations. The Employment Protection Act 1975 set out the constitution of the new service, and confirmed that ACAS was to be an independent body with the duty to promote the improvement of industrial relations. It attempts to discharge this duty through co-operation with employers, employees and their representatives, as it has no powers of compulsion. The service which it provides is free of charge, and it is controlled by a council which is responsible for policy matters. The council is composed of a chairman with nine part-time employer, trade union and independent members. All of the members are appointed by the Secretary of State for Employment.

One of the ways in which ACAS promotes harmony in industrial relations is by conciliation, which takes place both in trade disputes and in individual cases of complaint. Conciliation is a voluntary process, and in the case of trade disputes attempts are made through discussion and negotiation to enable parties to reach their own agreement. Conciliators do not impose or even recommend settlements. ACAS officers work with each party separately, and sometimes with parties together to promote discussion of the issue. If the parties to a dispute wish to involve ACAS there is no formal application procedure; they simply contact ACAS by telephone to arrange a conciliation appointment. Once conciliation has commenced then either party is free to bring the process to an end at any time, as it is voluntary.

Conciliation also takes place in individual cases of complaint, providing assistance, where applications are made to the Industrial Tribunal, in matters such as unfair dismissal, equal pay, sex discrimination and so on. When an individual makes an application to the Industrial Tribunal (on Form IT.1) the Central Office of Industrial Tribunals passes a copy of the form to ACAS, which then allocates to the matter a conciliation officer who tries to help the parties to settle the complaint without the need for a tribunal hearing.

The conciliation officer will contact the parties, and where a grievance procedure already exists he or she will encourage its use to settle the complaint. Conciliation can of course be refused by either of the parties to the complaint, as it is a voluntary process. The conciliation officer informs the parties of any options which might be open to them, and in doing so acts in a neutral and independent way. He or she cannot actually represent either party, but will explain the Industrial Tribunal procedure and the relevant law to the parties. However, he or she will not impose or even recommend a particular settlement, and it is up to the parties to decide upon the terms of settlement for themselves. It is important to note that this form of conciliation is available to parties even if a formal application has not yet been made to the Industrial Tribunal, where the circumstances are such that an individual has grounds to make such an application.

ACAS also assists parties by way of arbitration, although conciliation is a preferred approach. A dispute may, with the consent of the parties, be referred to ACAS, which may itself appoint an arbitrator (but not a member of ACAS staff, who are independent), or the dispute may be referred to the Central Arbitration Committee. Usually, however, arbitration takes place before a single arbitrator who will make a decision on the matter. Each party must set out its case in writing and agree to be bound by the decision of the arbitrator, and there is a prompt hearing, held either at the ACAS office or at a mutually acceptable venue. Each side will argue its case before the arbitrator, comment on the other side's case and answer any questions.

A third method of promoting agreement used by ACAS is mediation. It is a similar process to conciliation, except that the mediator takes a more active role and makes recommendations as to how the matter may be resolved. Both parties agree to consider the mediator's proposals, but they are not bound by them. Before a dispute goes to mediation, ACAS will request that both parties meet a conciliation officer to ensure that it cannot be resolved by conciliation.

A further role of ACAS is to provide advisory and information services to all kinds of people involved in employment, such as employers and workers, on such matters as pay systems, productivity and related matters, job evaluation and equal pay, job design and work organisation, new technology and so on. ACAS advisers seek to secure the involvement of employees and their trade unions, together with management, in a joint examination of their problems.

9.5 Exercise

You are approached by John Brown, who wishes to make an application to the Industrial Tribunal for unfair dismissal. John has been dismissed from work but wishes to be reinstated in his old job, ie to carry on working in his old job as before. The background to the case is as follows:

John was employed by a computer company, Omega Computers Ltd, as a sales representative. A few days ago he went with a friend to the pub for lunch, as usual, and then returned to his office. His lunch had consisted of a large pork pie and a glass of orange juice. Soon he felt rather unwell and put this down to dodgy pub food. He began to feel rather dizzy and faint, and he was aware that his speech sounded slurred. At that moment Miss Powers, the managing director of the company, entered his office with a valued client, Mr Chan. Seeing John in this state, she immediately jumped to the conclusion that he was drunk, and a heated row followed as John tried to deny the allegation. Finally, Miss Powers stated that enough was enough, and dismissed John with immediate effect for 'gross misconduct'.

You are supplied with an extract of John's contract of employment (Document A) and Form IT.1 (Application to an Industrial Tribunal with Guidance Notes) (Document B). You should read Documents A and B and then do the following:

1. Fill in, as far as you are able, the Application to an Industrial Tribunal (Document B), on the basis that you are John's adviser but that he wishes to represent himself before the IT.
2. Write to John in order to gather the remaining information which you need to fill in Form IT.1. Cover any other matters which you think may be appropriate.
3. Draft a covering letter to accompany Form IT.1, although you are still awaiting a response from John in relation to the outstanding details.

DOCUMENT A

Extracts from service contract

THIS AGREEMENT DATED 1 JANUARY 1990 IS MADE

BETWEEN

(1)   OMEGA COMPUTERS LIMITED whose registered office is at Unit 10, Industrial Estate, Blanktown ('the Company').

AND

(2)   JOHN BROWN of 100 Rose Terrace, Wolverton, Blanktown ('the Employee')

WHEREBY IT IS AGREED AS FOLLOWS:

*   *   *   *

APPOINTMENT

1   The Company shall employ the Employee and the Employee shall be employed by the Company as a full-time sales representative for the company's products in the county of Blankshire.

2   The Employee's period of continuous employment with the Company commenced on 1 January 1990. No employment with a previous employer will count as part of the Employee's said period of continuous employment.

3   **DURATION**

The employment may be terminated at any time by either the Company or the Employee giving to the other not less than three months' notice in writing.

4   **REMUNERATION**

The remuneration of the Employee shall be a fixed annual salary at the rate of £15,000 per annum to be paid by equal monthly instalments in arrears on the last working day of each calendar month.

*   *   *   *

7   **HOLIDAY ENTITLEMENT**

The Employee shall be entitled to twenty working days' holiday with pay per calendar year (plus bank holidays) at such times as may be agreed with the Sales Director.

8   **PENSION**

The Employee shall be entitled at completion of (   ) years' service to join the Company's pension scheme details of which are set out in a document entitled (   ) a copy of which is available upon request from the Company Secretary.

*   *   *   *

12   **CAR**

The Company shall provide a car for the Employee to enable him to carry out his duties under this agreement in accordance with the Company's scheme, details of which are obtainable from the Company Secretary.

DOCUMENT B

Application to an Industrial Tribunal

Notes for Guidance

Before filling in this form please read:
- these **GUIDANCE NOTES**
- **LEAFLET ITL1** which you were given with this form
- the correct **BOOKLET** for your type of case

Information: There are many things you can complain to a Tribunal about. LEAFLET ITL1 tells you what they are, which law (an Act of Parliament) covers your complaint, and which booklet you should get. Each of the BOOKLETS explains the law in simple terms. You can get the booklets free from any employment office, Jobcentre, or Unemployment Benefit Office. If you are in doubt, your Trade Union or a Citizens' Advice Bureau may be able to give you further advice or information.

Time limits: You must send in your application form so that it arrives at the Central Office of the Industrial Tribunals within the time limit. The time limit depends on which complaint you are making; for example, for unfair dismissal complaints it is three months beginning with the date of dismissal. So if you were dismissed on 10th January, the form must arrive by 9th April.

Qualifying periods: There are rules about how long you have to work for an employer before you can bring a case to a Tribunal. These rules are explained in the BOOKLETS.

If you are in any doubt about the time limits or qualifying periods, please contact your local employment office, Jobcentre, or Unemployment Benefit Office; or get in touch with the Advisory Conciliation and Arbitration Service (ACAS) – see the LEAFLET ITL1 for addresses and telephone numbers.

Representatives: You can present your own case at the Tribunal. If you want someone else to present your case, try to consult him or her before you complete your application form, but remember your form must arrive within the TIME LIMIT. If you name a representative, all future dealings will be with him or her and not with you. If you name a representative, you should ask him or her any questions you have about the progress of your case and when the Tribunal hearing will be.

If your complaint concerns EQUAL PAY or SEX DISCRIMINATION, you may wish to contact the Equal Opportunities Commission for advice or representation. If your complaint is about RACIAL DISCRIMINATION, you may wish to contact the Commission for Racial Equality for advice or representation.

Filling in the form

Help: Your Trade Union or local Citizens' Advice Bureau may be able to help you fill in the form if you have any problems, but make sure your form arrives within the TIME LIMIT.

Questions to answer: Try to complete all the boxes that apply in your case. You MUST answer the questions in boxes 1, 2, 4, and 10.

Be clear: This form has to be photocopied, so please use black ink, or type your answers, and use CAPITAL LETTERS for names and addresses.

Box 1
Put here the type of complaint you want the Tribunal to decide (for example, unfair dismissal, redundancy payment, equal pay, etc). A full list of types of complaint is given in the leaflet ITL1. If there is more than one complaint you want the Tribunal to decide, please say so. Give the details of your complaints in Box 10.

Box 2
Give your name and address and date of birth, and if possible a telephone number where the Tribunal or ACAS can contact you during the day about your application.

Box 4
Put here the name and address of the employer, person or body (the 'respondent') you wish to complain about. In the second box, give also the place where you worked or applied for work, if different from that of the respondent you have named. (For example, complete both boxes if you have named a liquidator, the Secretary of State for Employment, or your employer's Head Office as the respondent.)

Box 10
Give full details of your complaint. If there is not enough room on the form, continue on a separate sheet, and attach it to the form. Do NOT send any other documents or evidence in support of your complaint at this stage. Your answer may be used in an initial assessment of your case, so make it as complete and accurate as you can. (See **Help** above.)

When you have finished:

- Sign and date the form
- Keep these Guidance Notes and a copy of your answers
- Send the form to: **The Secretary of the Tribunals**
  Central Office of the Industrial Tribunals
  93 Ebury Bridge Road
  London SW1W 8RE
  Tel: 01-730 9161

FOR OFFICIAL USE ONLY

Received at COIT

Case No.

Code

Initials

ROIT

Application to an Industrial Tribunal

Please read the notes opposite before filling in this form

1 Say what type of complaint(s) you want the tribunal to decide.

2 Give your name and address etc. in CAPITALS.

Mr/Mrs
Miss/Ms

Address

Telephone

Date of birth

3 Please give the name and address of your representative, if you have one.

Name

Address

Telephone

4 Give the name and address of the employer, person or body (the respondent) you are complaining about.

Name

Address

Telephone

Give the place where you worked or applied for work, if different from above.

Name

Address

Telephone

5 Please say what job you did for the employer (or what job you applied for). If this does not apply, please say what your connection was with the employer.

IT 1 (Revised August 1986)

Please continue overleaf

6 Please give the number of normal basic hours you worked per week.

Hours [ ] per week

7 Basic wage/salary £ [ ] per [ ]

Average take home pay £ [ ] per [ ]

Other bonuses/benefits £ [ ] per [ ]

8 Please give the dates of your employment *(if applicable)*.

Began on [ ]

Ended on [ ]

9 If your complaint is **not** about dismissal, please give the date when the action you are complaining about took place (or the date when you first knew about it).

Date [ ]

10 Give full details of your complaint.

11 Unfair dismissal claimants only (Please tick a box to show what you would want if you win your case).

[ ] Reinstatement: to carry on working in your old job as before

[ ] Re-engagement: to start another job, or a new contract, with your old employer

[ ] Compensation: to get an award of money

You can change your mind later. The tribunal will take your preference into account, but will not be bound by it.

Signature _____ Date _____

10

Trial Procedure

10.1 Introduction

10.2 An outline of procedure in the civil courts

10.3 An outline of procedure in the criminal courts

10.4 Exercises

10.1 Introduction

This chapter considers the procedure in the civil courts and in the criminal courts. This information is relevant to understanding the jurisdiction of the courts described in Chapter 3 and is also necessary for the mooting technique given in the next chapter. The effective advocate will be familiar with court procedure. It is, after all, the context in which he or she works, and any procedural errors made by his or her opponent may sometimes be used to the advantage of his or her client.

10.2 An outline of procedure in the civil courts

Civil law and civil litigation are concerned with the resolution of disputes between individuals. The civil court system provides a framework within which this can take place. The judge acts as an umpire and ultimately, if necessary, will decide on the outcome of the dispute. Often it may not be necessary for the judge to do this as the parties themselves may come to an agreement and settle the matter without the need to go to trial or indeed to court at all.

The types of case that come under the classification of civil law, and thus will be dealt with, if necessary, in the civil courts, are actions for breach of contract, including debt, and those for negligence, including personal injury.

An important factor that the plaintiff must consider before commencing proceedings is the provisions of the Limitation Act 1980. The Limitation Act contains rules that limit the period of time within which an action can be brought. For most actions in contract and tort this period is six years from the date that the cause of action arose. For actions arising out of a claim for personal injuries, the period is three years from the date on which the cause of action arose or the date of the plaintiff's knowledge, if later.

In a civil case the party who brings the action is known as the 'plaintiff'. The person against whom the action is brought is known as the 'defendant'. Where the plaintiff decides to go to court, he or she must first consider whether to commence proceedings in the High Court or the county court. This is because both the High Court and the county court are courts of first instance in the civil court structure. The rules governing the choice of court (and also whether in certain circumstances there is any choice of court) are set out in the High Court and County Courts Jurisdiction Order 1991.

An outline will now be given of both High Court and county court procedure in turn.

High Court procedure

Commencing proceedings
In the High Court, the plaintiff usually commences proceedings by way of writ of summons. However, the plaintiff must choose the appropriate form of writ – that for a liquidated demand or that for an unliquidated demand. A liquidated demand arises where the damages claimed are exactly quantifiable from the outset (eg a debt action). An unliquidated demand arises where the damages claimed are not precisely quantifiable at the outset (eg an action for damages for personal injuries).

The plaintiff will take with him or her, or send to the court:

- at least three copies of the writ;
- the issuing fee;
- where relevant, a court copy of the Legal Aid Certificate.

Service
A writ is valid for *four months* once it has been issued. The plaintiff must serve the writ on the defendant within that time. The writ is usually served by means of ordinary first class post, but other methods of service are available (for example, the writ may be served personally on the defendant).

The plaintiff serves on the defendant:

- a sealed copy of the writ;
- a form of acknowledgment of service;
- where relevant, notice of issue of the Legal Aid Certificate.

Defendant's response
The defendant must complete the acknowledgment of service and return it to the court *within 14 days* of the service of the writ. If he or she does not return the form to the court, or does return it but indicates on the form that he or she does not

intend to defend the action, then the plaintiff may enter judgment against the defendant. This will be judgment in default of an intention to defend the action.

Where the defendant does intend to defend the action, the next stage in the procedure involves the pleadings.

Pleadings

A pleading is a formal document in which a party to the action will set out his or her case. Pleadings also have to be served on the party's opponent. There are four main types of pleading:

1. *The statement of claim* This is the plaintiff's first pleading. Somewhat confusingly there are two times at which a statement of claim may be served. It may be served with the writ initially (usually, for example, in debt actions where the statement of claim can be endorsed on the writ). Alternatively, the statement of claim may be served as a separate document later (usually, for example, in personal injury actions). In this instance, the statement of claim must be served *not later than 14 days* after the defendant has given notice of intention to defend.

    Note here the provisions of O.18, r12(1A), of the Rules of the Supreme Court 1965. In claims for damages for personal injuries, the plaintiff must serve a medical report and a statement of the special damages claimed with the statement of claim.

    Where the plaintiff fails to serve the statement of claim within the required time, the defendant may make an application for the action to be dismissed.

2. *The defence* This is the defendant's first pleading, his or her defence to the plaintiff's statement of claim. The defence must be served *within 14 days* of service of the statement of claim where this is a separate document. Where the statement of claim is served with the writ, then the defence must be served *within 28 days* of service of the writ.

    Where the defendant fails to serve the defence within the required time, then the plaintiff can obtain judgment in default of a defence.

3. *The counterclaim* Where the defendant wishes to make a claim against the plaintiff, he or she will do this by means of a counterclaim. The counterclaim will be added to the defence and will be served with it. However, where the defendant does not wish to make any claim against the plaintiff, then a counterclaim will obviously not be relevant.

4. *The reply* The plaintiff serves a reply on the defendant where he or she wishes to reply formally to any of the factual allegations raised in the defence. A reply is not compulsory. However, where the plaintiff does serve a reply it must be served *within 14 days* of the receipt of the defence.

The close of pleadings

Pleadings are deemed to be closed 14 days after service of the last pleading in the case. This stage in the proceedings is used as a reference point for the calculation of other time limits.

Directions

A direction is a means by which the court may give guidance as to the conduct of the matter to one or both parties. In the High Court, there are two types of direction:

1. *Automatic directions* These apply in personal injury actions only. The automatic directions *take effect immediately on the close of pleadings.*
2. *Directions obtained on a summons for directions* This is a formal application to the court for directions. The plaintiff should take out a summons for directions *within one month of the close of pleadings.*

   Note The summons for directions is an example of an 'interlocutory application'. This is an application made after the issue of the writ but before the final determination of the matter at trial.

The actual directions (whether automatic or obtained on a summons for directions) are similar in nature. They include the following:

- Discovery of documents within 14 days in accordance with O.24, r2, of the Rules of the Supreme Court and inspection *within seven days thereafter.*
- The action shall be tried at the trial centre for the place in which the action is proceeding or at such other trial centre as the parties may agree in writing.
- The action to be tried by judge alone as a 'category B' case and to be set down within six months.

In addition, the court when hearing a summons for directions must consider certain specific points. These include such matters as whether the action should be transferred to the county court, the exchange of expert evidence and of witness statements.

The number and nature of the directions (whether automatic or obtained on a summons for directions) will usually mean that they take some time to be carried into effect. During this time the parties may well engage in negotiations in order to arrive at a settlement of the action on mutually agreeable terms. This may include the use of 'formal tactics' such as payments into court. Many actions are settled in this way without the need for a trial. However, if the parties cannot agree then the matter will be set down for trial.

Setting down for trial

Setting a case down for trial is a process whereby the case is listed for hearing at the appropriate trial centre. In so doing the parties (and, in particular, the plaintiff) will be complying with the relevant direction.

The plaintiff will take or send to the court:

- a letter requesting formally that the action be set down for trial;
- the fee;
- two bundles of documents.

The bundles of documents will contain, for example, copies of the writ, the pleadings, any orders for directions and a statement of value of the action where relevant. One of the bundles is for the court record and the other is for the use of the judge at the trial.

It is now necessary to lodge at court a bundle containing copies of any witness statements that have been disclosed, together with a note as to whether the contents of such documents have been agreed.

It is now also necessary for the defendant to lodge at court any documents that he or she wishes to have included in the bundle as central to his or her case and those central to the plaintiff's case.

These bundles must be lodged at court *at least two clear days before* the date fixed for trial. This is so that all parties, including the judge, have time to read them. Each party must also lodge a note at court which summarises the issues involved and any propositions of law to be relied on. A list of authorities to be used and a chronology of relevant events must also be given.

The period of setting down for trial is a busy time for the solicitor. In addition to preparing the relevant bundles of documents, he or she must take steps to ensure that his or her witnesses attend trial (by means of a subpoena – an order to attend court – if necessary), brief counsel to conduct the trial, and generally 'tie up any loose ends'.

The trial

An outline of trial procedure has been given above, so it is only necessary here to highlight particular points of interest or divergence from the general rule.

At present only barristers (counsel) have a right of audience in the High Court in open court. This means that High Court trials are conducted by counsel. Proposals have been made to permit solicitors to have the same right of audience, but as yet these have come to nothing.

Note: Where no evidence is being called on behalf of the defendant, his or her counsel has the right to make his or her closing submission after counsel for the plaintiff.

As outlined above, the judge will give judgment on the issue and will thus decide on who has won the case and on the award of damages if appropriate. The judge may also make various orders ancillary to the main judgment. These will include the matters of interest on the damages, costs (the usual rule is that the loser pays the winner's costs) and legal aid taxation where relevant. The Associate's Certificate must also be obtained. (The associate is the clerk of the court at the trial, who in any action in the Queen's Bench Division in the High Court must certify, inter alia, the time that the trial has taken, any order made by the judge, and the judgment. This is for clarity and certainty, and also for the taxation of costs.)

Enforcement of judgments

The successful party often believes that once he or she has obtained judgment the case is over and finished. Unfortunately, this may not be so. The losing party may not, or at least may not willingly, pay the judgment debt owed to the winner. Thus, the successful party may need to go on to enforce judgment against the loser. He or she will first obtain information about the losing party's means by way of:

1. an oral examination of the judgment debtor; and/or
2. a company search;
3. the use of an enquiry agent.

The successful party will then go on to enforce judgment. The most common methods of enforcement in the High Court are:

1. writ of fieri facias;
2. garnishee proceedings;
3. charging order on land;
4. bankruptcy proceedings.

County court procedure

The county court has a wide jurisdiction. This means that it has power over a variety of matters. As mentioned above, this jurisdiction is now governed by the High Court and County Courts Jurisdiction Order 1991.

There is also provision for a district judge to try any case in which the sum claimed or in which the amount involved does not exceed £5,000. The district judge may also try any case where the parties consent to him or her doing so. Further, any proceedings in which the sum claimed or in which the amount involved does not exceed £1,000 must be referred to arbitration once a defence has been filed. Arbitration is a separate procedure taking place within the county court. (There is provision for the reference to arbitration to be rescinded in certain circumstances.)

Although the early stages of proceedings in cases not exceeding £1,000 and not exceeding £5,000 may be the same as, or at least similar to, cases where more than these amounts are involved, ultimately different court procedures will apply. These procedures are outside the scope of this section. The following outline procedure is concerned mainly with cases exceeding £5,000 in value.

Commence proceedings

The plaintiff commences proceedings usually by way of summons. There are two types of summons – a default summons and a fixed date summons. The default summons is used in respect of all claims for money, whether a liquidated or an unliquidated claim. A fixed date summons is used where a non-monetary remedy is claimed.

The plaintiff must take or send to the court office:

- a formal request for the summons *or* a completed summons, a copy of the completed summons and a letter containing an informal request for the summons;
- the issuing fee;
- the particulars of claim;
- where relevant, a court copy of the Legal Aid Certificate and notice of issue of the Legal Aid Certificate;
- in a personal injury action, a medical report and statement of special damages claimed.

Service

The summons must be served within four months of issue. The summons may be served either by the court or by the plaintiff or his or her solicitor. Otherwise, the rules concerning service are broadly similar to those in the High Court.

The plaintiff or the court serves on the defendant:

- the summons;
- the particulars of claim;
- the form of admission, defence and counterclaim;
- the notice of issue of the Legal Aid Certificate
- in a personal injury action, a medical report and statement of special damages claimed.

Defendant's response

The defendant must complete and return the form of admission, defence and counterclaim *within 14 days* of service of the summons.

The form of admission, defence and counterclaim is the county court equivalent of the High Court acknowledgment of service. However, it is also something in the nature of a pleading.

Thus, where a fixed amount is claimed, it is possible for the defendant to admit the claim. If he or she does so, the admission is sent direct *to the plaintiff.* Otherwise, the defendant returns the form to the court.

If the defendant does not respond *within 14 days* then the plaintiff may enter judgment in default.

Pleadings

The pleadings in the county court are essentially the same as those in the High Court. However, in the county court the plaintiff's first pleading is referred to as the particulars of claim and not the statement of claim. The particulars of claim are served on the defendant at the onset with the summons and other documents as set out above.

The close of pleadings

Again, the rules applying in the county court are essentially the same as those applying in the High Court. In the county court, pleadings are deemed to be closed 14 days after delivery of the defence or, where a counterclaim is served with a defence, 28 days after the delivery of the defence.

Directions

The nature of directions is the same in the county court as in the High Court. However, different rules do apply. In the county court, automatic directions now apply in most types of action.

There are general automatic directions that apply in all actions in the county court. In personal injury actions, these are supplemented by additional directions.

The content of the county court directions are similar to those of the High Court; for example, a direction provides for discovery and inspection of documents.

In the county court, the pre-trial review is the equivalent of the High Court summons for directions. This used to apply in all cases. However, the use of automatic directions now means that the pre-trial review is used only in limited circumstances.

As in the High Court, the parties may well have been negotiating and settlement may have been achieved by this stage.

Setting down for trial

Again, the procedure here is similar to that in the High Court. New rules now apply to any case in which the hearing date was fixed after 2 January 1991. These provide that:

1. *At least 14 days* before the day fixed for hearing, the defendant must inform the plaintiff of the documents that he or she wishes to have included in the bundle to be provided under the rule set out below.
2. *At least seven days* before the day fixed for the hearing, the plaintiff must file one copy of a paginated and indexed bundle comprising the documents which either party wishes to have before the court at the hearing, together with two copies of other specified documents, including witness statements that have been exchanged and expert reports that have been disclosed, together with a note as to whether the contents of any such documents are agreed.

Again, this is a busy time for the solicitor in preparing matters for trial. The solicitor must ensure that his or her witnesses attend court. The county court equivalent of the subpoena issued against recalcitrant witnesses is the witness summons.

The trial

Again, this has been dealt with above.

Both solicitors and barristers have rights of audience in the county court.

However, the parties are also more likely to represent themselves in the county court.

Trial procedure in the county court is also more informal than in the High Court. County Court Rules (O.21, r5A) now provide that the trial judge may give directions as to which party will begin, and the order and number of speeches, and also that he or she may dispense with opening speeches altogether.

The rules relating to judgment and to the orders sought after judgment are in general the same as or similar to those in the High Court.

Enforcement of judgments

Again, the provisions in the county court are similar to those in the High Court.

However, the county court equivalent of the writ of fieri facias is the warrant of execution. There is also an additional method of enforcement in the county court known as an attachment of earnings order. Obviously, appeal procedures do exist for the appeal of cases decided at first instance in the High Court and county court. However, again these are outside the scope of this chapter.

10.3 An outline of procedure in the criminal courts

The nature of criminal law is fundamentally different from that of civil law. While civil law is concerned with the resolution of disputes between individuals, criminal law is concerned with the imposing of a sanction on those who have been duly adjudged to be wrongdoers. Thus, in criminal law 'the State' takes a much more active role. This difference in the nature of criminal law and civil law is reflected in the difference in proceedings in the two courts. Proceedings in the criminal courts tend to be simpler than proceedings in the civil court. Again the information given below is intended as an outline only.

Procedure in the criminal courts

Commencing proceedings

Once the police have investigated the commission of a crime and have a suspect, they may proceed against him or her in one of two ways:

1. A summons may be issued against the suspect. This may be done, for example, where the suspect is thought to have committed minor driving offences. The police will lay an information at a magistrates' court, and a summons will then be issued against the suspect.

   The police usually serve the summons on the suspect. The summons will be served personally or by post to the suspect's usual or last known address. Registered post or recorded delivery may be used here.

2. The suspect may have been arrested by the police and charged with the

commission of the offence at the police station. In these circumstances the charge sheet will be handed to the suspect at the police station.

After these initial stages in the procedure, the prosecution will be taken over from the police by the Crown Prosecution Service (CPS).

Note In criminal cases a failure by the prosecution to institute proceedings within certain time limits prescribed by statute will, in effect, render the proceedings void.

The magistrates' courts
Most prosecutions begin in the magistrates' court. There are a few exceptions, but these are outside the scope of this course. Both the summons and the charge sheet will specify the date and time of the first hearing before the magistrates and also the locality of the court.

It is important to note that most offences begin in the magistrates' court. Thus, both very serious offences (eg murder) and more minor offences (eg careless driving) will begin in this court. The difference is that the more serious offences will later be referred or 'committed' to the Crown Court.

For procedural purposes, offences may be classified into three types:

1. *Summary offences* These are the more serious minor offences (eg careless driving). These offences can *only* be dealt with in the magistrates' court.

2. *Indictable offences* These are the more serious offences (eg murder, rape). These offences can only be dealt with in the Crown Court as they are regarded as being too serious to be dealt with by magistrates.

3. *Either way offences* These offences can be dealt with either in the magistrates' court or in the Crown Court – hence their name. They include offences such as theft and some assaults. How serious the offences are and thus how likely they are to be dealt with in the Crown Court will depend on the circumstances of the offence: for example, the degree of violence used in cases of assault or the value involved in cases of theft.

   With regard to this type of offence, a decision will be made as to which court, the magistrates' court or the Crown Court, will deal with the case.

Court venue
As mentioned above, summary offences can only be dealt with in the magistrates' court. In other words, such offences *stay* in the magistrates' court. However, with regard to either way offences, a decision has to be made as to whether the case will be dealt with in the magistrates' court or in the Crown Court. This is known as the *mode of trial enquiry*.

The procedure at a mode of trial enquiry is as follows:

1. The magistrate will ask for the charge to be written down and explained to the accused.

2. The Crown prosecutor will then be given the opportunity to make submissions to the magistrates upon the appropriate mode of trial.
3. The defendant's solicitor will make submissions as to the appropriate mode of trial (the prosecutor and the defendant's solicitor may be in agreement as to this).
4. The magistrates will consider all the submissions that have been made and decide whether or not they are prepared to hear the case themselves. If they are not prepared to hear the case, they will inform the defendant, and a date and time will be fixed for the committal proceedings.
5. Where the magistrates are prepared to hear the case, they will inform the defendant. The defendant's right to be tried by a judge and jury in the Crown Court will then be explained to him or her, as will his or her option to agree to summary trial. However, the defendant will be warned that if he or she does agree to summary trial before the magistrates, the magistrates may commit him or her to the Crown Court for sentencing if they consider that their own powers of sentencing are inadequate, having regard to the defendant's character and/or antecedents or to the seriousness of the offence.
6. The defendant is asked whether he or she agrees to summary trial. If he or she does agree, then matters will be dealt with in the magistrates' court, but will probably be adjourned (postponed) to a later date. If the defendant does not agree to summary trial, then the matter will be adjourned for committal to the Crown Court.

It is important to note that the defendant can decide that he or she wishes to be tried before a judge and jury in the Crown Court even where the magistrates have decided that they can deal with the matter. The defendant has the last word in this respect.

Committal proceedings

As mentioned above, both indictable offences and either way offences where a decision has been made to deal with them in the Crown Court must be heard in the Crown Court. In this context the magistrates act as examining magistrates (in other words, they examine whether there is sufficient evidence for the matter to be referred to the Crown Court).

This procedure is known as *committal proceedings*. There are two types of committal proceedings under s6 of the Magistrates' Courts Act 1980. These are:

Committal with consideration of the evidence. This is sometimes referred to as an 'old-style' committal because committal proceedings always used to take place in this way. It is governed by s6(1) of the Magistrates' Courts Act 1980. It is the prosecution's duty to persuade the magistrates that there is sufficient evidence upon which a jury in the Crown Court could safely convict the accused. The general rule is that all evidence upon which the prosecution intends to rely should be put before the magistrates at a committal hearing. The prosecution witnesses will be called to give evidence and will be subject to cross-examination by the defendant's solicitor or counsel. The defence case may not be given. The point is to show the weaknesses in the prosecution's case.

The advantage of an old-style committal as far as the defendant is concerned is that the defendant's representative may make a submission of 'no case to answer'. This is done after the conclusion of the prosecution's case. The defendant's representative will submit that no reasonable jury properly directed could reasonably find him or her guilty of the charge laid.

However, this submission can only be successful where either:

1. The prosecution evidence has been so discredited in cross-examination that no reasonable jury properly directed could reasonably think it adequate to make a conviction safe. (This will only usually happen where the witnesses admit that they are unsure of what they are supposed to have heard or seen, and there is no other evidence to support the charge, or where the witnesses admit that they have lied in giving evidence.)
2. The prosecution has not given any evidence to prove an essential element of the offence. (For example, in a case of alleged theft there may not be any evidence to show that the goods belong to another. This submission is rarely successful, not least because many elements of crime are proved by inference or presumption.)

A defendant can insist on a committal with full consideration of the evidence. However, he or she takes a risk in so doing. An old-style committal rehearses the prosecution witnesses, which is an obvious disadvantage to the defendant's case if the matter proceeds to the Crown Court. Such committals are therefore rare in practice and should only be used where the defence considers that the prosecution case is weak.

Note Even where a submission of no case to answer is upheld, the prosecution may bring fresh committal proceedings in respect of precisely the same facts or offence. This is because a discharge at committal is not regarded as an acquittal, and thus no plea of 'autrefois acquit' can be raised to prevent further attempts to try the accused.

Committal without consideration of the evidence. An old-style committal is rare – not least because it is relatively easy for the prosecution to show a prima facie case against the defendant.

New-style committal proceedings may be used by virtue of s6(2) of the Magistrates' Courts Act 1980. This procedure is cheaper and reduces delays in court. However, certain conditions must be satisfied:

1. The prosecution evidence (apart from real evidence) must be presented in the form of statements.
2. The defendant must be legally represented.
3. The prosecution statements must have been served on the defendant or on his or her legal representative before the opening of the committal proceedings.

4. The defendant consents to the short-form procedure and does not wish to make a submission of no case to answer.

The procedure at a short-form committal is straightforward:

1. The defendant is 'put up'.
2. The charge is written down and read to him or her. The defendant is asked whether he or she wishes to make a submission of no case to answer, or to call any evidence of his or her own, or to make any objection to the contents of the prosecution evidence at this stage. If the reply to any of these questions is in the affirmative, then a s6(1) committal must be held.
3. The prosecution statements are handed to the magistrates' clerk. The magistrates do not read them, but the clerk checks that they are all there.
4. The magistrates make an order committing the defendant for trial and may make all or any of the ancillary orders mentioned below.

There is some comment that the wide use of s6(2) committals has reduced the role of the magistrates from examining magistrates to mere administrators!

At both s6(1) and s6(2) committals, various other matters must be considered by the magistrates. These are:

1. *Place of trial* Committal will usually be to the Crown Court for the district in which the committal proceedings have been held.
2. *Witness orders* These orders instruct witnesses to attend court to give evidence. The order may be in the form of a full witness order – where the witness must attend court – or a conditional witness order – where the witness must only attend court if he or she subsequently receives an order telling him or her to do so.
3. *Alibi warning* If a defendant intends to rely on an alibi, the court will order that within seven days the defendant shall supply the prosecution with the names and addresses of all witnesses (and the defendant's own) that are proposed to be called at trial in support of an alibi defence. Before the alibi warning is given, the chairperson of the magistrates will usually first ask if it is required.
4. *Publicity at the committal* In certain circumstances, reporting restrictions may be imposed on the reporting of a case in the media.
5. *Legal aid* An order will be made extending the legal aid to cover the Crown Court proceedings where relevant.
6. *The costs of the committal* The magistrates may order the costs of the committal to be paid out of central funds where a submission of no case to answer is successful, or to be paid by the defendant where it is not. However, as the defendant is commonly legally aided, no order is usually made.

Obviously, the determination of where and by whom the case is to be heard may take some time. Any delays will be keenly felt by the defendant where he or she has been remanded in custody pending his or her trial or guilty plea. Alternatively, a defendant may be remanded on bail. Here, although at liberty, he or she may have to abide by bail conditions: for example, be subject to a curfew.

In certain circumstances a defendant may plead guilty by post. This procedure was introduced to save court time and expense. It is only available in certain limited circumstances involving the more minor offences. The procedure is most commonly used for motoring offences.

Procedure on guilty plea

Once the court venue has been ascertained (in cases where there is any choice), then the case needs to be dealt with. Many defendants plead 'guilty' to the offences with which they are charged.

In the magistrates' court, the magistrates will then go on to sentence the defendant or alternatively to commit him or her to the Crown Court for sentencing in cases where the magistrates consider their own powers of sentencing to be inadequate. In the Crown Court, the judge sentences the defendant (the jury decides only whether the defendant is guilty or not guilty where this is at issue).

In both courts, the prosecution will set out the facts of the case and may ask for a particular penalty in the circumstances of the case. The defendant's representative (counsel in the Crown Court) will then make a plea in mitigation, putting any points forward in favour of the defendant. In both the magistrates' court and the Crown Court, there may be adjournments for probation or psychiatric or other types of reports to be made concerning the defendant.

Procedure on not guilty plea

Where the defendant pleads 'not guilty', whether in the magistrates' court or the Crown Court, there will have to be a trial. Again, the basic trial procedure in a criminal case has been outlined above. Note that at the end of the prosecution evidence the defendant may make a submission of no case to answer. The prosecution has a right to reply to this submission.

The defendant's representative may make an opening speech in certain circumstances but may limit this to an address. This is because the defendant's representative may wish to concentrate on his or her closing speech. The prosecution does not usually have a closing speech in summary trial. The leave of the court to do so may be obtained, where, for example, there is a matter of law on which the prosecution wishes to reply. Where the prosecution does make a closing speech in the Crown Court or in the magistrates' court, it speaks first.

In the magistrates' court, the magistrates will retire to consider their decision. In the Crown Court the judge will sum up for the jury (and he may direct it on points of evidence); then the jury will retire to consider its verdict.

If the defendant is acquitted, he or she may be awarded his or her costs; if convicted, then his or her representative will make a plea in mitigation of the defendant's conduct. Again, there may be an adjournment for reports. The magistrates, in the magistrates' court, or the judge, in the Crown Court, will sentence the defendant and may also order him or her to pay costs.

Again, an appeals system is available but is outside the scope of this chapter.

10.4 Exercises

1. You are a legal assistant working for Megabank PLC. Write a memo to the head of the Legal Services Section outlining the provisions of the High Court and County Courts Jurisdiction Order 1991.
2. Prepare an oral presentation on the meaning of and the rules relating to discovery and inspection in High Court proceedings.
3. You are a trainee solicitor working for a firm that specialises in debt collection and the enforcement of court judgments. The senior partner has asked you to see a business client who wishes to enforce a judgment against a former customer. Write brief notes on the different methods of enforcement available in both the High Court and the county court in order to prepare for the appointment. What particular points would you wish to discuss with your client at the appointment?
4. You are a solicitor in a well-respected criminal law practice. Over the years your firm has acted for a well-known family of criminals, the Swaggs. The following members of the family now consult you on the following matters:

   a) Peter Swagg is charged with the murder of a police officer who disturbed him in the commission of the armed robbery of a bank.
   b) Susan Swagg is charged with theft from her employer over a period of two years. She worked in a trusted position in the accounts department and is alleged to have stolen £20,000.
   c) Jim Swagg is charged with careless driving.

   In each case, write a letter to your client, explaining briefly and as simply as possible the likely court that will deal with the matter and the procedures involved.

11

Mooting Technique

11.1 Introduction

A moot is the presentation and argument of a legal case by two opposing teams, each made up of two students or 'counsel'. Mooting is regarded as an essential part of legal education, testing as it does various legal skills. These include legal research and the preparation of a legal argument as well as advocacy skills. Many law schools organise internal mooting competitions, and they may also take part in external competitions, most notably the annual '*Observer* Mooting Competition' sponsored by the *Observer* newspaper.

Mooting provides a means of developing and practising various legal skills. Lawyers must be articulate, they must be able to spot issues, be able to sort out the relevant from the irrelevant, be able to present an argument and be able to explain points clearly. All of these skills are necessary for advocacy. However, not all lawyers work as advocates! Nevertheless, such skills will also be required by a lawyer when interviewing a client, explaining complicated matters to his client and when negotiating with other lawyers. Mooting is thus part of an overall foundation in legal skills.

The information given below is designed to provide general guidelines for students preparing for and taking part in a moot, and also to show that mooting is fun. Guidance on the order of speeches and on the formal speech used in submission is also given. In addition to these skills the advocate must also have a thorough understanding of trial procedure. This is essentially concerned with the rules that govern the conduct of a trial in court and an outline of trial procedure in the civil and in the criminal courts is given in Chapter 10.

11.2 Mooting personnel

The following people are required to take part in a moot:

1. senior counsel for the appellant;
2. junior counsel for the appellant;
3. senior counsel for the respondent;
4. junior counsel for the respondent;
5. the clerk of the moot;
6. the judge.

It can be seen from this that the moot will be made up of two competing teams, each of two members, those of counsel for the appellant and counsel for the respondent. The terms 'appellant' and 'respondent' are used because the mooting problem will usually take the form of an appeal to the Court of Appeal or to the House of Lords.

The role of senior counsel will be taken by the more proficient of the two students making up a single team. However, when mooting is first being taught the roles of senior and junior counsel may simply be allocated so as to give all students an equal opportunity to practice the necessary skills involved in mooting.

The role of clerk of the moot will also usually be taken by a student. The clerk is responsible for assembling in the mooting room the necessary case reports, statutes and other authorities to be relied upon by counsel. It is his task to pass such authorities to the judge at the appropriate moment in counsel's argument. It is also the job of the clerk to time counsel's speeches.

The person who acts as judge may vary depending upon whether the moot is part of a teaching programme or part of an internal or external competition. For a teaching programme or internal competition, this role will usually be taken by a member of the academic staff. For external competitions the role may be taken by a practising barrister or solicitor or even by a judge.

Sometimes a 'master of moots' may also be referred to in connection with mooting. The 'master of moots' is essentially the organiser of the moot or overall competition.

11.3 Preparing for a moot

Preparation is regarded as an essential element of both mooting and advocacy in general. However good a speaker a person may be, nothing can take the place of thorough preparation. This in itself is an important legal skill.

At the outset, the mooters will be told whom they are representing and whether they are to act as senior or junior counsel. Their first step will be to read and thoroughly familiarise themselves with the moot problem. They will then go on to pinpoint the various legal issues contained in the problem. The mooting problem will usually be designed so as to contain two major issues. Thus, the usual 'plan of action' will be for senior counsel to deal with one issue and for junior counsel to deal with the other. The argument or arguments prepared by counsel is or are referred to as their submission or submissions.

The question, as well as giving the facts of the case, will set out the decision of the judge in the court of first instance. It may give details of the cases relied upon by the judge and also give details of the grounds of appeal. Obviously the participants will need to consider these points carefully.

Preparation for a moot will require legal research into a particular area or areas of law. However, not all of the material and cases that are read will be relevant. Again, it is the task (and skill) of the mooter in preparing his or her case to sift the relevant from the irrelevant. Further, the mooter must emphasise the strong points of his or her client's case while seeking to minimise the weak points. It is usually better to engage in a spot of lateral thinking here! The mooter must try to anticipate what argument or arguments his or her opponent will be using and to prepare a response to it or them.

When preparing his or her submission, the mooter must remember that he or she is preparing a legal argument and not writing an essay or even a set of lecture notes! A common mistake is to make the submission too turgid and too heavily reliant on cases. It is difficult for a judge to follow such a submission and so it may be difficult for a mooter to keep the judge's attention. This is an obvious failing when a recognised skill of both mooting and advocacy is to gain and then keep the attention of the court.

Thus a submission should be concise but should also develop the necessary points. Cases can be used to support the legal argument but should not be allowed to take over that argument.

It is also essential to keep in mind at all times that the mooter needs to be thoroughly familiar with his or her submission or argument so that he or she can speak both naturally and with authority during the moot itself. It is not desirable for a mooter merely to read out notes or to repeat verbatim a submission or series of submissions that he or she has committed to memory. This point will be considered in more detail later.

11.4 The format of the moot and the order of speeches

As outlined above, the moot is made up of two teams of two counsel, one team for the appellant and one team for the respondent. Senior counsel for the appellant will speak first, usually followed by junior counsel for the appellant, senior counsel for the respondent and junior counsel for the respondent. Finally, senior counsel for the appellant will have the right to reply.

Each counsel will present his or her submission or submissions in turn, and he or she will have a limited time within which to speak. This time limit may vary but is usually about 20 minutes for each senior counsel and 15 minutes for each junior counsel. Senior counsel for the appellant then makes a formal reply, which is usually about five minutes in length. It is important that each mooter keeps within his or her allocated time – marks may well be lost if he or she does not. Having to speak within a prescribed time limit promotes conciseness and precision. When the speeches have concluded, the judge will give his or her decision.

The conduct of a trial is essentially the same whether it is taking place in a civil or a criminal court, although in some courts only barristers have a 'right of audience' whereas in others both solicitors and barristers can speak. The information given below is intended as an outline only of the rudiments of trial procedure.

The order of speeches in a trial is as follows:

1. In a civil trial, the plaintiff's opening speech.
   In a criminal trial, the prosecutor's opening speech.

2. In a civil case, the plaintiff then presents his or her case.
   In a criminal case, the prosecution then presents its case against the defendant.
   In both cases, this may well involve the calling of witnesses.

3. In both civil and criminal cases, the defendant and the defence, respectively, will then give its opening speech.

4. In both civil and criminal cases, the defendant and the defence, respectively, will then present its case.
   Again, this may well involve the calling of witnesses.

5. In both civil and criminal cases, the defendant and the defence, respectively, will then make a closing speech.

6. In a civil case, the plaintiff will then make a closing speech.

In a criminal case, the prosecution will only make a closing speech with the leave of the court in certain circumstances (see notes on criminal court procedure below).

To expand now on some of these points in more detail:

1. In his opening speech, the barrister or solicitor will outline the facts of the case and will also give a summary of the legal points involved. This is obviously to 'set the scene', as it were, for the presentation of his or her case.

2. When the barrister or solicitor goes on to present his or her case, this will usually involve the calling of witnesses. When a witness is called to give evidence, he or she will give that evidence on oath or make a declaration that he or she is telling the truth. The way in which a witness gives his or her evidence

is by responding to questions put to him or her by the barrister and/or solicitor for the party that has called him or her to give evidence and by the barrister and/or solicitor for the other party. This questioning will take three forms:

a) Examination-in-chief This is where a witness is questioned by the barrister or solicitor for the party who called the witness. The general rule is that leading questions cannot be asked of such a witness. A leading question is a question that suggests the answer to the witness and/or assumes the existence of a fact that is in dispute.

b) *Cross-examination* This takes place immediately after the examination-in-chief. The witness is now questioned by the barrister or solicitor for the other party. The purpose is 'to shake' the witness's evidence in some way; thus the questions will test the truthfulness and/or reliability of the answers given in response to the examination-in-chief. Leading questions may be asked.

c) *Re-examination* The barrister or solicitor for the party who called the witness may or may not choose to re-examine his or her witness. This will depend upon how well or otherwise his or her witness has stood up to cross-examination. If the witness has not performed well under cross-examination, then the barrister or solicitor may well wish to clarify certain points. During re-examination, questions must be limited to matters arising out of cross-examination, unless leave of the court has been obtained to do otherwise.

This three-stage process of questioning is repeated with each witness – at least where re-examination of the witness is carried out.

3. The closing speech is used to summarise the submissions that have been made, to comment on the evidence and to answer the arguments put by the party's opponent.

There are some variants on this basic structure depending upon whether it is a civil or a criminal trial. These will be dealt with later in connection with civil and criminal court procedure.

After the closing speech or speeches, the moment for the court's judgment (civil cases) or decision or verdict (criminal cases) has arrived. In civil cases the judgment may be given immediately or the judge may require time to consider all of the facts, evidence and legal issues and may adjourn the matter for judgment to be given later. In criminal cases the magistrates will usually retire to consider their decision, while in the Crown Court juries sometimes retire for some days to consider their verdict!

When the judgment, decision or verdict is given, other matters may then need to be considered, most notably any order for costs. These matters are dealt with below in connection with civil and criminal court procedure.

11.5 The presentation of an argument/submission

As already noted, senior counsel for the appellant will begin the speeches. As he or she is speaking first, various opening formalities will usually be included in his or her speech. Thus he or she will usually begin with these words, 'May it please your Lordship, my name is Mr/Mrs/Miss ... and I am appearing with Mr/Mrs/Miss ... for the appellant in this matter and my learned friends Mr/Mrs/Miss ... and Mr/Mrs/Miss ... are appearing for the respondent.'

Where the moot has an audience and copies of the mooting question are not available to its members, then senior counsel for the appellant should also begin by asking the judge whether he or she wishes senior counsel to set out the facts of the case. If the judge so wishes, then senior counsel should do this before proceeding with his or her submissions.

As will now be apparent, mooting does involve the use of some formal language. Most of this formal language is concerned with the way in which the participants address and refer to each other. Male judges are addressed directly as 'my Lord'. However, if counsel refers to the judge in the course of his or her submission, he or she should refer to him as 'your Lordship' – for example, 'as your Lordship has pointed out ...'. The equivalent ways of referring to female judges are 'my Lady' and 'your Ladyship'. However, barristers are taught that it is correct to address female judges as 'my Lord' and 'your Lordship'!

A mooter should not address his or her opponents as 'my opponents'. He or she should refer to them as 'my learned friends' or 'my learned friend' or 'my friends' or 'my friend'. Likewise, a mooter should refer to his or her colleague as 'my learned junior' or as 'my learned senior' as the case may be. If the matter is a criminal case, then a mooter should refer to it as 'The Crown against ...'. Another formality with which a mooter must comply is that he or she should stand while making his or her speech and remain standing while being questioned by the judge.

The formality of speech involved in mooting should not mean, however, that counsel should speak in a pompous way. Counsel should try to speak as naturally as possible but perhaps with something of a sense of occasion! Counsel must also speak clearly; while there is no need to shout, he or she should not mumble.

A mooter should establish eye contact with the judge. He or she should also try to avoid nervous habits which are irritating to others and, in particular, to the judge, such as clicking a pen constantly. An inexperienced student feeling nervous should nevertheless persevere. The more experienced a mooter or advocate is, the less nervous he or she becomes. It is not usually a good idea to speak as quickly as possible to get it all over with!

A mooter's argument will be presented in the form of numbered submissions. There may be only one main submission or there may be several, depending upon the nature of the mooting problem itself. It is important to establish the submission or submissions clearly at the outset and then to go on to develop each one in turn. Although a mooter should not read from a prepared speech, he or she may wish to use postcards on which certain key points have been noted in order to remind him or herself of these points.

Again, counsel should seek to emphasise the good points of the client's case without overloading his or her submissions with legal authorities. Neither should counsel express personal opinions. Again, a formal legal style is required. Thus counsel should say 'It is submitted ...' or 'It is suggested ...' and not 'I think ...'. Remember that it is for the judge to form his own opinion; counsel assists him or her to do so by the presentation of his or her legal argument.

Some final points to note on the use of authorities are, first, that they should be referred to in full and not in their abbreviated form: *Lloyd's Bank plc* and *Rosset* cited in volume one of the All England Reports for the year 1990 at page 1111, not *Lloyd's Bank plc* v *Rosset* [1990] 1 All ER 1111. Secondly, there may well be a preferred order of authorities. The mooters should check the rules of any competition they are taking part in on this point.

11.6 Answering questions

One of the most challenging parts of mooting is counsel's ability to answer questions well. It is challenging because obviously counsel will not know with certainty what the questions will be (although he or she may have a go at trying to predict them!). Thus, the ability to answer questions involves in turn counsel's ability to think on his or her feet and knowledge of the case, the law and his or her argument.

The guiding rule with regard to answering questions is 'DON'T PANIC!'. The judge will want to observe how counsel responds to questioning. It is better to take a few moments for silent reflection than to jump into a garbled immediate response. Where counsel considers that the judge's point is valid, he or she should respond by saying 'I am obliged to your Lordship'. Where, however, counsel considers that his or her own argument on the particular point is valid, he or she should persevere, perhaps beginning the answer with the words 'With great respect, my Lord ...'. The ability to answer questions may appear difficult, but senior and junior counsel can practise by questioning each other.

Counsel should never interrupt the judge before beginning his or her answer. Counsel should obviously treat the judge with courtesy and respect at all times.

11.7 Conduct during the moot

As already noted, counsel for the appellant speaks first. Once a mooter has finished speaking, his or her first reaction may well be an overwhelming sense of relief. However, it is not usually all over yet!

Senior counsel for the appellant must listen carefully to counsel for the respondent's submissions and prepare his or her reply. Here, he or she will deal with any particular points raised by the respondent and seek to answer them. Junior counsel for the appellant should assist his or her senior counsel. Obviously they cannot enter into a discussion in the middle of the moot, but they can whisper to each other and pass each other notes.

Counsel for the respondent will speak after counsel for the appellant. This may be difficult, not least because counsel may become increasingly nervous while waiting to speak. However, both junior and senior counsel must listen to the submissions of their opponents and incorporate any answers in response to those submissions into their own submissions. Counsel for the respondent should have allowed time for this when preparing their submissions so that they do not now run over their allotted time.

It obviously goes without saying that while a mooter is speaking, the other mooters should listen attentively and courteously. This is regarded as part of counsel's 'court room manner' and is one of the criteria that the judge will take into account when assessing counsel's overall performance.

11.8 Judging the moot

Once all of the mooters have finished speaking, the judge may well take a few moments to consider his judgment and to allocate marks. Judges usually make their assessment on the basis of the following criteria: clarity and presentation of argument, use of authorities, ability to answer questions and court-room manner.

It is possible for one team to win on the law and for another team to win the moot. Of course, it is also possible to win on both! The judge will usually give judgment on the law and also explain the reasoning behind his decision as to who has won the moot. How briefly or otherwise he deals with these points depends upon the individual judge.

The above outline is intended to provide some guidelines on mooting but also to show that mooting is fun.

11.9 Sample moot 'case'

Divide into teams, prepare and moot the following problem.

Julian was returning home from work. It was 7.15pm on a rainy November day and he alighted from the bus at his usual stop. He was late for an evening out with his fiancée, Jane, and began running along the pavement. Maria was reversing her car out of her driveway. She also was late – this time for a 'Bring and Buy sale'. Part of the rear window of her car was obscured by bags of 'goodies' that she was taking to the sale. Maria did not see Julian and ran him over with her car.

Julian was trapped underneath Maria's car. Peter, a member of the St John

Ambulance Brigade, who was passing at the time, advised that Julian should not be moved until the emergency services arrived.

During the short wait for the emergency services, Julian's mother, Anna, and his fiancée, Jane, walked past on their way to Anna's house. They saw a group of people gathered on the pavement and went to investigate. On seeing that Julian was trapped underneath the car, his mother collapsed and Jane became distraught. Both Anna and Jane have subsequently received medical treatment for shock and other after-effects. Julian made a complete recovery from his injuries.

At first instance, Mrs Justice Marvel held that Maria was negligent and that she was also liable to Anna and Jane in respect of damages for nervous shock. Mrs Justice Marvel based her decision on the cases of *Donoghue* v *Stevenson*, *McLoughlin* v *O'Brien* and *Jones* v *Wright*.

Maria now appeals to the Court of Appeal.

12

Legal Aid

12.1 Guiding principles and history of the scheme

It is axiomatic that having an elaborate structure of courts is of limited value in itself unless these courts are available to meritorious cases regardless of the parties' financial status. It is generally accepted that litigation and associated work is very expensive, and indeed the costs may be prohibitive – particularly for an individual. Many potential litigants see litigation as out of the question unless the cost can be in some way subsidised – usually by the state. Many countries have long recognised that the less affluent members of society will be denied access to justice unless such subsidies are available. This denial of justice has profound effects not only upon the individuals but also on society as a whole, since resentment and frustration are insidious. A common public perception of lawyers is that they have a 'taxi-meter' ticking as soon as a potential client makes contact, and it is incontrovertible that cases of public interest have either failed to be considered by the courts, or such consideration was delayed, due to the fear of the costs involved.

Prior to the introduction of the legal aid and advice scheme under the Legal Aid and Advice Act 1949 there was 'no organised provision for legal advice throughout the country' (per the Rushcliffe Committee), the only help being local ad hoc volunteer-run schemes. The 1949 Act was the result of a growing awareness of the need for a state-funded national scheme; it implemented the recommendations of the

Rushcliffe Committee, which saw the scheme as the second wave of the new welfare state (following on the introduction of the NHS).

Today's system is little changed from the original idea of a fund set up by government from central funds and controlled by the Lord Chancellor to pay lawyers in private practice to undertake litigation for the less-well-off section of the populace, with the fund rather than the individual meeting the legal bill (subject to recovery of the expenses should the case be successful). However, it is very contentious whether the overriding principle of ensuring that all persons have access to justice, regardless of their financial status, has now been breached in the light of recent developments. The simplistic analysis is that if you are rich, then you can afford to fund your litigation from your private means, and if you are poor and dependent upon state benefits, then you will almost certainly have your costs underwritten by the legal aid fund; but what happens to the millions of persons who do not fit into either of these categories – are their rights to be denied?

12.2 The administrative framework

The present organisation and regulations were introduced by the Legal Aid Act 1988 which created the Legal Aid Board as the fund's governing body. The administration is divided into civil legal aid, which is run by the legal aid area offices, and criminal legal aid, which is controlled by the relevant courts. The local legal aid area offices deal with applications, enquiries and complaints concerning civil legal aid in their designated area, with assistance from the area legal aid committee, while appeals and complaints concerning criminal legal aid are dealt with initially by the relevant court where the case is being heard (ie magistrates' court or Crown Court) and ultimately by the criminal legal aid committee.

The area offices are staffed by civil servants who consider the suitability of applications. Practising lawyers make a contribution by sitting on the area committees for both civil and criminal matters, and it must be borne in mind that these committees can ultimately decide if an application for legal aid is granted or refused.

The instructed solicitor will initially advise a client as to his or her likely eligibility for legal aid, and indeed this advice must be given whether or not that particular solicitor undertakes legally aided work. In the latter situation, should a client appear eligible, and wish to apply, for legal aid, the solicitor has to direct him or her to a solicitor who undertakes such legally aided work, since to fail to advise your client as to the advantages of applying for legal aid might lead to a successful claim in negligence by an inadequately advised client who subsequently suffers a loss. Indeed the Law Society may discipline solicitors who persistently fail to advise clients of their legal aid rights.

12.3 Civil legal aid

With the exclusion of certain local or specialised free advice lines or free initial interviews, such as may be set up in the wake of a disaster or in a group action, the following types of assistance are available:

1. legal aid and assistance scheme (euphemistically known as the 'green form scheme');
2. assistance by way of representation (ABWOR);
3. civil legal aid proper – ie under the terms of a legal aid certificate.

Legal aid and assistance scheme

This is usually a client's first contact with legal aid and is administratively the simplest and quickest type of help. The green form scheme is by far the most commonly used form of legal aid, but it is envisaged that, as a result of changes in the eligibility rates introduced by the Lord Chancellor in April 1993, far fewer persons will now be able to avail themselves of the scheme.

When is it available and what assistance can be given

The green form scheme can cover any question of English law (as opposed to Scottish or foreign law) and is therefore extremely wide-ranging. The most common areas covered are matrimonial law, criminal law, consumer problems and housing. The solicitor is allowed to give advice, send and receive communications, draft documents, undertake research and basically do any other connected work which falls short of actual conduct of court proceedings. Indeed it is perfectly possible for a solicitor to prepare a written case, for the client to go and argue personally in a court or before a tribunal, and *not* to represent the client in the hearing.

For the use of the green form scheme in relation to criminal matters, see section 12.4 below.

Limits imposed upon green form use

The green form scheme is intended to provide introductory and diagnostic help and is subject to strict limitations. A solicitor may undertake work until he or she reaches two hours' worth or, if the matter is matrimonial and he or she actually drafts a petition, three hours' worth of work. Once this limit has been reached an extension is possible on completion and submission of the appropriate form to the local area office. The purpose of the extension is to enable certain specified work to be done, all being well, to complete the matter.

Who can receive help under a green form

Eligibility for green form help is assessed by the solicitor without recourse to the legal aid office and is based upon the client's disposable income and capital, with set allowances for dependants. It should be noted that children are also eligible to apply through the medium of a parent or guardian.

The eligibility calculation for the green form only takes a couple of minutes (provided that the client has the relevant figures to hand) and does not take detailed figures into account. The client must be eligible as to both capital and income in order to qualify, and in each instance it is the disposable figure which is pertinent – that is, the available capital or income which could be used to meet the costs of legal advice.

The figures used are revised annually (each April) and are in line with the current income support allowances. In the year 1996/97, in order to qualify for green form advice an applicant must have a disposable weekly income of £75 or less and disposable capital of £1,000 or less. Anyone satisfying these financial criteria will be entitled to a maximum of two hours' (or where appropriate three hours') worth of work for no contribution.

However, clients have to be warned that if any property or money is recovered or preserved as a result of the green form work, then this will (subject to certain exceptions) be used to pay for the solicitor's work. For a more detailed explanation of this aspect, called the statutory charge, see below, pp268–270.

Clients who repeatedly seek advice upon the same matter, whether from one solicitor or from a series of solicitors, will have to obtain the area office's authorisation before the fund will meet the legal bill.

In the normal course of events, once the work is finished under the green form – the reverse of which is a pro forma bill – the instructed solicitor fills in the appropriate details and submits the form to the local legal aid office for payment.

Assistance by way of representation (ABWOR)

This is an extension to the cover given to a client who (usually) has already been receiving advice under a green form. The extension is not purely as to the length of time which may be spent on the work (indeed, once ABWOR has been granted, time limits are no longer applicable); it also expands the whole ambit of the assistance available by allowing the solicitor to appear in certain specified court proceedings on his or her client's behalf.

When it is available and what assistance can be given

ABWOR can be obtained for most civil cases to be dealt with by the Family Proceedings Courts (the magistrates' courts), covering such matters as disputes over residence and contact with children, and also for miscellaneous proceedings such as those before Mental Health Review Tribunals and on behalf of prisoners appearing before the Board of Prison Visitors.

The work covered includes all necessary preparation as well as the actual court appearance which, with prior authority on appropriate occasions, may be by counsel. The terms of the ABWOR certificate will clearly delineate the extent of the cover.

How ABWOR is obtained; eligibility

Unlike green form cover ABWOR has to be approved by the legal aid area office and involves completing a short form requiring greater detail than a green form. In most cases persons applying for ABWOR are already on green form advice, but it is possible to be eligible for the former and not the latter since the financial limits are higher. Once again the applicant must be eligible both as to disposable capital (here the 1996/97 limit is £3,000) and disposable income (1996/97 limit of £162 per week or less), with set deductions being made for dependants. In contrast to the green form scheme, a contribution towards the cost may be levied, being a third of the amount by which the income exceeds £67 per week (the green form upper limit) and £162 per week (the ABWOR upper limit).

Clients should be given advice and warning about the possible effects of the statutory charge, and the completed bill is passed to the area office for payment.

Civil legal aid

This is full legal aid and is available for cases in nearly any court except a coroner's court and tribunal proceedings. Full legal aid will be appropriate where the necessary work cannot be completed under a green form and ABWOR is insufficient or inapplicable. In contrast to the other types of legal aid, civil legal aid may, in restricted circumstances relating to children, be granted without either a means or a merits test, but for all other applications to be successful both of these tests must be passed.

A full certificate covers all the necessary preparatory work as well as representation in court by either a solicitor or a barrister, although a certificate may be limited to a certain aspect of the case.

Emergency legal aid

The normal processing of a civil legal aid application can take up to ten weeks, and in certain circumstances it is clearly unreasonable for someone to wait as long as that before being able to pursue his or her case. The classic example of an emergency arises in the case of domestic violence when a battered woman needs to obtain an injunction for her protection.

It is possible to obtain emergency legal aid within two to three working days, and in cases of the utmost urgency within a couple of minutes over the telephone. Effectively the emergency legal aid certificate covers the necessary work until an ordinary certificate (following full processing, assessment etc) replaces it. Obviously in emergency situations there is no time to assess finances, and so there is a danger that a person with emergency legal aid will be found to be ineligible financially some few weeks after the solicitor has done work under the emergency certificate – here the client will be entirely liable for all of the solicitor's costs.

Eligibility

An application for a civil legal aid certificate is both lengthy and detailed and takes anything between eight and 12 weeks to be processed, and the time spent completing the application is often claimed on the green form.

The tests as to eligibility are divided into *merits* test and *means* test.

Merits test

This is applied by the area director at the legal aid office, or his or her officer, and comes from s15(2) Legal Aid Act 1988, which states that no person shall be granted legal aid in connection with any proceedings unless he or she shows that 'he or she has reasonable grounds for taking, defending or being a party to those proceedings'.

Even if the applicant satisfies these criteria then he or she may still be refused legal aid if it is judged that any benefit arising out of successful proceedings would be trivial.

Means test

This calculation is carried out by an assessment officer of the DSS and is far more detailed and sophisticated than the comparable green form test. Additional expenses and liabilities, such as mortgage repayments or rent, pension contributions, and child care costs (if appropriate) feature in the calculations, and as before there are set allowances for dependants. The allowances are altered annually, and generally spouses' means are aggregated unless they are living apart or there is a conflict of interest, such as in a divorce.

The test is two-fold – on disposable income and disposable capital – and it is possible to be eligible on the figures for one and yet not be granted legal aid because of ineligibility on the other figures. Frequently, as shown below, legal aid will be granted subject to the applicant making a contribution from either income or capital.

Disposable income is assessed for the following 12 months and the deductions are: tax, national insurance, superannuation, pension contributions, employment expenses, rent, water rates, council tax, mortgage payments, and allowances for family and dependants.

Disposable capital assesses: savings, the surrender value of life assurance or endowment policies, items of substantial value, and the value of any dwelling other than your residence. It will not take into account the value of your principal dwelling house (but note that there is a principle in respect of equity exceeding £100,000), furniture and fittings, clothes, tools of your trade, and, if appropriate, the value of the item in dispute.

Only persons whose means are below the lower limits for both capital and income will qualify without a contribution. However, the error of viewing this as 'free legal aid' should not be made, for often, as will be explained later, the legal aid is a loan rather than a gift and in common with all other loans has to be repaid.

The figures in the following table show the eligibility limits for the year 1996/97. There are higher limits for capital eligibility for pensioners in recognition of the fact that their savings are literally life savings and there would be no opportunity to replenish them if they were used in legal costs.

Disposable income:

Below £2,498	No contribution.
Between £2,498 and £7,403 (£8,158 if the claim is for personal injury)	Contribution – assessed as balance of income over £2,498 ÷ 36 = monthly contribution – paid for so long as the applicant continues to receive legal aid.
Over £7,403 (or £8,158)	Ineligible.

Disposable capital

Below £3,000	No contribution.
Between £3,000 and £6,750 (£8,560 for personal injury)	A contribution from disposable capital in excess of £3,000 in payable
Over £6,750 (£8,560)	Ineligible unless the case is deemed to be very expensive, when legal aid may be granted.

Who pays what at the end of the case

The answer to this question depends upon factors such as who won the case, and was each party legally aided. The basic point is that the Legal Aid Fund is under a duty to try to remain in credit if at all possible and so it will attempt to recover costs paid out to legally assisted persons' lawyers.

There is a strict order in which the fund must attempt to recover such costs as it has paid out, until the deficit is made up, as follows:

1. Any order for costs made against the other party. In civil litigation there is a general rule that 'costs follow the cause' – ie the unsuccessful party will pay the costs of the successful party.
2. Any contribution assessed from the assisted person.
3. The statutory charge placed on 'property recovered or preserved which has been at issue in the proceedings'.
4. Finally, if there is still a deficit after the stages outlined above, the Legal Aid Fund has to bear the loss.

From the table below the following points become apparent:

1. A legally-aided person can budget far more accurately than a non-legally-aided party since he or she knows the amount of his or her contribution, which will only alter if his or her circumstances change and will not increase no matter how large his or her solicitor's bill. He or she can even budget for losing the case, since under s17 Legal Aid Act 1988 an order for costs in favour of the non-

legally aided winner will not exceed his or her own contribution unless he or she has been particularly vexatious or unreasonable in the conduct of the case. This can be summarised as follows: if a legally-aided person loses he or she will normally have to pay no more towards the winner's costs than he or she has paid towards his own.

2. It therefore follows that a non-legally-aided party in an action against a legally-aided party is in a vulnerable position – he or she may well find him or herself paying both his or her own and all his or her opponent's costs if he or she loses and yet will only recover a sum equal to the opponent's contribution (which may well be nil) if he or she wins and cannot get an order for the fund to make good the difference under s18.

3. A winning legally-aided party may find that a substantial part of the property he or she recovers or preserves is subject to the statutory charge, and so he or she has only a Pyrrhic victory.

LEGALLY-AIDED PARTY	NON-LEGALLY-AIDED PARTY
LOSES	**WINS**
He or she pays his or her maximum assessed contribution (if any) to the fund. If his or her solicitor's costs are less than this amount, he or she will be refunded the balance. The Court may order that he or she pay something towards the winner's costs: such sum as is 'reasonable having regard to the circumstances of the case' (s17 Legal Aid Act 1988). Generally this figure will be no higher than his or her assessed maximum contribution.	By s18 Legal Aid Act 1988 he or she may get an order that his or her costs be paid out of the fund to the extent that they have not been paid by the legally-aided opponent, if it is 'just and equitable' in all the circumstances: see *Hanning* v *Maitland (No 2)* [1970] 1 All ER 812 CA.
WINS	**LOSES**
He or she pays his or her maximum assessed contribution – this will be reimbursed by the fund if the loser pays all the winner's costs. NB: if the order for costs only partially covers the amount expended by the fund, and even taking into account the aided party's contribution there is still a deficit, the statutory charge will arise.	He or she pays his or her own legal costs and may well be ordered to pay all of the legally-aided winner's costs. NB: sometimes this costs order will not cover all of the legally-aided party's costs.

How the statutory charge operates

Simplistically, this is a means of ensuring that any deficit to the fund is repaid either from damages or from real property which has been recovered. In the case of damages or lump sums (except in matrimonial cases where the first £2,500 is exempt) the charge will bite immediately, and so the legally-aided person will only receive the balance of the damages once the deficit due to the fund has been deducted. In the case of real property the charge can be postponed in certain circumstances, but in that instance interest (currently 10.5 per cent) will be charged.

12.4 Criminal legal aid

With many civil proceedings the party has a choice as to whether to commence, defend, or be a party to, the action, whereas in criminal proceedings this element of choice is very often absent. Thus there may be great need for advice and help, with a tight time schedule linked to court appearances.

Help falls into three categories:

1. legal aid and assistance – see section 12.3 above;
2. duty solicitor scheme;
3. criminal legal aid.

Legal aid and assistance

For details as to eligibility etc, see section 12.3 above. The solicitor can provide advice to someone who is concerned or who has, for instance, received a summons, and can also help a client prepare his case, but *cannot* actually represent the client in court.

Duty solicitor scheme

This is essentially an emergency first aid scheme to ensure that each citizen has access to legal advice, no matter what the time of day or night, and whether or not he or she has his or her own family solicitor. The scheme is available to anyone being questioned by the police about an offence (whether he or she has been arrested or not) and is in operation 24 hours a day, 365 days a year. Local solicitors with criminal litigation experience are on call on a rota basis, and they go to police stations to give advice and assistance. Their costs are met under the green form scheme, and the advice is *free* to all regardless of financial status. The duty solicitors are also on call in the precincts of courts in case advice is needed.

Criminal legal aid

A criminal legal aid order covers all the work necessary to prepare the defence and also covers actual representation in court by a solicitor or, if appropriate, a barrister. The administration and assessment is dealt with by the clerk to the justices at the court dealing with the case.

Eligibility
As with civil legal aid, the applicant must satisfy the criteria as to both merits and means; failure to satisfy either will mean that a person will have to meet his or her own legal costs. Application is made on the appropriate form, which is then forwarded to the court for assessment.

Merits test
Certain categories of person – eg someone who has been committed for trial on a charge of murder – will automatically satisfy the merits test, but obviously these are a small minority. Most people are granted legal aid by the court where it is 'in the interests of justice' to do so and the applicant needs help to pay the legal costs. Courts follow what used to be called the 'Widgery criteria', which are now encapsulated in s22 Legal Aid Act 1988 and can be summarised as follows:

1. where the person will lose his or her liberty, job or reputation if convicted;
2. where the charges raise a substantial question of law;
3. where the accused is mentally ill;
4. where the accused does not understand English;
5. where it is necessary to trace witnesses or experts and interview and cross-examine them;
6. when it is in the interests of someone other than the accused that the accused be represented.

Means test
Disposable capital and disposable income are both considered, and the limits differ from those for civil legal aid. Similar allowances are given for dependants, account is taken of expenses such as housing, tax etc, and a contribution may be payable. The figures in the Table below relate to 1996/97.

Disposable income	
Less than £49 per week	No contribution.
More than £49 per week	Contribution is calculated as £1 per week for every £3 (or part of £3) by which the weekly disposable income exceeds £48.
Disposable capital	
Below £3,000	No contribution.
Above £3,000	Contribution will be the excess over £3,000.

Persons who are acquitted usually have their contributions repaid to them unless it is decided by the court that they brought the prosecution upon themselves. The Legal Aid Fund will meet the solicitor's costs.

12.5 Recent reforms

It has been clear for many years that adherence to the principle of legal aid was very expensive, but no one accurately foresaw how greatly the use of the scheme would expand. British society is far more aware of legal issues than ever before, due in part to massive media coverage. Our society is changing rapidly, and many more people wish to defend or protect their rights by recourse to the judicial system. This is not only true in relation to such things as consumer rights; people are also being forced to use the courts following the breakdown of relationships. Given today's economic climate, the full ideal of legal aid available to all who need help with the cost is now too expensive for the public purse to bear without other services suffering. Traditionally, successive governments had tried to curb the costs by refusing to extend the scope of legal aid even where there was patently a need – for example, to representation before tribunals – and by failing to increase eligibility limits in line with inflation. These devices led to some savings, but these were insufficient to keep control over spending.

The scale of the cost problem can be appreciated when one realises that the cost of the scheme in 1988 was £475 million while in 1992/93 it was estimated at £1,100 million – yet the numbers being helped have only risen from 2.3 to 3.1 million for the same period. In 1992 Lord Mackay of Clashfern, the Lord Chancellor, announced an intention to introduce changes which it was estimated would save £43 million in the first year of operating, rising to £173 million in 1995/96.

Lord Mackay's suggestions to save money fell roughly into the following proposals:

1. That solicitors' firms should tender competitively in order to win contracts to process legal aid work in volume at an agreed price, subject to strict quality controls. This is a logical extension of a pilot franchising scheme whereby firms are allowed to make some decisions as to legal aid eligibility without recourse to the area office, and receive preferential treatment in payments on account.
2. The financial eligibility for legal aid should be amended, and all legal advice and assistance at present available subject to a contribution should be withdrawn, so that anyone who did not qualify for 'free' green form advice would have to pay privately.
3. Persons eligible for legal aid would pay far greater contributions towards their legal costs.
4. Large cutbacks in the legal aid available for certain types of work, eg matrimonial matters.

5. The introduction of standard fee payments to solicitors in (initially) certain types of magistrates' court cases. Thus the solicitor would be paid a flat rate according to the type of work rather than on the amount of work expended on each individual case.

Lord Mackay encountered great opposition from, among others, the Law Society, the Bar Council, various consumer groups and, perhaps more surprisingly, members of the judiciary including the Lord Chief Justice, Lord Taylor. These groups felt that legal aid was becoming less readily available to the average citizen, and that thus there would be denial of justice and fragmentation into three groups: those who were so poor as to be able to obtain legal aid and thus pursue their actions; those rich enough to pay privately for legal help; and the remainder who would be forced to calculate whether they could afford to risk all their savings in a legal battle. The Law Society estimated that the effect of the cuts in eligibility rates would mean that ten million extra persons would no longer be able to get help. The practical outcome of this change is that generally, unless an applicant is on such a low income as to render him or her eligible for income support, he or she will not receive green form advice.

Lord Mackay's sweeping reform package encountered unprecedented opposition, with solicitors in some parts of the country refusing to undertake legal aid work in magistrates' courts. An attempt by the Law Society to obtain judicial review of the merits of the decision to introduce standard fees in magistrates' court was refused by the Queen's Bench Division on 30 April 1993 (*R* v *The Lord Chancellor, ex parte the Law Society* (1993) The Times 5 May). The Law Society and the Bar Council devised counter-proposals, but these were rejected, and the standard fees were introduced on 1 June 1993.

12.6 The future – if any

Since the new eligibility rates were introduced in April 1993 there has been a rash of prophecies of doom, mainly based upon the fear that people either now being ineligible for initial advice and assistance or only obtaining full legal aid subject to a significant contribution of potentially lengthy duration will not only cause individual denials of justice but also slow down the law's development by hampering judicial decisions on points of public interest and importance.

Due to the introduction of standard fees (which Lord Mackay eventually hopes to extend to certain types of civil proceedings) and franchising, it is forecast that many firms of solicitors will either voluntarily stop undertaking legal aid work, since it is viewed as uneconomic, or alternatively be unable to secure contracts. Clearly it will be the smaller firms, which are unable to handle a large volume of work and provide expensive, sophisticated support systems, which will suffer most. There is already incontrovertible evidence of firms that are no longer offering their services to legally aided persons, and for every firm that withdraws the client's choice of lawyer is diminished, with particularly hard implications for clients in rural areas where the majority of solicitors tend to be in small firms.

If the prophecies of doom and the effects of the changes, either already in place or proposed, are carried to their logical conclusion, then we shall be back to the nineteenth-century position where the law will be accessible only to the rich (and also to the very poorest members of society).

12.7 Alternative ways of funding legal work

In view of the foregoing, far greater emphasis is now falling on alternative methods of paying for legal costs. Basically these fall into two types – those that are free, and ultimately funded either by central or local government or by groups of lawyers, and those where the client pays but on a different basis from an hourly rate or set transaction fee.

The former sources of help with legal problems are bodies such as law centres and debt-counselling centres and Citizens' Advice Bureaux (CABx), which are found in most reasonably sized towns. They are able to give advice on a wide range of topics, and larger CABx have employed solicitors. Clearly they have to recoup their expenses if possible, and so if the client is eligible a claim for advice given will be made under the green form scheme. Free advice will also be offered by trading standards departments. On an irregular basis, following disasters, accidents or group actions, interested groups of lawyers will often set up telephone help and advice lines offering free oral advice, or alternatively for potential litigants the initial diagnostic interview will be free (regardless of financial status).

The latter methods of funding include the advice offered to members of organisations in specialised fields, such as motoring associations on matters connected with driving, the cost of such advice being covered by the members' annual subscriptions. Insurance is set to play a far greater role, with most house and car insurance policies now also offering the services of legal experts in matters connected with the policy. Clearly the cost of such help is built in as a weighting in each premium. There will also be a growth in specialist legal expenses insurance – that is, people taking out separate policies specifically to cover the costs of legal fees which may arise. It is interesting to note that this development stems from what has now become a shortcoming in the second arm of the welfare state, just as the increase in private health care insurance reflects perceived shortcomings in the first stage of that state. Possibly the most radical development is that of conditional fees agreements. Following lengthy consultation and research, by s58 of the Courts and Legal Services Act 1990, the way was opened for the limited introduction of such arrangements, whereby the solicitor agrees to undertake litigation on the basis that if the action is unsuccessful he will render no bill to the client, but if it succeeds he will send a bill calculated as at present on time spent, disbursements and VAT, but also with a modest percentage uplift. Clearly very strict controls need to be exercised over the type of case which can be dealt with in this manner, it being envisaged that the most common will be personal injury litigation, and regulations are yet to be made to permit such agreements in England (they have long been used in Scotland); yet it may be a way for a person ineligible for legal aid to fund his or her action, knowing from the outset that if he or she succeeds the damages will pay the lawyers, and if he or she fails there will not be a ruinous bill.

Given the present economic climate and the Lord Chancellor's drive for 'efficiency and quality', it may well be that self-help and more adventurous forms of funding will grow over the next few years as the use of legal aid becomes more restricted.

12.8 Exercises

1. Your client, a single mother with two children who is at present unemployed, seeks your advice as to a neighbour dispute. What would you tell her to allay her fears about the cost of your advice?

   Should your attempts to resolve the problem fail and your client take the law into her own hands and assault the troublesome neighbour, resulting in her being charged, to what help with legal costs might she be entitled?
2. Your client Mr Green is injured while using a lawn mower which appears to be faulty. The lawn mower manufacturers are maintaining that Mr Green did not follow their instructions for use and are contesting liability. Mr Green has today applied for legal aid in order to pursue the matter. Write to him giving advice as to the implications of applying for legal aid and explaining the differing scenarios as to cost if he should win or lose.
3. The facts are as above, but it is clear that Mr Green is financially ineligible for legal aid; how, in the foreseeable future, might he fund his action?

13

The Judiciary

13.1 Introduction

13.2 The categories of judge

13.3 The judiciary – general background

13.4 Judicial immunity

13.5 The function of judges

13.6 Extrajudicial activity

13.7 Cases

13.1 Introduction

The purpose of this chapter is to outline the involvement of judges in the English legal system. In his 1980 Richard Dimbleby lecture, 'Misuse of Power', Lord Denning said:

> 'Every judge on his appointment discards all politics and all prejudices. You need have no fear. The Judges of England have always in the past – and always will – be vigilant in guarding our freedoms. Someone must be trusted. Let it be the Judges.'

Consideration should be given to the role of a judge. Lord Radcliffe, a highly respected post-war judge, wrote in *Not in Feather Beds*:

> 'Say indeed that a judge must be fair, or that he must be impartial: that is essential. He must strip himself of all prejudices, certainly; except, I ought to add, those prejudices which on consideration he is prepared to stand by as his sincere convictions.'

Upon appointment a judge takes an oath to do 'right to all manner of people – without fear or favour, affection or ill will'. Each case must be considered by a judge in a calm and dispassionate way. The selection of a judge is based upon his or her experience of the law and of life, and also upon ability. A judge must have integrity, and he or she should cast aside any bias and prejudice, be it in respect of race, religion, morality or politics.

However, the role of a judge is not a simplistic matter. Lord Radcliffe indicates that a judge should not be biased but that a human mind does not have perfect balance. He refers to a judge as 'a mature man, of long and professional experience ...'. A judge's personal quality is important not only because of his or her reasoning powers or knowledge but also for 'his experience of life and the structure of thought and belief that he has built upon it'.

In 1921 Benjamin Cardozo, one of America's most renowned judges, wrote in *The Nature of the Judicial Process*:

> 'The great tides and currents which engulf the rest of men do not turn aside in their course and pass the judges by ...'

We can perhaps summarise this introduction by saying that a judge should be impartial and free of bias, and give a fair hearing to the respective parties. This should be tempered by bearing in mind that a judge is a human being and not a machine.

Judges are mature people who have professional experience and experience of life. They may, however, make mistakes, and they can be publicly reprimanded. For example, in 1978 a judge was rebuked for calling an Act a 'bugger's charter', and in 1982 Lord Hailsham repudiated a judge's comment that a rape victim who hitched a lift was guilty of contributory negligence and that the penalty should be reduced accordingly. Similarly, in 1992 a judge was rebuked by the Lord Chancellor, Lord Mackay of Clashfern, for kissing a female court usher. The Lord Chancellor's Department indicated that the incident was not one of sexual harassment but one of 'over familiarity' on the part of the judge. He was warned that a similar incident could result in his being dismissed. Further, in June 1993 the Lord Chancellor reprimanded a district judge following a second conviction for drink-driving. Lord Mackay considered invoking his powers of dismissal, on the ground of misbehaviour.

13.2 The categories of judge

The Courts and Legal Services Act 1990

Under this Act the qualifications for judicial appointment have been changed. Eligibility will *not* be based upon whether a person is a barrister or solicitor but upon specified rights of audience in the courts that are granted by authorised bodies. Solicitors will therefore be eligible for more judicial posts.

If a person, whether a barrister, solicitor or other authorised advocate, has rights of audience in *all* proceedings, then that person will be eligible for appointment to all levels of the judiciary. This removes the barristers' monopoly in higher courts and the joint monopoly by solicitors and barristers in the lower courts.

Before proceeding further, it should be pointed out that the term 'judge' is used in this chapter in its widest sense, namely, referring to all persons appointed to adjudicate. Further, although there are references to the varying retirement ages of judges, it should be noted that by virtue of the Judicial Pensions and Retirement Act 1993 the retirement age of all full-time and part-time judges is to be limited to 70. It is anticipated that this will become law during the summer of 1994.

Magistrates

With regard to magistrates as a whole, it is a measure of their importance that 98 per cent of criminal cases commence and finish in the magistrates' courts.

Lay magistrates

Magistrates are otherwise known as justices of the peace (JPs) or lay magistrates. There are approximately 28,000 lay magistrates, and although unpaid they receive allowances for travelling, subsistence and loss of earnings. On appointment, a magistrate must be over 21 but not over 60 years of age. Furthermore, he or she must reside in or within 15 miles of the commission area for which he or she is appointed. Certain people cannot sit as magistrates. These include undischarged bankrupts, serving members of Her Majesty's forces, members of the police, traffic wardens and persons convicted of certain offences.

Lay magistrates are sometimes found as a result of advertisements in the press which invite applications from the public at large, and one may put forward one's own name. Various organisations – for example, a local political party, trade union, Chamber of Commerce or voluntary body – may recommend the names of appropriate persons. Such people will generally be of good standing, and often they have some form of 'voluntary service' background.

Magistrates are appointed by the Lord Chancellor on the recommendation of a local advisory committee. Endeavours are made to balance the sexes, social classes, races and political parties, as magistrates provide experience from backgrounds other than legal ones and do not need a knowledge of the law. They do, however, undergo training. An induction course will comprise instruction, attendance at court as observers and also practical exercises. Training extends over one year and, apart from sitting in court, magistrates will visit penal institutions including prisons and remand centres. The *aim* of the training is to assist magistrates in understanding their duties. They will thus develop a sufficient knowledge of the law and a working knowledge of the rules of evidence.

When the Crown Court hears appeals or deals with people who have been committed for sentence by a magistrates' court, then it is compulsory for between two and four magistrates to sit with a High Court judge, circuit judge or recorder.

Lay magistrates do not officially retire, but at the age of 70 their names are entered in a 'supplemental list' which, inter alia, prevents their sitting judicially. Magistrates may, however, be removed by the Lord Chancellor for good cause.

Justices' clerks

An important office is that of a justices' clerk who must usually have a five-year magistrates' court qualification within s71 of the Courts and Legal Services Act 1990. This means a right of audience in relation to all proceedings in magistrates' courts.

Magistrates are independent of the clerk and must make their own decisions. In *R* v *Sussex Justices (ex parte McCarthy)* [1924] 1 KB 256 it was said by Lord

Hewart CJ (at 259) that it is of 'fundamental importance that justice should not only be done but manifestly and undoubtedly be seen to be done'. Following this principle, a justices' clerk should neither instruct magistrates as to their decisions nor appear to take part in those decisions. However, he or she *advises* the magistrates as to the law, practice and procedure. Other responsibilities of a justices' clerk involve administration and the training of magistrates.

Stipendiary magistrates
In addition to lay magistrates, there are also stipendiary magistrates who are full-time salaried professional magistrates. There are about 70 throughout the country. They must have a seven-year general qualification within s71 of the Courts and Legal Services Act 1990. This means that they have a right of audience in any part of the Supreme Court *or* in relation to all proceedings in county courts or magistrates' courts. Stipendiary magistrates are appointed by the Crown on the recommendation of the Lord Chancellor. They usually retire at 70 years of age.

County court district judges

County court district judges were formerly called registrars and are appointed by the Lord Chancellor. There is a requirement for a seven-year general qualification within s71 of the CLSA 1990. They have judicial and administrative functions, and their judicial role is emphasised. The Lord Chancellor may remove them, without the intervention of Parliament, on the grounds of incapacity or misbehaviour.

Recorders

Recorders are part-time judges appointed for a specific period by the Queen on the advice of the Lord Chancellor. The requirement in s71 is for a ten-year Crown Court or a ten-year county court qualification. Recorders sit in the Crown Court but may also sit in the county courts and the High Court.

It is argued that, to some extent, being a recorder is an apprenticeship in that a further appointment as a circuit judge or High Court judge could follow. Recorders may be removed by the Lord Chancellor, without Parliament's intervention, on the grounds of incapacity or misbehaviour, and they will not be appointed above 72 years of age.

Circuit judges

The Queen appoints circuit judges on the advice of the Lord Chancellor, and they are full-time permanent judges. Section 71 CLSA 1990 specifies that to be appointed a person must fulfil *one* of the following requirements: have a ten-year Crown Court or a ten-year county court qualification; be a Recorder; have had a full-time appointment of at least three years in one of various offices listed in part

1A of Schedule 2 to the Courts Act 1971 (Courts Act 1971 s16(3) as amended by the CLSA 1990). These offices include being a chairman of an industrial tribunal or a district judge or a stipendiary magistrate.

Circuit judges sit in the county courts and the Crown Court. They may also sit as additional judges of the High Court. The Lord Chancellor may remove them, without Parliament's intervention, on the grounds of incapacity or misbehaviour. In 1983 a circuit judge was dismissed for misbehaviour – that he had been fined £2,000 for smuggling whisky and cigarettes.

Circuit judges retire at 72 years of age, but they may continue until 75 if the Lord Chancellor considers it desirable.

High Court judges

High Court judges, sometimes referred to as 'puisne' judges, have high status, and officially they are called Justices of the High Court. The statutory maximum number has been 85, although this number is being increased (see below).

These judges are appointed by the Queen on the advice of the Lord Chancellor, and to become such a judge has been by invitation only. They are knighted or created DBE on appointment. The requirement in s71 CLSA 1990 is *either* a ten-year High Court qualification *or* having been a circuit judge for at least two years. High Court judges are assigned to a particular division. Their former practices are taken into account when they are so assigned, but they can be transferred to other divisions with the consent of both themselves and the presidents of their present divisions.

It is difficult to remove a judge of the High Court or above; this stems from the Act of Settlement 1701. Judges of the House of Lords, the Court of Appeal and the High Court hold office during good behaviour, subject to a power of removal by the Queen on an address presented to her by both Houses of Parliament. No judge of a superior court in England has been *removed* since the above Act was passed.

The retiring age for a High Court judge is 75, the age first imposed by the Judicial Pensions Act 1959. This does not, however, apply to judges appointed before 17 December 1959.

In October 1992 the Lord Chief Justice, Lord Taylor of Gosforth, described the delays in the High Court as 'intolerable'. Subsequently, Lord Taylor warned that there should be more High Court judges as otherwise the backlog of cases would become a 'national disgrace'. In the nineteenth Richard Dimbleby lecture, broadcast by the BBC, Lord Taylor said that the government's persistent failure to appoint enough High Court judges had caused unacceptable backlogs. As regards judicial appointments, he suggested that a 'lay observer' should be introduced into the process. In response the Lord Chancellor, Lord Mackay of Clashfern, although not promising more High Court judges, did appoint a working party to study how such judges were deployed. Chaired by Lord Justice Kennedy, it was set up jointly by the Lord Chancellor and the Lord Chief Justice.

In addition to the views expressed by Lord Taylor, the senior judge in the Commercial Court (a specialist court of the Queen's Bench Division), Mr Justice Saville, was extremely concerned about the shortage of judges in his court. The Commercial Court was operating with five instead of six judges and could reduce to four as retiring judges were not always replaced. There were difficulties in respect of delays in other courts which included the Criminal Division of the Court of Appeal, the Chancery Division of the High Court, and the Employment Appeal Tribunal, which is presided over by a High Court judge.

In March 1993 the Lord Chancellor announced that an extra ten High Court judges would be appointed as soon as possible. Accordingly, the statutory maximum number of High Court judges would be increased, although parliamentary and Privy Council approval would be required for this.

Interestingly, in June 1993 Michael Sachs, a former solicitor, became the first High Court judge appointed from outside the ranks of the Bar. He had been a circuit judge since 1984.

Lords Justices of Appeal

These are the judges in the Court of Appeal, and they can be up to 28 in number. They are appointed by the Crown on the advice of the Prime Minister after consultation with the Lord Chancellor.

The requirement in s71 CLSA 1990 is *either* a ten-year High Court qualification *or* having been a judge of the High Court. Accordingly, a Court of Appeal judge could be appointed straight from practice, that is, with no previous judicial experience. Removal is by joint address presented to the Queen by both Houses of Parliament (but see above, *High Court judges*, para 3).

The retiring age for such a judge is 75, but, again, this does not apply to judges appointed before 17 December 1959 – for example Lord Denning sat until he was 83 years of age.

Lords of Appeal in Ordinary

These are the judges in the House of Lords, otherwise known as the Law Lords. The President of the court is the Lord Chancellor. He is assisted by between seven and 11 Law Lords, the latter being the maximum permitted number. They are appointed by the Crown on the advice of the Prime Minister after consultation with the Lord Chancellor. The qualifications for appointment are:

1. the holding of high judicial office for two years;
2. the possession of a 15-year Supreme Court qualification within s71 of the CLSA 1990. A Supreme Court qualification means a right of audience in relation to all proceedings in the Supreme Court;
3. fifteen years of practice: as an advocate in Scotland, or as a solicitor entitled to

appear in the Court of Session and the High Court of Justiciary, or as a member of the Bar of Northern Ireland.

Removal is by joint address (see above), and retirement age for such a judge is, again, 75 years of age.

Promotion

There can be promotions from one level of the judiciary to another. A circuit judge with at least two years' experience can become a High Court judge. Any High Court judge will be eligible for appointment as a Lord Justice of Appeal. A judge in one of the superior courts for two years will be eligible for appointment as a Lord of Appeal in Ordinary.

13.3 The judiciary – general background

Social and educational background

The Bar was historically for the educated and wealthy, who went to public schools and Oxbridge (Oxford or Cambridge). Barristers could also have been in military service and possibly in politics. It appears, therefore, that the traditional view of judges has been that they are male, middle-aged, upper- and middle-class and white.

In 1970 a study of the background of 359 judges revealed that 81 per cent had been to public schools and 76 per cent to Oxbridge. In 1978, 74 High Court judges were listed, and over 75 per cent of these had attended public schools. Between 1 January 1980 and 1 May 1982, 17 High Court judges were appointed, of whom 76 per cent had been to public schools and 88 per cent to Oxbridge. Accordingly, with the occasional exception, the majority of judges had been to public schools and Oxbridge.

In March 1991 the *Sunday Times* published a study by Marcel Berlins which showed that of 123 senior judges in England and Wales more than half were over 60 years of age, and these included all of the Law Lords. Other points which arose were:

1. Two were 50 years of age or below.
2. Not one was from a racial minority.
3. Three were women (two in the High Court and one in the Court of Appeal).
4. Over two-thirds had been to public schools and Oxbridge.
5. They came from middle-class (or above) homes.
6. They were well off, conservative, Conservative also in the political sense, and they enjoyed 'the arcane, cosseted traditions of legal life'.

The situation, however, is slowly but surely changing. The legal aid scheme has assisted barristers to make a living at the Bar. Scholarships are now available, and legal education has increased, particularly in the former polytechnics which are now the new universities. The question which now arises is: will barristers or solicitors from such educational backgrounds become part of the judiciary?

Selection

On the Continent anyone wishing to become a judge selects such a career. This is not so within the English legal system, where judges are selected from the ranks of practising lawyers, mainly barristers, after years of professional practice. In effect, judges are appointed after demonstrating ability. The pool of lawyers for selection has generally been small, with correspondingly few candidates on short lists. The Courts and Legal Services Act 1990 should result in a larger pool.

What does selection involve?

Secrecy abounded, and little was known about the process of selection, until May 1986, when the Lord Chancellor's Department issued a pamphlet which gave a basic insight into the system of appointment and the policies involved. There is in-depth consultation and consideration, and a barrister may check facts about him or herself but not see the confidential opinions that have been expressed as to professional and personal suitability. Social and personal characteristics are obviously important, but if these are unconventional there could be a question-mark as to suitability. Reputation in court is very important.

In April 1993 the Lord Chancellor outlined reforms to modernise the appointment of judges and increase the numbers of women. He urged more women, particularly solicitors, to apply for judicial posts. Furthermore, selection would be dependent upon people *applying* as opposed to being invited, and a single individual's views would not block a candidate's appointment. However, the suggestion of a Judicial Appointments Commission was rejected as it was considered that it would lead to lobbying. The Lord Chancellor would retain his personal responsibility for appointments and maintained that he was in the best position to assess candidates.

In July 1993 it became clear that vacancies for judges were to be advertised, and the Lord Chancellor said that the new policy would help to freshen the public's image of the judiciary. Advertisements could appear in national newspapers as well as in legal journals. Bearing in mind the advertising of vacancies, and also that selection will be dependent upon application and not invitation, the selection process itself will be enhanced.

Do politics intrude into the appointment of judges?

There is a background of judicial independence which has to be borne in mind when considering this issue. Judges do not take part in politics, and a judge cannot be a Member of Parliament. Law Lords do not participate in party politics, although they may involve themselves in legal debates. A judge is neither dependent upon, nor dismissable by, a government.

Appointments generally involve the Lord Chancellor and the Prime Minister. The office of Lord Chancellor itself has a political basis, with appointment by the Queen on the advice of the Prime Minister. The Lord Chancellor is a member of the government and the Cabinet, and when there is a change of government there is a change of Lord Chancellor. He does, however, keep political activities separate from judicial responsibilities.

The Mastership of the Rolls is not only an important judicial office but also a strong political appointment. In former times there was party political influence. For some time now, however, it seems to have been accepted that the Lord Chancellor does not allow political considerations to influence his choice. Extreme radical views might prevent appointment, but membership of a party per se would not. Furthermore, promotion is not considered to be a political issue.

In essence, it is considered that there is no influence on promotion by ministers or civil servants.

Minorities

In May 1986 there were only three women among the 114 most senior judges. The first woman who was appointed to the Court of Appeal was Mrs (now Dame Elizabeth) Butler-Sloss, in December 1987. No woman has been appointed to the House of Lords. It should be remembered, however, that there have not been many women practising at the Bar at senior level. Nevertheless, over the years the number has increased; for example, in 1955 there were 64, but in 1986 there were 744. Furthermore, the number of female Queen's Counsel has also been very small, and until 1986 there were only 18 women out of 797 QCs.

In March 1992 Ann Ebsworth was the first woman appointed to the Queen's Bench Division of the High Court. She joined two other female judges in the High Court, Mrs Justice Booth and Mrs Justice Bracewell, both of whom sat in the Family Division. The Lord Chancellor's Department said that one reason for the lack of female judges was that there were very few applications from women for the post of assistant recorder, the lowest rung of the judicial ladder. Lord Justice Taylor, however, said that appointments must be on merit alone, and there should be no special procedures for women.

Although in April 1993 the Lord Chancellor made a plea for more women to apply for judicial posts, he did not approve of 'fast-tracking' women – that is, lowering the age for appointment to judicial posts. Further, there had to be preservation of 'the level of experience of both the law and of life in general' which was brought to the bench.

Quite apart from women, ethnic minorities, too, have not been represented to any great extent. As far as the advertising of vacancies for judges is concerned, the aim was to attract more women, blacks and Asians. Time, of course, will 'judge' the success of this new policy.

Salary

Is this why a barrister becomes a judge? The answer is generally no – QCs, for instance, earn a considerable amount of money. A judge, however, will receive a pension. A High Court judge will achieve status, as he or she will receive an automatic knighthood or DBE. Although in March 1993 the Prime Minister, John Major, declared an overhaul of the honours system, High Court judges were to retain such honours on appointment. Mr Major said that this was to 'preserve the independence of the bench'. A spokesman for the Lord Chancellor also said: 'If judges were not given their knighthoods automatically, the distribution of knighthoods could be seen as a comment on their judging ability.'

Apart from status generally, it is arguable that a judge will have a lesser burden of work, and there is also, of course, the possibility of higher judicial office.

Training

It has been said that an objection to judicial training is that it could undermine judicial independence (Report of the Working Party on Judicial Studies and Information 1978). Despite this, in 1979 a Judicial Studies Board was established, and it has played a very important part not only in the development of training for judges but also in identifying the need for such training.

In an informative and interesting article, 'Why judges are better trained', in *The Times* on 28 January 1992, David Pannick (now a QC) referred to the then newly published report of the Judicial Studies Board. The board itself had been exclusively concerned with criminal law and emphasised the training of Crown Court judges in sentencing. In 1985 the board's jurisdiction was extended to judicial training in the areas of civil and family law and also to the supervision of the training of magistrates and tribunal chairmen. The article explained that trainee assistant recorders and new circuit judges had induction courses and seminars, while there were refresher seminars for experienced circuit judges and recorders. Invitations to attend were extended to new judges at the Queen's Bench Division. Some judges feared that training would mean too high a risk of an 'official' view being imposed on the independent judiciary. Such a fear, however, was without foundation, and the judiciary's confidence in training had increased. David Pannick's article raised the issue of moving towards a Judicial College, with a judge seconded to act as full-time director of studies:

> 'The greater complexity of law and society, the enhanced powers of the judiciary, and the more rigorous media and public analysis of judicial pronouncements, mean that no longer is it appropriate to have acting as judges men and women who have received only the most rudimentary of guidance on the exercise of such onerous responsibilities.'

Training could encompass enhancing the knowledge of judges in respect of legal developments. Furthermore, they 'would benefit from the provision of broader information about subjects relevant to adjudication, such as jurisprudence, psychology, economics, and media relations'.

The article concluded:

> 'The work of the Judicial Studies Board has helped to make judges more competent, and more confident, than ever before. The creation of a Judicial College would further enhance the necessary training of a professional judiciary.'

The issue of proper training raised its head in March 1992 when one of the most experienced officers in the Fraud Squad retired and called for a special panel of judges to sit with juries in complex fraud cases. The officer considered that judges and barristers should be specialists and properly trained, and he claimed that some members of the judiciary were unable to follow the issues involved in such cases, while others did not have the ability to manage lengthy trials.

A constructive step towards training was taken during the latter part of 1992 with the first Annual Report of the Ethnic Minorities Advisory Committee under Mr Justice Brooke. The committee was established in 1991 to address the training of judges in racial awareness, and to combat discrimination. Guidelines, and also information packs, were to be sent to every judge in England and Wales. Recommendations included that facilities for Sikhs and Muslims to wash should be available at all courts, and certain holy books should be covered except when being touched by the witness. Training would encompass basic cultural differences of ethnic minority communities and identify areas which most commonly caused offence. In November 1993 the Lord Chancellor approved a two-year £1 million project to train judges in racial awareness. He accepted that every circuit judge, recorder and assistant recorder should attend a short residential course over the following two years. The courses were to be run by ethnic minority consultants.

It is doubtful whether the general public has been fully aware of developments in respect of training the judiciary. However, in May 1993 the BBC broadcast Amy Hardie's documentary 'Inside the Wig: Thinking Like a Judge'. This documentary filmed the four-day training course for assistant recorders and contributed to heightening the general public's understanding of the judge's role.

It is certainly necessary to enhance the image of the judiciary. The passing of lenient sentences and seemingly insensitive comments by judges do nothing to improve that image. Interestingly, in *The Times* of 10 June 1993 there was an article, 'When judges talk too much', by Fenton Bresler. He referred, inter alia, to the following comments by judges:

In 1987, in the Ealing Vicarage rape case, the judge described the victim's ordeal as 'not so very great'.

In April 1990, during a rape trial, an Old Bailey jury was told:

> 'As the gentlemen on the jury will understand, when a woman says "No", she doesn't always mean it. Men can't turn their emotions on and off like a tap like some women can.'

During September 1991, in a case involving aggravated burglary, the judge said:

> 'A lot of the excuse for your behaviour is that you have problems with a woman. Who do you think hasn't? I've had my girl friends. I've had a wife for the last 37 years. Even after 37 years they give you problems from time to time ... if a woman upsets you that's all right. It's part of their function in life.'

In June 1993 the sex attacker of an eight-year-old girl was given probation. The judge stigmatised the girl as 'no angel' (he indicated that he had received information which led him to think that the girl 'was not entirely an angel herself'.)

Fenton Bresler posed the question: 'Why do intelligent and able men, whose whole training as lawyers is to make them choose their words with care, sometimes do the exact opposite?' He considered that there were three possible explanations. First, a disease: 'Judgeitis' could 'afflict perfectly decent, modest lawyers the moment that they don the judicial ermine, giving them an exaggerated notion of their own importance ...'. Secondly, some judges become cynics and 'cannot resist the opportunity to tell it as they find it, even though sometimes they would be better advised not to do so'. Thirdly, when a defendant pleads guilty, some judges too readily accept everything that is said by defence counsel. 'How can they pick and choose what is true in what counsel tells them?'

The article concludes: 'Discretion is not only the better part of valour, it is the better part of judging.'

In August 1993 a judge described date rape as a lesser crime. The judge said: 'This is not in my view the more serious type of rape – that is the rape of a total stranger.' Women's groups called for the judge to be taken off rape cases.

Bearing in mind the above, guidance could be given to judges in their handling of sensitive cases, and a Judicial College (see above) could quite possibly provide more in-depth, structured training. The Judicial Studies Board has been successful, but there are limits on its resources.

In the light of the lenient sentence in the case involving the sex attack on the eight-year-old girl, new training was announced in July 1993. Judges would be sent on four-day residential courses to study case papers on sex offences, have lectures from experts who deal with sex abuse cases and also receive key advice from senior family law judges. Jane Simpson, the chairman of the Solicitors' Family Law Association, welcomed the move. She said: 'Judges can learn a lot from therapists, counsellors and child psychiatrists in this most difficult area which often arouses painful emotions.'

During the same month there was the report by the Royal Commission on Criminal Justice under Lord Runciman of Doxford. Radical measures were proposed both to improve the training of judges and to monitor their performance. The commission called for substantial funds for training and proposed compulsory refresher training every three years. Furthermore, it stated there should be 'an effective formal system of performance appraisal' set up by the judiciary and carried out by the presiding and resident judges. The Bar would have a channel through which to comment on judicial performance. The findings would be retained by the judiciary, so that there would be no risk to its independence. However, while giving the Leggett Lecture at the University of Surrey in November 1993, the Lord Chief Justice, Lord Taylor of Gosforth, said that judges being subject to performance appraisal was 'both dangerous and näive'. He considered that a secretive system would reassure nobody: 'It would just be said that judges were appraising judges behind closed doors.' In addition he said:

> 'Judges work in public. Their performance is on view all the time. If they make errors, the Court of Appeal can correct them. If they make outrageous remarks, the press is not noticeably slow in reporting them. In an extreme case, the Lord Chancellor has disciplinary powers.'

In general support of judges, it must be said that they are not beyond pursuing innovative ideas themselves. Scottish judges, for example, are considering the use of computers to aid more consistent sentencing. The idea stemmed from Lord Ross, the Lord Justice-Clerk, Scotland's second most senior judge. Strathclyde University is studying the feasibility of the scheme, and this project should be completed by the end of 1994.

Finally, it is argued that the adversarial process, involving oral argument, in which barristers participate is contrary to a judge's role, which is to sit and listen impartially without undue interruption. Does this mean, therefore, that it is *even more important* to train judges thoroughly in preparation for their role in court?

Age

On appointment, the average age of judges has been in the lower fifties. The average age of all in office has been about 60 years and, in respect of judges in the Court of Appeal and the House of Lords, 65 to 68 years.

The issue may be raised as to why judges are older people. The answer to this is that, bearing in mind that their task is a difficult one, judges need not only maturity but also experience of life and of the law. A judge has to determine the facts, supervise the trial, note all of the evidence, direct a jury where appropriate, and adjudicate accordingly.

13.4 Judicial immunity

Judges are not under the control of Parliament or the civil service. Their independence is a fundamental principle of constitutional law, and, arguably, judicial immunity is an extension of this fundamental principle.

Under the common law, no judge of a superior or inferior court can be sued for damages for the following:

1. an act within his or her jurisdiction (even where a judge is malicious);

2. an act which he or she honestly believes is within his or her jurisdiction.

The superior courts include the House of Lords, the Court of Appeal, the High Court and the Crown Court, and the inferior courts include the magistrates' courts and county courts.

In *Sirros* v *Moore* [1975] QB 118 Lord Denning MR said (at 136): '[A judge] should be able to do his work in complete independence and free from fear.' This case was a civil action against a circuit judge. A stipendiary magistrate had recommended the deportation of a Turkish citizen, but not that he was to be detained pending the decision of the Home Secretary (in respect of deportation). The plaintiff appealed to the Crown Court, but the appeal was dismissed. The circuit judge seemed to think that the Turkish citizen was in custody and so prevented him from leaving court, and he was taken to prison. There were habeas corpus proceedings, and the Turkish citizen was released. Action was then taken against the police and judge for assault and false imprisonment. It was held that the detention was unlawful, but that there was no liability upon the judge because he had acted judicially and in good faith. Neither was there an action against the police; they had acted on the judge's instructions and were entitled to immunity.

With regard to magistrates, s108 of the Courts and Legal Services Act 1990 has amended ss44 and 45 of the Justices of the Peace Act 1979. A justice of the peace is immune from action as regards any act or omission while executing his or her duty *and* acting *within* his or her jurisdiction (s44). If he or she acts outside his or her jurisdiction he or she will be liable to be sued *if* it is proved that he or she acted in bad faith (s45).

In the course of a trial, immunity extends to the advocates, the parties, the witnesses, the jury's verdict, and fair, accurate reporting. This is done because it is considered that such freedom will lead to the easier discovery of the truth and will stop further civil actions. There is *not*, however, complete freedom, bearing in mind perjury and contempt of court. Furthermore, an advocate may be disciplined by a professional body.

13.5 The function of judges

Lord Diplock maintained that the British Constitution is based solidly on the separation of powers. Parliament makes the laws and the judiciary interprets them.

A judge supervises the conduct of a trial, interprets the law, decides any legal issue and gives effect to the law. He or she decides the quantum (the amount) of damages in civil cases, sums up for a jury in criminal cases and, of course, passes sentence.

The traditional view is that judges apply existing rules of law. The judge applies the law to the facts and a decision is made. Reaching a decision may involve binding precedent and the interpretation of statutes. Ostensibly, the judicial function goes no further. In *Scruttons* v *Midland Silicones* [1962] AC 446 Viscount Simonds indicated that he would not

> '... easily be led by an undiscerning zeal for some abstract kind of justice or ignore our first duty, which is established for us by Act of Parliament or the binding authority of precedent'.

The declaratory theory

Walker and Walker's *The English Legal System* says (at 142):

> 'A decision may be overruled either by statute or by a higher court. If it is overruled by a higher court the earlier decision is deemed to have been based on a misunderstanding of the law. The earlier rule of law is deemed never to have existed. This is the declaratory theory of the common law. The common law is never changed; it is merely restated correctly. Consequently all judicial overruling operates retrospectively.'

The declaratory theory was important for a long period of time – the role of the judge was to declare what the law was, and not to make law. Now, however, it is argued that judges are capable of 'making law'. Lord Denning considered not only that judges made law but also that they *should* do so. In 1972 Lord Reid, in his address 'The Judge as Law Maker', said:

> 'We do not believe in fairy tales any more. So we must accept the fact that for better or worse judges do make law, and tackle the question how do they approach their task and how they should approach it.'

Consideration should be given to the following:

1. Judicial precedent – case law. It is here that we find principles of law which are the reasons for decisions. These principles accumulate, and thereby a body of law develops. The Practice Statement is, of course, of considerable importance with regard to the development of the law. An example is the case of *Miliangos* v *George Frank (Textiles) Ltd* [1976] AC 443 in which the House of Lords effected an important change in the law, namely that damages could be awarded in the currency of any foreign country specified in the contract.
2. Statutory interpretation – Parliament says what the law *is*, but what do the words mean? It should also be noted that where, in relation to a given situation, there is neither an appropriate statute nor a precedent, *then* a judge has to make a decision and thereby create law. These are cases of 'first impression'.
3. In *Central London Property Trust Ltd* v *High Trees House Ltd* [1947] KB 30 there was the principle of equitable estoppel which, although obiter, has been subsequently adopted and is now an accepted rule of equity. Also, in *Donoghue* v *Stevenson* [1932] AC 562 the 'neighbour principle' was strictly obiter, but it became the basis for the modern tort of negligence.
4. In the sphere of criminal law, judges seem to have adopted the role of enforcing public morality by creating new criminal offences: see *Shaw* v *Director of Public*

Prosecutions [1962] AC 220. This case involved the publication of a 'Ladies' Directory' which was a list of prostitutes. The defendant was convicted of a 'conspiracy to corrupt public morals'. Counsel had vigorously denied that there was such an offence. Viscount Simonds said (at 267–268):

> 'In the sphere of criminal law I entertain no doubt that there remains in the courts of law a residual power to enforce the supreme and fundamental purpose of the law, to conserve not only the safety and order but also the moral welfare of the State.'

In *Knuller (Publishing, Printing and Promotions) Ltd* v *Director of Public Prosecutions* [1973] AC 435 the case involved a similar publication, but this time in respect of homosexuals. *Shaw*'s case was followed in respect of the same offence. In addition the House of Lords, obiter, considered that there were further offences of outraging public decency and conspiring to do so known to the criminal law.

In *R* v *Manley* [1973] 1 KB 529 the defendant falsely alleged that she had been attacked and robbed. She was convicted of public mischief but appealed on the ground that no such offence was known to the law. The appeal was dismissed. In similar circumstances there would now be a summary offence under s5(2) of the Criminal Law Act 1967.

Wider aspects of a judge's function

In some areas a judge's function extends to more than giving a decision; for example, the appellate courts provide guidelines for judges with regard to the exercise of discretionary powers, and the Chancery Division may exercise an administrative function where judges supervise the affairs and administer the property of persons of unsound mind. Note also the Supreme Court Rule Committee and the Crown Court Rule Committee which make rules of court to regulate and prescribe practice and procedure; these committees include judges. The judiciary is also involved in the issue of Practice Directions.

13.6 Extrajudicial activity

Royal Commissions and Departmental Committees

The Crown appoints Royal Commissions to enquire into specific areas of concern, for example the Royal Commission on Criminal Justice. The same purpose is served by departmental committees which are appointed by ministers. Both the commissions and the committees are chaired most frequently by judges, then by academics and lastly by businessmen. The Law Commission, a full-time law reform body, has a judge as its chairman.

The judiciary in politics

Judges should be politically neutral, but consider the Restrictive Practices Court, industrial relations and Northern Ireland:

The Restrictive Practices Court

This court comprises at least one judge and two laymen. Its function is to decide whether restrictive agreements may continue – are they contrary to the public interest? The argument here is that judges are involved in making political and economic decisions.

Industrial relations

The National Industrial Relations Court was established by the Industrial Relations Act 1971. Both the Act and the court were unpopular with some trade unions, and there was political protest.

Under a Labour government the court was abolished by s1 of the Trade Union and Labour Relations Act 1974. However, by virtue of the Employment Protection Act 1975, the court was effectively revived by the creation of the Employment Appeal Tribunal, which was called a 'tribunal' for psychological reasons but is, in fact, a superior court of record. It is duly constituted when there are a judge and either two or four other members who are laymen with specialist knowledge of industrial relations.

Northern Ireland

There have been important official enquiries relating to Northern Ireland, including the Diplock Commission which reported on the legal procedures to deal with terrorist activities. Does such activity involve judges in political controversy?

Generally, if judges are meant to be politically neutral, should they be involved in the areas referred to under these last three headings?

13.7 Cases

Following the consideration of the background of judges and the possible intrusion of politics, the question arises as to whether judges are influenced by their own education, background, social positions and political views.

In his book *The Politics of the Judiciary*, J A G Griffith devotes a great deal of attention to the various influences upon judges' decisions. Therefore, to reflect upon this question, reference will be made to some cases dealt with by Griffith within a variety of areas of interest. In examining these cases, consideration should be given to whether the judges were biased for either party *or* whether their decisions were just legally correct.

Trade unions

Allen v Flood [1898] AC 1

The ironworkers' union objected to certain work being done by woodworkers. The ironworkers informed one of their officials that they would stop working if the woodworkers continued to be employed. The official told the employers, who dismissed the woodworkers, who brought an action against the official. The action was not successful, and the union remained protected.

Quinn v Leathem [1901] AC 495

Leathem supplied meat to a butcher. A trade union endeavoured to persuade Leathem not to employ non-union men. This did not succeed, and the union then told its members who worked for the butcher to cease work if Leathem's meat was still bought. The butcher therefore bought no more meat from Leathem, who took action against the union officials for conspiracy to injure him. The action was successful. Consequently, the effect of *Quinn v Leathem* was to curtail the powers of trade unionists in certain ways.

As a result of political upheaval the Trade Disputes Act 1906 was passed. This protected trade unions from actions for civil conspiracy if the acts were done in furtherance or contemplation of a trade dispute.

Taff Vale Railway Co v Amalgamated Society of Railway Servants [1901] AC 426

This case concerned a dispute involving trade union funds. A trade unionist led a wage demand, and it was alleged that the Taff Vale Railway Company victimised this person. The House of Lords held that trade unions could be sued for losses suffered by employers because of strike action.

This decision was a blow to trade unions, but the decision was effectively reversed by the Trade Disputes Act 1906.

Rookes v Barnard [1964] AC 1129

There was an agreement with BOAC that all workers should be union members. Rookes left the union in 1955, following a disagreement. BOAC was threatened, by two members and a district official, that if Rookes was not dismissed then labour would be withdrawn. Rookes was given notice to leave, and he sued the two union members and the official for conspiracy.

By virtue of the Trade Disputes Act 1906 there was no action for conspiracy unless the act would be unlawful if it were carried out by a person alone. It was held by the House of Lords that a threat to strike could be unlawful in this context. Lord Hodson said:

> 'The injury and suffering caused by strike action is very often widespread as well as devastating and a threat to strike would be expected to be certainly no less serious than a threat of violence.'

The decision was reversed by the Trade Disputes Act 1965.

Express Newspapers v *McShane* [1979] 2 All ER 360

There was a dispute between provincial newspapers' proprietors and members of the National Union of Journalists. The union called out all members who worked for the provincial newspapers. The union also called for Press Association journalists to strike (the Press Association supplied news copy for the provincial newspapers). The strike by Press Association journalists affected *national* newspapers. The plaintiffs sought an injunction to restrain the union from instructing union members to refuse to use Press Association copy. The defendants said that what they were doing was in furtherance of their dispute with the provincial newspapers. An injunction was granted, and this was upheld by the Court of Appeal which said that the acts were not done in furtherance of a trade dispute. The courts would test 'furtherance' objectively as well as considering the defendants' intentions subjectively.

The House of Lords did not agree. It held that 'in furtherance' concerned a defendant's subjective state of mind, and he or she acted 'in furtherance' if his or her purpose was to help the parties in a dispute to achieve their objectives, and if he or she honestly and reasonably believed that his or her actions would do so. For the House of Lords to have supported the Court of Appeal in this case would have brought the judiciary into sharp confrontation with the trade unions.

As regards the claim that judges are totally biased against trade unions, a survey was carried out in respect of judicial decisions concerning disputes between workers and employers from 1871 to 1966. The survey did not support such a claim. Of 127 decisions, including appeals, 38 per cent were determined in favour of the workers.

Individual freedoms and rights

Liversidge v *Anderson* [1942] AC 206

There were Defence Regulations to detain persons without trial. The powers were expressed to be exercisable only if the Secretary of State had reasonable cause to believe that a person had 'hostile associations'.

The House of Lords held that the courts were not able to review the reasonableness of the cause. Was this, during a period of national emergency, an abdication of the courts' controlling authority? The effect of the decision was that the Secretary of State's order could not be questioned as he could not be required to clarify the basis of the order.

R v *Secretary of State for Home Affairs, ex parte Hosenball* [1977] 1 WLR 766

An American journalist appealed against a deportation order, alleging a breach of natural justice. The basis for this was that the Home Secretary refused to provide the details which had caused him to decide that the appellant was a security risk. The appeal was dismissed. Lord Denning said (at 783):

'There is a conflict here between the interests of national security on the one hand and the freedom of the individual on the other. The balance between these two is not for a court of law. It is for the Home Secretary. He is the person entrusted by Parliament with the task. In some parts of the world national security has on occasions been used as an excuse for all sorts of infringements of individual liberty. But not in England. Both during the wars and after them, successive ministers have discharged their duties to the complete satisfaction of the people at large. They have set up advisory committees to help them, usually with a chairman who has done everything he can to ensure that justice is done. They have never interfered with the liberty or the freedom of movement of any individual except where it is absolutely necessary for the safety of the state.'

Consider also the following two cases:

Duncan v *Cammell Laird & Co* [1942] AC 624

In this case the Crown claimed that certain documents should not be disclosed on the ground that the public interest would be harmed by their production. Ninety-nine men had lost their lives when a submarine sank during tests. The defendants had built the submarine, and the plaintiffs had called for the disclosure of plans and specifications. The objection to disclosure was upheld by the House of Lords.

Chandler v *Director of Public Prosecutions* [1962] 3 WLR 694

The defendants, who were endeavouring to further the aims of the Campaign for Nuclear Disarmament (CND), were involved in organising a demonstration at an airfield which was occupied by the US air force. The airfield was a 'prohibited place' under the Official Secrets Act 1911. The six defendants were charged with conspiring to commit, and to incite others to commit, a breach of the Official Secrets Act, namely to enter the airfield 'for a purpose prejudicial to the safety or interests of the State'. Their counsel was not allowed to cross-examine or to call evidence as to the defendants' purpose *not* being prejudicial to the safety or interests of the State. The defendants were convicted, and their convictions were upheld by the Court of Appeal and the House of Lords.

The control of discretionary powers

Secretary of State for Education and Science v *Tameside Metropolitan Borough Council* [1976] 3 WLR 641

By virtue of s68 of the Education Act 1944, if the Secretary of State was satisfied that any local education authority had acted or was proposing to act unreasonably he or she could give such directions as appeared to him or her to be expedient.

In 1975 the Labour-controlled Tameside Council proposed that comprehensive education should be brought into effect in September 1976. The proposals were approved. In May 1976 the Conservatives won control of the council and told the Secretary of State that they did not wish to proceed. The Secretary of State gave a direction under s68 which required implementation of the plans, and the Divisional

Court ordered the council to comply. The Court of Appeal overturned this decision, and the House of Lords upheld the Court of Appeal.

The basis for the decision was that the Secretary of State could only give a valid direction if he was satisfied that no reasonable local authority could have reached a decision such as that decided by the Conservative majority, *and* he could not have been so satisfied.

R v *Greater London Council, ex parte Bromley London Borough Council* [1983] 1 AC 768

This case appears to be regarded as involving a political decision. In July 1981 the Greater London Council (GLC) passed a resolution implementing a commitment in the Labour Party election manifesto to reducing fares charged by the London Transport Executive (LTE). There was a supplementary rate for all London Boroughs. The GLC policy also resulted in a lost rate-support grant from the government.

Bromley LBC applied to the High Court to quash the supplementary rate as being ultra vires. The GLC was empowered to make grants to the LTE. The GLC intended thereby to reimburse the LTE for revenue lost by the fares reduction and thus enable the LTE to balance its books. The LTE was under a duty to exercise and perform its functions in accordance with GLC principles and in such manner as to provide or secure with due regard to efficiency, economy and safety of operation the provision of such public passenger transport services as best met the needs of Greater London. The GLC had authority to give general directions, and GLC approval was required for the level and structure of fares to be charged by the LTE.

The Divisional Court refused the application. However, the Court of Appeal and House of Lords upheld the application and quashed the supplementary rate. The House of Lords agreed that the GLC's power to make grants to the LTE included a large degree of discretion to supplement revenue received by the LTE from fares. Limitations, however, were placed on this discretion.

The decision was founded on the ground that the LTE was under a general duty to run its operations on ordinary business principles, and this had been breached by the reduction of fares. The GLC, when making a grant, had to have regard to the LTE's obligation to run its operations on a break-even basis. Grants were only to make good unavoidable losses and not to further a particular social policy. Also, the GLC was under a fiduciary duty to its ratepayers which it had breached by the scheme – in particular, by the loss of rate-support grant and by acting without thought for thrift.

Was it the way in which the Labour majority carried out their election promises, as opposed to their statutory powers to do so, that upset the Court of Appeal and the House of Lords?

Morality

Shaw v *Director of Public Prosecutions* [1961] 2 WLR 897

Were the Law Lords the most appropriate people to prescribe codes of moral behaviour (see p61 above)? Lord Reid dissented, and he concluded that there was 'no such general offence known to the law as conspiracy to corrupt morals'.

Ward v *Bradford Corporation* (1972) 70 LGR 27

Miss Ward was a student at a teacher training college. She and four others were found to have men in their rooms one night. Miss Ward moved to lodgings. The man had been with her for nearly two months.

Only the principal could refer cases to the disciplinary committee, and she did not wish to do so. The governing body, however, wanted action to be taken and amended the rules to enable *it* to refer cases. The amended rules were *then* applied retrospectively, and the disciplinary committee became involved. An Assistant Education Officer joined the committee, although he was not a member of the committee as such. The other students were reprimanded, but Miss Ward was expelled from the college.

The courts were asked to declare the expulsion invalid. It was argued, in effect, that justice was not seen to be done by such proceedings. Lord Denning was, it seems, unimpressed. He said (at 35):

> 'Instead of going into lodgings she had this man with her, night after night, in the hall of residence where such a thing was absolutely forbidden. That is a fine example to set to others! And she a girl training to be a teacher! I expect the governors and the staff all thought that she was quite an unsuitable person for it. She would never make a teacher. No parent would knowingly entrust their child to her care.'

Gillick v *West Norfolk and Wisbech Area Health Authority and DHSS* [1985] 3 All ER 402

This case involved doctors giving contraceptive advice to girls under 16 years of age. There was a DHSS circular indicating that in certain circumstances it might be legitimate to give such advice. Mrs Gillick challenged the validity of the circular. The Court of Appeal made a declaration that the advice was unlawful. This was set aside by the House of Lords.

Race relations

Ealing London Borough Council v *Race Relations Board* [1972] AC 342

Stanislaw Zesko was born and bred a Polish national. In 1939 he escaped to France and subsequently came to the United Kingdom where he joined the Royal Air Force. He remained in the United Kingdom, married, and lived in Ealing, London. Mr Zesko applied for his name to be added to the council's housing list. This was refused because of a council rule that the applicant had to be 'a British subject within the meaning of the British Nationality Act 1948'.

A complaint was made to the Race Relations Board, which decided that there had been unlawful discrimination because the special treatment of a person on the ground of his national origins was made unlawful under the Race Relations Act 1968. Ealing Borough Council applied to the courts to determine that its rule was not unlawful. A majority (four-to-one) decision of the House of Lords supported the council. The basis for the decision was that 'national origins' did not mean 'nationality', and the council's rule was concerned with the latter. Consider s2(1) of the Race Relations Act 1968:

> 'It shall be unlawful for any person concerned with the provision to the public or a section of the public (whether on payment or otherwise) of any goods, facilities or services to discriminate against any person seeking to obtain or use those goods, facilities or services by refusing or deliberately omitting to provide him with any of them or to provide him with goods, services or facilities of the like quality, in the like manner and on the like terms in and on which the former normally makes them available to other members of the public.'

Charter v *Race Relations Board* [1973] AC 868
A Mr Shah applied to join East Ham South Conservative Club. The chairman indicated that Mr Shah's colour was relevant, and membership was rejected. There was a complaint to the Race Relations Board but this was rejected by a majority (four-to-one) decision of the House of Lords. It was considered that the club members were not 'a section of the public'.

Dockers' Labour Club v *Race Relations Board* [1974] 3 WLR 533
Mr Sherrington was a coloured man; he was taken, as a guest, to a dockers' club in Preston but was told to leave. In fact, Mr Sherrington was a member of another club in Preston where there was no colour bar. Both clubs were in a union of approximately 4,000 clubs. Any member of one club was an associate member of the other clubs in the union. Were associates 'a section of the public'? The House of Lords decided unanimously in favour of the club.

Mandla v *Dowell Lee* [1982] 3 WLR 932
A headmaster refused to admit a Sikh boy unless his hair was cut and he stopped wearing a turban. Were Sikhs a racial group and thereby entitled to the protection of the Race Relations Act 1976? The difficulty concerned the meaning of the word 'ethnic' in s3 of the Act. The House of Lords reversed the Court of Appeal and held that Sikhs were a racial, not solely a religious, group, and that there had been unlawful discrimination.

14

The Jury System

14.1 Introduction

14.2 Qualifications for jury service

14.3 Juries in criminal cases

14.4 Juries in civil cases

14.5 The advantages and disadvantages of the jury system

14.6 Alternatives to the jury system

14.7 A source of interest – but what of the future?

14.1 Introduction

Judgment by one's peers has long been upheld as an entrenched principle of the English legal system. In *Ford* v *Blurton* [1922] 38 TLR 801, Atkin LJ said, at 805, that jury trial was 'the bulwark of liberty, the shield of the poor from the rich and the powerful'.

The jury system has evolved over the centuries and presents a fascinating insight into the protection of the rights of a citizen. Many important developments have included the introduction of majority verdicts, Practice Directions as to when jury vetting should take place, and the abolition of the peremptory challenge, ie a challenge *without* cause. Jury decisions have influenced the law; for example, it was partly due to the reluctance of juries to convict motorists of drunken driving that, in 1967, the 'breathalyser law' was introduced, based upon the level of alcohol in the blood. Juries may react to unsatisfactory laws or to defendants being unfairly treated, and cases of interest include the acquittal in 1979 of the politician Jeremy Thorpe of conspiracy to murder and incitement to murder, and also the acquittal in 1985 of Clive Ponting, a senior civil servant with the Ministry of Defence, in respect of charges under the Official Secrets Act. A short but informative article, 'From Norman Conquest to Terrorist Trial', by Stewart Tendler (*The Times* 24 October 1988) traced an outline history of the jury system.

There are distinctions between the English jury system and the jury systems in many other countries, for example, in Scotland a jury is comprised of 15 people and a simple majority is sufficient for a verdict.

In 1988 there was an inquiry by *The Times* which indicated that consideration should be given as to whether the jury system had become a stumbling block in the path of justice. Tony Dawe and Jack Crossley reported that there were grave doubts that justice was being done in 'Twelve good men and true ... the myth of the English jury? The Jury on TRIAL Part 1', *The Times* 24 October 1988. Interviews were conducted with former jurors, although it should be noted that the interviews were not concerned with individual cases. It is contempt of court to question jurors 'about their deliberations in specific cases'. The former jurors talked about their experiences in court but did not discuss details of identifiable cases. The report showed

> 'that "12 good men and true" in the jury room can too often be swayed by ignorance, boredom with the whole process, or prejudice against other social groups or the police. Sometimes they might be influenced, too, by real and justified fear.'

Douglas Hurd, the then Home Secretary, had announced that the right of peremptory challenge of jurors by defence counsel was to be removed, and that the age limit for jurors would also be raised from 65 to 70 years. Mr Hurd had said: 'Jury service is a solemn duty. It should not be regarded flippantly or carelessly.' *The Times* report, however, showed that almost every former juror provided examples of flippancy and prejudice. Furthermore:

> 'Many people complained of the inability of their fellow jurors to reason logically. The foreman of one jury said "Only two members of the jury had any obvious education and the ability to remember the evidence and make deductions." Several cases of illiterate jurors were reported.'

Also:

> 'The conditions in some courts seem bad enough to instil anti-establishment feelings. A man from Windsor said that the Old Shire Hall, Reading, was so cramped and uncomfortable that jurors were ready to reach any verdict as long as they could go home.
>   Several jurors recalled an increasing lack of objectivity as the end of the week approached. It appeared that occasionally another British institution, the weekend, was more prized by jurors – and the judiciary – than the jury system itself.'

One juror considered that a convincing case had been presented by the prosecution, together with supporting documents. It was a matter of believing either the man's story or the evidence of two police officers, two customs men and two immigration officers:

> 'Most of my fellow jurors preferred to believe the man. Some said it was an obvious "fit-up" by the authorities. They seemed to admire the man's ability to get round the immigration laws and to invest on the black market. "You would be a mug to do anything else out there," one juror said.
>   A couple of young women jurors were impressed by the man's smart appearance in court. One even said: "He's a good-looking darkie. I wouldn't mind him living next door." '

The juror was convinced of the man's guilt but was accused of being racist. A majority verdict of not guilty was returned.

In another case, one of alleged assault, a juror said:

'It was the clearest case of the man being guilty that you could imagine. I was asked to be foreman and suggested that everyone should state their initial views. To avoid embarrassment, I suggested they write them on pieces of paper which were then mixed up and handed to me. I was amazed to find eight Not Guilties and three Don't Knows.

I asked the other jurors to explain their views ... some showed an inbuilt reluctance to believe the police ... it became clear some could not distinguish whether witnesses had been giving evidence for the prosecution or the defence.'

As a result of these and other interviews, it is clear why there was concern about the jury system.

Despite the above, no reasons have to be given for a jury's verdict and it cannot be questioned. A jury is able to reach a decision based on justice and can look to its conscience in spite of the dictates of the law. Juries are randomly selected, and they should be free from bias.

14.2 Qualifications for jury service

The Juries Act 1974 s1, as amended by the Criminal Justice Act 1988 s119(1), provides that, to qualify for selection as a juror, a person must:

1. be between 18 and 70 years of age, although persons over 65 years old may be excused from service as of right (see below).
2. have lived in the United Kingdom for any period of at least five years since the age of 13; and
3. be registered as a parliamentary or local government elector.

All persons who satisfy the above requirements are, basically, qualified to serve, but some are disqualified, ineligible or excused from jury service:

Persons disqualified

Schedule 1, Part 2, of the Juries Act 1974, as amended by the Juries (Disqualification) Act 1984, disqualifies, inter alia, the following:

1. anyone who, *at any time*, has been sentenced in the United Kingdom to life imprisonment or custody, or a prison term or youth custody of five years or more;
2. anyone who, within the previous ten years, has in the United Kingdom served any part of a prison term or been detained in a borstal institution or received a suspended sentence or a community service order;
3. anyone who, within the previous five years, has been placed on probation in the United Kingdom.

If an accused person's guilt or innocence was left to be decided by people whose own conduct had been reprehensible in the past, then this would hardly encourage public confidence in the legal system. It is therefore both sensible and desirable to disqualify such people.

Persons ineligible

Schedule 1, Part 1, of the Juries Act 1974 specifies four groups:

1. all present and past members of the judiciary, including magistrates and chairmen and vice-chairmen of tribunals;
2. all members of the legal profession and of the police force, including civilian employees; court employees; probation officers, and anyone who in the previous ten years has been within one of these categories;
3. clergy, monks and nuns;
4. the mentally ill.

It is felt that people from groups 1 and 2, with experience of the law, might exert undue influence as jurors.

Persons excusable as of right

By s9(1) and Schedule 1, Part 3, of the Juries Act 1974, as amended by the Criminal Justice Act 1988 s119(2), certain people may be excused as of right if they so wish. This group includes peers and peeresses entitled to attend the House of Lords, and also Members of the House of Commons, together with full-time serving members of the armed forces and members of medical and other similar professions, such as dentists, vets and pharmacists.

Persons more than 65 years of age may also be excused as of right; when called for service they are entitled to inform the appropriate court officer that they do not wish to serve.

In addition s8 of the Juries Act 1974 grants excusal as of right if a person has:

1. served on a jury (but not a coroner's jury), or attended to serve on a jury within the last two years; or.
2. been excused from jury service by any court for a period which has not terminated.

Discretionary excusal

Section 9(2) allows for discretionary excusal on certain occasions if there is a good reason, such as illness, pregnancy, a holiday having been booked or a person having to sit an examination. A refusal to excuse a person may be subject to appeal. *Practice Note* [1988] 3 All ER 177 listed examples of circumstances sufficient to satisfy s9(2):

1. personal involvement in the facts of the case;

2. close connection with either a party or a prospective witness in the case;
3. personal hardship;
4. conscientious objection to jury service.

Furthermore, where a person seeks discretionary excusal then the matter should be dealt with 'sensitively and sympathetically'. During the formative stages of the Criminal Justice Act 1988 there was an Opposition amendment which sought to allow people to be excused jury service as of right if their objection to such service was on religious grounds. This amendment was narrowly defeated. Although such people, eg Plymouth Brethren, will not therefore be excused as of right, their requests to be excused will, under the guidelines, be treated sympathetically.

Discretionary deferral of jury service

Where a person has been summoned to attend for jury service, s9A of the Juries Act 1974 (inserted by s120 of the Criminal Justice Act 1988) allows an appropriate officer to *defer* attendance if there is a good reason. Attendance may be deferred only once. Crown Court Rules provide a right of appeal against the refusal of an appropriate officer to defer attendance.

Capacity

Section 10 of the Juries Act 1974 provides that a judge will decide whether a person will act as a juror if there is doubt about that person's capacity to be an effective juror because of 'physical disability or insufficient understanding of English'.

Penalties

There are fines for failing to attend for jury service, for serving on a jury when disqualified and, indeed, for being unfit to sit on the jury because of drink or drugs.

The summoning of jurors

Despite the problem that electoral registers do not accurately reflect the population (for example, people may have moved or died), the court officer obtains a random list from the electoral register, and each person on the list is summoned by written notice to attend for jury service. To establish whether a person is, in fact, qualified to sit on a jury, the court officer may, at any time, ask questions of that person. The object of this is to avoid people maintaining that they are disqualified when they are not and, conversely, to ensure that people who *are* disqualified do not sit.

The persons who have been summoned become the jury panel, and the jury for a specific case is selected by ballot from that panel in open court. Each juror swears separately:

'I swear by Almighty God that I will faithfully try the several issues joined between our Sovereign Lady the Queen and the prisoner(s) at the bar and give a true verdict according to the evidence.'

Jurors may be summoned in exceptional circumstances. Where it appears to a court that a jury will be incomplete, s6 of the Juries Act 1974 provides that the court may require any persons who are in the vicinity to be summoned, without written notice, for jury service. The court will proceed as if their names had initially been included in the jury panel.

It is rare for a judge to make such an order, that is, to 'pray a tales', as it is known. Officials may go out into the street or, indeed, into the nearby offices, to approach people to complete a jury panel. 'Tales' is the latin plural of talis and means such (or the like) persons from those standing about. People who are approached in this way may refuse, but only for reasons that they would have been able to cite on receipt of a summons. Such orders were made in January 1992 when there was a dire shortage of jurors at some London Crown Courts following the Christmas holiday.

14.3 Juries in criminal cases

Jury trials take place at the Crown Court when a defendant pleads not guilty. There is, however, a relatively small number of jury trials, first, because the vast majority of criminal cases are tried in the magistrates' courts and, secondly, because a very high percentage of the defendants committed to the Crown Court do, in fact, plead guilty and therefore jury trial is not required.

The jury listens to the evidence presented by the prosecution and the defence and to the summing-up of that evidence by the trial judge. The judge then directs the jury as to the law and, bearing this in mind, the jury decides guilt or innocence on the facts.

Jury vetting

Vetting involves looking into the background of jurors, and this could be contrary to the random selection of jurors. Consideration should be given to the *Attorney-General's Guidelines on Jury Checks* [1988] 3 All ER 1086, which cover the following topics.

Basically, the principles to be observed are that there must be random selection from the jury panel; only those identified in the Juries Act 1974 and the Juries (Disqualification) Act 1984 may be disqualified or ineligible; and to prevent a member of the jury panel from sitting on a jury, the correct procedure for the Crown is to ask for a 'stand by' or 'challenge for cause' (see below).

Further guidelines include these:

'Parliament has provided safeguards against jurors who may be corrupt or biased. In addition to the provision of majority verdicts, there is the sanction of a criminal offence for a disqualified person to serve on a jury. The omission of a disqualified person from the panel is a matter for court officials, but any search of criminal records for the purpose of ascertaining whether or not a jury panel includes any disqualified person is a matter for the police ...'

The recommendations of the Association of Chief Police Officers in respect of checks on criminal records for disqualified persons are annexed to the guidelines (see below).

The provisions as to majority verdicts and the disqualification of jurors may not be sufficient to ensure the proper administration of justice in certain *exceptional* types of case of public importance. In such cases it is in the interests of justice, and also of the public, for there to be further safeguards against possible bias, and in these instances checks which go beyond the investigation of criminal records may be necessary.

These are cases involving *national security*, where some evidence is likely to be heard in camera (the hearing of a case in private), and *terrorist cases*. In national security cases there may be improper use of sensitive evidence given in camera, and in both national security and terrorist cases biased political beliefs may reflect extreme views, leading to either interference with the fair assessment of facts or improper pressure being exerted on jurors by their fellows.

After criminal records have been checked, further investigations may only involve records of police Special Branches. No such further investigation may be made without the personal authority of the Attorney-General on the application of the Director of Public Prosecutions. The checks of the records of police Special Branches are referred to as 'authorised checks'.

The result of any authorised check will be sent to the Director of Public Prosecutions, who will decide what information ought to be brought to the attention of prosecuting counsel. Where there is 'strong reason for believing that a particular juror might be a security risk, be susceptible to improper approaches or be influenced in arriving at a verdict ...', then counsel for the Crown may exercise a right of stand by.

There is no duty to disclose to the defence the information which is the basis for a potential juror being asked to stand by for the Crown. Counsel, however, has a discretion to disclose the information if its nature and source permit it.

If the information which has been revealed does not justify a juror being asked to stand by but nevertheless suggests possible bias against the accused, then an indication of this should be given to the defence.

Accordingly, the judge does not need to authorise the vetting. It should further be noted that there is no statutory basis for the Attorney-General's guidelines.

As referred to above, annexed to the guidelines are the recommendations of the Association of Chief Police Officers. These include a check against records of previous convictions when, in all the circumstances, the Director of Public

Prosecutions or a chief constable considers that such a check would be in the interests of justice, for example where endeavours were made to interfere with a juror or jurors in a previously connected and abortive trial, *or* to make sure that a disqualified person does not serve on a jury.

No further checks should be made unless the Attorney-General authorises them under his guidelines. Where a person is not disqualified as such, but in the light of the checks of criminal records there is information suggesting that he or she is nevertheless unsuitable for jury service, then the police or Director of Public Prosecutions may pass this information to the prosecuting counsel for a decision as to its use.

The concept of jury vetting has proved controversial. In *R v Crown Court at Sheffield, ex parte Brownlow* [1980] 2 All ER 444, Lord Denning MR and Shaw LJ said, obiter, that it is unconstitutional for the police authorities to engage in jury vetting. If a person is eligible for jury service under the Juries Act 1974, then it is wrong for the police to check his or her record covertly, as a result of which he or she could then be asked to stand by or be challenged by the defence. The courts should not assist in the extraction of further information over and above that provided for in the Juries Act 1974.

However, in *R v Mason* [1980] 3 All ER 777, *Brownlow* was not followed. There had been obiter dicta in respect of jury vetting and therefore, in that respect, the case was not binding. It was held in the *Mason* case that the practice in a criminal trial of supplying prosecuting counsel with information about the convictions of potential jurors is not unlawful. Because it is a criminal offence for a disqualified person to sit on a jury, the police by engaging in jury vetting are only carrying out their duty. Some vetting was necessary and, indeed, welcome, to prevent disqualified persons from sitting on a jury. Accordingly, *R v Mason* upheld the legality of vetting, although the case restricted itself to vetting for the purpose of checking for criminal convictions.

It is argued that vetting undermines random selection and that there is no common law or statutory provision providing a basis for it. In addition, is the procedure open to abuse and capable of different interpretations? Conversely, is it not desirable to exclude disqualified persons and also those with extreme and radical views?

Vetting is not necessary in the 'Diplock courts' because trials are conducted without juries. This is because s7 of the Northern Ireland (Emergency Provisions) Act 1978 allows terrorist offences to be judged by a single judge alone. It should be noted that, by way of safeguard, there is an automatic right of appeal to three judges.

The challenging of jurors

Prior to the Criminal Justice Act 1988 the defence had a right to make a peremptory challenge (a challenge *without cause*) in respect of up to three jurors. Reasons for this included that a person on trial should have confidence in the jury trying him or her, and that it was not unreasonable for the defendant to object to some jurors because he or she had certain reservations about them. Furthermore, a defendant might well have had genuine reasons for objecting to a juror but have lacked the necessary evidence to make a challenge for cause which could be tried by the judge as a preliminary matter. Peremptory challenges could also be justified where, for example, the circumstances surrounding an offence involved a racial minority and it was deemed desirable to ensure that members of the minority were on the jury.

Conversely, there was concern that defence counsel used peremptory challenges to manipulate the composition of a jury. This was particularly so with regard to multi-defendant trials where there could be a significant influence as to who sat on the jury by virtue of defence counsel pooling their peremptory challenges. It was further maintained that challenges without cause were contrary to the random selection of juries, were insulting to the juror concerned, and helped to bring about unjustified acquittals.

The situation was clarified by s118 of the Criminal Justice Act 1988, which abolished the right of the defence to make a peremptory challenge. The defence, however, may still challenge any juror *for cause*.

The prosecution's position is arguably more advantageous. A challenge for cause may be made by the prosecution, but apart from this there is also the right to 'stand by' a juror and, if necessary, the whole jury panel. This does not mean that the prosecution will 'support' a juror – the right to stand by is still, technically, a challenge for cause. To explain further, if there is a specific challenge for cause by the prosecution then this will be a preliminary matter tried by the judge. If, however, the prosecution exercises the right to stand by a juror, then investigating the cause behind this challenge is postponed until the jury panel has been exhausted. In practice, a jury will generally be formed from the remaining members of the jury panel and there will actually be no necessity to investigate why, ostensibly, a juror was stood by. The trial will then proceed.

There are, however, limitations upon the right to stand by. These are the Attorney-General's Guidelines on the Exercise by the Crown of its Right of Stand By specified in *Practice Note* [1988] 3 All ER 1086, which refer to it having been

> 'customary for those instructed to prosecute on behalf of the Crown to assert that right only sparingly and in exceptional circumstances. It is generally accepted that the prosecution should not use its right in order to influence the overall composition of a jury or with a view to tactical advantage.'

The guidelines clarify the circumstances in which it would be proper to exercise the right to stand by:

1. where an authorised check has revealed information justifying the exercise of the right to stand by and the Attorney-General personally authorises the exercise of the right; or

2. where a juror is 'manifestly unsuitable', and it is agreed by the defence that exercising the right to stand by would be appropriate.

The guidelines also give an example of 'exceptional circumstances' which could justify stand by: when a juror selected to hear a complex case is illiterate.

Death or discharge of a juror

By s16(1) of the Juries Act 1974, where there is a trial for an offence on indictment (including murder) and a jury member either dies or is discharged for a valid reason, then, as long as there is a minimum number of nine remaining jurors, there will still be a properly constituted jury and the trial may proceed; but the judge may discharge the jury if he wishes. If, however, the offence is punishable with death (eg treason), then subs(1) may only apply if there is agreement, in writing, by both the prosecution and the defence.

Majority verdicts

The Criminal Justice Act 1967 introduced majority verdicts; the requirement that verdicts be unanimous was relinquished. Section 17 of the Juries Act 1974 is now all important; s17(1) specifies that in the Crown Court or the High Court verdicts need not be unanimous if

'a) in a case where there are not less than eleven jurors, ten of them agree on the verdict; and
b) in a case where there are ten jurors, nine of them agree on the verdict.'

Section 17(4) stipulates minimum time limits for the jury's deliberations under subs(1).

In addition *Practice Direction* [1967] 1 WLR 1198 indicated that if the jury return before two hours has elapsed, and there is no unanimous verdict, then they will have to deliberate further to reach, if possible, a unanimous verdict. *Practice Direction* [1970] 1 WLR 916 clarified this and specified that a majority verdict shall not be accepted until a period of two hours and ten minutes has elapsed between the time when the last member of the jury left the jury box to go to the jury room and when, upon their return, the first question is put to the jury about their verdict.

To outline the sequence of events briefly, a jury should endeavour to reach a unanimous verdict, and any verdict within a period of two hours would have to be unanimous. Accordingly, if such a verdict was not agreed within two hours, the jury would have to deliberate further. If a period of at least two hours ten minutes has elapsed and a unanimous verdict has not been reached, then, if the judge, bearing in mind the nature and complexity of the case (subs4), considers that the jury has had a reasonable time for deliberation, he will direct that a majority verdict will be acceptable. The judge will also direct the jury that they should still endeavour to reach a unanimous verdict. If, after all this, there is still no agreement, then the jury may be discharged and a retrial be held before a fresh jury. Where there is a majority verdict of *guilty*, the requirement in s17(3), that such a verdict cannot be accepted by the Crown Court 'unless the foreman of the jury has stated in open court the number of jurors who respectively agreed to and dissented from the verdict', must be satisfied. However, although the requirement in s17(3) is mandatory, compliance with the *substance* of the requirement is sufficient, and as long as the words used made it clear to an ordinary person how a jury was divided, then the precise form of the words used would not be material. The authority for this is *R* v *Pigg* [1983] 1 WLR 6. It was further clarified in this case that if subs(3) was not observed at all, then the jury's verdict could not be accepted. No similar requirement to that in subs(3) is necessary where there is a majority verdict of *not* guilty.

Questions for consideration include the following: does a majority verdict:

1. Reduce the fear of jury 'nobbling'?
2. Avoid the cost of a second trial in terms of expense and time?
3. Increase the risk of convicting the innocent?
4. Lessen the credibility of the standard of proof, ie proof beyond a reasonable doubt?

Points of interest

- Prior to 1972 a juror had to be the occupier of a house, ie there was a property qualification. This requirement, however, was abolished by the Criminal Justice Act 1972, and the electoral register became a basic requirement. The composition of juries has changed since that time, and jurors have become younger and less middle class. Does this mean that juries are now fully representative of society as a whole? The answer would still seem to be 'no' as, arguably, there should be more involvement of ethnic minorities and women.

- Jurors are *not* paid for their services although they are in receipt of travelling and subsistence expenses and also compensation for loss of earnings.

- When the jury retire to consider their verdict, they do so privately, and it is very important that no one should come into contact with them. It is the responsibility of the jury bailiff to ensure that this is so. Any breach could result in the discharge of the jury or a conviction being subsequently quashed. What happens if the jury have retired to deliberate but require further information or clarification in respect of a particular matter? First, a judge and jury should not indulge in *private* communication. Secondly, unless a communication from the jury includes details which should not be disclosed in open court or relates to a personal matter which has nothing to do with the trial in question, the judge should deal with the communication in open court. The defendant and his counsel should be present and, if necessary, the jury will be brought back to court for further guidance.

- A jury must not be subjected to pressures, whether these are external (such as threats and intimidation) or even stemming from the judge. In *R* v *McKenna* [1960] 1 QB 411, after deliberating for over two hours a jury were still unable to reach a verdict. The trial judge indicated to the jury that they would be locked up for the night unless they reached a verdict within ten minutes. Verdicts of guilty were returned within this period of time. The convictions were quashed by the Court of Criminal Appeal because of the material irregularity in the trial.

- What is said in the jury room should remain secret. Under s8(1) of the Contempt of Court Act 1981 it is a contempt to obtain, disclose or solicit any particulars of statements made, opinions expressed, arguments advanced or votes cast by members of a jury in the course of their deliberations in criminal or civil proceedings, which would include a coroner's jury. Proceedings for such a contempt can only be brought by, or with the consent of, the Attorney-General or on the initiative of a court having jurisdiction to deal with it. Mr Justice McHugh has raised various arguments both for and against the secrecy of the jury room. Arguments *in favour* of secrecy include, inter alia:

(a) it is necessary to ensure freedom of discussion;
(b) it is necessary to ensure the finality of jury verdicts;
(c) it protects a juror's privacy and prevents harassment;
(d) jurors are protected from pressure to explain their reasons;
(e) it prevents vendettas against jurors; and
(f) it prevents jurors from being subjected to enormous public pressures.

The arguments *against* secrecy include, inter alia:

(a) juries will be more accountable;
(b) there could be worthwhile reforms of the legal system;
(c) there could be an educational effect upon the public; and
(d) openness is necessary for a proper examination of jury trial to see if it is working.

The full arguments for and against appear in 'Jurors' Deliberations, Jury Secrecy, Public Policy and the Law of Contempt' in *The Jury Under Attack*, by Mark Findlay and Peter Duff, at 62–67.

- Whether a verdict is given in a civil or a criminal case it is final and cannot be altered. Would it be in the public interest if the rule were otherwise? It is not even acceptable for a juror, following a verdict being given, to swear an affidavit that when he agreed to a verdict he was under a misapprehension. An interesting case is that of *Boston* v *W S Bagshaw & Sons* [1966] 1 WLR 1135n; this was a libel case, and the jury mistakenly found no malice. The jury were surprised that the plaintiff's case failed, and an affidavit was sworn by each juror to the effect that he wanted to change what he had said. The Court of Appeal refused to allow a new trial.

- In 1986, Lord Roskill's Committee on Fraud Trials recommended that juries should be abolished in complex criminal fraud trials and be replaced by a judge sitting with two lay financial experts. The government rejected the proposal.

In April 1989 the defendants in the first Guinness trial appeared before Southwark Crown Court. However, because of legal argument, the selection of the jury did not begin until February 1990. The judge, Mr Justice Henry, had to be convinced that the jurors had no links with the Guinness company and could cope with the anticipated hearing of three months. Over 100 potential jurors had to complete a questionnaire. Two jurors dropped out and were replaced. The prosecution opened the case, but two more jurors withdrew. The jury was discharged, 100 more jurors were called, and the questionnaire was repeated. The case again commenced, but in June of that year another juror had to stand down, and the case continued with 11 jurors. However, the trial, which ran to 112 days, was vindication that juries could cope with complex fraud trials. Nevertheless, considerable support remained for the Roskill proposal, and a committee member said that the Guinness trial did not alter the findings:

> 'Just because one jury has coped, it does not follow that all can. I still don't think it right for people to be asked to give this amount of time, which puts an enormous strain on everyone.'

In August 1990 a Bar Council report urged the retention of juries for such trials. Tudor Owen, who was a committee member of the Criminal Bar Association, said:

> 'This case demonstrates that despite the criticisms made by some factions about juries in complicated fraud cases, when the case is properly and simply presented, which is the Bar's specialist skill, juries are well capable of understanding it.'

The Bar report did, however, make recommendations, including an increase in the allowances for jurors to provide a more representative cross-section of people, and to ensure the inclusion of businessmen and the self-employed. It also suggested that, in lengthy trials, guidance should be given to jurors in respect of their taking notes. Detailed notes are taken by a judge, and juries should take notes of counsels' closing speeches and the judge's summing up. Furthermore, a specialist panel of experienced judges should sit on such cases. The report said that the case for retaining juries was 'an overwhelming one' and was strongly against the recommendation of the Roskill Committee:

> 'We do not accept the premise that 12 ordinary members of the public, selected at random, cannot be relied upon to produce satisfactory verdicts in complex fraud cases. Juries have consistently produced verdicts which are sensible, responsible and entirely just.'

In February 1992 the second Guinness trial was halted because a defendant was too ill to carry on. Members of the jury were disappointed and angry, and one of the jurors spoke out after suggestions that there should be urgent reforms in dealing with complex fraud cases. She challenged the idea that such cases were beyond the understanding of ordinary people and accused the legal profession of presuming that juries were 'vastly inferior in understanding to their august selves'.

The Lord Chancellor, Lord Mackay of Clashfern, rejected the suggestion that the jury system should be abandoned in complicated fraud trials and said that defendants in such cases had as much right to trial by their peers as any other persons. He did, however, agree that an improvement in the handling of such trials was needed, although he knew of no quick way of achieving it.

David Pannick QC, in his article 'What verdict on juries' (*The Times* 25 February 1992), made the point that to discuss, sensibly, whether jury trial is a fundamental right in serious fraud cases can be done 'only if we know how the jury reach their decisions'. This was difficult, however, because s8(1) of the Contempt of Court Act 1981 makes it a contempt

> 'to obtain, disclose or solicit any particulars of statements made, opinions expressed, arguments advanced or votes cast by members of a jury in the course of their deliberations in any legal proceedings'.

Accordingly, no research into a jury's deliberations is permissible. The article concludes:

> 'Juries do not necessarily understand all the issues. In a New Jersey case, the jury foreman was asked: "Have you agreed upon a verdict, Mr Foreman?" The juror replied: "My name isn't Foreman. It's Admerman."
>
> The less we are allowed to know about how juries determine guilt or innocence in serious fraud trials, the stronger must be the suspicion that jury trial itself is a serious fraud on the public. As all first-year law students know, ignorance is no defence.'

14.4 Juries in civil cases

The provisions of the Juries Act 1974 apply to civil trials as they do to criminal trials, including the qualifications necessary for jurors and the procedure for summoning and selecting them. Majority verdicts may also be accepted in civil cases.

Jury trial is now very rare in both the county courts and the Chancery and Family Divisions of the High Court. There is jury trial in the Queen's Bench Division of the High Court, albeit in a relatively small number of cases. Section 69 of the Supreme Court Act 1981 provides for a right of jury trial in certain cases and a discretion to order it in other cases

By way of comparison, in the United States of America nearly all civil trials are required to be tried by juries. This means that, with complex issues, trials can last for months and even years and must, therefore, result in various pressures upon the jurors.

Right to trial by jury

There is a right to trial by jury in the following cases: fraud, defamation (libel and slander), malicious prosecution and false imprisonment. It must be noted, however, that by virtue of s69(1) of the Supreme Court Act 1981 the right to jury trial is qualified and will be refused if

'the court is of the opinion that the trial requires any prolonged examination of documents or accounts or any scientific or local examination which cannot conveniently be made with a jury ...'.

In these circumstances, therefore, the trial would be by judge alone.

Whether or not jury trial will be granted involves consideration of the probable length of a trial as well as the points mentioned above, as opposed to the desirability of allowing jury trial when there are, for example, important issues involved – part of the problem of how best to achieve the efficient administration of justice.

In *Orme* v *Associated Newspapers Group Ltd* (31 March 1981, unreported) there was a libel trial lasting more than five months, with 117 witnesses. Was the jury overburdened? Furthermore, the costs of the action, including appeal proceedings, were estimated at £800,000. In the light of this case, an amendment was proposed in the early stages of the Supreme Court Act 1981 (ie, an amendment to the bill) that in civil cases there should be no jury trial where a jury could not conveniently try a case because of the probable length of a trial, and in *Practice Direction* [1981] 2 All ER 775 it was pointed out that lawyers, in estimating the length of civil trials, should be careful to avoid hardship to jurors. In *Beta Construction Ltd* v *Channel Four TV Co Ltd* [1990] 2 All ER 1012, liability for libel was admitted, and the only issue to be tried was the amount of damages which, in turn, involved a lengthy investigation of documentary evidence. The plaintiffs wanted a jury to assess damages, whereas the defendants wanted the damages to be quantified by a judge. A decision in favour of the latter was upheld on appeal. The Court of Appeal held that whether such a lengthy examination could be dealt with conveniently by a jury, in accordance with the efficient administration of justice, was dependent upon whether a jury added to the length and cost of the trial. Furthermore, would there be practical difficulties for a jury, and could special complexities result in the jury misunderstanding issues in the case?

The dichotomy is between the desirability of jury trial (for example, in defamation cases when a person's reputation is at stake) and a pragmatic view as to a jury's capabilities.

Discretion to order jury trials in other cases

The governing provision regarding discretion to order jury trials is s69(3) of the Supreme Court Act 1981. From the case of *Ward* v *James* [1966] 1 QB 273 it can be ascertained that the discretion is *not* absolute – that is, unfettered and unrestricted, and not subject to review by any court. When a judge has a discretion conferred on him by statute, the Court of Appeal has jurisdiction to review the exercise of that discretion. Lord Denning MR said (at 295):

'Whenever a man is on trial for serious crime, or when in a civil case a man's honour or integrity is at stake, or when one or other party must be deliberately lying, then trial by jury has no equal.'

It may be seen from the case, however, that a judge should order jury trial only in exceptional circumstances, and it will not be easy to persuade him to do so. An important factor, referred to by Lord Denning, is uniformity in deciding the amount of damages. A judge will be experienced in this area compared with a jury.

• The severity of injuries will not be sufficient a reason to order jury trial. For injuries to be sufficient a reason, they would have to be unique. The authority for this is *Hodges* v *Harland and Wolff Ltd* [1965] 1 WLR 523.
• In *Williams* v *Beasley* [1973] 1 WLR 1295 Lord Diplock indicated that trial without a jury is more speedy and less expensive. In additionr, a conflict of evidence will not be sufficient to depart from trial by a judge alone. Accordingly, trial by jury in civil cases will be the exception rather than the rule. The question lingers as to whether jury trial will continue to exist in civil cases.

In the mid-1970s the Faulks Committee on Defamation recommended that a judge should have discretion (as opposed to the qualified right) to order jury trial. There was no implementation of the recommendation. The committee indicated that a civil jury has the function of considering facts impersonally and recompensing for sustained injury. Juries, however, have no training for this, whereas a judge has many years of experience.

Arguably, however, lay involvement is desirable in the administration of justice. Despite general disadvantages (see below) it is unlikely that jury trial will be completely abolished in civil trials. As regards defamation, there was an interesting development in December 1992. The Lord Chancellor announced reforms which would probably result in smaller libel actions being settled more quickly, cheaply, and without a jury. Under a summary procedure, cases would be dealt with by a High Court judge who would decide the damages. The Lord Chancellor also announced an 'offer of amends' procedure – this would enable newspapers to make an offer where it was recognised that a plaintiff had been defamed and deserved an apology and where there was a willingness to pay damages assessed by a judge.

14.5 The advantages and disadvantages of the jury system

Advantages

1. There is emotional support for trial by jury. Defendants generally consider that it is preferable to entrust their liberty to 12 of their peers rather than to a judge alone. This leads back to our original concept that jury trial is 'the bulwark of liberty, the shield of the poor from the rich and the powerful'.
2. The random selection of members of the public ensures lay participation in the

administration of justice. We must, however, bear in mind that there are relatively few jury cases, and there is influence upon a jury by a judge.

However, lay participation:

a) provides a wealth of experience, various viewpoints and the application of current social attitudes;

b) keeps the law and its procedures comprehensible and responsive to the ordinary person; and

c) gives society the responsibility for deciding guilt and thereby punishment.

3. It is sometimes maintained that judges live in 'ivory towers'; their rarefied standards can be replaced by jurors' general standards of behaviour and morality. The jury therefore become a restraining influence upon the judiciary.

4. Secrecy equates to a guarantee of civil liberty. Because the jury do not have to explain and justify their verdict they are able, in effect, to make a stand against unsatisfactory and oppressive laws. This indirect criticism of the law may pave the way for law reform.

Disadvantages

On the other hand, a number of significant criticisms can be levelled at the jury system. For example:

1. Juries involve more time and additional expense.

2. Is it unreasonable to expect that jurors should understand complex and technical evidence?

3. Are jurors competent to understand difficult issues of law?

4. Counsel thus have the burden of explaining complex evidence and difficult issues of law.

5. It is maintained that jurors are susceptible to rhetoric and can thereby be greatly influenced, bearing in mind particularly their lack of experience in the weighing of evidence and in understanding legal terminology.

6. Verdicts can be unpredictable. It has often been asked whether juries reach 'perverse' verdicts. Perverse, in this context, means against the weight of the evidence or the judge's direction. In considering the case of Clive Ponting, was his acquittal acceptable because the verdict was given according to the jury's conscience, even though the decision flew in the face of the law? Should juries be allowed to give such verdicts? If the law needs to be changed, should this change be brought about by a more reasoned process?

Smith and Bailey's The Modern English Legal System (2nd ed) make the point that, quite apart from whether it is acceptable for juries to decide according to their consciences, an argument may arise 'about "perverse" verdicts in a different sense'. The perception of the role of the jury will affect whether or not a verdict is considered to be perverse.

Smith and Bailey say, at 815:

'If a narrow approach is taken, a verdict is right if it is reached by the jury after an honest, careful and reasonable attempt to apply the law (as explained by the judge in the summing up) to the facts as it finds them, taking no other circumstances into account. What is then achieved is both greater certainty in the outcome of trials and greater consistency in juries' decisions. A broad approach might perceive a verdict to be right where it is a verdict of acquittal, say, after a consideration of the evidence which indicated guilt or even without any consideration of the evidence at all, provided it nevertheless results from a reasonable exercise of discretion in favour of the accused reflecting the jury's sympathy, clemency or disapproval of the prosecution.

The narrow approach will view more acquittals as perverse verdicts and hence leads to the argument that reform of the jury is necessary.'

Despite the limitations, research has been carried out as to whether juries *do* reach perverse verdicts. There were two studies where the views of professionals were taken into account. In 1972 there was a survey by S McCabe and R Purves, *The Jury at Work*, which covered a two-year period and concentrated on 115 accused who were acquitted by jury trial. In 58 other cases, the accused were acquitted on the directions of the judges. The professionals regarded many of the acquittals as correct; the proportion of perverse verdicts in relation to *jury* acquittals was only one verdict in eight, and in relation to *all* acquittals one verdict in 11.

In 1979 there was a second survey, *Jury Trials*, by J Baldwin and M McConville, which spanned an 18-month period and concentrated on 500 contested cases in the Birmingham Crown Court. This survey did not just examine acquittals but looked at all jury verdicts. There was a similar proportion of perverse verdicts. The authors concluded that trial by jury was '... an arbitrary and unpredictable business'.

Overall, therefore, it appeared that there were perverse verdicts in a relatively small number of cases.

7. Juries are not accountable for their verdicts.
8. Instead of being impartial, jurors may be prejudiced either in favour of or against the defendant. Interestingly, because juries were reticent about convicting drivers for drunken driving, specific legislation was passed in 1967 in respect of the permitted level of alcohol. Furthermore, juries often have common prejudices, for example, in relation to race, being against 'red tape', favouring the motorist, or being anti-newspapers in actions for libel; juries may well also be anti-police.
9. Jurors suffer hardship and inconvenience in lengthy cases. The compulsory element of jury service is also unpopular because there is a loss of time, and possibly a loss of money, despite travelling and subsistence expenses and also compensation for loss of earnings.
10. Jurors may not spend a large proportion of their jury service actually in court. They will be subject to delays caused, inter alia, by pleas being changed or witnesses failing to appear.

11. It is obviously more difficult to protect all jurors from intimidation than it is to protect a judge. In August 1991 a Crown Court fraud trial was abandoned after four months because of allegations of jury-nobbling. The jury was discharged, and a retrial was ordered, over two days after the jury had retired to consider their verdicts. The case was estimated to have cost £2 million already. A drugs trial at Southwark Crown Court was halted after three jurors said that they had been the victims of death threats., During the second trial, the jury were given round-the-clock protection.

In August 1993 it was reported that, according to one of Britain's senior judges, criminals were intimidating increasing numbers of people, to stop them giving evidence or to change their stories. Warning letters were also being sent to jurors and thousands of pounds being offered to secure 'not guilty' verdicts. Because senior members of the judiciary and police had become so alarmed, the Lord Chancellor set up a committee to consider measures to provide greater protection for witnesses. Finally, the difficulty in protecting jurors from intimidation is one of the reasons for the existence of 'Diplock courts' in Northern Ireland.

12. Jurors are not usually offered counselling, although the Lord Chancellor's Department said that it would look sympathetically upon any such requests from the jurors in the James Bulger murder trial. They had to listen to the most harrowing and sickening evidence as well as look at photographs of the child victim. It appears that some psychiatrists believe that being involved in murder trials can induce post-traumatic stress disorder similar to that suffered by the survivors of disasters.

13. The variability of juries' verdicts. Compare, for instance, the circumstances and the amounts of damages awarded in the cases of Jeffrey Archer (unreported) and Sonia Sutcliffe (*Sutcliffe* v *Pressdram Ltd* [1990] 1 All ER 269 CA).

14. In the context of awards of damages, consideration must now be given to s8 of the Courts and Legal Services Act 1990. The position in law had been that if both parties agreed, then the Court of Appeal could reassess damages; otherwise the court could only order a new trial. Under s8 the Court of Appeal can still order a new trial *or* award an amount of damages which it considers to be proper instead of the amount decided by the jury. The point to be borne in mind is that the Court may alter the amount of damages *without* the parties agreeing to this being done.

15. In 1967 Lord Devlin levelled at the average jury the criticism that it was 'predominantly male, middle-aged, middle-minded and middle-class'. The original basis for this was that the age limits were too narrow (21 to 60 years of age), and the property qualification restricted those eligible for jury service. As mentioned in section 5.2 above, the property qualification was abolished by the Criminal Justice Act 1972, and the qualifications for jury service, including the extension of age limits, are now governed by the Juries Act 1974 as amended by

s119 of the Criminal Justice Act 1988. In the light of these statutory provisions, it is argued that Lord Devlin's criticism has now lost its justification.

14.6 Alternatives to the jury system

After consideration of the functions and involvement of juries in criminal and civil trials, and also the advantages and disadvantages of the present jury system, it must be asked if there could be a better alternative which still nonetheless upheld the efficient administration of justice. The present jury system may be compared with the methods listed below.

A single judge

As we have seen, most civil cases are already decided by a single judge, and it should be remembered that a stipendiary magistrate sitting alone tries summary offences. If this system were extended to the Crown Court, the concern would be that judges might become pro-prosecution or case-hardened. There would be distrust and a lack of confidence if judges were not impartial and fair-minded. It is also argued that for a judge alone to determine guilt or innocence in serious cases would impose too heavy a burden and would therefore be unacceptable to the public. In this context it seems that the 'Diplock courts' in Northern Ireland are considered to be unsatisfactory. Moreover, there would be no lay participation and no 'voice of conscience'.

There are arguments for decisions being made by a judge alone, however. The saving of time, and thereby of expense, is one. Judges would not be subject to the same external influences as would a jury. Furthermore, verdicts would not be so unpredictable and would not 'fly in the face of the law'.

A bench of judges

Benches of judges are already in use for appeals heard in the divisional court of the Queen's Bench Division, the Court of Appeal and the House of Lords. The concept of a bench of three or five judges would avoid some of the difficulties referred to above, but there would be problems in the light of the increased number of judges required, and there would, of course, be considerable expense. Would such an increase in the number of judges dilute the quality of the bench and also deplete the legal profession? Furthermore, such a system would again lose lay participation and therefore the experience of 'everyday life', to be replaced possibly by a much more narrow legalistic attitude.

Concern followed the case of *Stafford* v *DPP* [1974] AC 878. This involved the matter of fresh evidence, which might have resulted in a jury considering that there was reasonable doubt, coming to light after the trial. Was the verdict unsafe or unsatisfactory? The House of Lords considered that it was not a matter of asking whether a *jury* would have returned a verdict of not guilty in the light of new evidence. If the Court of Appeal was satisfied as to the defendant's guilt then the conviction should not be quashed despite the possibility that a different view might have been reached by the jury. The appeal in this case was dismissed, and so there was, in effect, a verdict by the *judges*. The concern related therefore to the Court of Appeal allowing convictions to stand where a jury might say there was reasonable doubt because of new evidence. Indeed, Lord Devlin criticised the approach of judges determining guilt instead of a jury. He considered that if new evidence could have influenced a verdict then the court should order a new trial.

A mixed tribunal

This could encompass lay experts sitting with a legally qualified chairman – as, for example, in an industrial tribunal. In the Crown Court a judge *must* already sit with lay magistrates where there are appeals from magistrates' courts and also where there are committals for sentence. A mixed tribunal could comprise a judge and lay people – in effect, there is such a system in France. What would be the advantage of a composite tribunal? A judge would use his legal expertise to decide points of law and punishment, but he would also have the benefit of the lay people's experience. The judge's involvement would save time, and if he could be outvoted by the lay members of the tribunal, then lay participation would be ensured.

Special juries

Lay people could sit with other experts, such as accountants in a complicated fraud trial or doctors in cases where medical issues are in dispute. Such experts would assist in the understanding of complex cases, thereby saving time. If there was again the qualification that the experts could be outvoted by the lay people, then lay participation would remain of great importance.

Alternatively, there could be an appointed jury of lay people who would be trained to understand and competently carry out jury service. However, this would be to the detriment of *random* selection. Which of these aspects would be preferable?

14.7 A source of interest – but what of the future?

Juries provide a wealth of interesting, and sometimes amusing, incidents. In September 1992 barristers complained that a juror had been seen filling in an application form, placing tickets or vouchers in envelopes, examining her cheque book and flipping through a diary. After six days of a trial, she was asked to leave the jury.

A juror may sometimes have to be extra careful. In May 1993 it was reported that a gun which was being examined by an Old Bailey juror in a robbery case, suddenly went off. The gun was a replica Colt .45 which fired pellets and in this instance damaged the ceiling. In the same month, during the first few hours of a murder trial a juror, remarkably, fell asleep and awoke when given a nudge by another juror. The jury were discharged and a different set of jurors sworn in. It is thought that, although the judge could have discharged a single juror, the option taken may have seemed the best as the trial had only just commenced. A point to be borne in mind is that a spokeswoman in the Lord Chancellor's Department said that £6850 was the average daily cost of a Crown Court trial.

During a Crown Court case, when the jury returned to court to give their verdict a man in the public gallery wolf-whistled and then winked at a female juror, a 'willowy beauty'. The judge ordered the man's arrest, refused to accept his apology and gave him 14 days' imprisonment for contempt of court. He was released on bail after one night in jail. Subsequently, the Court of Appeal allowed him to go free.

A jury was dismissed at Snaresbrook Crown Court when, after listening to three days of evidence and argument, and having retired to consider their verdict, the jurors sent a note to the judge asking: 'Is it a question of whether we have to decide if he is guilty or not guilty?'

In July 1993, during a case involving assault, 11 jurors wrote to the judge to say that they could not stand the twelfth juror and were worried that there would be difficulty when they had to consider their verdict. The juror was described as: 'a pain in the arse from the start' and 'a self-opinionated, bullying know-all'. The judge consulted the prosecution and defence counsel and decided:

'It is a unique situation. I have never come across it before. We obviously have to start afresh.'

The jury was discharged and there was an estimated figure of £10,000 in lost court time.

In September 1993 it was reported that a blind juror had arrived at Liverpool Crown Court but was told that his visual handicap disqualified him from doing his duty. He had been eager to take part in the proceedings; he felt humiliated and considered that it was an absolute injustice. John Wall, the chairman of the Royal National Institute for the Blind and also Britain's first blind judge, said: 'Every trial is a hearing – not a viewing.' A spokesman for the Lord Chancellor's Department said: 'Blind jurors are able to sit, but it depends on the nature of the case ...'

In November 1993, during a burglary trial at the Old Bailey, the judge had to order a retrial because two jurors nearly came to blows. There had been a clash of personalities, and when the flat of one of the men was burgled he accused the other of being the 'swine' responsible. This man had a cast-iron alibi, but they could not be left to reach a verdict because of the bad feeling. During the same month, after ten hours of deliberation in a spy case, the jury was asked whether they had reached unanimous verdicts on any of the four charges under the Official Secrets Act. The jury foreman announced that they had found the accused guilty on two counts but had not yet reached verdicts on the two further charges. They retired to consider the two outstanding verdicts but sent out a note which expressed concern about the two guilty verdicts. The jury were called back into court, and the judge explained that he took the note to mean that they might have had reservations about the two guilty verdicts. He took the *rare* step of revoking those verdicts and said that the jury would be free to return verdicts on all four charges.

Jury trials have, therefore, given rise to varying experiences, amusing and otherwise. Nevertheless, there are also serious issues which ought to be addressed. For instance, have educational standards fallen to such an extent as to affect the process of the law? Can we expect jurors to understand and evaluate evidence if they are illiterate or semi-literate? Furthermore, if jurors are biased against the police and determined *not* to convict, it is obvious that the guilty are allowed to go free. Should there be an educational requirement to improve the quality of jury members? If so, would the result be predominantly middle-class jurors? Even if that were so, would it not be worth it, to improve justice?

In 1993 there was an article, 'Twelve Biased Men', by Ian Robertson (*The Times* 26 August 1993) which related to a book, *Inside the Juror: The Psychology of Juror Decision Making* edited by Professor Reid and Hastie of the University of Colorado. Robertson wrote:

> 'Surely jurors simply listen carefully, weigh up the evidence and apply rules of logic in order to decide on guilt or innocence? [But] if that is the case, then why are the vast majority of cases (in America at least) majority verdicts, with unanimity among jurors being relatively rare? This means that something else other than the evidence itself is influencing the jurors, and that something can only reside inside jurors themselves. Justice is at least partly at the mercy of the personalities, abilities and attitudes of the jury sitting at the time.'

As regards consideration of the evidence, Professor Hastie's book suggests that jurors reach 'a global conclusion about important issues' and seek evidence to support it. This may involve mishearing evidence which is actually against their opinion and considering that it supports their conclusion. Furthermore, for example:

> '... the fact that two witnesses said that they saw the accused throw something into the sea does not constitute two separate pieces of evidence that the defendant actually disposed of a murder weapon.'

Jurors tend to give double weight to this kind of evidence 'as being separate corroborative points in favour of the view they have come to'. Robertson's article concludes: 'Maybe there is truth in the old adage that people who love sausages (and jury decisions) should never watch them being made.'

Certainly, not everyone is sympathetic to the jury system. This can be seen from a letter published in *The Times* on 10 May 1993, in response to an article, 'By God and my peers', by Bernard Levin. An interesting viewpoint was expressed by the writer, James G Bradshaw of York:

> 'If some wise and impartial being from another planet were to descend upon us and be told that our method of determining guilt or innocence of crime is to put together 12

persons who have never been in a court of law in their lives, who may be barely literate or numerate, and whose level of education or any other reasonable qualification is of no relevance whatsoever, he would without doubt conclude, in a phrase coined by a very eminent lawyer in another context, that we are stark raving bonkers.

One of the very telling moments of truth in a criminal trial is when you look at the faces of jury members who have just acquitted someone of a serious crime but convicted on a minor alternative charge, and they hear read out a list of convictions for the serious offence they have rejected. The very simple reason why virtually every defendant goes for trial by jury and why our courts are clogged up with cases of no merit is the substantial possibility (which is supported by statistics) of an acquittal, however weighty the evidence.'

There was a public furore when a 19-year-old male was cleared by a jury of the murder and manslaughter of a 40-year-old music teacher who had remonstrated with him for vandalising cars. Some people argued that even if the jury had made a mistake, there was nothing wrong with the system. Others argued that the case was an example of the jury system being in disrepair, and that there could be radical improvements.

There is concern about soaring crime figures and falling conviction rates. Various tactics are used by people accused of crimes to escape conviction, including wearing smart clothes, having a neat haircut, smiling pleasantly at the jury, carrying commendable newspapers such as *The Times* to create a good impression, feigning illness and endeavouring to keep disagreeable tattoos out of the sight of the jury.

Proposals have been made to improve the jury system, although sometimes their objective is to save time and expense. In 1975 the Interdepartmental Committee on the Distribution of Criminal Business between the Crown Court and the Magistrates' Court recommended that thefts of property not exceeding £20 in value should be dealt with by summary trial. The reasoning behind this was that such cases were not only not serious but also did not 'justify the elaborate and expensive method of Crown Court trial'. This was not accepted by Parliament.

In 1992, at their association's annual meeting, magistrates passed a resolution that thefts involving £200 or less should be tried at the Crown Court only at the justices' discretion. In effect, this would end the defendant's right to elect for trial at the Crown Court. Reference may be made to an article, 'Counting the Cost of Justice', by Adrian J Turner (*The Times* 22 December 1992). He said:

'The main objection to the proposal is that *all* thefts are serious and anyone facing such a grave allegation should be able to elect trial by jury. I do not for one moment suggest that theft is not serious. It is a fundamental wrong, but its commission is commonplace.'

Although in 1990 the number of people proceeded against for theft and handling was 160,400, the total number of notifiable offences of theft of less than £100 in value, as recorded by the police, was 1,000,192. Do such numbers support the stigma of 'disgrace' and justify opposing summary trial? Furthermore, certain other more serious offences involving dishonesty and violence, such as interfering with a motor vehicle with intent to steal it, and assaulting a police officer in the execution of his duty, *must* be tried in a magistrates' court. Is it inconsistent and illogical that these offences must be dealt with by a magistrates' court whereas a trivial theft case could go to the Crown Court? Such an argument is supported by a case in May 1993 when an unemployed young man was found not guilty of a £2 burglary following a Crown Court trial where the costs were estimated to be at least £15,000.

In an interview with *The Times* in April 1993 Barbara Mills QC, the Director of Public Prosecutions, recommended the abolition of the defendant's right to choose trial by jury. Such a right resulted in the Crown Court having to consider many cases unnecessarily and at huge expense. Mrs Mills was questioning not the worth of the jury system but the reckless cost. Lord Taylor of Gosforth, the Lord Chief Justice, rejected the DPP's call for defendants to lose the right to choose trial by jury. The change might be convenient for those involved in managing the courts, but Lord Taylor did not think that it was in the interests of justice to abolish a defendant's right to trial by jury.

In July 1993 the Royal Commission on Criminal Justice (the Runciman Commission) published its proposals for reform of the criminal justice system. Proposal 114 is that in either way offences (where a case may be heard in a magistrates' court or in the Crown Court) the defendant should no longer have the right to insist on trial by jury. Where the Crown Prosecution Service (CPS) and the defence agree that the case is suitable for summary trial, it should proceed to the magistrates' court. It should go to the Crown Court if both the prosecution and defence agree that it should be tried on indictment. Where the defence does not agree with the CPS, the matter should be referred to the magistrates. Proposal 115 says that legislation should refer to various matters (including potential loss of reputation) which magistrates should take into account in determining the mode of trial.

Professor Michael Zander served on the Royal Commission. In a letter to *The Times* published on 16 July 1993 he explained the reasoning behind the proposal to remove the right to insist on jury trial. The proposal concerned the 30 per cent of defendants who opted for jury trial. Of this number, 83 per cent pleaded guilty, with a waste of time and resources in preparing cases. For these defendants the issue of jury trial becomes irrelevant. Therefore, in effect, the proposal affected the remaining 17 per cent of the 30 per cent who opt for jury trial, that is, 5 per cent of *all* Crown Court defendants. In many cases defendants would still get jury trial under statutory criteria. Furthermore:

> '... it should be for the system, not the defendant, to decide whether the case is appropriate for the full panoply of a jury trial, which is nearly ten times as expensive as a trial in the magistrates' court.'

Later in the same month, at the 'Criminal Justice after the Royal Commission' conference, the Director of Public Prosecutions was strongly in favour of the commission's recommendation to abolish the defendant's right to elect trial by jury. Referring to people defending the right as an 'inalienable right' stemming from

Magna Carta, Mrs Mills said: 'We do not usually go back to the thirteenth century to decide how to run things.' As far as magistrates' discretion was concerned, guidelines could be devised which would be acceptable in every case. Defendants who pleaded not guilty and then changed their minds at the court door caused great inconvenience, and the majority received sentences which could have been imposed by magistrates.

Lord Taylor, on the same occasion, said that he did not doubt the integrity or capacity of magistrates' courts.

> 'However, it is essential not only for justice to be done but for those concerned to have confidence in the process. We must have regard to our history, our culture and the perception of many that trial by jury is a fundamental right.
>
> ... the commission say jury trial has long been recognised as appropriate for cases involving loss of reputation. They add: "But it should only be one of the factors to be taken into account and will often be relevant only to first offenders."
>
> I do not accept that a defendant with a criminal record has, by that token, a weaker claim to jury trial. On the contrary, he or she may well feel specially vulnerable.'

Lord Taylor, referring to the James Report in 1975 which aimed to remove the right of election for trivial offences, for low-value thefts, said that he had supported the view prevailing hitherto that the stigma of dishonesty did not depend on the amount taken.

> 'But if limits are to be put on the present right of election, the *de minimis* approach of the James committee is surely preferable to the socially divisive regime which may well result from the commission's more sweeping proposal. Insignificance of the offence is a fairer test than insignificance of the offender.'

('De minimis' refers to 'de minimis non curat lex', which means the law does not concern itself with trifles.)

It was reported by *The Times* on 5 August that George Carman QC defended the right to choose jury trial. He considered that the commission's proposal would be socially divisive. Magistrates would decide the court of trial in respect of either way offences, and one of the factors to be taken into account would be whether the defendant was faced with a loss of reputation. The newspaper report referred to Mr Carman writing in *Counsel*, the Bar magazine, that the middle classes would be favoured:

> 'The middle-class professional is more likely to obtain trial by jury on a shoplifting charge than the defendant of humble background.'

Furthermore, magistrates would probably take into account the likely effect of a conviction:

> 'So the possible loss of lucrative employment by a defendant would place him in a more favoured position for jury trial than the unemployed defendant. The recommendation undermines the basic principle of equality before the law. It would constitute a very grave erosion of existing rights of trial by jury. It may be seen by many to be something of a charter in favour of the middle-class defendant.'

In November 1993 it was reported that government ministers were expected to shelve the controversial plans for removing the right to trial by jury. This was because of strong opposition from Lord Taylor and the legal profession. Ministers favoured instead the reclassifying of some either way offences as summary offences.

Other proposals of the Runciman Commission include the amending of s8 of the Contempt of Court Act 1981 to enable research into juries' reasons. Proposal 216 specifies that clergymen and members of religious orders should be removed from the list of those who are ineligible for jury service, and proposal 217 says that practising members of a religious sect or order who find jury service to be incompatible with their tenets (principles) or beliefs should be entitled to be excused.

By virtue of proposal 222, in exceptional cases where compelling reasons can be advanced for such a course, it should be possible for either the prosecution or the defence to apply to the judge before the trial for the selection of a jury containing up to three people from ethnic minority communities. Under proposal 223, it should be open to the defence or prosecution to argue the need for one or more of those three jurors to come from the same ethnic minority as the defendant or the victim. The judge should be able to order this in appropriate cases. America, of course, is not without its difficulties in selecting jurors for such cases. In February 1993, following five days of questioning, a multi-racial jury was selected in the federal trial of the police officers accused of beating the black motorist Rodney King. By contrast, in the first trial the jury which acquitted the officers of most charges, in April 1992, was mainly white. The jury's verdicts in that trial provoked the worst riots in the US this century.

Proposal 226 specifies that the judge, in his or her opening remarks, should cover the extent to which jurors may ask questions during the trial, and explain that they may take notes. There are many other proposals relating to juries, and reference may be made to the edited version of the Runciman Commission's summary of its proposals for reform of the criminal justice system in *The Times* of 7 July 1993.

If a general conclusion is drawn that the jury system needs radical improvement, then, apart from the Runciman proposals, should prospective jurors be given a literacy test and should their minimum age be raised from 18? With regard to the challenging of jurors, is it equitable that the prosecution has such a right of stand by? Should perverse verdicts be allowed, and should trials be judged by alternative means?

Section 8(1) of the Contempt of Court Act 1981 has complicated research into how juries perform their functions. David Pannick QC, in an article, 'Juries must stand up and be counted' (*The Times* 17 August 1993), refers to the Royal Commission having pointed out, in the first chapter of its report, that it was 'barred by s8 from conducting research into juries' reasons for their verdicts', and recommending that:

> 'such research should be made possible for the future by an amendment to the Act so that informed debate can take place rather than argument based only on surmise and anecdote'.

Pannick said:

'Every so often, light is thrown on what we all suspect: that jurors, being human beings, will include ignorant, prejudiced and offensive persons.'

He referred to the trial at the Old Bailey where jurors sent a note to the judge appealing to him to remove a juror. He further referred to the robbery case at Snaresbrook Crown Court where the jury enquired as to whether they had to decide if the accused was guilty or not guilty. (Both of these cases have been referred to above.)

Furthermore, Pannick says:

'The sanctity of the jury room has a long legal history. In 1785, Lord Mansfield, the Chief Justice, declined to consider affidavit evidence from two jurors that a divided jury had tossed a coin to determine a verdict.'

And:

'In 1961, the Court of Criminal Appeal was told that several jurors had favoured acquittal until the jury foreman produced a list of the defendant's previous convictions. The court accepted that if such information had been provided, "it would be highly improper". "Public policy", however, prohibited the court from considering what had occurred in the jury room.'

The article concluded:

'Champions of jury trial should consider whether the institution really requires such an extraordinary degree of immunity from analysis of the manner in which it has performed its functions. If juries can work only if they are exempt from procedures that might identify miscarriages of justice, then the fewer cases tried by juries, the better.'

The proposal for amendment to s8 of the Contempt of Court Act 1981 should, if accepted, enable in-depth research to be carried out to identify pertinent problems, which may, in turn, be rectified. Jury trial could then be strengthened, and confidence in the system restored.

15

The Legal Profession

15.1 Introduction

15.2 Solicitors

15.3 Barristers

15.4 Fusion

15.5 Other practitioners

15.6 The Courts and Legal Services Act 1990

15.7 Not all is doom and gloom

15.1 Introduction

This chapter outlines the involvement of the legal profession in the English legal system. The legal profession itself is divided into two main branches, namely solicitors and barristers. The origins of this division date back to the twelfth and thirteenth centuries. Although the law was developing it was not without its complexities, and experienced representatives became involved with cases; a legal profession thereby developed. Subsequently, various groups of lawyers came into existence, and the two main branches now remain. They each have their own purposes, organisations, rules and traditions.

15.2 Solicitors

There are about 61,000 solicitors throughout the country, compared with approximately 7,000 barristers. The controlling body for solicitors is the Law Society, which regulates their conduct and discipline. In addition, by virtue of the Solicitors Act 1974, the Law Society makes regulations relating to the training of solicitors, particularly in respect of examinations and articles.

A roll of solicitors is maintained by the Law Society. To practise as a solicitor, a person's name must be entered on the roll and he or she must have a current practising certificate.

The number of female solicitors is increasing. Between 1980 and 1985 female admissions rose from just above 13 per cent to over 41 per cent. There has, however, been concern that, although more women have been admitted to the roll, many more subsequently leave the profession compared with their male counterparts. In 1988 a Law Society report, *Equal in the Law*, showed that a 'significant and alarming number' of women were temporarily retiring after a few years, mainly, it seemed, to have children. The Law Society was urged to sponsor refresher and returning courses for women. Although this recommendation was not implemented, some firms have subsequently introduced flexible arrangements and policies for women with family commitments. There is, no doubt, great scope for further progress to be made.

Qualification

To become a solicitor an aspiring lawyer must initially obtain a law degree. However, it may be that someone with a non-law degree, eg in languages, decides to become a solicitor or a barrister. In these circumstances he or she must pass the Common Professional Examination, which encompasses six core legal subjects. In a recent article, 'Rough Justice for Students' by Professor Peter Birks (*The Times* 14 September 1993), concern was expressed over the increase of non-law graduates being recruited by firms of solicitors and, similarly, to the taking of places on the Bar's vocational course. The responses made to this article are dealt with below.

Thereafter, having obtained either a law degree *or* a non-law degree and a pass in the Common Professional Examination, a student must register with the Law Society and then pass the Legal Practice Course (LPC) which has replaced the fact-based Law Society Finals (LSF) course. The LPC is *skills-based*, and teaching commenced in September 1993. Although academic institutions now set their own examinations, the Law Society ensures national consistency and also monitors and controls the standards. Generally, the previous LSF course involved too much emphasis upon rote-learning – that is, learning by memory without thought for the meaning – and too little in respect of teaching the skills required in daily practice. Accordingly, the institutions now teaching the LPC, and not the legal profession, basically have the responsibility for assessing students. Overall, of course, there is concern to ensure that the changes do not result in any lowering of standards.

Finally, to complete the road to qualification, there is a two-year training contract, otherwise known as 'articles', which may be with a firm of solicitors or a local authority, or possibly with the Crown Prosecution Service. In essence, a person must be of good character and suitable to practise as a solicitor.

A continuing problem is the funding of students, and this has been exacerbated by, on the one hand, a shortage of local authority discretionary grants, and, on the other, the prospect of increases in fees. The legal profession should be drawn from the community as a whole and not just from those privileged enough to be able to afford the fees. In May 1993, 21 per cent of students were receiving discretionary grants, together with one in five obtaining sponsorship from law firms, and others relying on loans or assistance from parents. The Law Society had previously urged the Department of Education to provide mandatory grants and said that the funding crisis 'will tend to narrow the social base of the profession' and 'have a serious and adverse effect on access to justice'. By November 1993, however, it appears that education ministers had made it clear that they would not favour conferring mandatory grant status.

There is the further problem of the shortage of traineeships (articles) caused by more students completing their vocational courses in comparison with the number of training places available. How do firms whittle down the large numbers of applications? They will obviously consider academic success and carefully scrutinise tutors' references. In November 1992 a recruitment partner from one City firm said that they were 'looking for focused ambition, the ability to manage hard work and clients, willingness to work and a sense of responsibility'. The senior partner from another City firm said:

'We are looking for that spark, that combination of intelligence, commitment and common sense: the ability to be able to show as much concern and sympathy to the director of a major company one day and to a battered wife the next.'

The role of a solicitor

Initially, it must be borne in mind that a member of the public does *not* have to instruct a solicitor and, indeed, is entitled to appear in person. This could, however, give rise to other difficulties, such as lack of the skill and expertise to present a case properly or lack of familiarity with practice and procedure.

A considerable number of solicitors are in private practice. Here they form partnerships or are employed as assistant solicitors. In private practice the broad role of a solicitor encompasses a very wide range of legal issues including, inter alia, litigation (court work), which involves civil, domestic (matrimonial) and criminal cases; conveyancing; the drafting of wills and the administration of estates; and commercial and company law matters.

Usually members of the public approach a solicitor, and it is the solicitor who prepares the case even though the hearing may subsequently be in a higher court with representation by a barrister. Preparation involves interviewing the client – and may necessitate speaking to the witnesses – the collation of evidence generally, and liaison with various people and/or organisations, eg the Crown Prosecution Service. Proceedings may have to be commenced, and negotiation could also take place. If necessary, a solicitor will instruct a barrister.

In private practice many solicitors are general practitioners, while others specialise in particular areas of law. Apart from private practice, solicitors may be found working in the Crown Prosecution Service, local government, industry and education.

The Law Society places great importance, and rightly so, upon the handling of clients' money and the keeping of accounts. Solicitors must be insured, and there is also a compensation fund. The purpose of the fund is to relieve the hardship of clients where loss has been caused because of a solicitor's failure with regard to the handling of their money.

The Solicitors' Disciplinary Tribunal is very important and has a major involvement in dealing with complaints against solicitors regarding professional misconduct and also offences under the Solicitors Act 1974: for example, failure to comply with the Solicitors' Accounts Rules. The tribunal may suspend and fine a solicitor and may also remove his or her name from the roll. An appeal generally lies to the divisional court of the Queen's Bench Division and subsequently, on a point of law, to the Court of Appeal and the House of Lords. A solicitor is also an officer of the court, and disciplinary jurisdiction may therefore be exercised by the High Court, the Crown Court and the Court of Appeal.

Rights of audience

Solicitors may appear in the magistrates' courts, county courts, coroners' courts, tribunals and, in certain circumstances, the Crown Court. The matter of rights of audience now has to be considered in the light of the Courts and Legal Services Act 1990 (see section 15.6 below).

A solicitor may be appointed as a district judge, formerly called a registrar, a stipendiary magistrate, a recorder and subsequently a circuit judge.

Liability

In civil proceedings a solicitor may be liable to a third party as well as to a client. The law of agency will generally resolve whether a solicitor is liable to a *third party* in contract. Apart from contract, there may be liability in tort.

As regards negligence, it was decided in *Hedley Byrne & Co Ltd* v *Heller & Partners Ltd* [1964] AC 465, that a duty of care in the giving of advice could arise where there was a special relationship. Accordingly, liability for negligence has been wider since this decision. In *Midland Bank Trust Co Ltd* v *Hett, Stubbs and Kemp* [1979] Ch 384 there was such a relationship between a plaintiff client and a defendant solicitor. In *Ross* v *Caunters* [1980] Ch 297 there was liability in tort although there was no contractual relationship between the plaintiff and solicitor. In this case the solicitor did not inform the testator that the will must not be witnessed by any beneficiary's spouse. The plaintiff's husband (the plaintiff was the beneficiary) witnessed the will, and the plaintiff was thereby prevented from inheriting under the will. The plaintiff was successful in her negligence action even although there was no contractual relationship between herself and the solicitor.

A client gives a retainer to a solicitor and thereby a *contractual* relationship arises. The duty of care will exist while there is a retainer. Where there is a contentious matter a solicitor may require some money on account of costs, and if this is not paid the solicitor may, subject to giving notice, withdraw from the retainer.

Where there is negligence by a solicitor he may be sued for damages in contract and also in tort. However, in *Rondel* v *Worsley* [1969] 1 AC 191 four of their Lordships said, obiter, that a solicitor, as an advocate, should have the same immunity as a barrister, namely no liability in tort for a case being negligently presented in court or for the preliminary work connected with it. In the subsequent case of *Saif Ali* v *Sydney Mitchell & Co* [1980] AC 198 there were similar dicta.

Section 62 of the Courts and Legal Services Act 1990 is now of great importance. Section 62(1) states:

'A person–
(a) who is not a barrister; but
(b) who lawfully provides any legal services in relation to any proceedings,
shall have the same immunity from liability for negligence in respect of his acts or omissions as he would have if he were a barrister lawfully providing those services.'

It should be noted that where there is such immunity, there is no liability for breach of any contract (s62(2)).

The relationship between a solicitor and his client is *fiduciary*, ie the solicitor must act in good faith when dealing with his client. Communications between a client and his solicitor are 'privileged'; this means that there is protection against disclosure in evidence. This privilege may be waived by the client but *not* by the solicitor.

15.3 Barristers

Barristers are otherwise known as 'counsel'. They do not form partnerships but are self-employed and work in 'chambers' which comprise a number of rooms where there is a sharing of a barristers' clerk and secretarial staff. The barristers' clerk is an important figure as he or she controls administration, deals with fees and liaises with solicitors.

All barristers have to belong to one of four Inns: Inner Temple, Middle Temple, Lincoln's Inn or Gray's Inn. There are three types of members of Inns – students, barristers and benchers. Benchers comprise senior barristers and active and retired judges.

Barristers themselves are of two types: Queen's Counsel (known as QCs or 'silks' because of their silk gowns) and junior barristers. In other words, any barrister who is not a Queen's Counsel is, strictly speaking, a junior barrister. A Queen's Counsel is appointed by the Queen on the advice of the Lord Chancellor. He or she will thereby acquire status, have less paperwork and should earn considerably more money. He or she will still usually be accompanied in court by a junior barrister, although the rule requiring this was abolished in 1977.

Queen's Counsel are chosen on the basis of views obtained from the profession by the Lord Chancellor's officials. Personal files are kept, but they are not open to the individuals concerned. Names of those considered to be suitable are sent to the Queen by the Lord Chancellor. Many barristers, however, would like to see an end to the secrecy involved in selecting Queen's Counsel and a more open system with wider consultation. It is also considered that more women should apply, as they only comprise approximately 5 per cent of all Queen's Counsel. Similarly, there are too few applications by ethnic minority candidates. In 1992 Gareth Williams QC (now Lord Williams of Mostyn, a former Bar chairman) said the system was 'deeply flawed'.

One of the main criticisms has been that barristers have not been given reasons for their rejection. That having been said, advice from officials may be sought by disappointed candidates, although it is debatable whether frank reasons are given for their rejection. As evidence of general progress, in April 1993 Harry Wolton QC, the head of a leading Birmingham chambers, said that the system was changing fast:

'We don't go in for anybody because of school, university or parental background. We go for individual character, talent and personality. Background doesn't carry the weight it used to. It will gradually disappear as a stepping-stone.'

On 29 September 1993 a letter from Sir Robert Megarry FBA was published in *The Times* in response to an article, 'Barristers challenge QC secrecy', in that paper on 27 September; he wrote:

'The essence of the process was that the decision was based on the personal knowledge of those with no axe to grind who had seen and heard the applicants in court; and both as to character and ability, such appearances are wonderfully revealing.

Views on individual applications were not, of course, bruited abroad; but why the process itself should be called "secret" I do not know. I have often spoken of it openly at meetings and dinners ...'

Sir Robert was referring to the system of selection in which he was involved when he was Vice-Chancellor (1976–85). With reference to how judges choose QCs, an interesting point was made by Piers Ashworth in a letter to *The Times* printed on 5 October 1993. This letter referred to the fact that, because of a shortage of judges, the majority of common law cases in the Queen's Bench Division were tried by deputies, and thus experienced and competent barristers lost 'the opportunity of arguing cases before the very judges whose views on their suitability for silk are so important'.

Sir Thomas Legg, the permanent secretary at the Lord Chancellor's Department, has said that the selection system is as fair and open as the Lord Chancellor can make it. Opinions about applicants and their work have to remain confidential. Furthermore, he said, the system is not informal but organised and systematic. As regards fee income, the Lord Chancellor accepts that it is relevant but rejects that a minimum amount is necessary before an individual is considered. There is no upper or lower age limit, and no account is taken of any particular set of chambers that an applicant comes from. In 1992 more than 470 barristers applied to become Queen's Counsel and

70 were chosen. The first black female barrister 'took silk' – that is, became a Queen's Counsel – in 1992. It is also worth noting that the percentage of female barristers and those from ethnic minorities has been increasing (see Chapter 3.3, above).

In March 1992 new research was announced to remedy sex discrimination. In November 1992 the Bar published the findings of the first survey into sex discrimination in the profession, and reference may be made to an article, 'Rough justice at the Bar', by Frances Gibb (*The Times* 1 December 1992). There was evidence of 'substantial and continuing unequal treatment between the sexes at many levels of the profession'. The report found that women suffered discrimination in obtaining pupillages (training places) and tenancies (permanent seats in chambers); in the allocation of work by clerks; in earnings; and in selection for promotion to senior ranks. Lesley Holland, a principal consultant with TMS Management Consultants, Bournemouth, who conducted the survey, said:

> 'It is not that barristers want to exclude women. But the Bar has a set of traditions, cultures and values which quite unconsciously and unintentionally favour men and provide extra hurdles for women.'

The recommendations included '... selection criteria at every level, from entry to the bench. These should be defined, job-related and publicised, bringing more objectivity into recruitment.' Furthermore, with reference to applications for the judiciary and to become QCs, the article continued by stating that there should be an overhaul of the procedures 'to make them more open, systematic, objective and, therefore, fair'.

Barristers are governed by the General Council of the Bar of England and Wales – the Bar Council. As well as maintaining standards, and promoting and improving the services and functions of the Bar, it also regulates the Bar's practices and activities. There is also the Council of the Inns of Court which consists of representatives of the four Inns, the Bar Council and the Council of Legal Education. The last of these is responsible for the Inns of Court School of Law.

It should be noted here that if there is disagreement between the Council of the Inns and the Bar Council, it is the policy of the latter body which will be followed as long as two-thirds of the profession supports it.

The Bar has not in the past been regulated by statute, although the Bar Council enforces a strict 'code of conduct'. The Courts and Legal Services Act 1990, however, does now have importance.

Qualification

For anyone wishing to become a practising barrister, either a good law degree or a non-law degree and a pass with commendation in the Common Professional Examination is needed. There is also a vocational course of one year which is skills based. Reference has previously been made to the article 'Rough justice for students' by Professor Birks. In the light of that article, did the increase in recruitment of non-law graduates, inter alia, mean a danger of an under-qualified profession and a threat to law schools if the legal profession as a whole turned away from law graduates? The article did not go unchallenged, and reference may be made to three other articles, 'How to select the best' by Clare Deanesly, 'Leave a door open' by Roger Jones and 'Lower the barriers' by Rhodri Davies, all of which were published in *The Times* on 28 September 1993.

Clare Deanesly, a recruitment partner with a London firm, said:

'True, law undergraduates may study more legal subjects, but these are not always relevant to commercial practice. Most law faculties offer a diverse range of options to supplement the six core subject elements. Many students will have used their time to explore a legal topic they will not pursue in practice. Subject choice is as diverse as criminology, legal history, human rights, Roman law, housing and welfare law, family law and women and the law.'

Roger Jones, a partner with a Cardiff firm, who is the chairman of the Law Society's training committee and CPE board vice-chairman, said:

'The Law Society believes there must be a route into the legal profession for those who decide on a legal career later in life than the typical law student. Some students prefer to pursue another intellectual interest before studying law and making this their career. A growing number feel the call to retrain as lawyers after spending time in a different occupation. Such people have a right to an alternative path to the legal profession that recognises their existing intellectual abilities and experience of life.'

And further:

'In 1992–93, 69 per cent of those admitted as solicitors were law graduates, compared with 14 per cent non-law graduates. The rest were mostly lawyers transferring from other jurisdictions.'

Rhodri Davies, a barrister, said:

'The conversion course is itself a barrier to non-law graduates; it should not be raised to a full three-year second degree. As for whether non-law graduates know enough law, the answer is that the essentials for a successful start in practice – apart from basic legal knowledge – are the abilities to think rigorously, grasp detail and communicate effectively.

Professor Birks almost suggested non-law graduates should be excluded from practising because the competition for jobs they provide is unfair to law graduates and hence to universities' law schools. This is a challenge to be risen to, not shut out by a monopoly constricting entry to the profession.'

The student must join one of the four Inns of Court, and subsequently he or she has to eat a required number of dinners at the Inn. The purpose of 'eating dinners' is to meet one's peers and seniors, engage in stimulating conversation and, in effect, develop an understanding of the Bar. A student used to have to eat 24 dinners, but this has now been reduced to 18, and they must have been eaten before a student can be 'called to the Bar' (see below).

Reference has previously been made to the problem of funding students, and, although there are scholarships and awards from Inns of Court, the percentage of full local authority grants has fallen, and only about 4 per cent of students receive any grant at all. In 1992 Lord Donaldson, the then Master of the Rolls, said that the public could no longer afford to have a legal profession recruited and trained on a 'pre-qualification means test', and that that was a tragedy 'not only in personal terms for the students concerned, but also for the profession and the wider public which it serves'. The legal profession has endeavoured to persuade the government to provide mandatory grants, as it does for doctors, but so far this has been unsuccessful.

Still on the issue of training, an informative article, 'Bar trainees go live', by Frances Gibb, was published in *The Times* on 24 August 1993. During 1993, for the first time in England, a small group of students was involved in real cases and assessed on them, in order to qualify at the Inns of Court School of Law. Such 'live' work was, and is, rare. The article refers to voluntary work having always been carried out by law students at a referral unit known as the Bar's Free Representation Unit (FRU). The students deal with tribunal cases sent by law centres and advice bureaux, and they act without charge. From this basis the Council of Legal Education (CLE) developed a structured option for students in their third term. During the summer of 1993, for the first time, 24 students chose the FRU option, and in 1994 it will be offered to 36 students. The Bar Council would like to see more barristers being involved in FRU cases, and also FRU units being developed elsewhere. It may be that the CLE will subsequently license institutions to offer the Bar's finals course at centres around the country. The article concludes:

> 'With the growing emphasis on practical training for the Bar, regional training centres could tie up with local FRU units, giving students vital on-the-job training, as well as plugging a gap in legal services to the public.'

Having successfully completed the academic or vocational course, and having eaten the required number of dinners, a student is 'called to the Bar'. To practise, however, a student must complete pupillage, which is for 12 months. It is not until the second half of pupillage that 'instructions' may be accepted by the pupil. There are now various funded pupillages, awards and grants to assist entry into the profession.

The role of a barrister

Generally, barristers are instructed by solicitors to provide specialist advocacy and specialist advice. Advocacy, involving the oral presentation of cases, is obviously important. Barristers will write opinions on legal points and advise as to the strength of a case. They will also draft pleadings, ie formal documents such as a statement of claim, a defence, or defence and counterclaim. There is specialism among barristers – for example, those involved with Chancery cases will probably have more paperwork in the context of written advice and the drafting of pleadings.

A barrister is *not* an officer of the court (unlike a solicitor). A duty is, however, owed to the court as well as to the client, and a barrister must bring to the court's notice all relevant authorities even though they do not support his or her client's case. The court must not be misled by the concealing of any material facts, and a barrister must not present a defence where an admission has been made by the client. A prosecuting counsel should not endeavour to obtain a conviction by all means at his disposal; he should present the facts impartially and generally assist the court.

Note should also be taken of the cab-rank principle: basically, that a practising barrister is bound to accept any brief to appear before a court. There must be no regard for the barrister's personal feelings in respect of either the accused or the type of offence involved.

Barristers have rights of audience to appear in any court and have, in the past, had sole rights of audience in the higher courts. This is now subject to the Courts and Legal Services Act 1990 (see 15.6 below). In addition, the higher judiciary has historically been chosen from barristers, but this too will be affected by the 1990 Act.

In 1992 the chairman of the barristers' annual conference in London was Anne Rafferty QC, who chaired it under the theme of reform. Miss Rafferty considered that the aim of the Bar was to advance appropriately but not to lose '... those aspects of our tradition of standards which we need to hold on to'. She felt that the Bar was vulnerable to a public perception that 'we do an enervating two hours in court, have our briefs carried back by our clerks to chambers prior to a quick sherry before nipping home to dinner'. There were various debates at the conference, including [whether the Bar was] 'an expensive anachronism or the cornerstone of liberty?'. Miss Rafferty predicted that within ten years there would be a smaller, leaner Bar.

In 1993 another woman, Heather Hallett QC, was appointed the Bar's director of public affairs. The fact that there is such a high-profile role indicates how the profession has changed. Frances Gibb wrote an article, 'Model of a modern barrister', in *The Times* on 9 March 1993:

'The Bar has made great efforts to shed its fusty image. Its new public affairs director is committed to continuing the task.'

Ms Hallett said:

'We have managed to get across that you don't have to be public school, to be moneyed, male and middle-class – that we are a meritocracy rather than an old-boy network.'

It appeared that she would endeavour to continue to underline the Bar's image as a reformist body promoting ideas and concerned with access to justice.

Finally, in another article by Frances Gibb, 'Will the Bar face collapse?', published in *The Times* on 16 November 1993, there was a reference to 'a drastic reduction of work' over the preceding three years. Furthermore:

'The difficulties of finding work are exacerbated by the shortage of both training and permanent places in chambers (pupillages and tenancies), reducing more young barristers to "squatting" temporarily in chambers which will let them in.'

The shortage of work had coincided with a growth in the Bar 'to the record size of 7,735' in October 1993. A report on the young Bar warned:

> 'Unless the Bar recruits sufficient young barristers of ability who can train, gain experience, practice [sic] and go on to be senior and leading members of the profession, the profession will have no future.'

There was a decline in magistrates' courts work and also a drop in work given to the Bar by the Crown Prosecution Service. Solicitors were carrying out much more of the work which had previously been passed to young barristers. Nicholas Vineall, the chairman of the Young Barristers' Committee, said:

> 'This has nothing to do with the battle over rights of audience. This is work that solicitors have always been able to do, in the magistrates' and county courts, but which, when they were busier, they put out to junior counsel.'

There was increased competition from solicitors in the criminal courts, and there would be greater loss when solicitors gained the rights to appear in the Crown Courts. The Bar, it seemed, would reduce in size. The report's recommendations included repackaging and reorganising of the Bar's services to be more attractive, and the provision by barristers of competitive quotations to compare with solicitors' charges.

Liability

It was held in *Rondel* v *Worsley* (see section 15.2) that a barrister is not liable in tort for the negligent presentation of a case in court or its preparation.

In *Saif Ali* v *Sydney Mitchell & Co* (see section 15.2) the House of Lords considered that professional immunity would only extend to advice given by a barrister if it was 'so intimately connected' with the conduct of the case in court that 'it could fairly be said' to be a preliminary decision affecting the way the case was conducted when it came to trial.

15.4 Fusion

The question has often been raised as to whether there should be fusion of the two branches of the legal profession. The Royal Commission on Legal Services (the Benson Commission) was formed in 1976. Consideration was given to the cost of conveyancing services and to the structure, organisation, training and regulation of the legal profession. Arguments concerning the inefficiency of the two branches of the legal profession were submitted to the commission.

Arguments for fusion

1. It would avoid repetition of work – at present a client instructs a solicitor who, in turn, may instruct a barrister.

2. The quality of service could improve if one lawyer prepared a case. The lawyer would be familiar with the facts, and there would be no possibility of problems in communication between a solicitor and a barrister and therefore no risk of any oversight. It would also avoid the possibility of a barrister not being as well prepared as he might have been.

3. There would be no representation by a barrister on a last-minute basis, caused by either the original barrister still being involved in a court hearing or the solicitor sending late instructions.

4. It would avoid the criticism that a barrister might not see his client until the day of the trial, especially so where there is a plea of guilty. The question arises as to whether seeing the barrister at such a late stage increases confidence or makes matters more intimidating.

5. Theoretically, costs would be reduced. The question must be asked, however, as to whether a solicitor's costs would, in fact, be less if he or she was doing *all* the work.

6. Fusion would avoid a wrong career decision – a solicitor wishing that he or she had originally become a barrister and vice versa.

7. There would be a wider scope for the selection of judges as the pool would be increased.

8. The loss of public confidence caused by a divided profession would be lessened. This loss of confidence would perhaps have arisen from a barrister becoming involved in a case and not being familiar with the circumstances, or from the late return of a brief resulting in different counsel at the hearing.

Arguments against fusion

1. There would be the loss of the specialist expert: the 'detached second opinion'. Where counsel is fully and properly briefed by a solicitor, then a divided profession provides a superior service.

2. The high standards of advocacy would be reduced. Advocates would have to spend more time in the office, whereas it is frequent practice in court which is the basis for specialisation.

3. Specialists/senior barristers would no doubt be employed by large firms of solicitors, but where would this leave small firms? Would the latter be able to join forces economically with barristers or, indeed, be able to brief a barrister equal to the one instructed by their opponents?

4. Although there would be a larger pool for selection of the judiciary, there would also be an increase in the possibility of an unsuitable choice being made. The Lord Chancellor would not have the same knowledge of all prospective candidates.

5. What would become of the important cab-rank principle? Would it disappear? A barrister cannot refuse a case, but small firms of solicitors could not deal with all types of problem.

The Royal Commission on Legal Services was unanimously in favour of there being a divided legal profession. The commission was concerned about the lowering of the standards of advocacy if fusion took place. Where there is an adversarial system of law, then high standards of advocacy are very important. If the standards are low then pertinent points may not be considered, the right questions may not be asked, and the evidence may not give the full picture, and all this would affect the decision of the judge. Logically there could then be a decrease in the quality of judicial decisions.

Furthermore, with fusion there could be more expense in certain circumstances and small firms would disappear. Solicitors should also be able to avail themselves of a specialist Bar.

In 1986 the Law Society published a discussion paper, *Lawyers and the Courts: Time for Some Changes*. There were compromise proposals, namely that all lawyers should undergo the same initial training followed by general practice. A lawyer could subsequently become a barrister and would be a specialist advocate. Lawyers in general practice would have rights of audience in lower courts for two to three years and no restrictions thereafter. The Bar was opposed to these proposals.

15.5 Other practitioners

Licensed conveyancers

In 1983 Austin Mitchell sponsored a Private Member's Bill, the House Buyers' Bill, whose purpose was to remove restrictions on conveyancing. The bill was opposed, although the government indicated that it intended to allow banks and building societies to carry out conveyancing and would consider allowing suitably qualified non-solicitors to compete with solicitors in this field. Subsequently the bill was withdrawn on the basis that the government would give an undertaking with regard to non-solicitors carrying out conveyancing, subject to a committee's advice in respect of ensuring consumer protection.

The committee reported in 1984, and legislation was based upon its recommendations; a system of licensed conveyancers was established by the Administration of Justice Act 1985. Subsequently the Council for Licensed Conveyancers was given powers under s53 of the Courts and Legal Services Acts 1990 to enable it to become an authorised body for the purposes of granting rights of audience under s27(2)(a) and rights to conduct litigation under s28(2)(a).

Legal executives

Legal executives are employed within firms of solicitors. They have their own examinations and legal qualification, and there is an Institute of Legal Executives.

15.6 The Courts and Legal Services Act 1990

Background

As a result of the Royal Commission on Assizes and Quarter Sessions, the Beeching Report was published in 1969 (Lord Beeching had been chairman of the commission). Following the report's recommendations, the courts of Assize and Quarter Sessions were abolished by the Courts Act 1971 and a single court, the Crown Court, was established. Lord Beeching's only concession to solicitors was that the Lord Chancellor was given power to allow solicitors rights of audience where there were insufficient barristers to do the work.

In 1972 a Practice Direction specified that solicitors could appear before the Crown Court where there were appeals from the magistrates' courts, or committals from the magistrates to the Crown Court for sentence, *as long as* the solicitors had acted for the clients in the magistrates' court.

In its evidence to the Royal Commission on Legal Services (see 15.5 above), apart from desiring limited rights of audience in the High Court, the Law Society considered that solicitors should have rights of audience in the Crown Court for appeals and committals for sentence from magistrates' courts, triable-either-way offences and the least serious offences in the Crown Court. There would be a choice of advocate and a reduction in costs, and pressure on the Bar would be eased. The Bar, however, was strongly opposed, and maintained that there would be a lowering of advocacy standards and also serious financial consequences for the junior Bar. The commission recommended that there should be no change, but only by eight votes to seven, whereas its decision against fusion was unanimous (see 15.4 above).

In 1984 the Home Office proposed that solicitors in the Crown Prosecution Service should have rights of audience in the Crown Court, but there was again great opposition from the Bar, and the proposals were not pursued.

In *Abse* v *Smith* (1986) QB 536 a High Court judge had refused to allow the solicitor acting for the Member of Parliament Cyril Smith to read a seven-line agreed statement in court in settlement of a libel action. The Court of Appeal upheld the judge's ruling. Sir John (later Lord) Donaldson, the then Master of the Rolls, said that it was for judges to decide whom they should hear as advocates.

A Legal Aid Scrutiny Report in 1986 indicated that there was no good reason why solicitors should not have rights of audience for 'guilty' pleas in the Crown Court. However, in the following year a Legal Aid White Paper said that the government had no intention of extending rights of audience in the Crown Court.

In 1986 a committee was appointed, chaired by Lady Marre, who had previously distinguished herself in her work for the Citizens' Advice Bureaux and was also a former member of the Lord Chancellor's Legal Aid Advisory Committee. The Marre Committee comprised six barristers, six solicitors and six independent figures. It was concerned with whether the public's needs and demands for legal services were met by the legal profession. Where, in the public interest, could changes be made in the education, structure and practices of the profession?

The committee reported in July 1988 and basically preserved the status quo. There was a recommendation that solicitors should have a qualified right of audience in the Crown Court, which would encompass solicitors appearing for the defence, provided that they had been approved as competent by an Advisory Board established in each circuit. A majority of the committee did not consider that there should be an extension in respect of the High Court or of conducting prosecutions in the Crown Court.

In October 1988 Lord Mackay of Clashfern, the Lord Chancellor, unexpectedly announced that he would be publishing a Green Paper. In fact, on 25 January 1989 *three* radical Green Papers were published containing his proposals for large-scale changes in the working and organisation of the legal profession.

The Green Papers
The three Green Papers were as follows:

1. *The Work and Organisation of the Legal Profession* (the main Green Paper)
2. *Contingency Fees*
3. *Conveyancing by Authorised Practitioners*

The Lord Chancellor said:

> 'The whole idea is to improve access to justice, encourage fair competition, and at the same time maintain professional standards.'

Furthermore, he added that his aim was not to 'fuse' the solicitors' and barristers' branches of the profession.

The important aspects of the Green Papers were: competition; the removal of restrictive practices; and a better service to the public involving a wide choice of cost-effective legal services provided by competent practitioners, with professional standards being upheld. Clearly, also, the interests of justice had to be safeguarded. The proposals included, inter alia, the following:

1. The establishment of a lay-dominated advisory committee on legal education and conduct, with members being appointed by the Lord Chancellor.
2. Lawyers who obtained certificates of competence and training should have rights of advocacy in all courts. The right of audience in a particular court would depend upon appropriate education, training and qualifications, and codes of conduct would also have to be followed. Professional bodies would issue the certificates, but it appeared that the Law Society and the Bar would not be the only bodies involved. There would be parliamentary scrutiny and control with regard to rights of audience.
3. Cases could be accepted on a 'no win, no fee' basis, thereby giving greater access to the courts for members of the public. Such contingency fees, so it seemed, would not be applicable to criminal cases but would be appropriate in claims for personal injury. It was considered that justice would thus be more readily

available, for example to people who were ineligible for legal aid but nevertheless could not afford to pursue their claims. A controlled system was proposed, with some type of incentive for lawyers to become involved in speculative cases. Clearly, also, the situation should not arise whereby settlements for claims would result in less damages than if the claim had been hard pressed.

4. The appointment of a Legal Services Ombudsman.
5. Banks and building societies would be able to offer conveyancing services for their customers – 'one-stop shopping' for house buyers.
6. Barristers would be allowed to form partnerships, and solicitors to form multi-disciplinary practices, with members of other professions (eg surveyors and estate agents).
7. Barristers were to decide if they wished to take instructions from members of the public.

The Bar, understandably, was reluctant to forgo its monopoly of advocacy rights in the higher courts. It was extremely concerned about control by the government over the administration of justice, for example the licensing of advocates and the involvement of an advisory committee on legal education and conduct. Lord Denning, the former Master of the Rolls, in effect considered that a Bar of specialists must be retained, and that solicitors should be general practitioners but able to instruct the specialists.

In early May 1989 responses were received from the Law Society and the Bar Council, and later in the same month from the judges.

The Law Society's response ('Striking the Balance'). The Law Society supported an independent legal affairs commission to govern the profession (instead of the suggested advisory committee, which it described as 'a dangerous accumulation of power in the hands of a government minister'). It opposed lending institutions being able to provide conveyancing, and also multi-disciplinary practices between lawyers and members of other professions (this could, inter alia, create conflicts of interest and make it more difficult to pursue complaints). The society supported solicitors having full rights of audience in higher courts.

The Bar Council ('Quality of Justice: the Bar's Response'). The Bar opposed rights of audience for solicitors in the higher courts. It supported the system controlled by judges, which it saw as being of benefit to the public. It also wished judges, rather than Parliament, to retain control over who appeared before them. This involved independent control of the higher courts and the independence of the profession. The cab-rank rule was important – its purpose was to ensure that every person could have the services of an independent barrister. If solicitors were given rights of audience, then this should be on equal terms with barristers. The cab-rank rule should apply to everybody or nobody.

Lay access to barristers was opposed as being both expensive in terms of time, cost and quality and incompatible with consultant status.

Advocacy certificates were felt to be inadequate in respect of controlling and judging ability, and contingency fees were opposed.

It was maintained that the proposed advisory committee on education and conduct threatened the independence of the judiciary and the legal profession. The Lord Chancellor would have power to decide the standards of education and training, codes of conduct, disciplinary procedures and which bodies should be recognised as practitioners. The Bar considered that judges should supervise the code of conduct and the professional standards of both barristers and solicitors, and proposed that there should be a legal professional standards committee.

It was considered that barristers entering partnerships with each other, or with solicitors or members of other professions, would reduce choice, competition and standards and lead to an increase in costs. For instance, with multi-disciplinary practices there would be conflicts of interest and difficulties of supervision, and the distinctions between professions would be blurred.

Judges ('The Green Papers: the Judges' Response'). The judges felt that the rule of law might be undermined; there could be a decline in advocates' conduct and competence, with the added possibility of a 'potentially very dangerous' transfer of power from the judiciary to a government department.

With regard to advocacy, the judges defended the existing system and its contribution to the quality of justice. They opposed non-lawyers being allowed to practise in the Supreme Court and insisted upon retaining ultimate control over the conduct of those practising there.

The judges opposed extending the rights of audience of solicitors. They considered that, as a result, there was a possibility that advocates' skills would decline, that there would be fusion of solicitors and barristers, and that there would be an adverse effect upon recruitment to the Bar. Furthermore, they felt that the proposal in respect of licensing advocates was unsound and the idea of multi-disciplinary practices objectionable.

After all the responses to the Green Papers had been received, the government published a White Paper in July 1989.

The White Paper (*Legal Services: A Framework for the Future*)

'The government's aim in all these changes is to make the legal system of this country more straightforward, more flexible, and above all more responsive to the citizen's choices and needs, whilst at the same time maintaining the standards necessary to achieve justice.'

Furthermore, there would be legislation to redistribute civil cases between the High Court and the county courts.

The criticism of the proposed advisory committee on education and conduct had been that there would be too much power in the hands of the executive. It had been maintained that the powers over education and conduct constituted a threat to the independence of the judiciary. Lord Mackay endeavoured to offset some criticism by emphasising that the advisory committee would have a purely advisory role. Its main functions would be to advise on arrangements for education and training and on the rules of conduct to be observed by those providing legal services. In addition it would advise the Lord Chancellor on the suitability of professional bodies or organisations to grant to their members rights of audience or the right to conduct litigation. There would have to be agreement by the Lord Chancellor, professional bodies and senior judges to the rules on the competency of advocates.

The Green Papers had proposed a complex system of certification for rights of audience. There were, however, *revised proposals* in the White Paper: a statutory framework would be created, allowing an extension of rights of audience for present advocates and new classes of advocates. The professional bodies representing lawyers would determine the persons qualified to appear in the courts. Those who wished to appear in the higher courts would have to undertake a period of practical training in advocacy plus a test. Furthermore, the proposals would not be a restriction on the judges' discretion to control proceedings in the courts over which they presided.

The government was to end the statutory ban on multi-disciplinary and multi-national partnerships; the legal profession would have to decide whether they would be allowed. A Legal Services Ombudsman would be established to investigate how complaints had been handled by the relevant professional body.

Banks, building societies and authorised practitioners would be able to undertake conveyancing, with safeguards to protect the public from possible abuses.

There would be a contingency fee system, but this would not be appropriate in respect of criminal and family matters.

There would be wider eligibility for high judicial office; suitably qualified solicitors would be allowed to be appointed as High Court and appellate judges.

The Courts and Legal Services Bill
This was announced in December 1989. Fundamental changes were proposed, and restrictive practices were to be swept away:

1. The Bar's monopoly was to end in the higher courts and on higher judicial appointments.
2. Regarding rights of audience, senior judges and the Lord Chancellor would have the final word on the new rules allowing solicitors into the higher courts. Further, the proposed advisory committee on legal education and conduct (lay-dominated) would be important in respect of recommending approval of these rules.
3. Banks, building societies and insurance companies would be able to undertake conveyancing, subject to safeguards. A new Authorised Conveyancing Practitioners' Board would oversee those providing conveyancing services. The Lord Chancellor would have power to appoint a conveyancing ombudsman.
4. There would be a transfer of certain areas of jurisdiction from the High Court to the county court, with a probable expansion of the jurisdiction of the small

claims court, and at least a doubling of its limit. The aim of this would be to cut costs and delays.

5. A legal services ombudsman would investigate how professional bodies oversaw complaints.
6. There would be the removal of statutory prohibitions in respect of professionals forming partnerships with one another or with professionals in another country.
7. Conditional fee arrangements were proposed.

Lord Mackay said that the Bill was a 'a significant step in the further evolution of a healthy, competitive and competent legal profession for the needs of the coming decades'.

The Act

The Act received the Royal Assent in 1990. Section 17(1) states:

> 'The general objective of this Part is the development of legal services in England and Wales (and in particular the development of advocacy, litigation, conveyancing and probate services) by making provision for new or better ways of providing such services and a wider choice of persons providing them, while maintaining the proper and efficient administration of justice.'

The Advisory Committee on Legal Education and Conduct

This is a very important body and is independent of the government. It has a broad advisory function, and its duties relate significantly to those persons offering legal services. Section 19 states:

> '(1) There shall be a body corporate to be known as the Lord Chancellor's Advisory Committee on Legal Education and Conduct (in this Act referred to as 'the Advisory Committee').
> (2) The Advisory Committee shall consist of a Chairman, and 16 other members, appointed by the Lord Chancellor.
> (3) The Chairman shall be a Lord of Appeal in Ordinary or a judge of the Supreme Court of England and Wales.
> (4) Of the 16 other members of the Advisory Committee –
> (a) one shall be a judge who is or has been a Circuit judge;
> (b) 2 shall be practising barristers appointed after consultation with the General Council of the Bar;
> (c) 2 shall be practising solicitors appointed after consultation with the Law Society;
> (d) 2 shall be persons with experience in the teaching of law, appointed after consultation with such institutions concerned with the teaching of law and such persons representing teachers of law as the Lord Chancellor considers appropriate; and
> (e) 9 shall be persons other than –
> (i) salaried judges of any court;
> (ii) practising barristers;
> (iii) practising solicitors; or
> (iv) teachers of law,
> appointed after consultation with such organisations as the Lord Chancellor considers appropriate.'

The Advisory Committee's general duty is to assist 'in the maintenance and development of standards in the education, training and conduct of those offering legal services': s20(1). Schedule 2 confers various further functions upon the Advisory Committee. Paragraph 1 states:

'(1) The Advisory Committee shall –
(a) keep under review the education and training of those who offer to provide legal services;
(b) consider the need for continuing education and training for such persons and the form it should take; and
(c) consider the steps which professional and other bodies should take to ensure that their members benefit from such continuing education and training.
(2) The Advisory Committee shall give such advice as it thinks appropriate with a view to ensuring that the education and training of those who offer to provide legal services is relevant to the needs of legal practice and to the efficient delivery of legal services to the public.'

Also under Schedule 2, other functions of the Advisory Committee relate to the adequate training of those entitled to exercise rights of audience and to those entitled to exercise rights to conduct litigation. This leads to a consideration of ss27 and 28.

Rights of audience
Section 27(2) specifies when a right of audience will be granted:

'A person shall have a right of audience before a court in relation to any proceedings only in the following cases –
(a) where –
(i) he has a right of audience before that court in relation to those proceedings granted by the appropriate authorised body; and
(ii) that body's qualification regulations and rules of conduct have been approved for the purposes of this section, in relation to the granting of that right;
(b) where paragraph (a) does not apply but he has a right of audience before that court in relation to those proceedings granted by or under any enactment;
(c) where paragraph (a) does not apply but he has a right of audience granted by that court in relation to those proceedings;
(d) where he is a party to those proceedings and would have had a right of audience, in his capacity as such a party, if this Act had not been passed; or
(e) where –
(i) he is employed (whether wholly or in part), or is otherwise engaged, to assist in the conduct of litigation and is doing so under instructions given (either generally or in relation to the proceedings) by a qualified litigator; and
(ii) the proceedings are being heard in chambers in the High Court or a county court and are not reserved family proceedings.'

Section 27(2)(a) is where an *authorised body* has granted the right of audience, and there has been approval of the authorised body's regulations and rules of conduct. Note s27(9):

' "authorised body" means –
(a) the General Council of the Bar;

(b) the Law Society; and
(c) any professional or other body which has been designated by Order in Council as an authorised body for the purposes of this section;
"appropriate authorised body", in relation to any person claiming to be entitled to any right of audience by virtue of subsection (2)(a), means the authorised body –
(a) granting that right; and
(b) of which that person is a member ...'

Section 27(2)(b) is where *any enactment* has granted the right of audience; for example, the Lord Chancellor, under s11, may by order specify rights of audience in county court proceedings. Section 27(2)(c) relates to *a court having discretion* to grant a right of audience, while s27(2)(d) relates to *litigants in person* having rights of audience; s27(2)(e) would, *by way of example*, protect the rights of audience enjoyed by *legal executives*. A 'qualified litigator' includes any practising solicitor (s27(9)). With regard to family proceedings, rights of audience will be at the discretion of the court.

Section 27(7) states:

'Where, immediately before the commencement of this section, no restriction was placed on the persons entitled to exercise any right of audience in relation to any particular court or in relation to particular proceedings, nothing in this section shall be taken to place any such restriction on any person.'

This provision will cover the rights of audience in *tribunals* in respect of an applicant being represented by another person who may or may not be professionally qualified.

There have been difficulties in the negotiations relating to advocacy rights for solicitors, although in October 1992 it appeared that solicitors employed in government, industry and commerce would be able to exercise rights of audience alongside their private practice colleagues. There was, however, a problem in respect of crown prosecutor solicitors.

The Bar was opposed to wider advocacy rights for crown prosecutors, but in November 1992 Barbara Mills QC, the Director of Public Prosecutions, said that the Crown Prosecution Service and the Government Legal Service would not be deflected from their 'goal of further limited rights of audience'. In March 1993 the Bar warned the Office of Fair Trading that if solicitors were allowed into the higher courts there could be a drastic reduction in the size of the independent Bar. This was indicative of the Bar continuing its strong resistance to higher rights of advocacy for solicitors. In July 1993 it was reported that the committee set up by the Lord Chancellor to resolve the dispute over rights of audience had decided that solicitors should not be allowed into higher courts 'for the present'. The long-running campaign by solicitors continued.

If they are eventually to exercise their rights of audience in higher courts, litigation solicitors will need to develop advocacy skills. In David Mayhew's article 'Peculiar, but good practice' (*The Times* 7 September 1993) there was reference to the traditional view that advocacy skills could be learnt only by experience. Nevertheless, it is arguable that such skills could be learnt, if taught correctly. The

National Institute of Trial Advocacy (Nita), established in 1970, trains American lawyers in advocacy skills. There is learning-by-doing in small groups, combining simulated court-room settings with constructive critiques. Nita's method of teaching has spread to other common law jurisdictions, and in August 1993 a firm of solicitors, Clifford Chance, designed and ran a Trial Advocacy Programme in conjunction with Nita.

> 'The skills covered included opening statements, examination of witnesses (both evidence-in-chief and cross-examination), techniques in discrediting evidence and examining expert witnesses and closing argument. The week culminated in a full trial at which these skills were brought together.'

After an intensive week, the conclusion was that learning advocacy skills not only helped solicitors to become competent advocates but also enhanced their existing litigation skills, ie fact-gathering, legal analysis, negotiation and giving advice.

Reference may also be made to an article by Frances Gibb, 'Enter the renaissance lawyer', published simultaneously. City firms had been embarking on training courses to prepare their advocates for work traditionally passed to counsel. Such advocacy courses are perhaps indicative of the way ahead for firms of solicitors to develop advocacy skills. The Bar questions whether training sessions and seminars can be compared with hands-on experience through pupillage. City firms appear, however, to accept that there will always be a need for an independent Bar, as many firms would not be capable of handling all of their own advocacy.

Right to conduct litigation

Section 119 states:

> '[the] "right to conduct litigation" means the right
> (a) to exercise all or any of the functions of issuing a writ or otherwise commencing proceedings before any court; and
> (b) to perform any ancillary functions in relation to proceedings (such as entering appearances to actions) ...'

It is the provisions of s28 which relate to the right to conduct litigation; s28(2) states:

> 'A person shall have a right to conduct litigation in relation to any proceedings only in the following cases –
> (a) where
> (i) he has a right to conduct litigation in relation to those proceedings granted by the appropriate authorised body; and
> (ii) that body's qualification regulations and rules of conduct have been approved for the purposes of this section, in relation to the granting of that right;
> (b) where paragraph (a) does not apply but he has a right to conduct litigation in relation to those proceedings granted by or under any enactment;
> (c) where paragraph (a) does not apply but he has a right to conduct litigation granted by that court in relation to those proceedings;
> (d) where he is a party to those proceedings and would have had a right to conduct the litigation, in his capacity as such a party, if this Act had not been passed.'

It will be seen that these provisions follow very closely the provisions of s27(2) and may be compared accordingly. Section 28(5) defines 'authorised body' and 'appropriate authorised body'. Section 29 and Schedule 4 deal with professional or other bodies applying to become authorised bodies and the requirements for approving their regulations and rules. It is an authorised body which will subsequently be able to certificate those persons entitled to rights of audience and those persons entitled to conduct litigation.

The Advisory Committee again plays an important part in the recognition of professional or other bodies *as* authorised bodies; s29(1) states:

> 'In order to be designated as an authorised body for the purposes of section[s] 27 or 28 a professional or other body must –
> (a) apply to the Lord Chancellor under this section, specifying the purposes for which it is seeking authorisation; and
> (b) comply with the provisions of Part 1 of Schedule 4 as to the approval of qualification regulations and rules of conduct and other matters.
> (2) Where –
> (a) an application has been made to the Lord Chancellor under this section;
> (b) the requirements of Part 1 of Schedule 4 have been satisfied; and
> (c) the application has not failed,
> the Lord Chancellor may recommend to Her Majesty that an Order in Council be made designating that body as an authorised body for the purposes of section 27 or (as the case may be) section 28.'

It is Schedule 4 which provides the details of the procedure whereby approval as an authorised body may be obtained. The procedure is different from that envisaged in the original Green Paper in that, arguably, there is a compromise between appeasing the senior judiciary and at the same time enlarging the group of people who will have rights of audience in the higher courts. Under Schedule 4, a professional or other body has to send the following to the Advisory Committee:

1. a draft of the qualification regulations it proposes to use;
2. a draft of the proposed rules of conduct;
3. a statement of the rights which it wishes to grant;
4. explanatory material considered necessary for the Advisory Committee.

Following consideration of the application, the Advisory Committee may require amendments to be made. An applicant must take due notice of any advice given to it by the Advisory Committee.

After the above requirements have been complied with, an application is made to the Lord Chancellor. This application has to be in writing and must specify whether it is for the purposes of s27 or s28 that approval is being sought. A copy of the regulations and rules has to be provided, together with explanatory material considered likely to be necessary, a statement of the proposed rights and any additional information reasonably required by the Lord Chancellor. The Lord Chancellor has to forward a copy of the application and documents provided to the Advisory Committee and each of the designated judges. These designated judges are the Lord Chief Justice, the Master of the Rolls, the President of the Family Division and the Vice-Chancellor. The Lord Chancellor asks for the advice of the Advisory Committee as to whether there should be approval of the regulations and rules for the purposes of s27 or s28. Copies of the documents are also sent to the Director-General of Fair Trading, who will give advice after considering whether the regulations and rules would have any contrary effect upon competition.

Having received the advice of the Advisory Committee and the Director-General of Fair Trading, the Lord Chancellor will then send a copy of the advice to the applicant. A period of 28 days is allowed for representations by the applicant. Following this period the Lord Chancellor has to consider whether the regulations and rules and the application should be approved. The Lord Chancellor sends to each designated judge copies of the advice received and the representations made by the applicant, together with his own proposed decision. Each designated judge considers the application and must notify the Lord Chancellor, in writing, of his decision and his reasons. For approval, an application must have the support of the Lord Chancellor and all of the designated judges.

The Lord Chancellor then notifies the applicant of the decision. A successful application means a recommendation by the Lord Chancellor to the Queen for the making of an Order in Council designating the particular body as an authorised body for the purposes of s27 or s28.

Sections 31 (relating to the General Council of the Bar) and 32 (relating to the Law Society) provide that these two bodies shall be deemed to have in force qualification regulations and rules of conduct which have been properly approved for the purposes of s27. If, however, any particular provision of those regulations or rules would not have been approved for the purposes of s27, had it been submitted for approval under Schedule 4, then it shall not be deemed to have been approved. Any such provision may be referred for advice to the Advisory Committee and a subsequent decision be made by the Lord Chancellor and each of the designated judges.

The Legal Services Ombudsman

The ombudsman may *not* be anyone who is authorised to provide legal services under the Act, and neither may the ombudsman be a Member of Parliament.

There may be investigation of any allegation made properly to the ombudsman which relates to the manner in which a complaint made to a professional body has been dealt with by that body.

The immunity of advocates

Section 62(1) and (2) are of great importance (see 4.2 above).

Multi-disciplinary and multi-national practices

Section 66 clears away any statutory barriers to multi-disciplinary and multi-national practices; s66(1) states:

'Section 39 of the Solicitors Act 1974 (which, in effect, prevents solicitors entering into partnership with persons who are not solicitors) shall cease to have effect.

(2) Nothing in subsection (1) prevents the Law Society making rules which prohibit solicitors from entering into any unincorporated association with persons who are not solicitors, or restrict the circumstances in which they may do so.

(5) It is hereby declared that no rule or common law prevents barristers from entering into any unincorporated association with persons who are not barristers.

(6) Nothing in subsection (5) prevents the General Council of the Bar from making rules which prohibit barristers from entering into any such unincorporated association, or restrict the circumstances in which they may do so.'

Conveyancing

The appropriate provisions of the Courts and Legal Services Act 1990 are ss34–52 and Schedules 5–7. An Authorised Conveyancing Practitioners' Board is established by s34, and the composition of the board must 'provide a proper balance between the interests of authorised practitioners and those who make use of their services'. By virtue of s35 the board must endeavour 'to develop competition in the provision of conveyancing services' and 'supervise the activities of authorised practitioners in connection with the provision by them of conveyancing services'. In accordance with s40 the Lord Chancellor may by regulation ensure that satisfactory standards of competence and conduct are maintained by authorised practitioners; that when providing conveyancing services they act in a way 'which is consistent with the maintenance of fair competition between authorised practitioners and others providing conveyancing services'; and that there is satisfactory protection of their clients' interests. Under s43 provision is made for establishing a Conveyancing Ombudsman scheme to investigate complaints against authorised practitioners.

Reference may also be made to ss104–7. Under these provisions a bank or building society would be prevented from providing a mortgage if it was only given on condition that a borrower used other services of the bank or building society. The statute prohibits such a 'tying-in arrangement' and supports the Law Society's view that competition in conveyancing should be upon an equal footing.

Conditional fees

The response to the Green Paper on contingency fees was that such a basis for funding litigation was wrong in principle. (Contingency fees involved a lawyer receiving a slice of any damages recovered.) Section 58, however, sets out the concept of *conditional* fee arrangements and removes any barriers in their way.

An agreement would provide for the payment of fees in specified circumstances and would have to comply with any requirements which might be set by the Lord Chancellor. Interestingly, he had decided to allow fees to be increased by 20 per cent if lawyers took a speculative case. There was criticism that this would not be worth the risk. In August 1993 the Lord Chancellor agreed that lawyers would be able to charge an uplift of 100 per cent on top of their normal fees – ie double their fees – *if* they had taken a case on a 'no win, no fee' (conditional) basis.

Conditional fees will not be applicable in criminal proceedings, matrimonial proceedings or cases involving children. Where someone is represented on a conditional fee basis then an opponent will not be liable to pay any of the percentage increase, ie will not be liable to pay higher costs.

Jurisdiction of the High Court and county courts
Changes in the jurisdiction of the above courts are mentioned elsewhere in this book; see Chapter 2 above.

15.7 Not all is doom and gloom

Barristers are, of course, easily recognised at court by the wigs which they wear. Lord Taylor of Gosforth, the Lord Chief Justice, feels that they make judges 'look slightly ridiculous'. Indeed, the question has been raised as to whether judges should abandon wigs to promote a 'user-friendly' judiciary. After a period of consultation, the public and most of the 500-plus responses from the legal profession indicated that they wished wigs to be retained. The decision was announced jointly, at the end of September 1993, by Lord Taylor and Lord Mackay of Clashfern, the Lord Chancellor.

In particular, there was support for wigs to be worn in the criminal courts, and, indeed, many defendants thought that a wig conferred authority. However, judges in the Court of Appeal and the Commercial Court decided, as an experiment, to shed their wigs for a short period. It is not surprising that there was a move towards change in the Commercial Court because of the more international atmosphere involving clients who were not accustomed to lawyers and judges wearing wigs. Heather Hallett QC, the Bar's director of public affairs, considered that wigs disguised both youth and age, neutralised a barrister's sex and could tip the scales in favour of ensuring that a defendant told the truth: 'If there is anything that will help stop miscarriages of justice, let's keep it.'

It must not be forgotten that odd, and perhaps hilarious, incidents sometimes occur within legal circles. In this context David Pannick QC wrote an amusing article, 'It's been a funny old year at the Bar' (*The Times* 22 December 1992). He recounted that it had been a difficult year for some advocates:

'In Bridgend, Mid Glamorgan, the chairman of the magistrates' bench interrupted the sentencing of a defendant in a drink-drive case to order the defence solicitor to leave the court because his shoelaces were undone. At Southwark Crown Court, in London, a judge ordered the arrest of defence counsel arguing a criminal case because the barrister persisted in making submissions despite the judge's direction that he sit down and be quiet.'

Judges also encountered distractions:

'A young woman burst topless into Cardiff Crown Court in protest at the arrest of her boyfriend. A Crown Court judge in Newcastle upon Tyne, angered by a noisy display of pleasure from the public gallery after a jury acquitted a defendant on a charge of wounding, ordered 12 members of the public to be detained in prison for the night. The acquitted defendant sadly explained that he "was hoping to celebrate with my friends, but they were all locked up".'

Neither does it seem that legal developments in the United States of America are always beyond reproach:

'The chief judge of the New York court of appeals was arrested and charged with blackmailing his former lover by threatening to publish compromising photographs of her with her new boyfriend. A woman sued Bill Clinton on the ground that the prospect of "a draft-dodger and communist sympathiser" being elected president was causing her "serious emotional and mental stress". And a US district court judge accepted that "counsel have a constitutional right to regard each other as schmucks".'

Finally, for mitigation above and beyond the call of duty, reference may be made to a solicitor who, several years ago, addressed a magistrates' court at Stafford. While speaking to the magistrates, he leaned forward and Christmas songs filled the court. It appeared that his children had given him a present of a pair of musical underpants which he inadvertently 'pressed into action'. The songs had to run their course but, despite the tears of laughter, he completed his address to the bench. Life as a lawyer is not always doom and gloom.

16

Interviewing and Client Counselling

16.1 Introduction

The lawyer must be adaptable so that he or she can meet the needs of the various types of clients with whom he or she will be dealing; he or she will have to get on with timid people as well as aggressive, demanding types. He or she must extend the relationship of mutual trust built up with long-standing clients to new clients, some of whom will find articulating their problem difficult, and to others who may be visiting a solicitor for the first time. The problem facing the lawyer is compounded when one takes into account the potential differences between the social background, education and class of the solicitor and that of his or her clients. Nevertheless at the end of the first interview the client must feel confident that his or her problem is understood and will be dealt with in an efficient way, and that he or she is informed simply of the initial steps which are to be taken. Similarly, the solicitor should have a clear idea of what the problem is and how it is to be solved.

16.2 Communication skills

From the clients' point of view, resolving a legal problem without professional help would be extremely difficult. The first problem is the terminology used by lawyers and in legal textbooks, which is both unfamiliar and intimidating to the lay person. The way in which the lawyer communicates with his or her client may create a barrier between them. It is therefore important for the lawyer to be aware that a problem exists and also to be prepared to take steps to overcome it. One of the most crucial points to grasp is that if you can communicate information as simply as possible to your client you will save yourself valuable time at a later date by avoiding lengthy and possibly frustrating telephone conversations with the client who has not understood the point during the interview. It therefore makes sense to avoid the use of legal jargon and to discuss the problem in language the client understands. However, you must be careful not to patronise or 'talk down' to him or her. Just remember that your client is likely to be as unfamiliar with the law's specialised language as he or she is with the law itself.

16.3 Putting the client at ease

Ease of communication is a two-way process; if a client does not understand the language you use he or she will feel intimidated and unable to talk to you. If, however, he or she realises that the problem can be discussed 'at his or her level', the chances are that he or she will tell you all the facts you need to know. The way in which you arrange your room is a factor to take into consideration. A room informally furnished with comfortable chairs is more likely to provide a relaxed atmosphere that is more conducive to a confidential discussion of a problem (particularly if the issue is marital breakdown) than two chairs separated by a desk. The latter arrangement tends to put up a psychological barrier between the parties. You must experiment with the arrangement of the furniture in your office in order to create the most pleasant environment for you and your clients.

It may be possible to set aside a room solely for interviewing clients which means that you are less likely to be interrupted during interviews. An additional advantage is that you will not have to tidy your desk! If this arrangement is impracticable, however, ensure that the secretarial staff know you are engaged so that you are not disturbed except for urgent telephone calls.

16.4 The initial interview

The purpose of the interview is to obtain the following information about the client:

1. what he or she thinks the problem is; and
2. what he or she intends to do about it (although at this point it may be an unrealistic expectation).

You can then offer advice.

Greeting a client

Try not to keep a client waiting, but if a delay is inevitable explain why he or she will have to wait and give an indication of how long the delay will last.

Make sure you present yourself in a business-like way; for example, you are formally dressed, your desk is reasonably tidy and the relevant files/papers are in front of you. Remember the client will be influenced by his or her first impression of you, so attention to details is important.

Before the interview you should make every effort to discover whether the client is known to your firm. There may be information about him or her which is useful for you to know on file in the office. In any case, even if you are new the client will expect you to know that he or she has been dealing with your firm for many years.

The client should be shown to your office by a member of staff or, better still, you should go to reception yourself and greet him or her personally. He or she should not be allowed to wander around alone trying to find your office. If he or she is shown to your room by a member of the reception staff do not forget to show the basic social skills which can help your client to feel at ease; for example, get up out of your chair, shake hands and introduce yourself, giving your name and your position in the firm. (Clients sometimes forget their lawyers' names, so it would be helpful to hand over a card with your name on it before your client departs.) Try to create a good impression from the start.

If the client is new to the firm the next task is to find out various personal details, eg name, address and telephone number both at home and at work. Then you will need to know why he or she has come to see you.

Discussion of fees

At some point in the interview you must advise the client about costs, for example how much it is likely to cost, whether legal aid applies to the case and if he or she is entitled to it, having first considered his or her financial circumstances. Details of whether a fee has been agreed, or the way in which you are to be paid, should be given to the client in writing when confirming his or her instructions, together with an estimate of how much the final account is likely to be. It may be impossible to give such an estimate with any accuracy, and for this reason some lawyers give only a vague idea. The timing of discussion of fees give rise to concern with a few lawyers, which explains an accepted practice of making a nominal charge for the first half hour. New lawyers will normally not have to face this problem as policy will have been formulated by the senior partners. Make sure you know what the policy is.

Explanation of confidentiality

You may have to ask questions which will reveal intimate details about your client. Where he or she is worried about giving information of this kind, it should help considerably if you stress that the confidential nature of your relationship with him or her does not allow you to disclose any information given in the interview. In addition it is a wise precaution to clear your table/desk of other clients' files. Some people may like to have a friend or relative with them during their initial interview, but at some stage you will have to talk with your client alone.

Introductory questions enabling interaction with client to commence

It is sometimes necessary to help a client to begin to tell you the problem with an opening question, such as 'How can I help you?', or by identifying the area of law to which the problem refers, for example 'You have a problem with your marriage I believe?'. You may have to prompt the client throughout the interview, particularly if he or she finds it difficult or upsetting to talk freely about the problem. Try not to restrict him or her, while relating the story, with a lot of questions which need one-word answers. A good lawyer will be able to adapt to differing clients' needs. Periods of silence on the lawyer's part can sometimes be effective.

Listening to the client

Part of the skill of communicating with your client is the ability to listen to what he or she is saying. Allow him or her the time to tell you, uninterruptedly and in his or her own words, the basic outline of the problem, bearing in mind that you will have time constraints imposed upon you from the office which you must not, of course, communicate to the client. It is therefore obvious that you need to be patient, as some people will not tell you their stories in a straightforward way. Listening to someone recounting information that you will need later on is different from listening to a social type of conversation and needs different skills. Inevitably the lawyer is told irrelevant as well as relevant information; a lay person is unlikely to be aware of what is legally significant. He or she may omit to tell you something of vital importance because of feelings of guilt or sorrow or simply through not realising its importance. It is, therefore, necessary to allow the client to tell you his or her full story so that you can establish why he or she has come to see you. It is helpful at this stage to make short notes so that you will have a record of the problem for later reference. At the same time you can continue to listen to your client while maintaining eye contact and encouraging him or her in the story. You will have the chance later on to fill in the details or omissions by relevant questions. It is important that the client feels you are interested in what he or she is saying.

It is very easy when listening to someone speaking to jump to conclusions before the speaker has finished, particularly if you have heard similar cases before. Avoid falling into this trap; maintain an open mind. Even if you have heard a similar scenario several times before, remember that no two cases are identical because the people involved are different. If you do not allow the speaker to finish his or her story you may miss the most relevant part of the problem. Similarly, do not omit the questioning part of the interview as, again, you may only have the facts as related by the client, which may not be the whole story.

Empathy with the client

The 'human element' must not be lost during the interview, so by showing an understanding of the problem and remaining interested you will help to build a relationship based on confidence. If you can develop the attitude whereby the client feels important you are much more likely to have a successful career, because, more often than not, when people need legal advice they ask friends to recommend a lawyer.

Encouraging the client where necessary

Your involvement at this stage depends on what type of person your client is. In order to continue the story some people need more encouragement in the form of prompting statements or questions, whereas others will need only an occasional word or gesture.

Questioning the client

The purpose of asking the client questions is to find out more detail about specific facts which he or she has mentioned in order to explore the issues for any hidden problem. In addition the lawyer is beginning the process of sorting out the relevant points from the irrelevant in the client's story.

There are different types of question that clients can be asked:

1. General questions which allow freedom of answer.
2. Questions which control the client by giving guidance as to what information is required.

Both are useful in interview techniques. The first type, the general question, allows the client the freedom to choose how to tell the story without any guidance from the lawyer – for example, 'What happened next?'. Although there are no limits on what the client can answer to this type of question, the obvious disadvantage is that it allows for irrelevant information to be included, and therefore time can be wasted.

The second type of question gives guidance as to what information is required – for example, 'What colour coat were you wearing?'. The answer is limited, which can be both an advantage and a disadvantage. The lawyer controls the situation and obtains specific information, but the client, realising that a particular fact is important, may be tempted to exaggerate. Sometimes an explanation of why the lawyer is asking the question is successful in these circumstances, especially if the client realises it is in his or her interests to tell the truth. Involving the client in the problem-solving process often minimises exaggerated answers.

In addition to the two types of question explained above there is a third category, the half-way house type of question – for example, 'What did he do with the knife?'. The client knows what information is required and therefore what is relevant, but there is an element of freedom in the response.

Reviewing the interview and recapping the key issues with the client

At this point you can summarise the facts of the case to your client in order to ensure that you have not omitted anything and that you have understood the problem fully.

It is advisable to approach this task as sympathetically as possible, for it may seem to the client, hearing his or her problem summarised by an objective third party, that it is a trifling matter after all and unworthy of all this attention. Tact is needed when ascertaining whether the client agrees with the way in which you see the problem. The danger is for a client to be intimidated into agreeing when in reality he or she feels that you have not represented his or her feelings correctly. Bear in mind that your command of words and language may be far superior to that of your client. You should aim to achieve the skill of re-telling the facts of the client's story in such a way that he or she feels able to correct any inaccuracies.

Advising on the relevant legal issues

You should now be in a position in which you can offer advice, which means that you tell the client what the legal situation is and what choices, both legal and non-legal, are available to him or her.

Offering advice does not necessarily mean that you give in-depth details of the area of law with which the problem is concerned. Generally speaking, advice of a general nature on the specified area will be sufficient at this stage. A client will usually be satisfied at this stage with a certain amount of advice and information together with the knowledge that you intend to research the area of law in order to discover the most recent cases etc. There will be times when you will not be competent to deal with the area of law involved in your client's problem. When this happens there is normally another lawyer within the same firm who specialises in similar problems, to whom the client can be referred.

As a general rule it is better to be cautious when giving advice, even if by doing so you have to tell the client that his or her worst fears are realised. Experienced lawyers, and other professionals whose job includes giving bad news, tend to cultivate an objective manner in order to prepare themselves for the recipient's reaction.

Planning a course of action

Even if you are able to give only a very general application of the relevant law to your client, you must endeavour to formulate some sort of plan of action. Do not restrict yourself to legal remedies; a non-legal solution may be the most appropriate in the circumstances. If the case is hopeless you must say so from the outset. Often a client will have a reasonable chance of success but will run the risk of having to pay the costs of both sides. It may be too costly for him or her to proceed, and he or she must be warned of the dangers. Similarly, if the other party is short of funds it is sensible to advise your client not to proceed, for even when he or she has a high chance of success there is the risk of being inadequately compensated. A client may ask for the lawyer's opinion as to the best course of action. The lawyer will then have to counsel him or her, taking into consideration the point of view, objections and what he or she hopes to achieve.

Is the client aware of the course of events?

The important thing to remember is that *the client* must choose the course of action, having been advised on any alternatives. Once he or she has made this choice the client must be told general information about each step in the procedure, for example how long it will take, how much it will cost, and the likely outcome.

It should also be made clear to the client what should happen next, who should do what and the date by which it should be done. He or she must realise that the final decision on a course of action is his or her own. In addition you must ensure that he or she is satisfied with the agreed course. Whether he or she will agree or not depends to a great extent on:

1. whether the client understands the advice given,
2. the degree of control the client feels that he or she has had in the decision-making process, and
3. the type of relationship the client has with the lawyer.

As discussed earlier (see section 16.2 above), it is vital that you advise your client in simple language. An individual seeking advice of a professional nature is often unable to comprehend, let alone remember, what his or her adviser is saying on the first occasion, simply because of the potentially momentous effect it will have on his or her life. For this reason it is a good idea to repeat the advice and send a letter to the client giving written details. Time spent now will lessen the amount of telephone calls you would otherwise receive from a bewildered, uninformed client.

Reducing the client's emotional stress

When the client has been given the maximum amount of information he or she can prepare him or herself for future events which may be unpleasant. Discussing the points of the problem that cause the client particular anxiety can help the lawyer to advise on the best course of action. It has the additional advantage of strengthening the relationship between client and lawyer.

Bringing the interview to an end

Before you close the interview you should ask if there is anything else your client wants to discuss with you. This is a useful tactic for revealing any hidden problem which the client has either forgotten to tell you or has been too shy to discuss. All being well, there will be nothing left to reveal at this point. If, however, a client introduces an entirely new fact which changes the whole problem, try not to show the frustration you may feel; you must partly take the blame for the breakdown in communication.

At the end of the interview act courteously towards the client; get up and shake hands with him or her. By your so doing the client will depart with the sense of having received a satisfactory professional consultation. It is not good practice to leave a client at the door of the interview room; if possible escort him or her back to the reception area or ensure that he or she is accompanied by a member of the secretarial staff.

16.5 After the interview

Confirm in writing to the client the information discussed in the interview together with a summary of the advice you gave and the course of action you agreed upon after careful consideration of the alternatives. Both lawyer and client know what they have to do next and the time limit they have in which to fulfil their tasks. In addition they have agreed the time and date of their next meeting.

16.6 Exercises

Work with a partner and another pair.

For the first exercise you and your partner take the role of the solicitors who are instructed by one of the other pair. The fourth person is to observe, make notes and assess the performance of the solicitors.

Exchange roles for the second exercise.

Exercise 1

Mr Jones lives next door to Mr and Mrs Smith who own a Rottweiler dog. The Smiths leave the dog alone all day because they both work; as a result the dog is lonely and barks incessantly until they return. Because of the constant noise Mrs Jones is a nervous wreck. She has been on tranquillisers for many years, but since the Smiths moved in next door with their dog her condition has deteriorated. Mr Jones tells you that he has had words with the Smiths about the dog on several occasions, but to no avail. Indeed Mr Smith has been very aggressive and threatened to throw Mr Jones off his property if he ever dared to darken his doorstep again.

One day while Mr Jones was gardening he found the noise so annoying that he went round to his neighbour's house to pacify the dog. Unfortunately Mr Smith was at home and was greatly displeased at finding Mr Jones shouting at the dog through the letter box. What happened next, according to your client, is that Mr Smith, a 'six-foot body builder', was rolling up his sleeves while rapidly advancing towards the front door. Mr Smith caught up with your client just as he was opening the garden gate. Mr Jones was so frightened at the sight of Mr Smith, who is twice the size of Mr Jones, that he punched Mr Smith, who fell and hit his head on the garden gate. Mr Jones then ran into his own house and has not seen his neighbour since. The incident happened two days ago.

The Joneses are a retired couple. Mr Jones used to work as a hospital porter, and Mrs Jones had to retire early because of her nervous disorder.

Advise Mr and Mrs Jones.

Exercise 2

Fred owns a small business making speciality chocolates. Having visited a trade exhibition he decided to buy one of the machines on display which would double his output of chocolates. Having taken his name and telephone number at the exhibition, the sales manager of Cheap'n'Nasty, the manufacturers of the machine, telephoned Fred and offered the machine at a price which Fred thought was excessive. The sales manager of Cheap'n'Nasty told Fred that the price was going to be increased in the next few weeks and that this was the last machine at the old price. Fred said he was interested in that case but would like to think about it. The sales manager told Fred that he would keep the machine for him for one week, after which time he would offer it elsewhere.

Four days after this telephone conversation Fred decided he would buy the machine as it was an offer too good to miss and faxed his decision to Cheap'n'Nasty. Meanwhile, however, Chocolates Ltd, a rival business to Fred, bought the machine for cash at a considerably lower price.

Fred is angry and wants to sue Cheap'n'Nasty because he fears his rivals may now be able to put him out of business.

Advise him.

Use the general assessment criteria below when marking the performance of the solicitors. Mark each category out of ten.

1. Greeting a client.
2. Introduction of self.
3. Putting the client at ease.
4. Discussion of fees.
5. Explanation of confidentiality.
6. Introductory questions.
7. Ability to listen to client.
8. Encouragement of client where necessary.
9. Control of client when necessary.
10. Picking up relevant issues.

11. Questioning client on relevant points.
12. Asking client his or her expectation.
13. Reviewing interview.
14. Advising on relevant legal issues.
15. Advising on relevant non-legal issues where necessary.
16. Empathising with client.
17. Planning a course of action with client.
18. Obtaining agreement of client.
19. Taking leave of client.
20. Arrangement of furniture.

17

Negotiation Skills

17.1 Introduction

In order to be able to negotiate you need to understand just exactly what negotiation is. The *Shorter Oxford English Dictionary* defines it thus:

> 'To confer with others for the purpose of arranging some matters by mutual agreement; to discuss a matter with a view to settlement or compromise.'

An alternative interpretation comes from Nierrenberg in his book *Fundamentals of Negotiation*:

> 'Whenever people exchange ideas with the intention of changing relationships, whenever they confer for agreement they are negotiating.'

So there you have it! Negotiation is about mutual agreement, settlement, compromise and changing relationships. What is the significance of this as a lawyer's skill, you may well be thinking?

The aim of any lawyer should be to do the best for his or her client. Proceeding with litigation and appearing in court are costly procedures, especially with the current scenario of restrictions on the availability of legal aid. It may well be that in the future the ability to negotiate a speedy or an early settlement will be a crucial skill in terms of client satisfaction and commercial expediency. However, negotiation is not new. All individuals, and lawyers in particular, do effectively negotiate in all situations. Away from the court room a solicitor undertaking a conveyancing transaction may well negotiate moving dates and financial deposits for his or her client.

As a student of law you can be reassured; the skill of negotiation, both style and strategies, can be learnt. Individual personality traits and approaches will influence negotiations undertaken – these are not disadvantages, but can be used positively once you know how.

In undertaking a negotiation you will have to remember that you will have a client (or clients) for whom you are acting, and you must act on the basis of your client's decision. Furthermore, you will have to keep in mind your client's objectives, as well as keeping to your instructions, and you must be prepared to communicate with him or her throughout. As well as the client you will also have to bear in mind the opposition. Here you will have to consider the situation, try not to make wrong assumptions, appreciate the art of persuasion, have authority for your ideas, and again keep in communication with the opposing parties.

When negotiating you will need to communicate, analyse, be flexible, consider unusual solutions, be objective, have confidence and assess risks. In doing this you will also have to bear in mind ethical considerations. One of the key points of ethics is not to go back on your word; you would soon have a poor professional reputation if you could not be relied on. It is also important that you do not lose your objectivity. In other words, do not become so personally involved and determined on one particular outcome that you lose all possibility of a settlement when that intended outcome proves not to be attainable. Other key points are: do not commit your clients without receiving their instructions; do not hide vital information; and finally, do not deliberately mislead either the opposition or your client.

17.2 Negotiation in context

It is perhaps important to put negotiation in context for a while. One of the first questions is: with whom could a lawyer negotiate? The following list gives a comprehensive answer:

1. another lawyer;
2. your own side (ie those in your team who will be involved with the case);
3. the client;
4. the Crown Prosecution Service;
5. a judge;
6. court officials (eg finding a time on the list for your case);
7. a social worker;
8. a probation officer;
9. a lay person;
10. Everyone!

Some areas of law may seem more suitable than others for a negotiated settlement, for example family law. It would be much easier for all the parties in a domestic situation if there could be a well-negotiated financial settlement rather than, say, a well-publicised and contested divorce. Contract and tort are other areas where negotiation is a prime practical strategy, saving costs and providing a speedier settlement than perhaps a court case would. As well as these areas, commercial issues and cases, and landlord and tenant cases, lend themselves to negotiated settlements.

There is no need for a formal arena to accommodate the process of negotiation. It is possible to negotiate by letter, perhaps suggesting a financial settlement and admitting some liability. Again it is possible to negotiate by telephone and fax, as well as at a meeting in the office, or in the cells, or at a police station. Finally, as always, negotiation can and does take place within the courtroom.

When to negotiate is an important consideration. Financial restraints, flexibility of the client, the existence of a range of desired outcomes, or the client's instructions to negotiate, would all be positive factors to take into account when making the decision whether or not to do so.

In answer to the question 'What can be gained by a negotiation?' the following may be suggested. First, in terms of the range of solutions, a court solution would normally involve merely the award of damages. It is possible, however, to negotiate beyond damages; for example, a negotiation could result in compensation and the return of property that is the subject matter of the dispute, or money could be the outcome – and indeed there could be more money available to solve the problem as less would have been spent in incurring legal costs. Secondly, a negotiated settlement can also involve a consideration of the future. For example, a short-term solution may be fixed which is dependent on other factors, so that there can be a review of the settlement in the long term. Finally, it is possible to reach a structured settlement by means of negotiation, which would be ideal in a divorce settlement.

17.3 Negotiation strategies

A definitive text on negotiation must be *Getting to Yes* by R Fisher and W Ury, in which the authors state:

> 'Every negotiator wants to reach an agreement that satisfies his substantive interest, that is why one negotiates. Beyond that, a negotiator also has an interest in his relationship with the other side'.

From this it can be seen that in order to negotiate we need a plan or strategy! In our own domestic and social lives we may have come across various negotiating strategies. Some of the most familiar might include: a child that cries until it achieves what it wants; parents who promise rewards for success in exams; sulking spouses! Nonetheless, these familiar strategies do achieve success and may give a hint on how we should proceed when negotiating professionally.

That hint would appear to be that we need a strategy or plan. In order to attain a strategy we need a style or a combination of styles and approaches. Different texts will suggest a variety of these. For our purposes I would like to consider four possible styles and/or approaches:

1. the co-operative style;
2. the competitive style;
3. the problem-solving approach;
4. the positional approach.

We now need to analyse these in turn.

Co-operative style

In using this style you would put the client first, and try to maintain a good relationship with him or her. Rather than simply stating a position for your client to the other side, you would appear reasonable to the opponent, since you would be making reasonable concessions in return for favourable responses to your problem.

Self-interest is not the key motivator in using this style. You would try to take account of the needs of the other side by creating an open and trusting atmosphere. Using this style you would analyse the problem from both sides and look for mutual interests. However, you would have to remember not to underestimate your own client's needs!

A co-operative negotiator will commence in a friendly and open way, reviewing strengths and weaknesses of each side. You would need to avoid making concessions with no return if the other side were not as co-operative. This style of negotiation has advantages and disadvantages.

Its main aim is that the negotiator should make concessions and so encourage the other side to make concessions. The parties here will build up trust in each other. Co-operative negotiations psychologically require a negotiator to move towards his or her opposition. Once this has been achieved an outcome can be reached that covers common ground and will thus be a result from which both parties may benefit. Here information will be shared. The behaviour of the negotiator is fair and reasonable; for example, reasons would be given to explain a concession. Further attempts would be made to review and reconcile the parties' interests and areas of conflicts. As the parties are co-operating it is less likely that the negotiations will break down, and consequently it is more likely that the parties will not have to resort to court action.

In terms of disadvantages, if this style were to be used against a competitive opponent he or she would be likely to accept all the concessions made but would offer nothing at all in return. The second disadvantage rests in any inequality between the parties. Thus it is a poor style to use where one party is very wealthy and the opponent is very poor, as the wealthy party would have little to gain from being co-operative.

Competitive style

The essential characteristics of the competitive style are straightforward. The main tactic is to try to make the opponent come to a favourable settlement by persuading him or her that the case is not as good or as strong as they think. Initially a competitive negotiator will not want to make concessions because he or she will feel that the case is a strong one and all can be won for the client. A competitive negotiator will view making concessions as weakening his or her position, as appearing less able. Furthermore, when using this style you would make large demands of the other side to emphasise to the opponent your confidence in your arguments.

This style can be seen as having a 50/50 chance of success: you would either win all or lose all. However, it is possible that compromise positions could be attained.

In terms of advantages, this style is essentially a manipulative one. You would never make the first move or reveal your client's true objectives. This style puts pressure on the opposition; threats, bluffs, and exaggerations will persist. An opponent subjected to this style would lose confidence, and it would be possible to persuade him or her to accept your demands.

However, there are disadvantages. First, by adopting this style you may encourage your opponent to adopt a similar one. Secondly, new or innovative solutions are unlikely to arise. The outcome, although initially favourable, may result in the failure of the other side to pay up because of unhappiness with the way in which the negotiation proceeded. Also, people may not wish to negotiate with you in the future because they know your style and resent it. In the long term the style may also seem unsuccessful, since it will appear to yield fewer rewards as it is anticipated by the opposition, resulting in more issues having to be resolved by the courts.

Problem-solving approach

In adopting this style as a negotiator, you will see the subject matter of the negotiations as a shared difficulty, not as a contest. A problem solver will try to seek the best solution, not just the largest amount of money. Furthermore, this approach will require consideration of psychological factors and of the feelings of both parties, the client and the opponent. It will also have to be remembered that different clients will have different values, and these will have to be ascertained before you start; for example, financial compensation may not be the only target if your client is keener on seeing justice done. In adopting the problem-solving approach you are seeking the best for both sides, with consequent cost-saving and the achieving of a quick settlement. That there is justice for both parties will again be an important consideration.

Positional approach

This style is seen as a conventional method of negotiating and is clearly related to 'bargaining'. It requires an opening position and a 'bottom line'. In other words, you state your opening position but at the same time you know how far away from that position you are prepared to move.

In moving from your opening position in the direction of your bottom line you are in fact making concessions. If you are going to use this approach you will have to determine what concessions you might be prepared to make, ie your fall-back positions or the steps to your bottom line.

There are advantages to this particular approach. The main one is perhaps flexibility, followed by the other side's awareness that you may be willing to make concessions which could be mutually beneficial. A disadvantage of this style is the fact that the other side will be aware that you have a bottom line and will seek to move towards this; in other words, your opponent may not take your opening position seriously.

17.4 Choosing a style

When you are faced with a negotiation the most important question is which style to adopt. The first point to consider is what is the likely style of your opponent. If you wish to adopt the co-operative and problem-solving approach, both parties really need to adopt that style. It would not be wise to attempt a co-operative style when faced with a competitive opponent as the latter would exploit anyone using a co-operative style.

However, a problem-solving approach alone might be a better strategy when dealing with a competitive negotiator, because it proceeds along the basis of offering a new position for a creative solution. Be warned, though: a competitive negotiator may not exchange the information that this particular approach requires. A non-competitive style, as indicated earlier, is useful when dealing with a more powerful opposition, since any threats from you will not be believed when you are in the weaker position.

In conclusion, your chosen strategy may be a particular approach or style, or a combination of these. However, you will have to bear in mind the opposition, your client's wishes, the strength of your case and your own personality before making a final decision on which style to adopt.

It is also important that you separate the people from the problem, and focus on the interests, not on positions; in other words do not become entrenched and see the positions in terms of personalities and so personalise the argument. Concentrate on the problem and the interests of your client. You will also need to have options available in order to make suggestions during your negotiation. Thus, before commencing a negotiation, know your position, know your styles, decide on your strategies and prepare well.

17.5 Phases of negotiation

There are four phases to a negotiation:

1. preparation;
2. discussion;
3. proposal;
4. bargain.

Each phase will occur one at a time and in the order above.

Preparation phase

Preparation is obviously of vital importance. The first point to consider is if the given situation is suitable for negotiation, and the next is whether your client's case is best suited by negotiation or if there is an alternative means of settling the dispute. If these questions are satisfactorily answered the third stage is the arrangement of a meeting, agreeing the location and items for the agenda. This can be done by telephone or letter, or in person. The location would normally be the office of one or other of the negotiators.

In order to negotiate for a client you must ensure that you have his or her authority, and the full scope of that authority must be ascertained; for example, have you total authority to act and reach any solution, or has your client suggested limitations? Time and any statutory time limitations should also be borne in mind.

In terms of written work, it would be sensible to prepare written statements or lists of an overview of the situation, the actual facts and figures, reports and documents. It would also be useful to list confirmed facts and areas of factual confusion.

Next, consider your chosen style and that of your opponent. Prepare lists of both your and your opponent's strong and weak points, and in addition list any points you wish to deny; also consider any solutions and concessions you may wish to introduce.

Discussion phase

This phase is where you are able to clarify assumptions that you have made during the preparation stage, gain additional information, check on common ground and agree on the issues which are open for negotiation.

At this phase you will find it useful to listen to what the other side says, even if that means you have to remain silent! Indeed, silence from the opponent can be an indication of his or her position. It would be useful at this stage to use open questions to try to find a solution. Open questions are those where the response is not 'yes' or 'no', as in a closed question, but more extensive, so that information is likely to be given.

Summarising is also an important procedure at this stage – recapping on common ground and clarifying agreed areas as the negotiation progresses. Remember to keep notes with details of all negotiation meetings.

Both listening and the use of open questions are very important skills in the negotiation process; do not be afraid to use them. Remember too that your non-verbal communication, such as body language, may give you away! Playing with pens or paper clips, fiddling with your hands or clothes, touching your eyes and ears are all seen as indicators of a lack of confidence, as is the inability to make eye contact. Aggression is seen through exaggerated facial expression, including staring. Confidence, on the other hand, is seen through smiling, nodding at others when they speak, and leaning slightly forward. Yawning, sighing, playing with your watch and moving your body away from the speaker are additional negative non-verbal communications that could irritate the other side and spoil the negotiations.

Finally, at the discussion stage, adjournments might be sought by yourself or the other side. Do not be afraid of using these to reconsider objectives, check facts, consider options, structure attitudes, and to brief your own team.

Proposal phase

The proposal phase is where you 'test the water', in other words the 'what if you ...', 'then I ...' scenario. It is an opportunity to assess the scope for movement. If you see yourself as making the proposal 'what if you ...' in a vague way, you then appear to be doing something. When this stage seems acceptable to your opponent, you can first propose firmly a condition that he or she should do something and then respond, either vaguely or, at a later stage, firmly, with your offer towards the proposal.

It is important at this stage to remember to try to gain concessions, to structure attitudes, to pitch offers at the right level, and to aim for a 'win-win' situation – one where each side feels that it has won something out of the negotiations, where each believes itself to be the winner. This is to be compared with the approach of the competitive negotiator, who feels that his or her clients should win and the other side lose.

At the proposal phase it is important to avoid responding to any attack from the opposition, whether real or perceived. It is also important not to gloat over the opponent, particularly if you feel that you have won or have had all the advantages. Also, avoid concluding too quickly and, most importantly, having any uncontrolled discussion which could lead to additional unplanned proposals.

Bargaining phase

This final phase is where you move to agreed solutions. The previous 'if you, then I' of the proposal stage becomes the exact term of the bargain as proposed in a conditional format.

It is important to ensure that there is time for acceptance to be considered, that decisions are written down, that there are 'face-savers' (back to the 'win-win' situation), and that there is an intention to abide by the agreement. Without the last item the whole negotiation would be pointless.

Remember finally that that which may be cheap to you to give away as a concession may seem dear to the other side, and if you do give a concession, ensure that it does not affect your main principles or stance on the issue.

Conclusion

Having been through the four phases you will have concluded the negotiation. When you have done this you can assess how successful you have been if you consider some of the following issues. First, you should have addressed the clients' objectives as far as possible. Secondly, the outcome must be comprehensive and clear and must have given due consideration to the future. Thirdly, the conclusions should be enforceable, and in view of this you may need to write letters, draft a contract, sue, obtain an order of a judge or exchange letters to ensure that enforcement takes place.

Do remember that it is possible to have a very successful negotiation when both parties feel they have won! Negotiation does not have to be a 'one winner, one loser' situation. This could be seen as its advantage over litigation.

17.6 Criteria for assessment

In your negotiation sessions you will be assessed according to the following criteria:

1. Opening. Your opening introduction of the other party and initiation of discussions will be reviewed. It will be important to have a structure for your discussions.
2. Conduct of the negotiation. Here you will be assessed in terms of how you pursue your client's objectives and how you analyse both client's and opponent's issues. It will be important that you identify your own strengths and weaknesses. Credit will be given for both selecting and pursuing an appropriate strategy. Remember, do not disclose too much information too soon. Deal with difficulties as they arise.
3. Conduct of negotiator. Assessment here will include points such as:

   - Do you listen to your opponent?
   - Are you dominated or dominating?
   - Are you too trusting?
   - Are your emotions under control?
   - Do you argue without making progress?

4. Closing. Finally, it will be considered whether you have concluded an appropriate settlement for the client, including the following criteria:

- Did you plan a means of ensuring the outcome of the negotiation?
- Did you pursue a practical approach to the client's needs?
- Did you show a professional approach to the needs of the client?

17.7 Exercises

1. Happy is a well-known, charismatic and very popular professional football player with a leading first division club, Westend Rovers. At 33 he is coming to the end of his first division playing days, a fact further compounded by some ligament injuries he has suffered. These injuries are unknown to anyone other than Happy, his medical advisers and the directors of Westend Rovers.

   Eastend United are a team recently promoted to the second division. They are well supported by Elton Jackson, an international pop star, who is also a director of the club. Elton wishes to buy more players and is very interested in Happy. It is well known that Elton is on the lookout for new players, and that money is no object. As a guide, a suitable transfer fee for Happy would be in the order of £600,000 if he were uninjured.

   Eastend United approach Westend Rovers with a view to purchasing Happy. If Happy were to be sold he would have to move home, send his young children to new schools, and move away from his family and roots. Negotiations are now being entered into.

   Complete the following tasks:

   a) Identify the strengths of Westend Rovers in the negotiations.
   b) Identify the weaknesses of Westend Rovers in the negotiations.
   c) Identify the strengths of Eastend United in the negotiations.
   d) Identify the weaknesses of Eastend United in the negotiations.
   e) Assume the role of negotiator for Eastend United. Plan out your negotiations, indicating styles and strategies you will adopt.

2. Prepare a report highlighting the advantages and disadvantages of the co-operative and competitive styles of negotiating.
3. You are a headwaiter in a large restaurant. You are called over to a table to find Mrs Goldworthy, a wealthy and regular client on whose recommendation the restaurant has acquired many other clients, in a state of distress. It seems that one of your waiters has tripped and spilt a sauceboat of gravy over Mrs Goldworthy's dress (a Dior original worth £5,000). Describe the style and strategies you would adopt and solutions you would offer.
4. Chris, a fellow student, asks to borrow your textbook (just for today) to prepare for her seminar. You too will need the textbook to prepare for your seminar in

ten days' time. You would like to help Chris, as you know she is hard up and cannot buy the book, but the last time you lent her a book it came back covered with coffee stains.

Choose a partner; one of you is to adopt the role of Chris, the other that of her fellow student. What different solutions or ideas could you come up with to address this problem?

Index

Law Update 1997

Law Update 1998 edition – due March 1998

An annual review of the most recent developments in specific legal subject areas, useful for law students at degree and professional levels, others with law elements in their courses and also practitioners seeking a quick update.

Published around March every year, the Law Update summarises the major legal developments during the course of the previous year. In conjunction with Old Bailey Press textbooks it gives the student a significant advantage when revising for examinations.

Contents

Administrative Law • Civil and Criminal Procedure • Commercial Law • Company Law • Conflict of Laws • Constitutional Law • Contract Law • Conveyancing • Criminal Law • Criminology • English Legal System • Equity and Trusts • European Union Law • Evidence • Family Law • Jurisprudence • Land Law • Law of International Trade • Public International Law • Revenue Law • Succession • Tort

For further information on contents, please contact:

Mail Order
Old Bailey Press
200 Greyhound Road
London
W14 9RY
United Kingdom

Telephone No: 00 44 (0) 171 385 3377
Fax No: 00 44 (0) 171 381 3377

ISBN 0 7510 0782 X
Soft cover 234 x 156 mm
396 pages £6.95
Published March 1997

Old Bailey Press

The Old Bailey Press integrated student library is planned and written to help you at every stage of your studies. Each of our range of Textbooks, Casebooks, Revision WorkBooks and Statutes are all designed to work together and are regularly revised and updated.

We are also able to offer you Suggested Solutions which provide you with past examination questions and solutions for most of the subject areas listed below.

You can buy Old Bailey Press books from your University Bookshop or your local Bookshop, or in case of difficulty, order direct using this form.

Here is the selection of modules covered by our series:

Administrative Law; Commercial Law; Company Law; Conflict of Laws (no Suggested Solutions Pack); Constitutional Law: The Machinery of Government; Obligations: Contract Law; Conveyancing (no Revision Workbook); Criminology (no Casebook or Revision WorkBook); Criminal Law; English Legal System; Equity and Trusts; Law of The European Union; Evidence; Family Law; Jurisprudence: The Philosophy of Law (Sourcebook in place of a Casebook); Land: The Law of Real Property; Law of International Trade; Legal Skills and System; Public International Law; Revenue Law (no Casebook); Succession: The Law of Wills and Estates; Obligations: The Law of Tort.

Mail order prices:

Textbook £10

Casebook £10

Revision WorkBook £7

Statutes £8

Suggested Solutions Pack (1991–1995) £7

Single Paper 1996 £3

Single Paper 1997 £3.

To complete your order, please fill in the form below:

Module	Books required	Quantity	Price	Cost
		Postage		
		TOTAL		

For UK, add 10% postage and packing (£10 maximum).
For Europe, add 15% postage and packing (£20 maximum).
For the rest of the world, add 40% for airmail.

ORDERING

By telephone to Mail Order at 0171 385 3377, with your credit card to hand

By fax to 0171 381 3377 (giving your credit card details).

By post to:

Old Bailey Press, 200 Greyhound Road, London W14 9RY.

When ordering by post, please enclose full payment by cheque or banker's draft, or complete the credit card details below.

We aim to despatch your books within 3 working days of receiving your order.

Name

Address

Postcode   Telephone

Total value of order, including postage: £

I enclose a cheque/banker's draft for the above sum, or

charge my   ☐ Access/Mastercard   ☐ Visa   ☐ American Express
Card number

☐☐☐☐ ☐☐☐☐ ☐☐☐☐ ☐☐☐☐

Expiry date   ☐☐☐☐

Signature: ....Date: ....